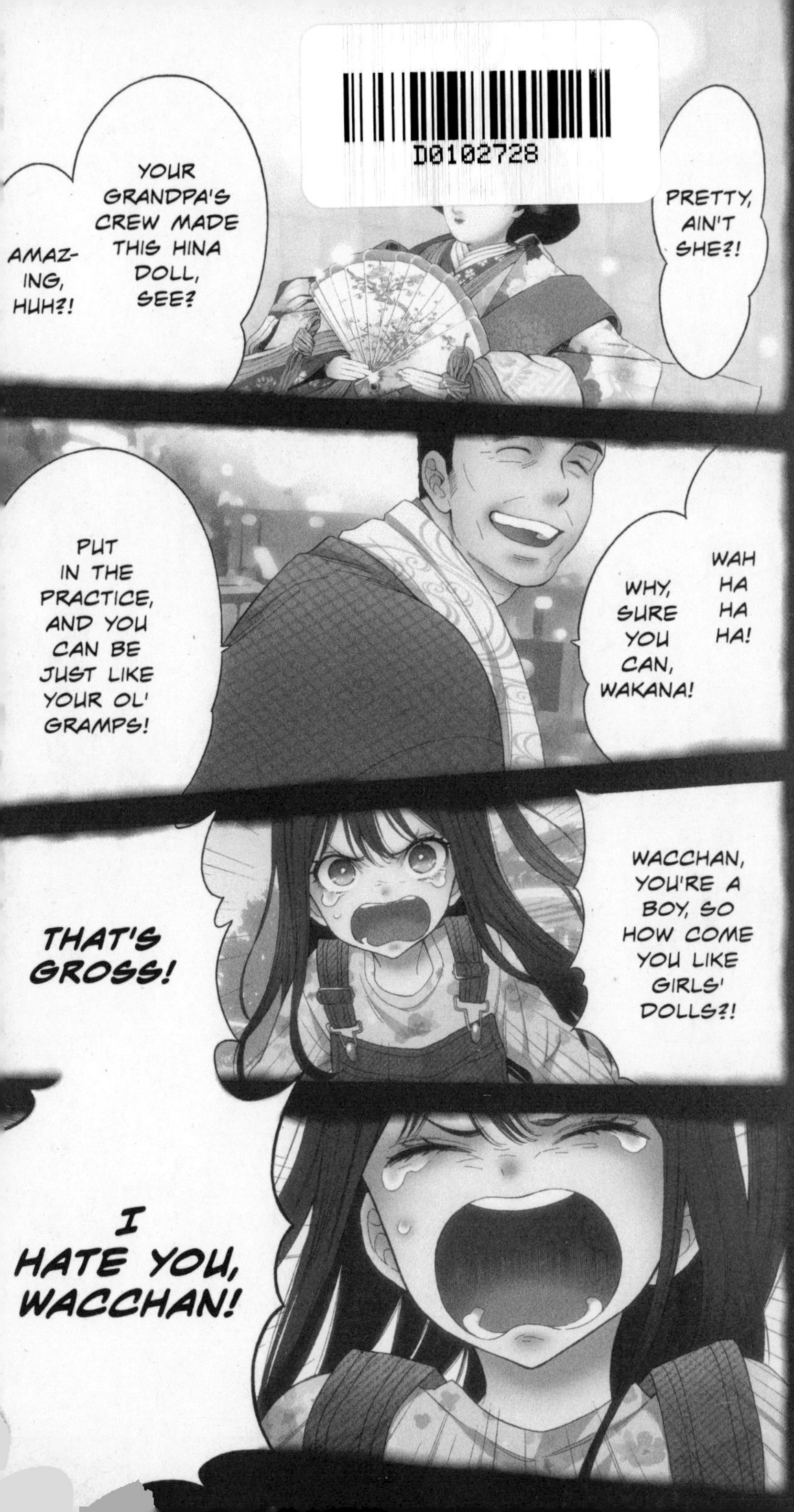
PRETTY, AIN'T SHE?!
YOUR GRANDPA'S CREW MADE THIS HINA DOLL, SEE?
AMAZ-ING, HUH?!
WAH HA HA HA!
WHY, SURE YOU CAN, WAKANA!
PUT IN THE PRACTICE, AND YOU CAN BE JUST LIKE YOUR OL' GRAMPS!
WACCHAN, YOU'RE A BOY, SO HOW COME YOU LIKE GIRLS' DOLLS?!
THAT'S GROSS!
I HATE YOU, WACCHAN!

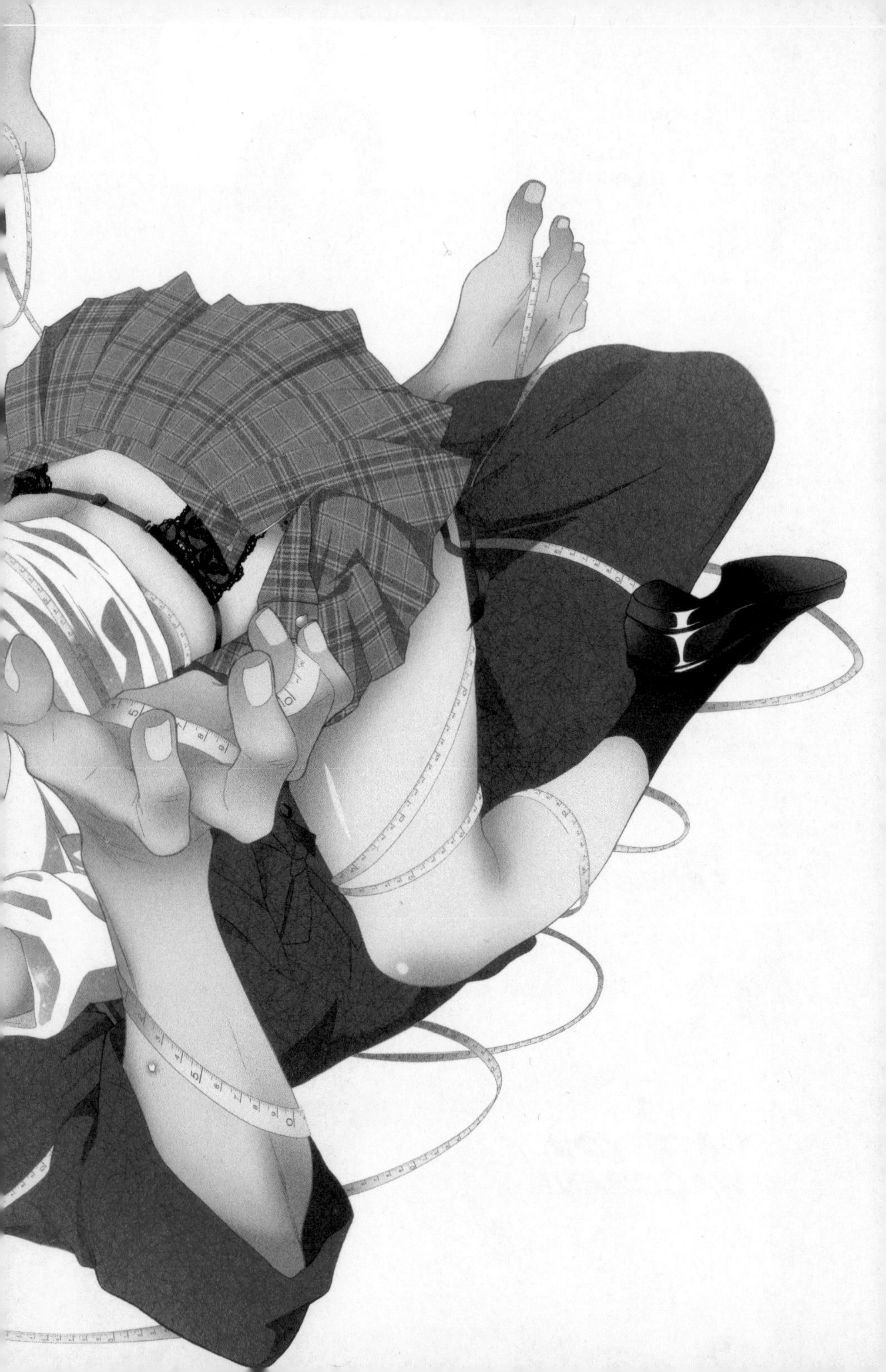

CHAPTER 1

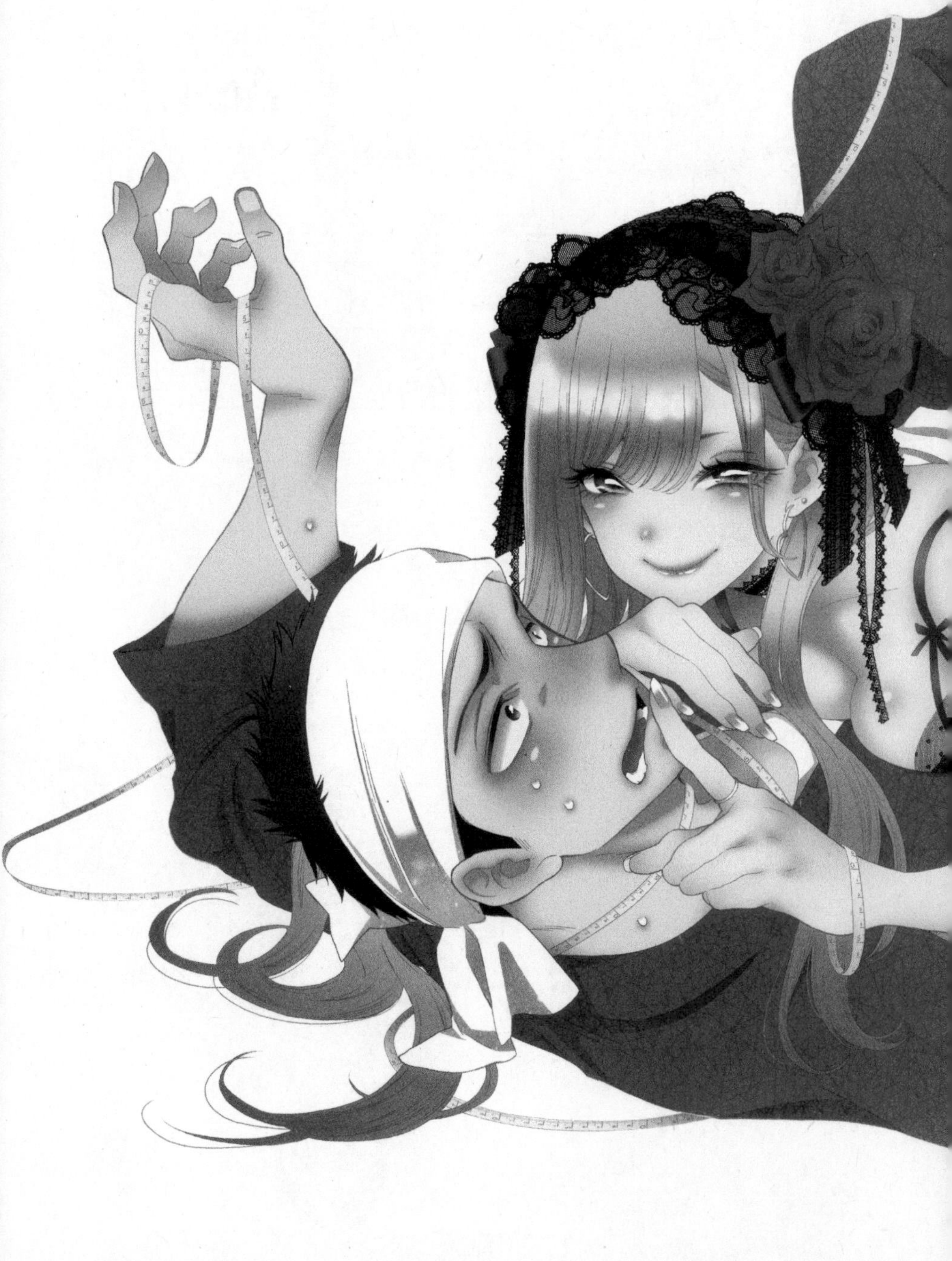

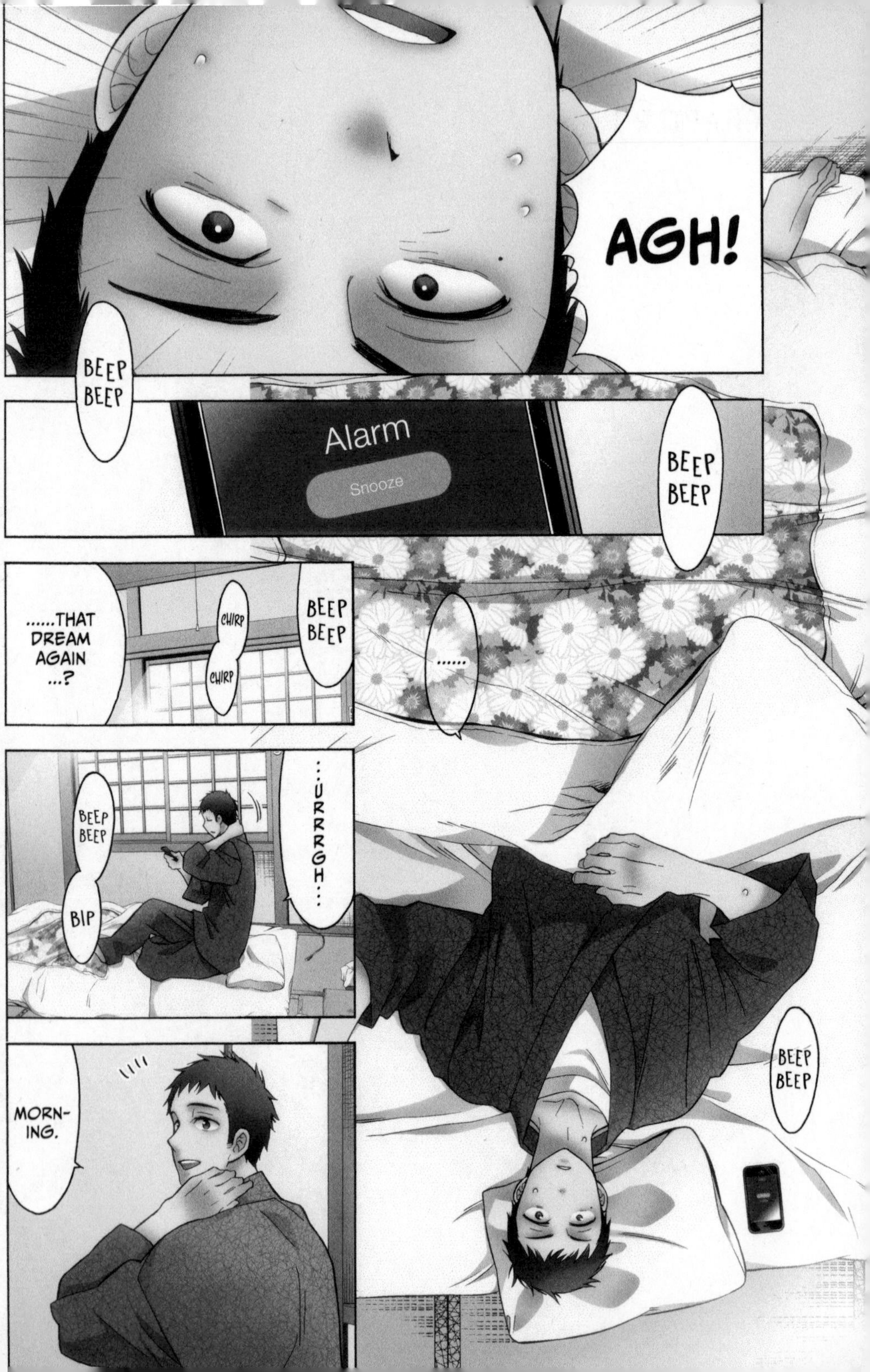
AGH!
BEEP BEEP
BEEP BEEP
......
BEEP BEEP
Alarm
Snooze
BEEP BEEP
CHIRP
CHIRP
......THAT DREAM AGAIN ...?
...URRRGH...
BEEP BEEP
BIP
MORN-ING.

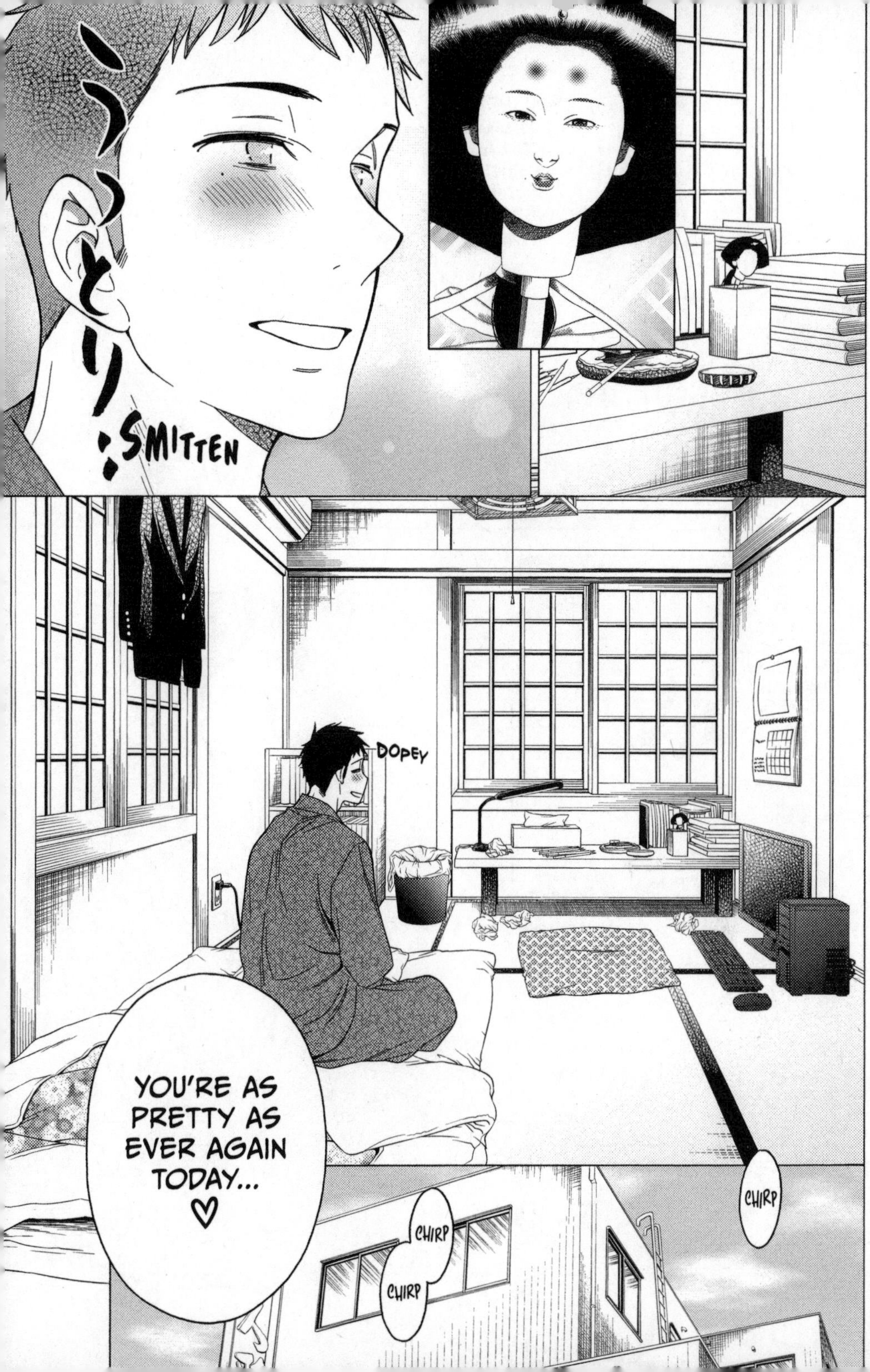

うっとり
SMITTEN
DOPEY
YOU'RE AS PRETTY AS EVER AGAIN TODAY... ♡
CHIRP
CHIRP
CHIRP

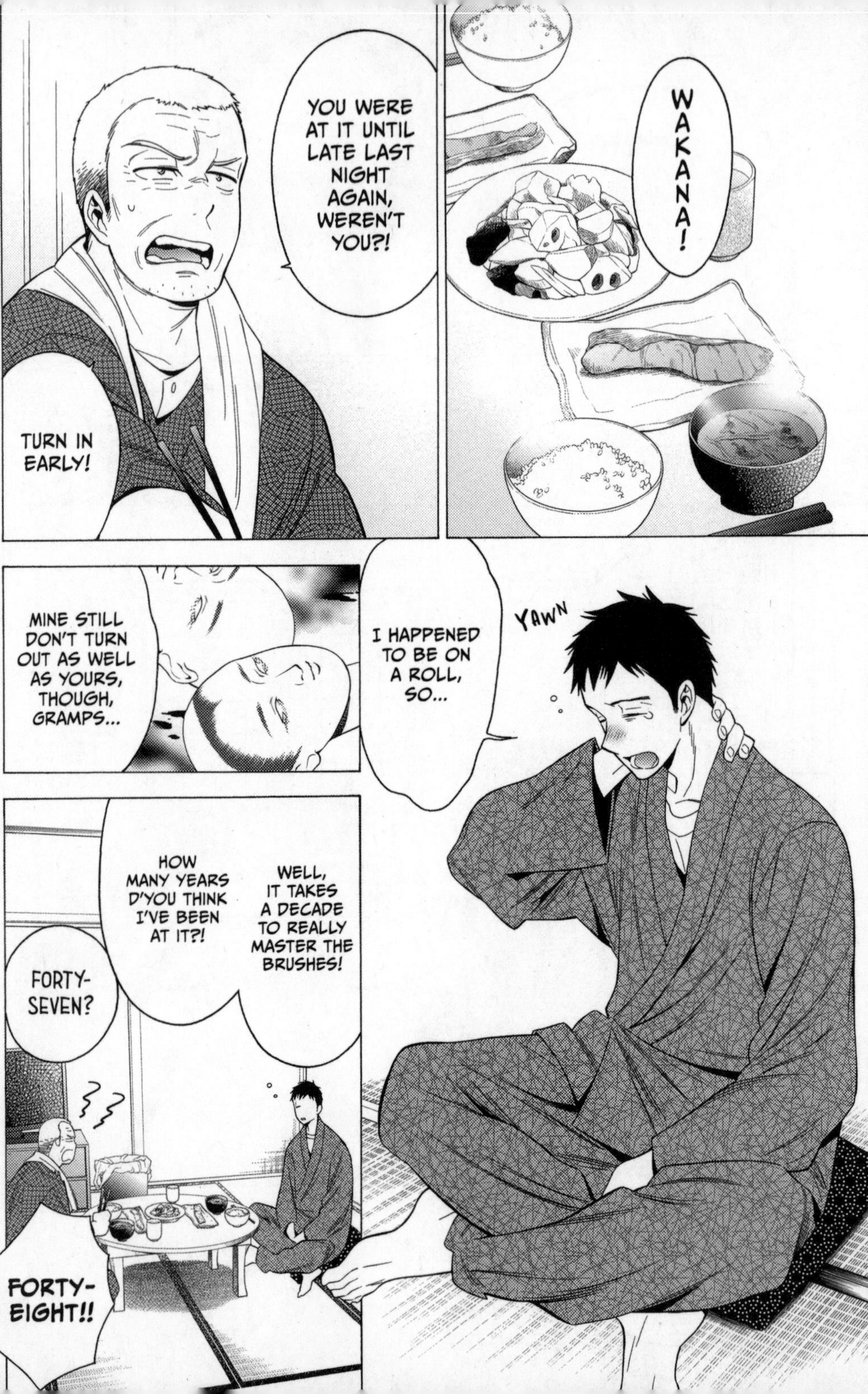
WAKANA!
YOU WERE AT IT UNTIL LATE LAST NIGHT AGAIN, WEREN'T YOU?!
TURN IN EARLY!
YAWN
I HAPPENED TO BE ON A ROLL, SO...
MINE STILL DON'T TURN OUT AS WELL AS YOURS, THOUGH, GRAMPS...
WELL, IT TAKES A DECADE TO REALLY MASTER THE BRUSHES!
HOW MANY YEARS D'YOU THINK I'VE BEEN AT IT?!
FORTY-SEVEN?
FORTY-EIGHT!!

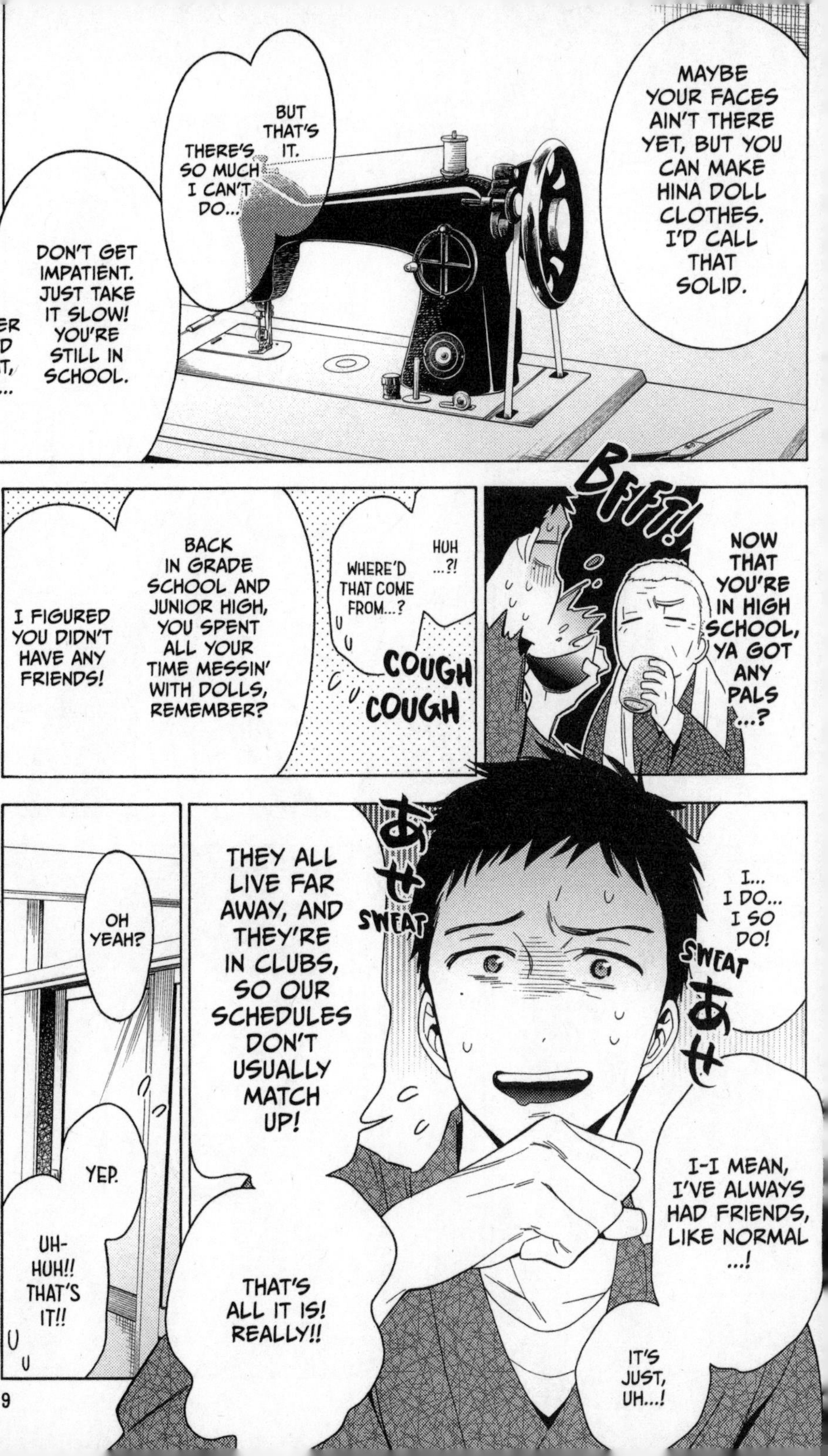
MAYBE YOUR FACES AIN'T THERE YET, BUT YOU CAN MAKE HINA DOLL CLOTHES. I'D CALL THAT SOLID.
BUT THAT'S IT.
THERE'S SO MUCH I CAN'T DO...
DON'T GET IMPATIENT. JUST TAKE IT SLOW! YOU'RE STILL IN SCHOOL.
NEVER MIND THAT, KID...
BFFT!
NOW THAT YOU'RE IN HIGH SCHOOL, YA GOT ANY PALS...?
HUH...?!
WHERE'D THAT COME FROM...?
COUGH
COUGH
BACK IN GRADE SCHOOL AND JUNIOR HIGH, YOU SPENT ALL YOUR TIME MESSIN' WITH DOLLS, REMEMBER?
I FIGURED YOU DIDN'T HAVE ANY FRIENDS!
I... I DO... I SO DO!
SWEAT あせ
SWEAT あせ
THEY ALL LIVE FAR AWAY, AND THEY'RE IN CLUBS, SO OUR SCHEDULES DON'T USUALLY MATCH UP!
I-I MEAN, I'VE ALWAYS HAD FRIENDS, LIKE NORMAL...!
IT'S JUST, UH...!
THAT'S ALL IT IS! REALLY!!
OH YEAH?
YEP.
UH-HUH!! THAT'S IT!!

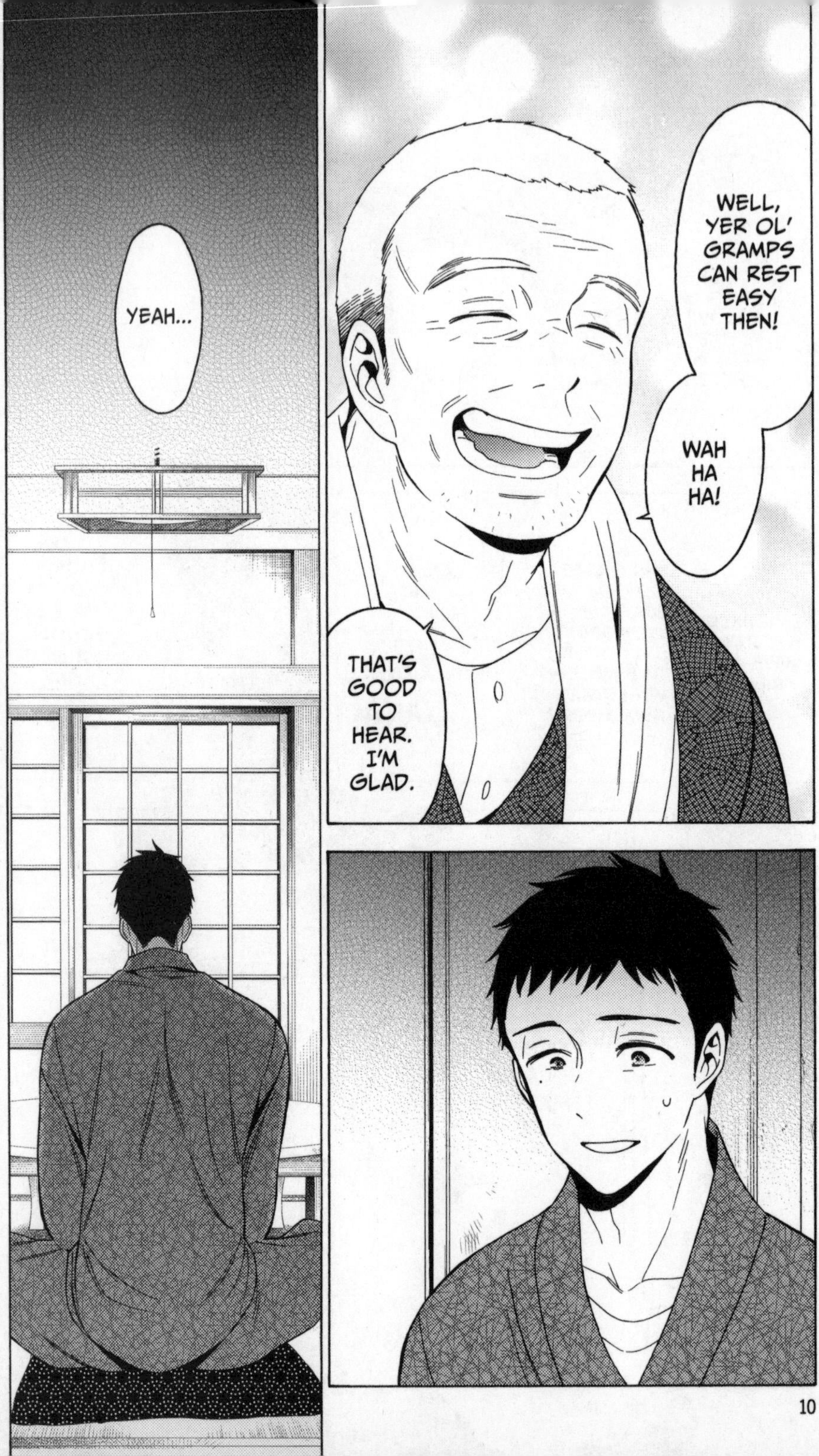
WELL, YER OL' GRAMPS CAN REST EASY THEN!
WAH HA HA!
THAT'S GOOD TO HEAR. I'M GLAD.
YEAH...

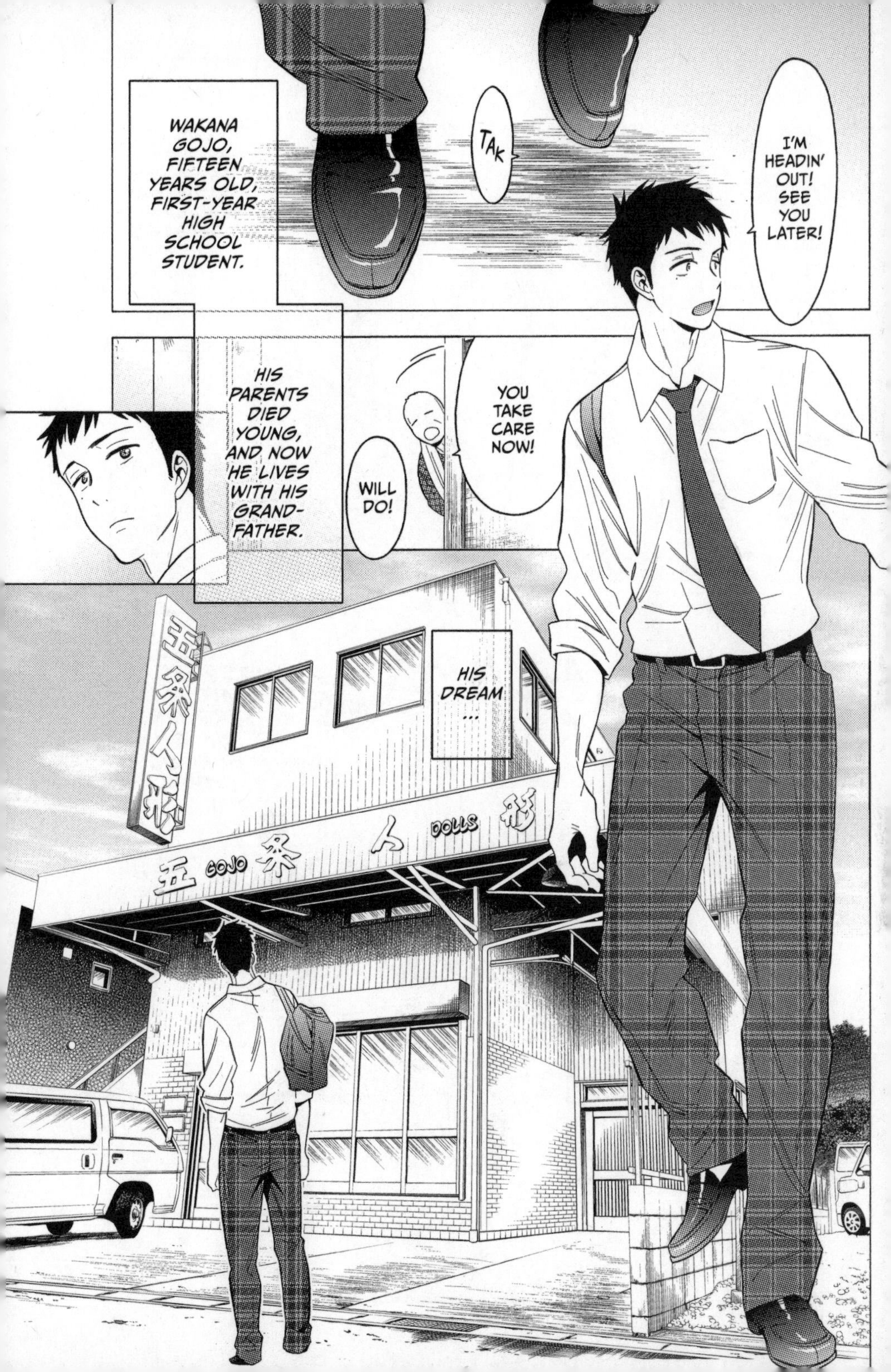
I'M HEADIN' OUT! SEE YOU LATER!
TAK
WAKANA GOJO, FIFTEEN YEARS OLD, FIRST-YEAR HIGH SCHOOL STUDENT.
YOU TAKE CARE NOW!
WILL DO!
HIS PARENTS DIED YOUNG, AND NOW HE LIVES WITH HIS GRAND-FATHER.
HIS DREAM ...
五条人形
五 GOJO 条 人 DOLLS 形

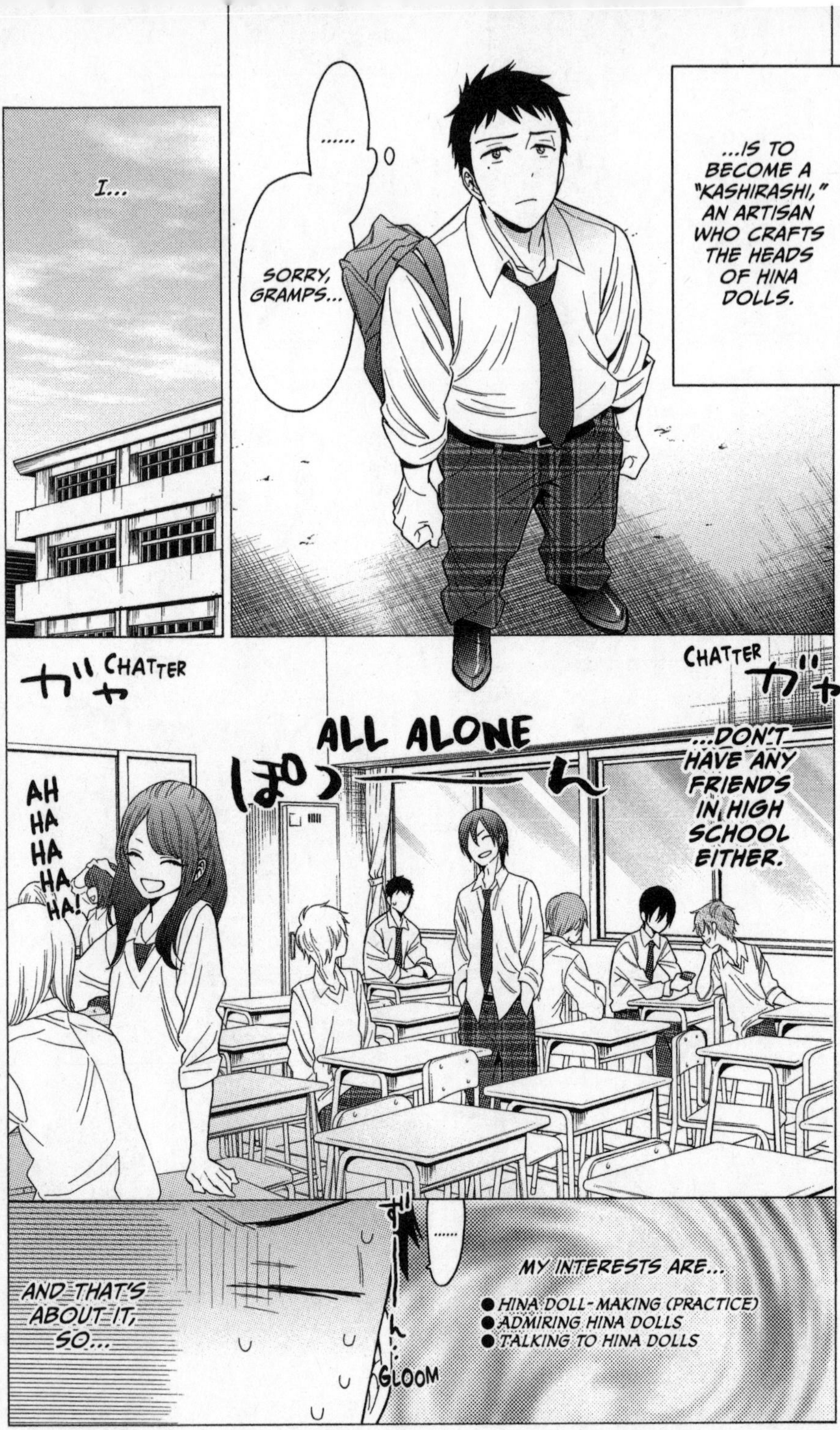

...IS TO BECOME A "KASHIRASHI," AN ARTISAN WHO CRAFTS THE HEADS OF HINA DOLLS.
......
SORRY, GRAMPS...
I...
CHATTER
ガヤ
CHATTER
ガヤ
ALL ALONE
ぽつーーん
...DON'T HAVE ANY FRIENDS IN HIGH SCHOOL EITHER.
AH HA HA HA HA!
MY INTERESTS ARE...
● HINA DOLL-MAKING (PRACTICE)
● ADMIRING HINA DOLLS
● TALKING TO HINA DOLLS
......
GLOOM
AND THAT'S ABOUT IT, SO...

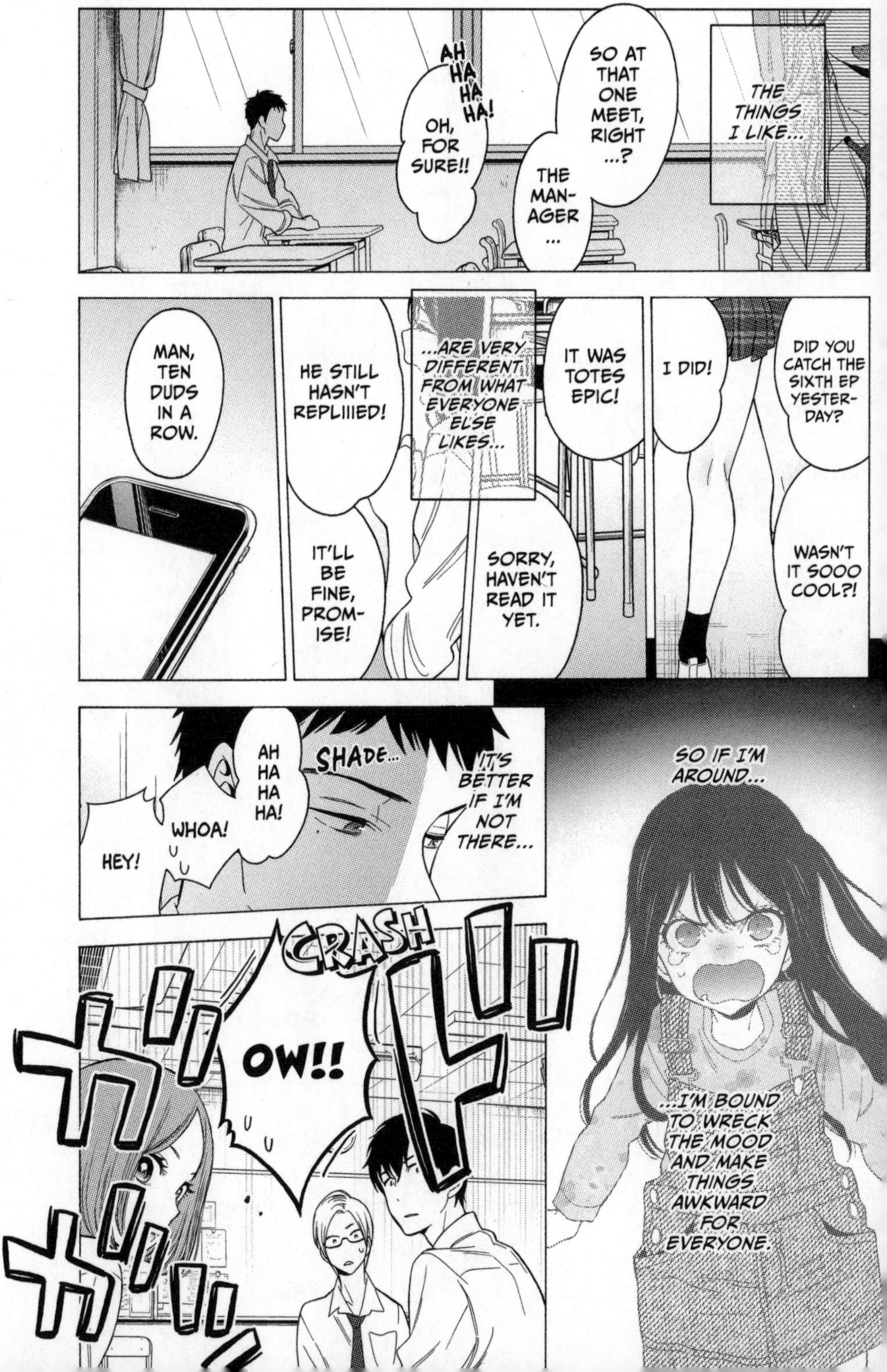
THE THINGS I LIKE...
SO AT THAT ONE MEET, RIGHT ...?
THE MANAGER ...
AH HA HA HA!
OH, FOR SURE!!
DID YOU CATCH THE SIXTH EP YESTERDAY?
I DID!
WASN'T IT SOOO COOL?!
IT WAS TOTES EPIC!
...ARE VERY DIFFERENT FROM WHAT EVERYONE ELSE LIKES...
SORRY, HAVEN'T READ IT YET.
HE STILL HASN'T REPLIIIED!
IT'LL BE FINE, PROMISE!
MAN, TEN DUDS IN A ROW.
SO IF I'M AROUND...
...I'M BOUND TO WRECK THE MOOD AND MAKE THINGS AWKWARD FOR EVERYONE.
IT'S BETTER IF I'M NOT THERE...
SHADE...
AH HA HA HA!
WHOA!
HEY!
CRASH
OW!!

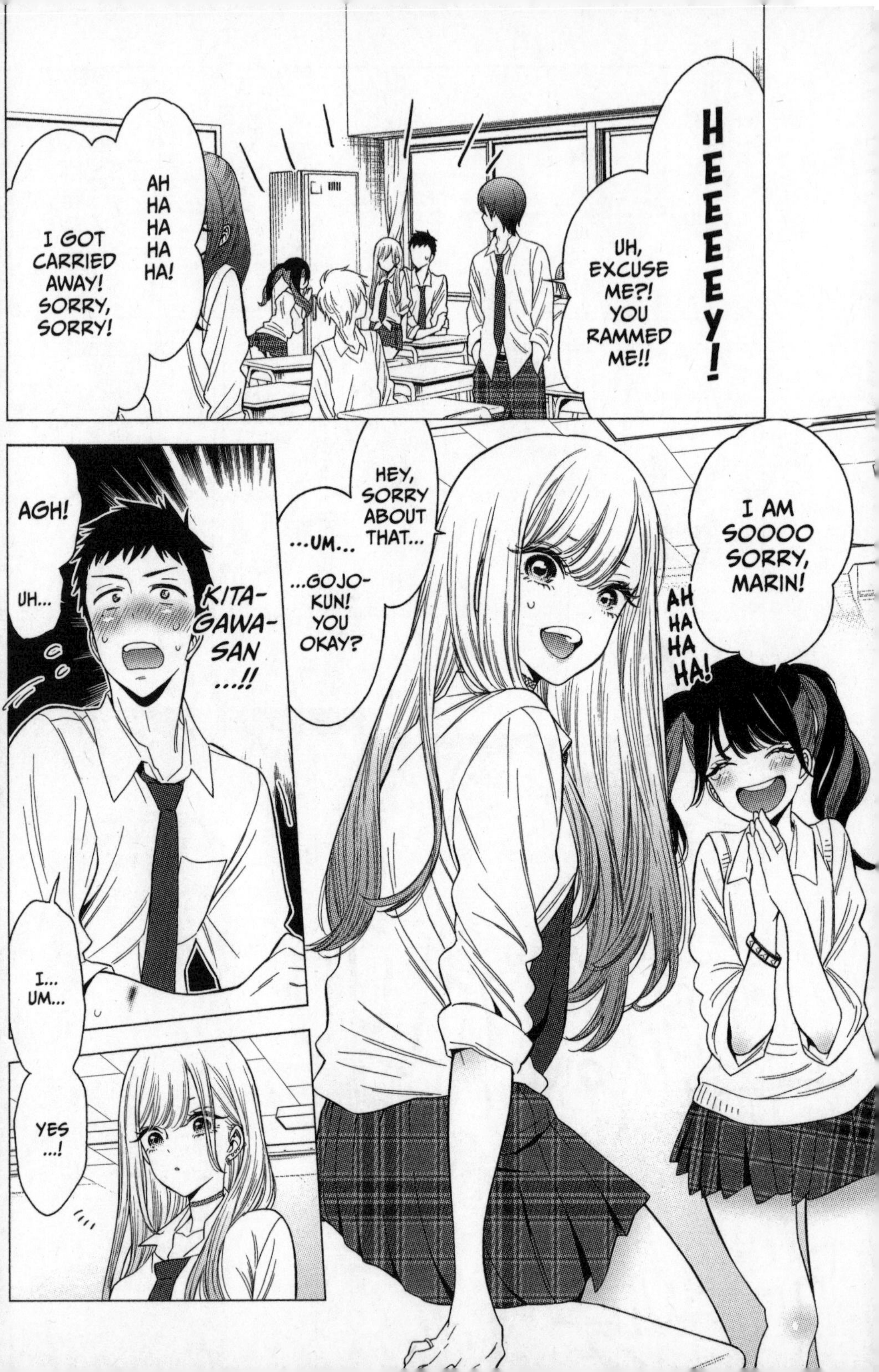
HEEEEY!
UH, EXCUSE ME?! YOU RAMMED ME!!
AH HA HA HA HA!
I GOT CARRIED AWAY! SORRY, SORRY!
I AM SOOOO SORRY, MARIN!
AH HA HA HA!
HEY, SORRY ABOUT THAT...
...UM...
...GOJO-KUN! YOU OKAY?
KITA-GAWA-SAN ...!!
AGH!
UH...
I... UM...
YES ...!

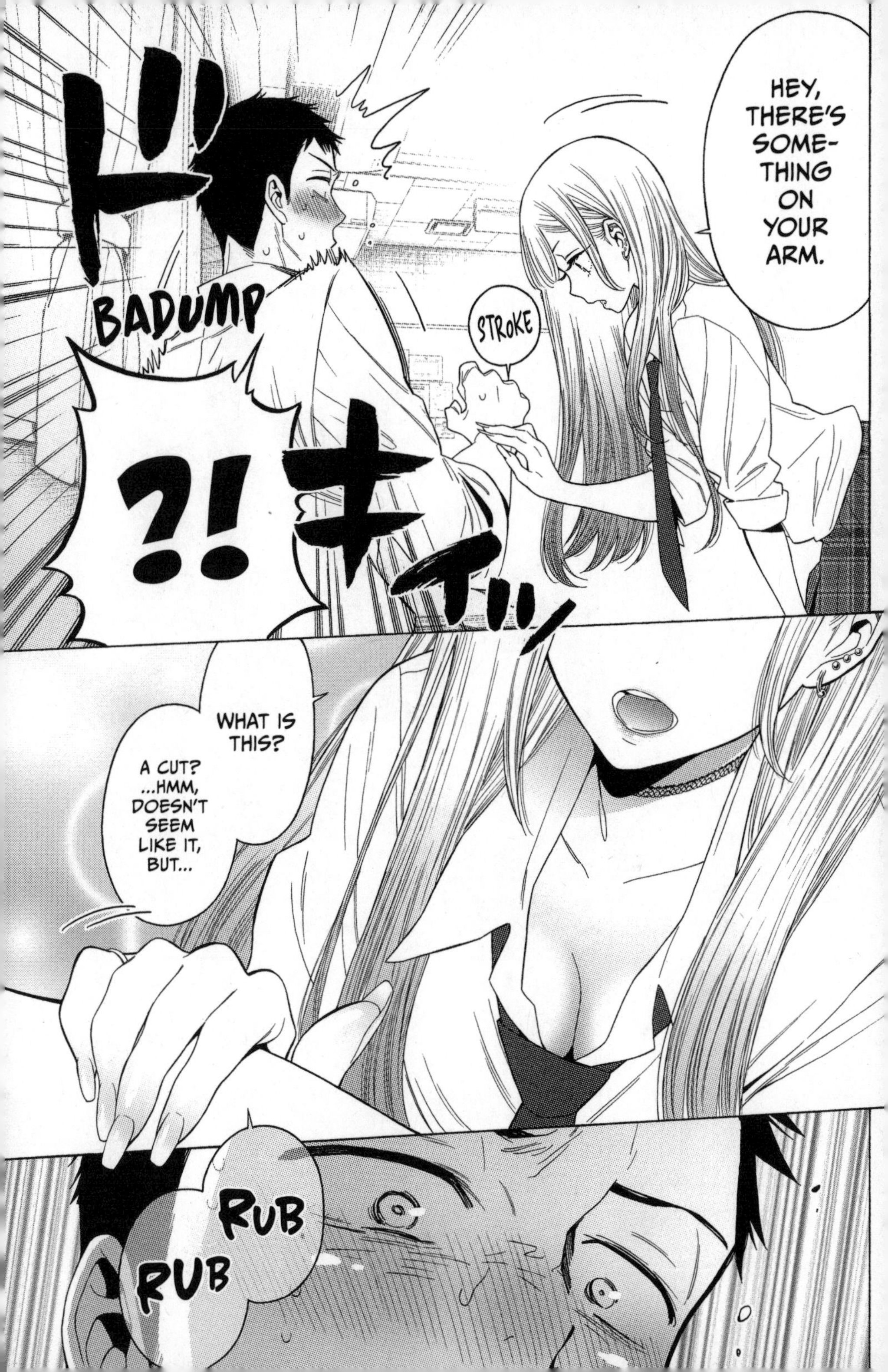

HEY, THERE'S SOME-THING ON YOUR ARM.
STROKE
ド
BADUMP
キ
?!
WHAT IS THIS?
A CUT? ...HMM, DOESN'T SEEM LIKE IT, BUT...
RUB
RUB

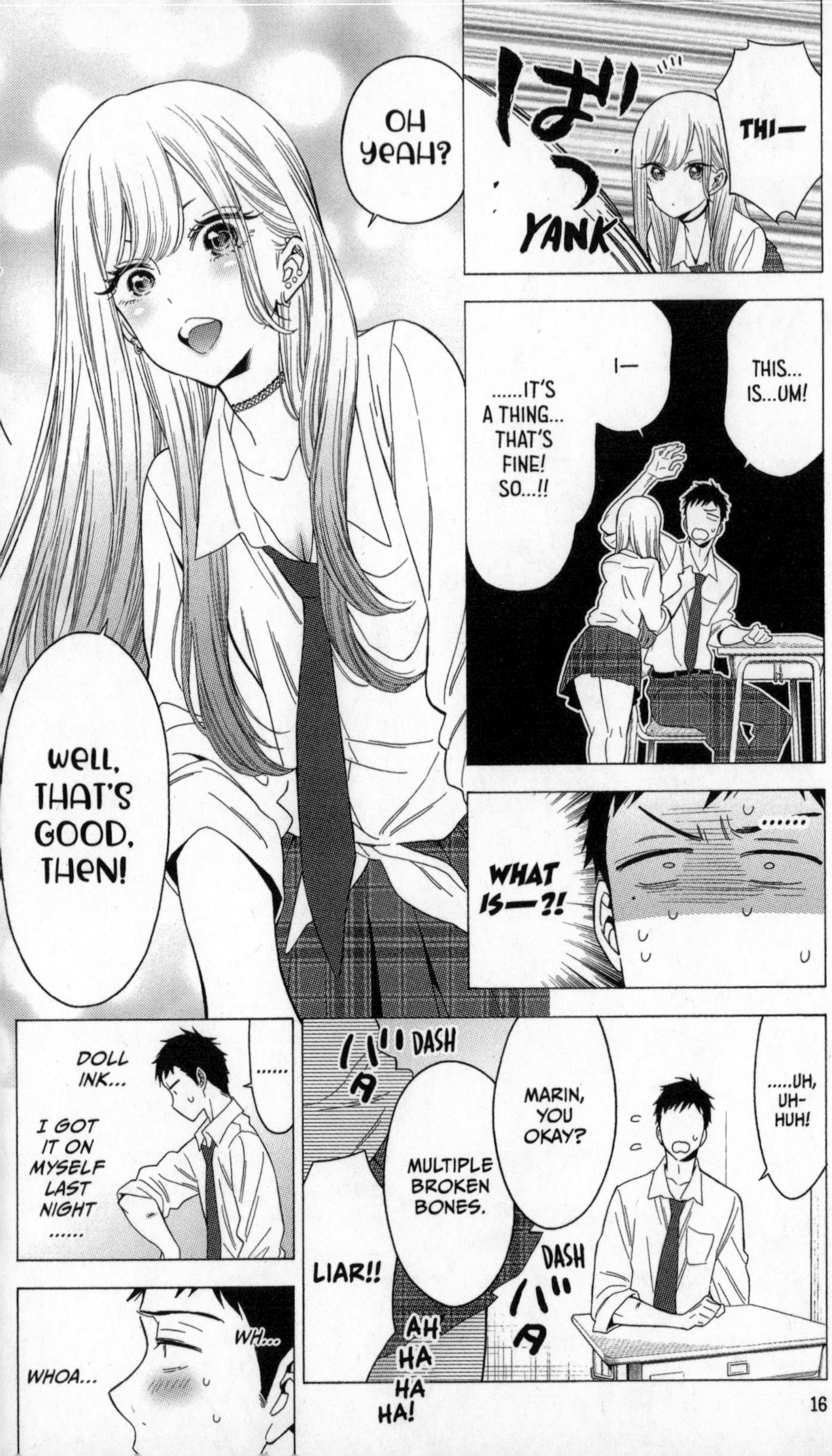
ぱっ
YANK
THI—
THIS... IS...UM!
I—
......IT'S A THING... THAT'S FINE! SO...!!
......
WHAT IS—?!
OH YEAH?
WELL, THAT'S GOOD, THEN!
.....UH, UH-HUH!
MARIN, YOU OKAY?
バッ
DASH
MULTIPLE BROKEN BONES.
DASH
バッ
LIAR!!
AH HA HA HA!
......
DOLL INK...
I GOT IT ON MYSELF LAST NIGHT ......
WH...
WHOA...

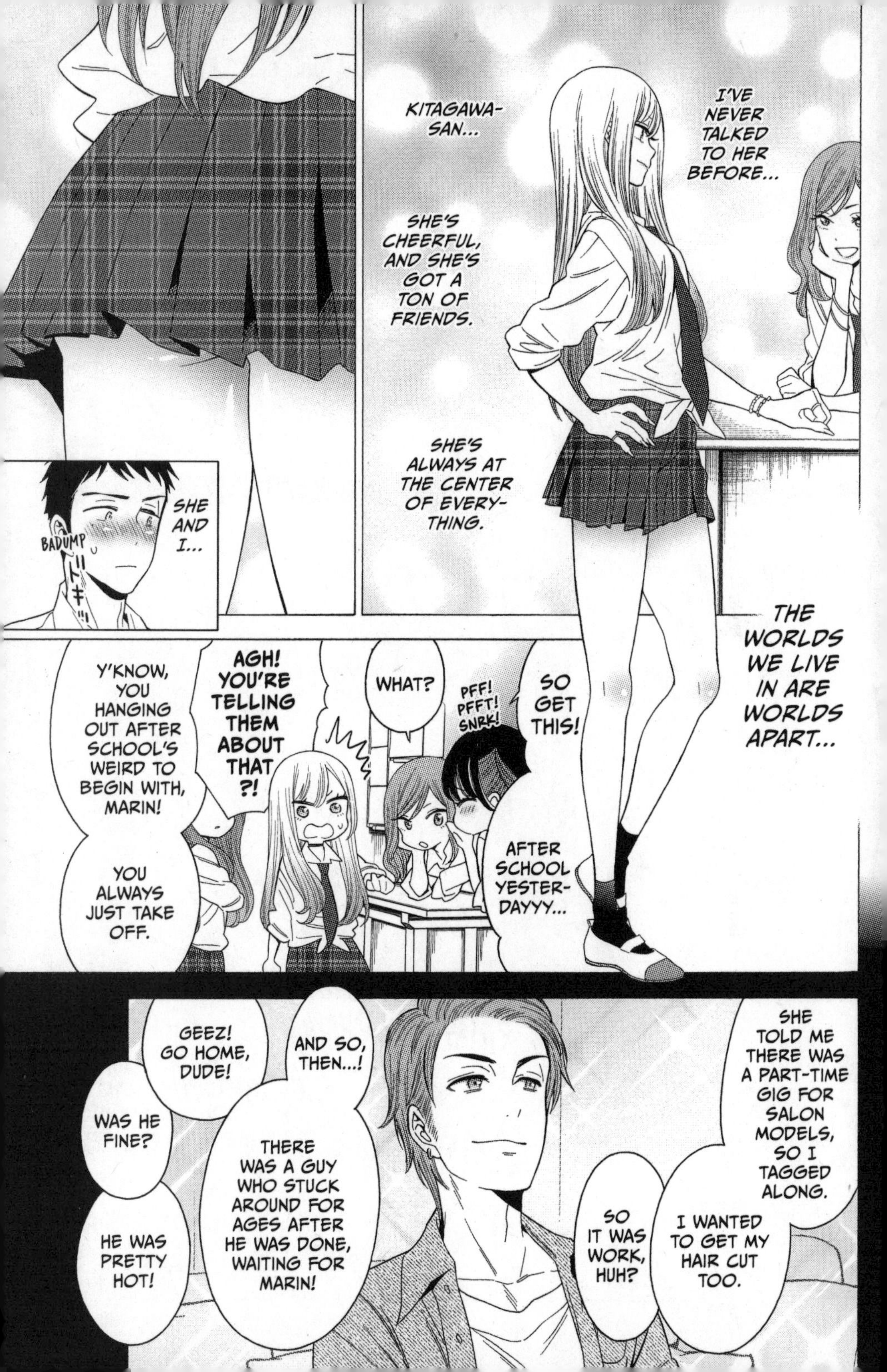
I'VE NEVER TALKED TO HER BEFORE...
KITAGAWA-SAN...
SHE'S CHEERFUL, AND SHE'S GOT A TON OF FRIENDS.
SHE'S ALWAYS AT THE CENTER OF EVERY-THING.
SHE AND I...
BADUMP
THE WORLDS WE LIVE IN ARE WORLDS APART...
SO GET THIS!
PFF! PFFT! SNRK!
WHAT?
AGH! YOU'RE TELLING THEM ABOUT THAT?!
Y'KNOW, YOU HANGING OUT AFTER SCHOOL'S WEIRD TO BEGIN WITH, MARIN!
AFTER SCHOOL YESTER-DAYYY...
YOU ALWAYS JUST TAKE OFF.
SHE TOLD ME THERE WAS A PART-TIME GIG FOR SALON MODELS, SO I TAGGED ALONG.
I WANTED TO GET MY HAIR CUT TOO.
SO IT WAS WORK, HUH?
AND SO, THEN...!
GEEZ! GO HOME, DUDE!
THERE WAS A GUY WHO STUCK AROUND FOR AGES AFTER HE WAS DONE, WAITING FOR MARIN!
WAS HE FINE?
HE WAS PRETTY HOT!

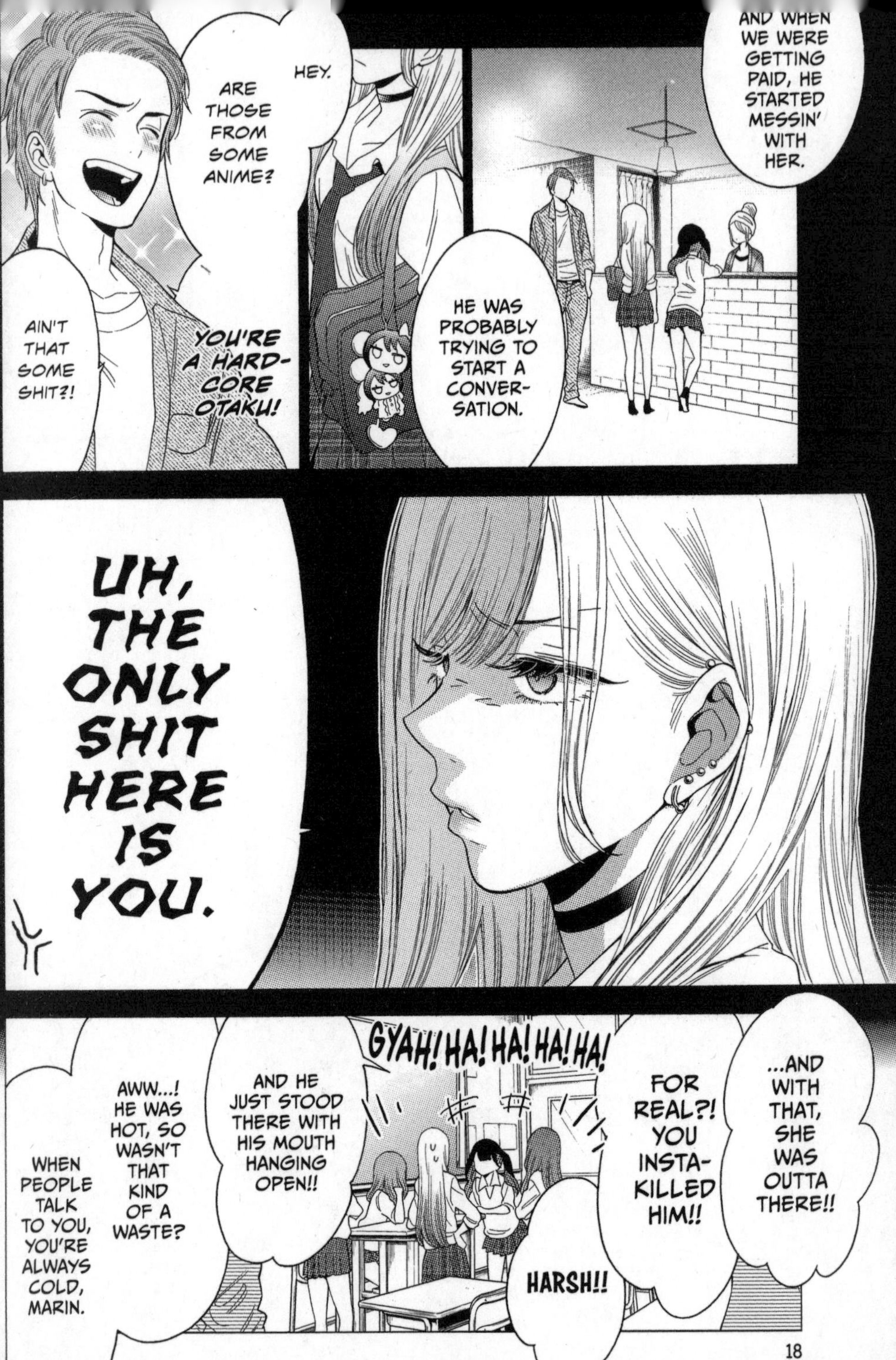
AND WHEN WE WERE GETTING PAID, HE STARTED MESSIN' WITH HER.
HE WAS PROBABLY TRYING TO START A CONVERSATION.
HEY.
ARE THOSE FROM SOME ANIME?
YOU'RE A HARD-CORE OTAKU!
AIN'T THAT SOME SHIT?!
UH, THE ONLY SHIT HERE IS YOU.
...AND WITH THAT, SHE WAS OUTTA THERE!!
FOR REAL?! YOU INSTA-KILLED HIM!!
HARSH!!
GYAH! HA! HA! HA! HA!
AND HE JUST STOOD THERE WITH HIS MOUTH HANGING OPEN!!
AWW...! HE WAS HOT, SO WASN'T THAT KIND OF A WASTE?
WHEN PEOPLE TALK TO YOU, YOU'RE ALWAYS COLD, MARIN.

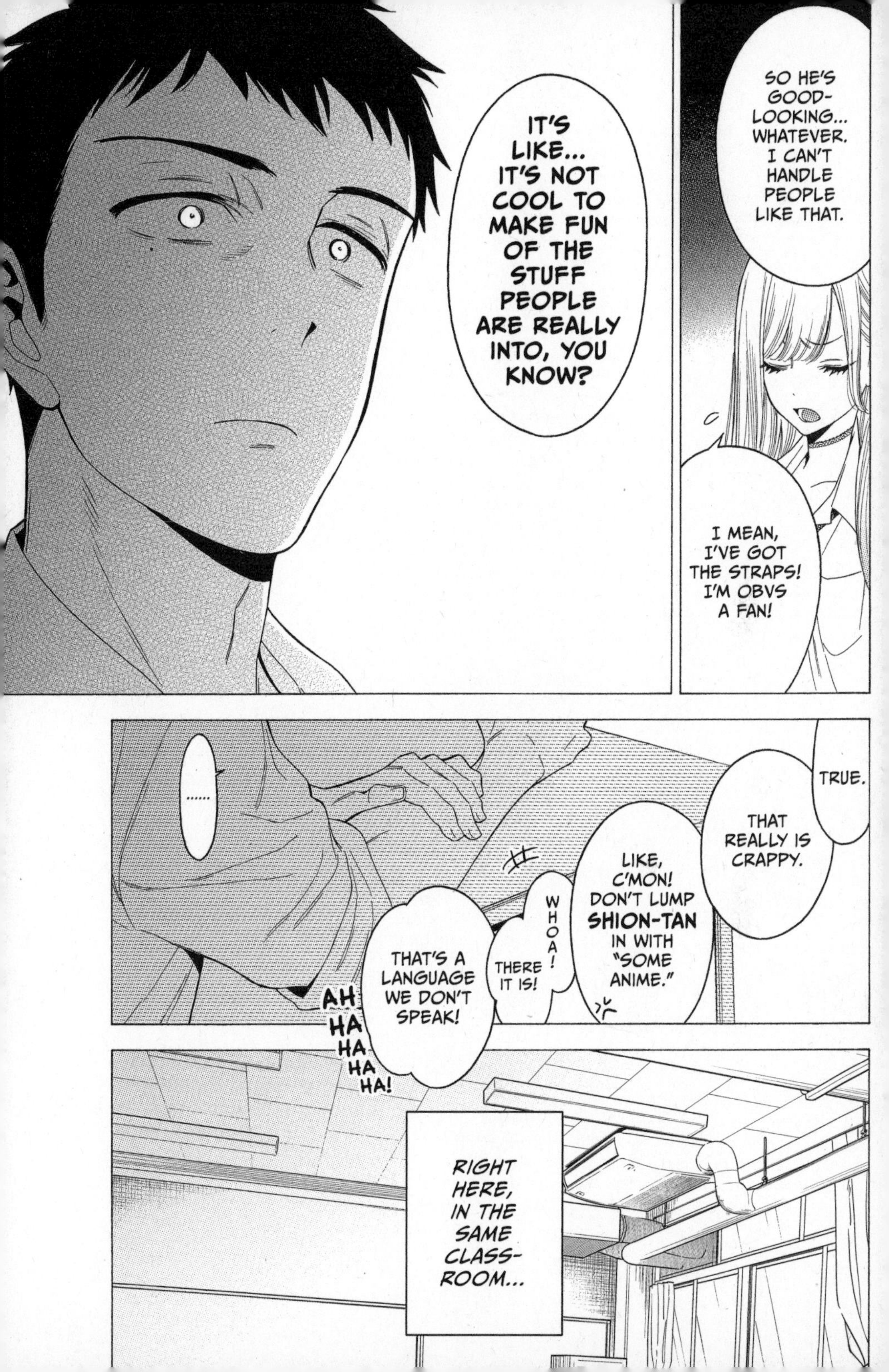
SO HE'S GOOD-LOOKING... WHATEVER. I CAN'T HANDLE PEOPLE LIKE THAT.
I MEAN, I'VE GOT THE STRAPS! I'M OBVS A FAN!
IT'S LIKE... IT'S NOT COOL TO MAKE FUN OF THE STUFF PEOPLE ARE REALLY INTO, YOU KNOW?
TRUE.
THAT REALLY IS CRAPPY.
LIKE, C'MON! DON'T LUMP SHION-TAN IN WITH "SOME ANIME."
WHOA!
THERE IT IS!
THAT'S A LANGUAGE WE DON'T SPEAK!
AH HA HA HA HA!
......
RIGHT HERE, IN THE SAME CLASS-ROOM...

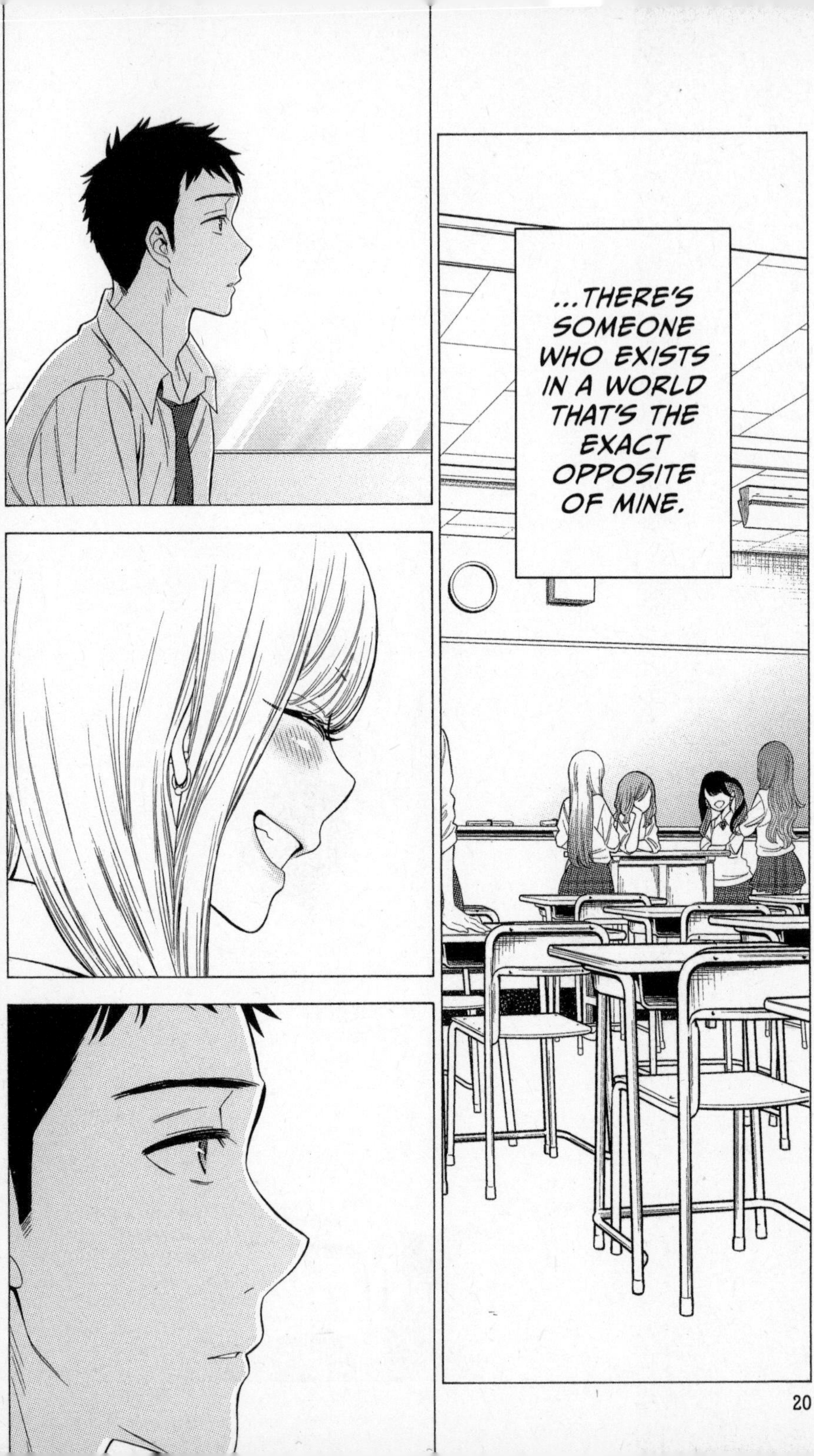
...THERE'S SOMEONE WHO EXISTS IN A WORLD THAT'S THE EXACT OPPOSITE OF MINE.

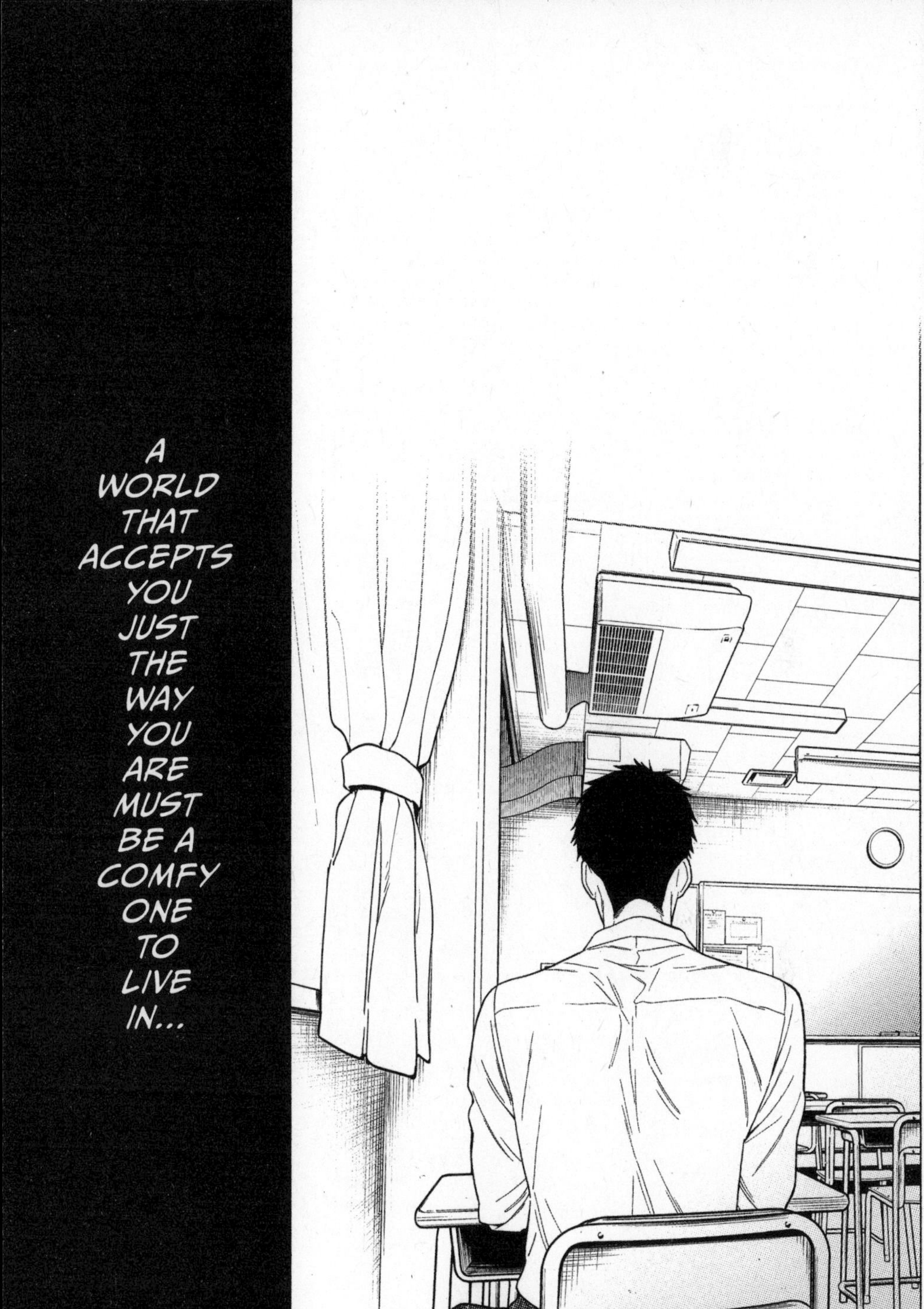
A WORLD THAT ACCEPTS YOU JUST THE WAY YOU ARE MUST BE A COMFY ONE TO LIVE IN...

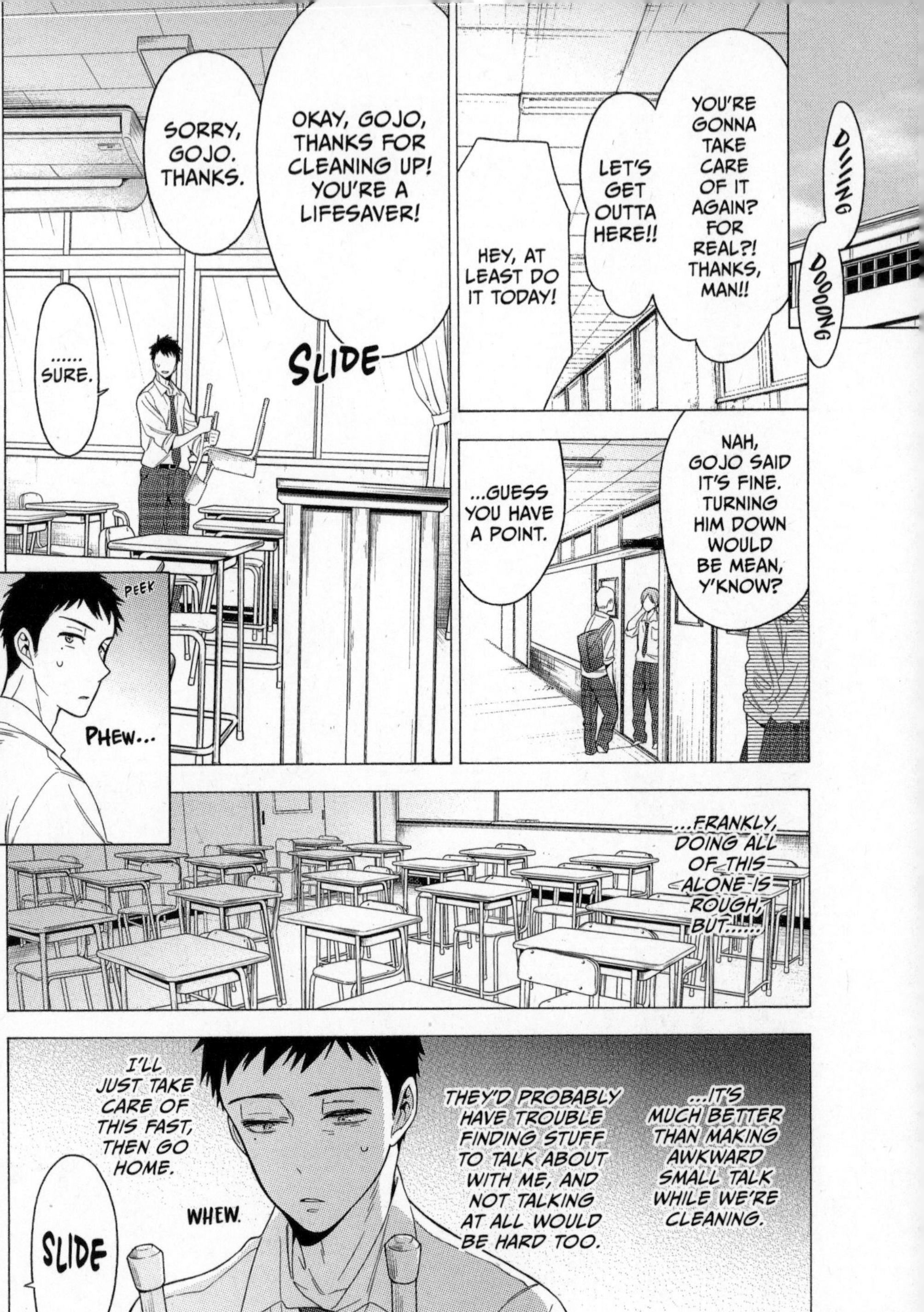
DIIING DOOOONG
YOU'RE GONNA TAKE CARE OF IT AGAIN? FOR REAL?! THANKS, MAN!!
LET'S GET OUTTA HERE!!
HEY, AT LEAST DO IT TODAY!
NAH, GOJO SAID IT'S FINE. TURNING HIM DOWN WOULD BE MEAN, Y'KNOW?
...GUESS YOU HAVE A POINT.
OKAY, GOJO, THANKS FOR CLEANING UP! YOU'RE A LIFESAVER!
SORRY, GOJO. THANKS.
SLIDE
......SURE.
PEEK
PHEW...
...FRANKLY, DOING ALL OF THIS ALONE IS ROUGH, BUT......
...IT'S MUCH BETTER THAN MAKING AWKWARD SMALL TALK WHILE WE'RE CLEANING.
THEY'D PROBABLY HAVE TROUBLE FINDING STUFF TO TALK ABOUT WITH ME, AND NOT TALKING AT ALL WOULD BE HARD TOO.
I'LL JUST TAKE CARE OF THIS FAST, THEN GO HOME.
WHEW.
SLIDE

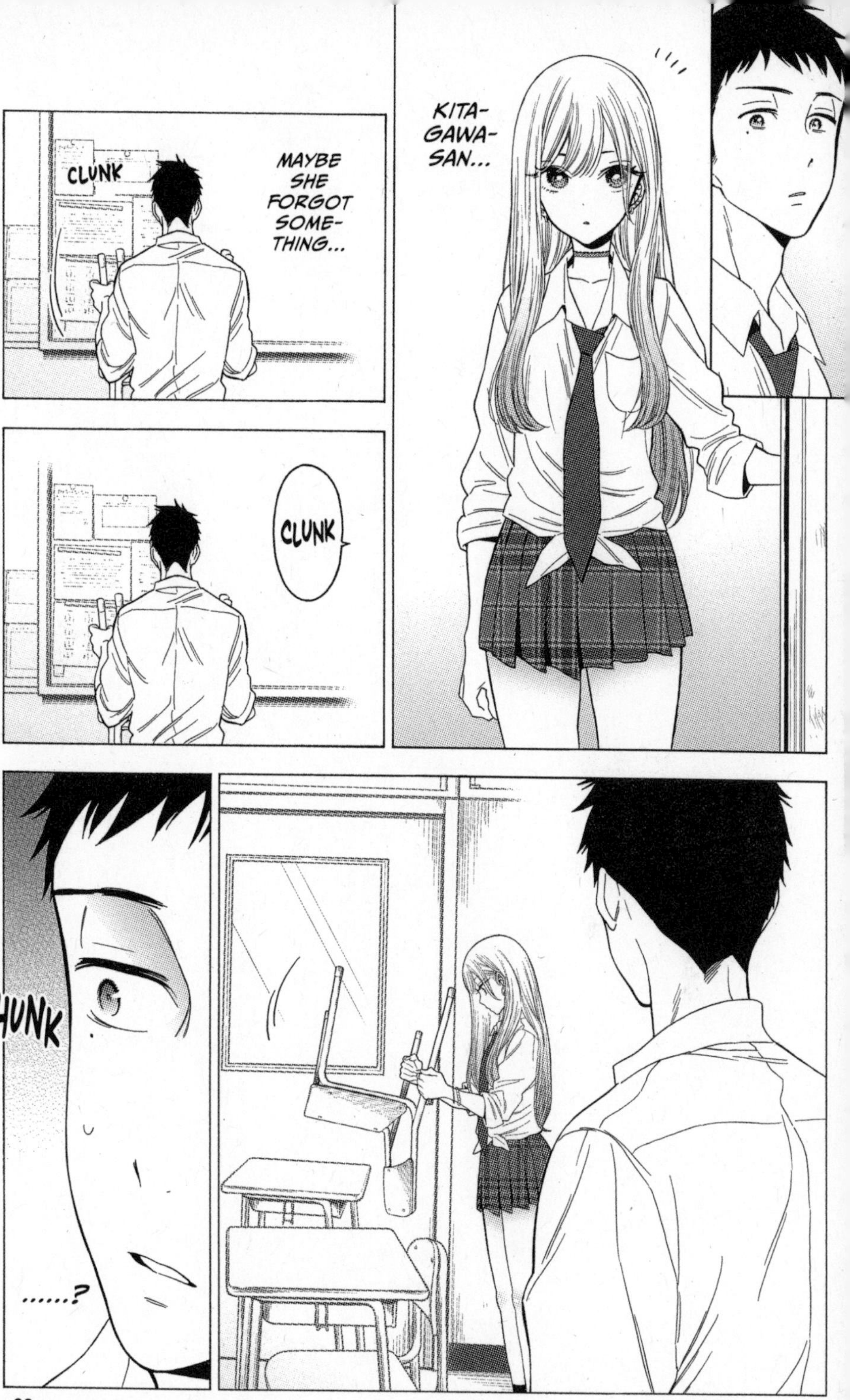
KITA-GAWA-SAN...
CLUNK
MAYBE SHE FORGOT SOME-THING...
CLUNK
THUNK
......?

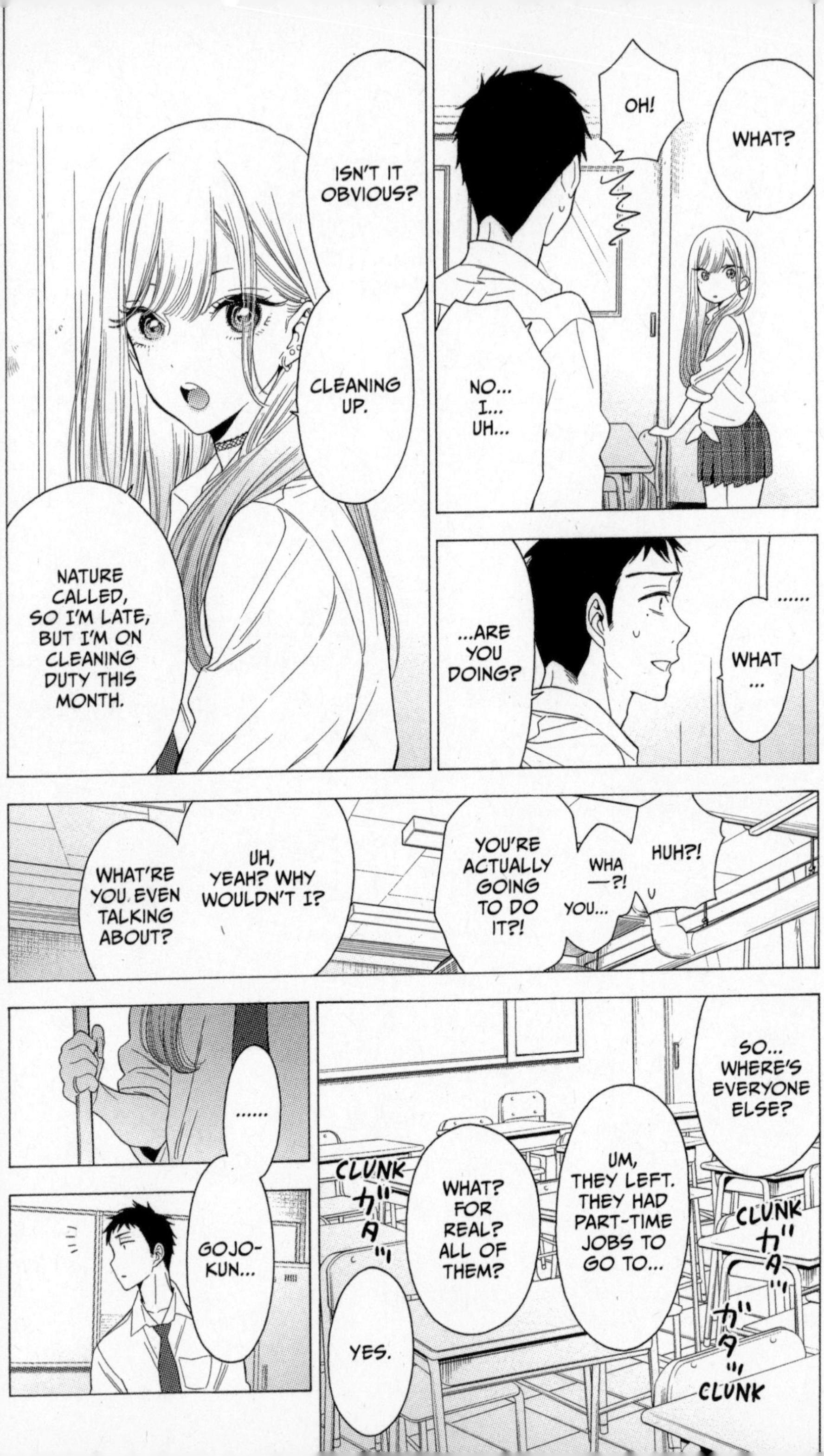
WHAT?
OH!
NO... I... UH...
......
WHAT ...
...ARE YOU DOING?
ISN'T IT OBVIOUS?
CLEANING UP.
NATURE CALLED, SO I'M LATE, BUT I'M ON CLEANING DUTY THIS MONTH.
HUH?!
WHA—?! YOU...
YOU'RE ACTUALLY GOING TO DO IT?!
UH, YEAH? WHY WOULDN'T I?
WHAT'RE YOU EVEN TALKING ABOUT?
SO... WHERE'S EVERYONE ELSE?
UM, THEY LEFT. THEY HAD PART-TIME JOBS TO GO TO...
CLUNK ガタッ
CLUNK ガタッ
WHAT? FOR REAL? ALL OF THEM?
CLUNK ガタッ
YES.
......
GOJO-KUN...

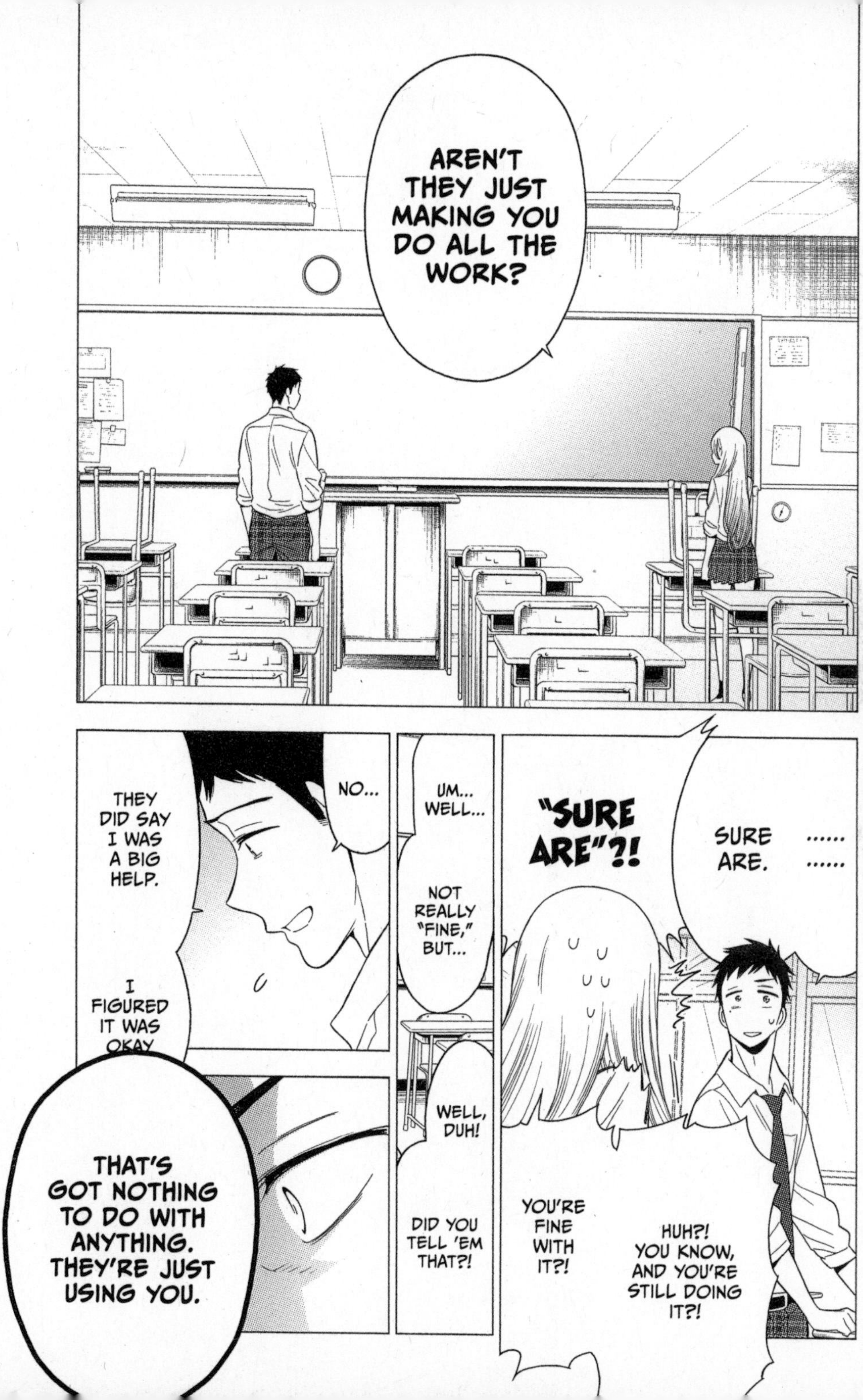
AREN'T THEY JUST MAKING YOU DO ALL THE WORK?
......
SURE ARE.
......
"SURE ARE"?!
HUH?! YOU KNOW, AND YOU'RE STILL DOING IT?!
YOU'RE FINE WITH IT?!
UM... WELL...
NOT REALLY "FINE," BUT...
WELL, DUH!
DID YOU TELL 'EM THAT?!
NO...
THEY DID SAY I WAS A BIG HELP.
I FIGURED IT WAS OKAY
THAT'S GOT NOTHING TO DO WITH ANYTHING. THEY'RE JUST USING YOU.

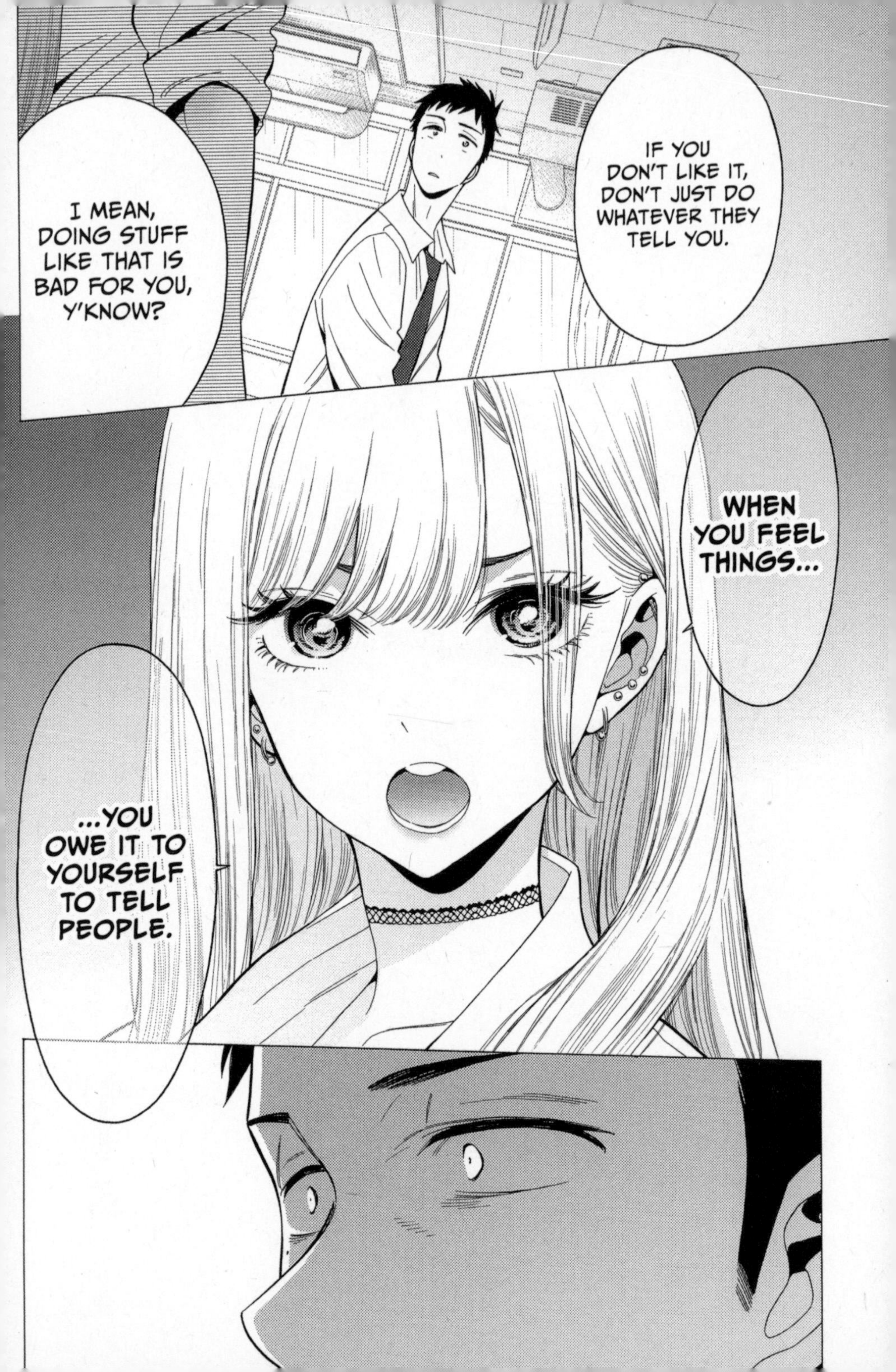
IF YOU DON'T LIKE IT, DON'T JUST DO WHATEVER THEY TELL YOU.
I MEAN, DOING STUFF LIKE THAT IS BAD FOR YOU, Y'KNOW?
WHEN YOU FEEL THINGS...
...YOU OWE IT TO YOURSELF TO TELL PEOPLE.

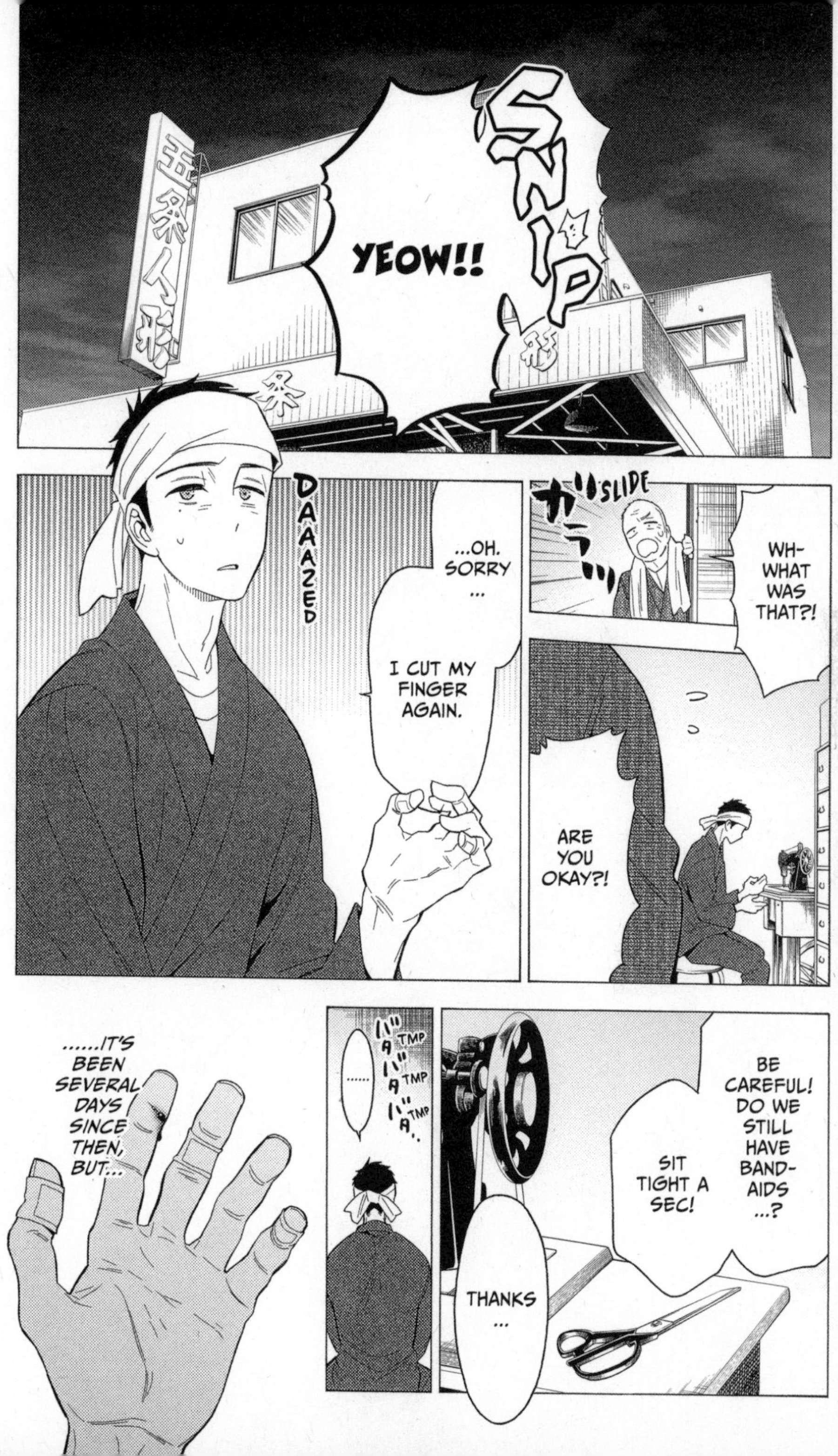
SNIP
YEOW!!
SLIDE
WH- WHAT WAS THAT?!
ARE YOU OKAY?!
DAAAAZED
...OH. SORRY ...
I CUT MY FINGER AGAIN.
BE CAREFUL! DO WE STILL HAVE BAND-AIDS ...?
SIT TIGHT A SEC!
THANKS ...
TMP TMP TMP
......
......IT'S BEEN SEVERAL DAYS SINCE THEN, BUT...

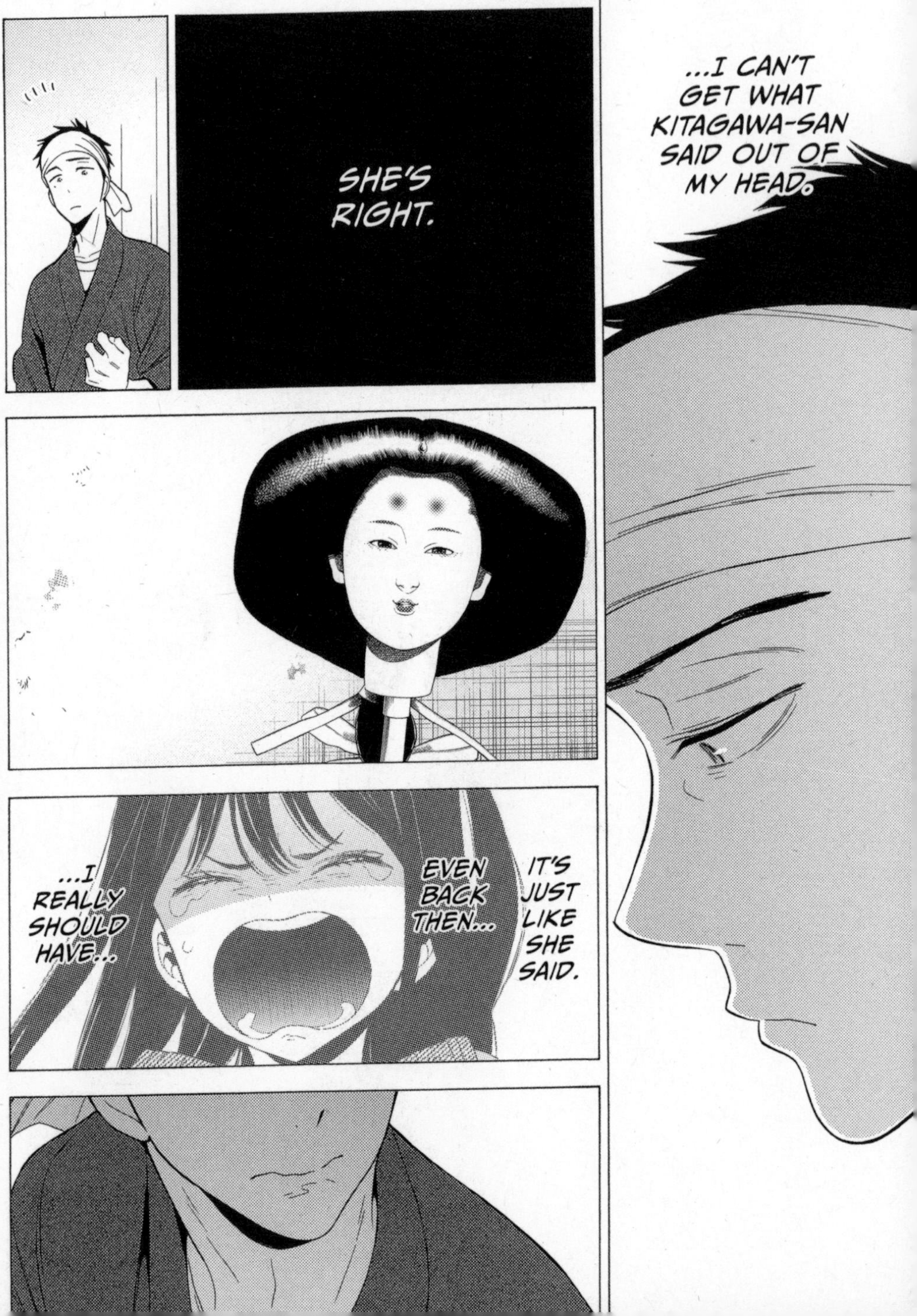
...I CAN'T GET WHAT KITAGAWA-SAN SAID OUT OF MY HEAD.
SHE'S RIGHT.
IT'S JUST LIKE SHE SAID.
EVEN BACK THEN...
...I REALLY SHOULD HAVE...

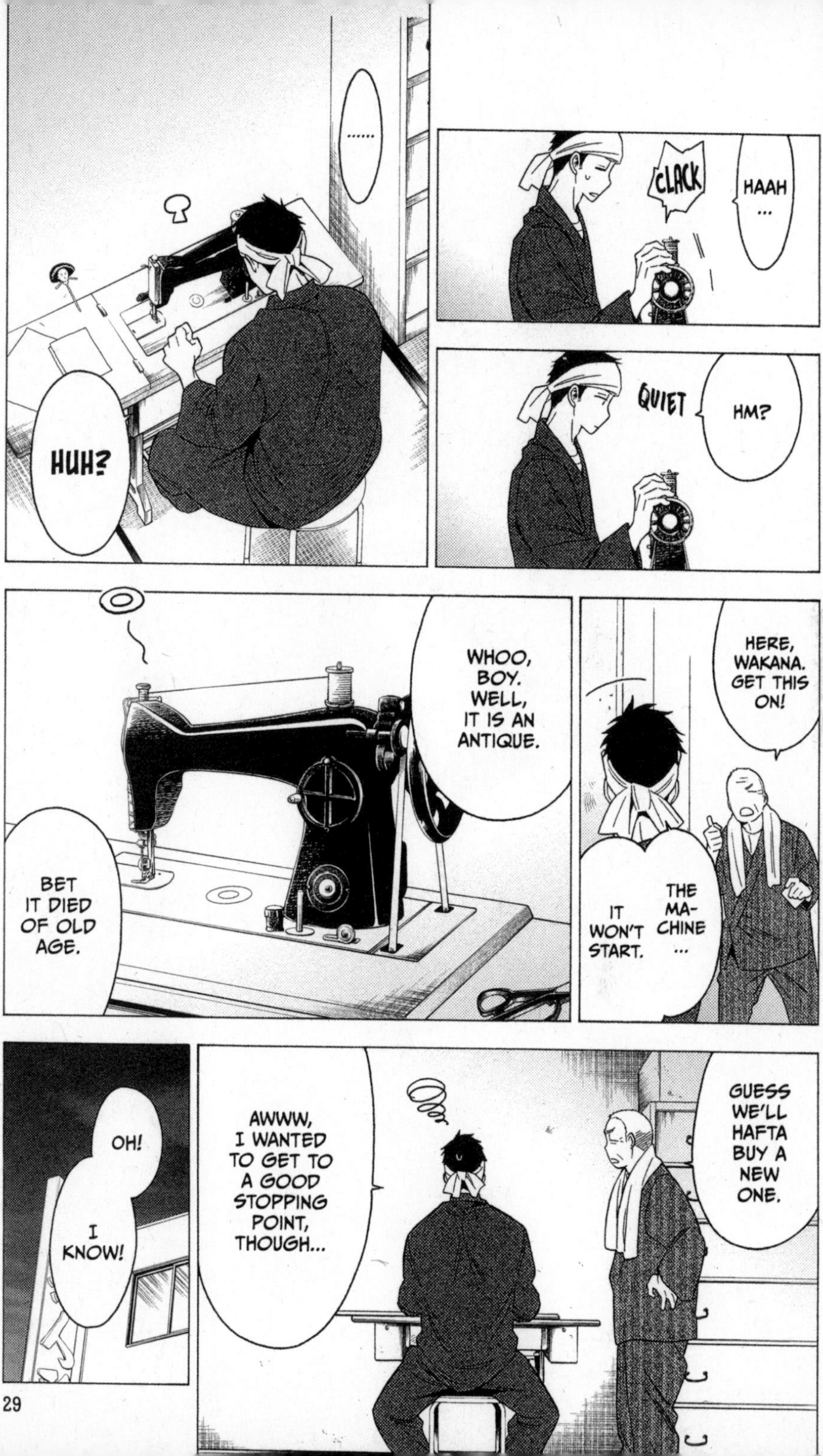

CLACK
HAAH ...
QUIET
HM?
......
HUH?
HERE, WAKANA. GET THIS ON!
THE MA-CHINE ...
IT WON'T START.
WHOO, BOY. WELL, IT IS AN ANTIQUE.
BET IT DIED OF OLD AGE.
GUESS WE'LL HAFTA BUY A NEW ONE.
AWWW, I WANTED TO GET TO A GOOD STOPPING POINT, THOUGH...
OH!
I KNOW!

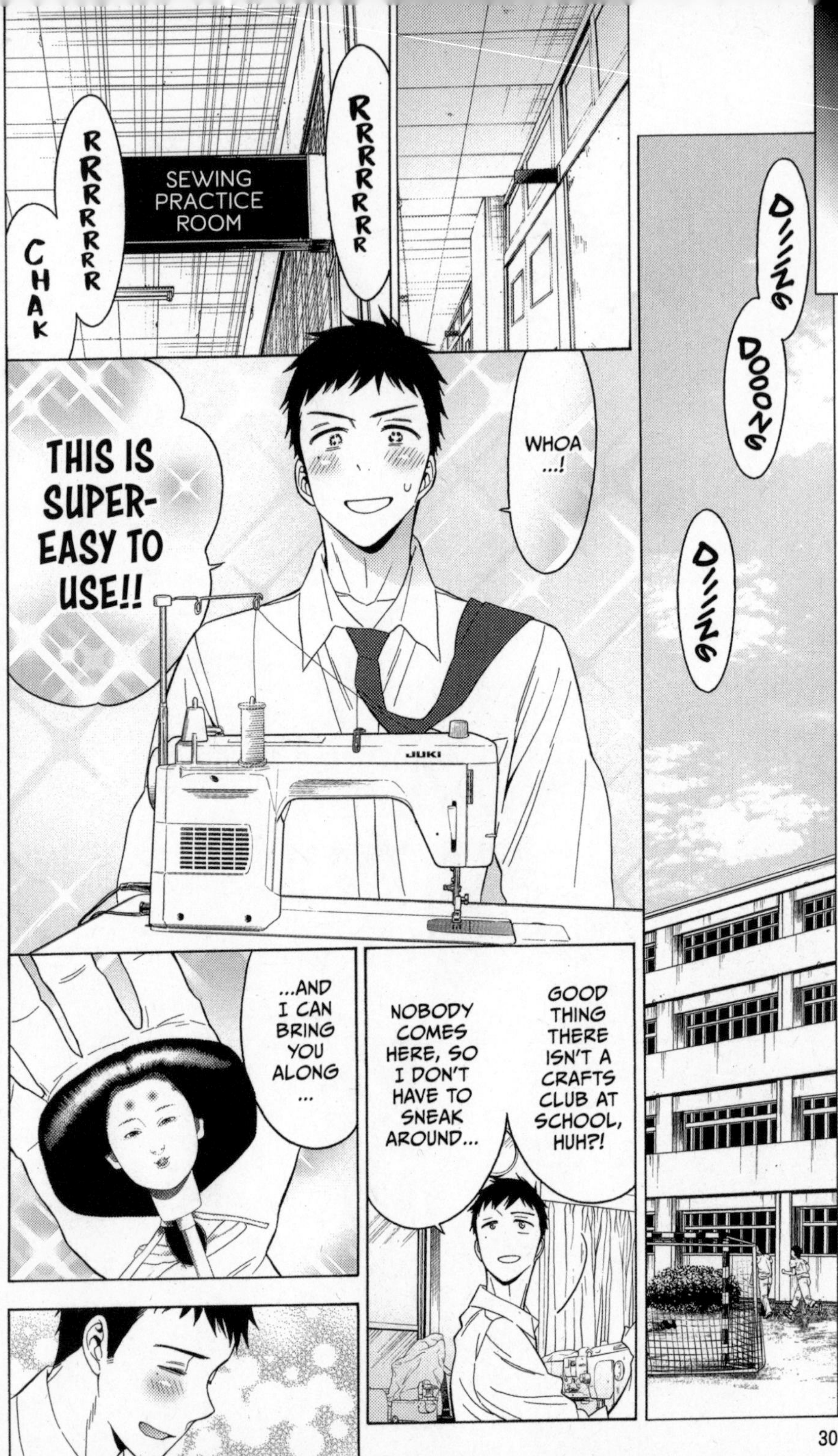
DIIING DOOONG
DIIING
RRRRRRR
SEWING PRACTICE ROOM
RRRRRR
CHAK
WHOA ...!
THIS IS SUPER-EASY TO USE!!
GOOD THING THERE ISN'T A CRAFTS CLUB AT SCHOOL, HUH?!
NOBODY COMES HERE, SO I DON'T HAVE TO SNEAK AROUND...
...AND I CAN BRING YOU ALONG ...

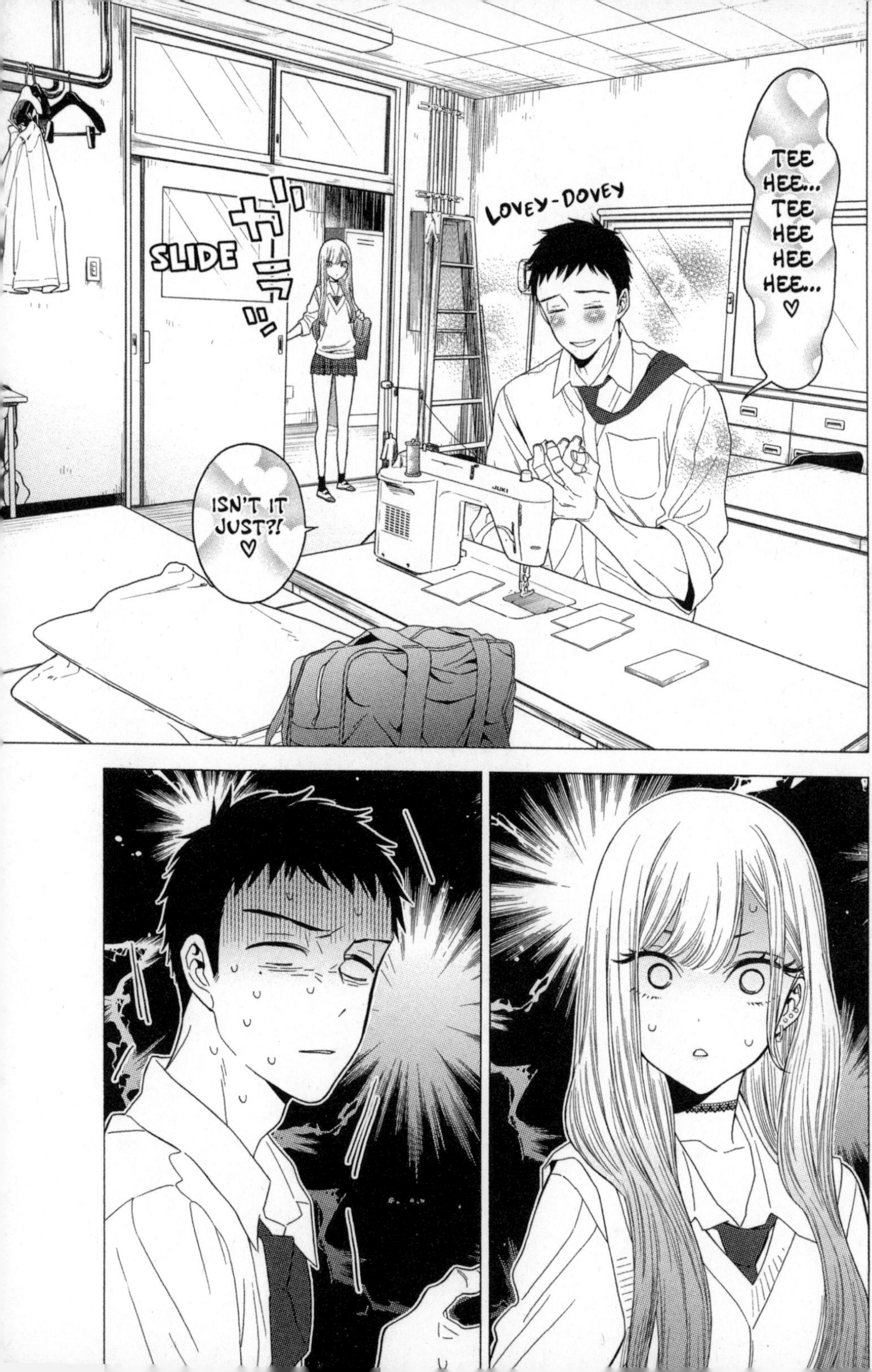
TEE HEE... TEE HEE HEE HEE... ♡
LOVEY-DOVEY
SLIDE
ISN'T IT JUST?! ♡

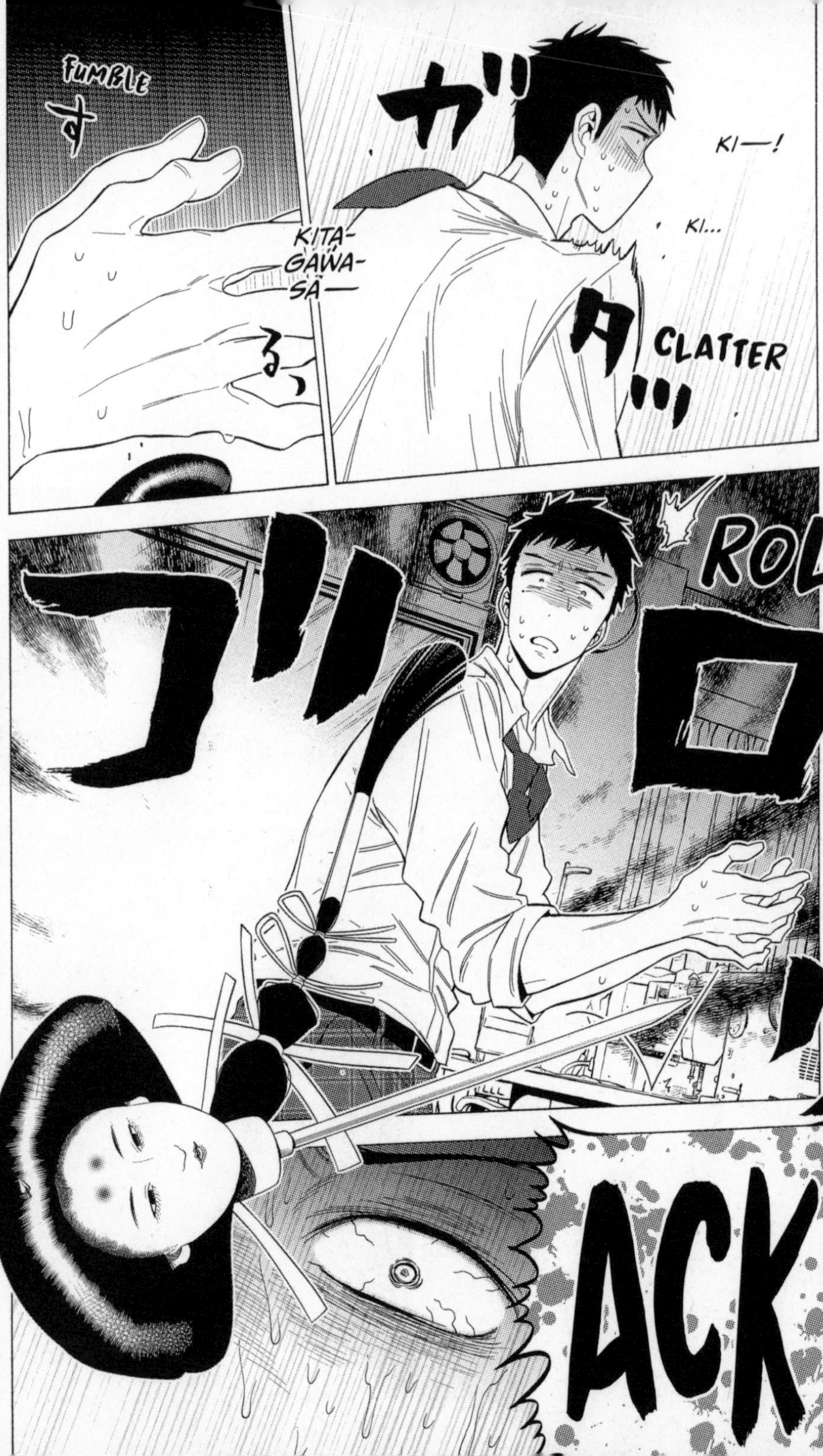
KI—!
KI...
CLATTER
FUMBLE
KITA-GAWA-SA—
ROLL
ACK!

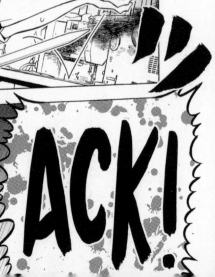

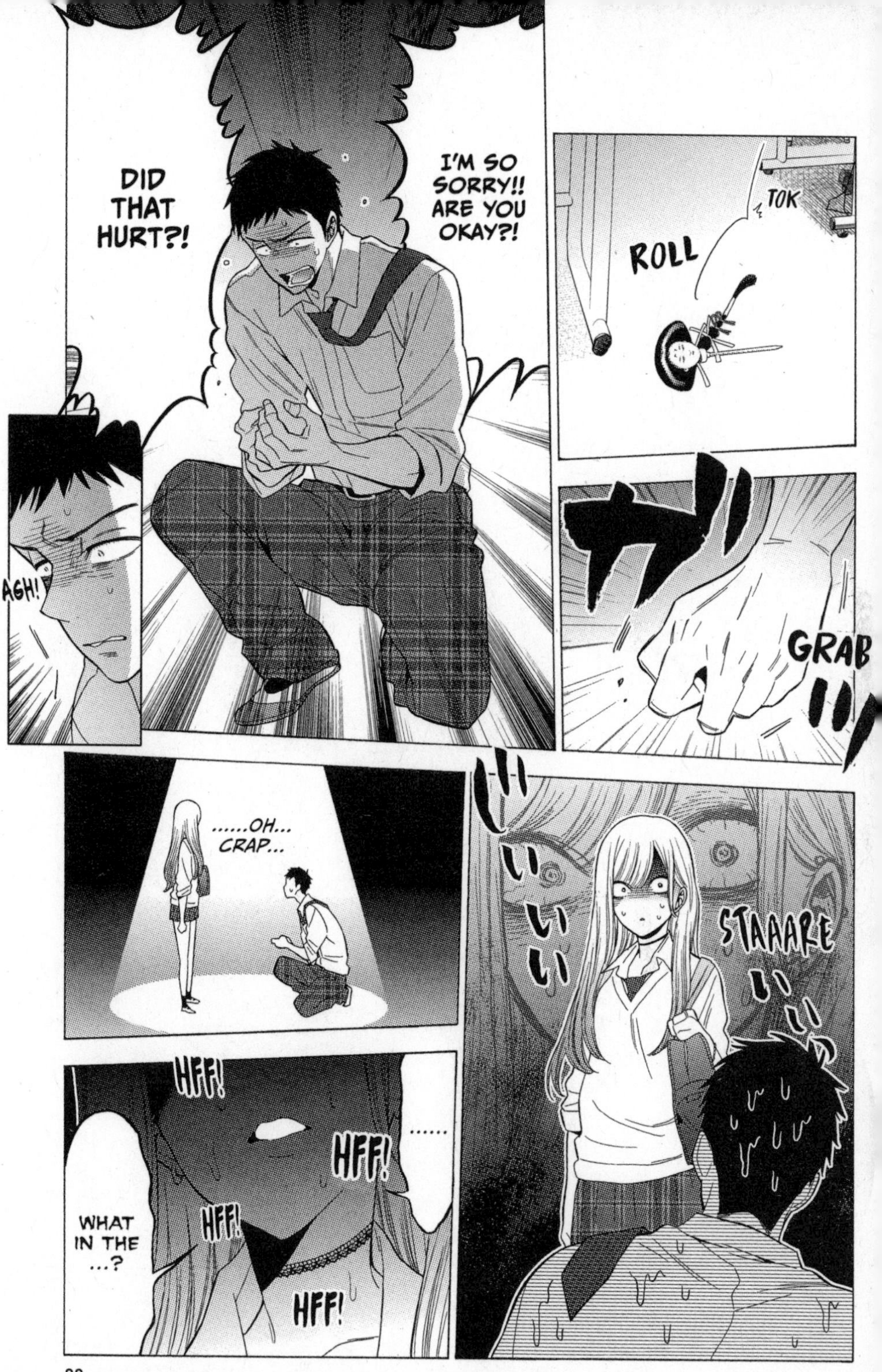
TOK
ROLL
GRAB
I'M SO SORRY!! ARE YOU OKAY?!
DID THAT HURT?!
AGH!
STAAARE
......OH... CRAP...
HFF!
......
HFF!
WHAT IN THE ...?
HFF!
HFF!

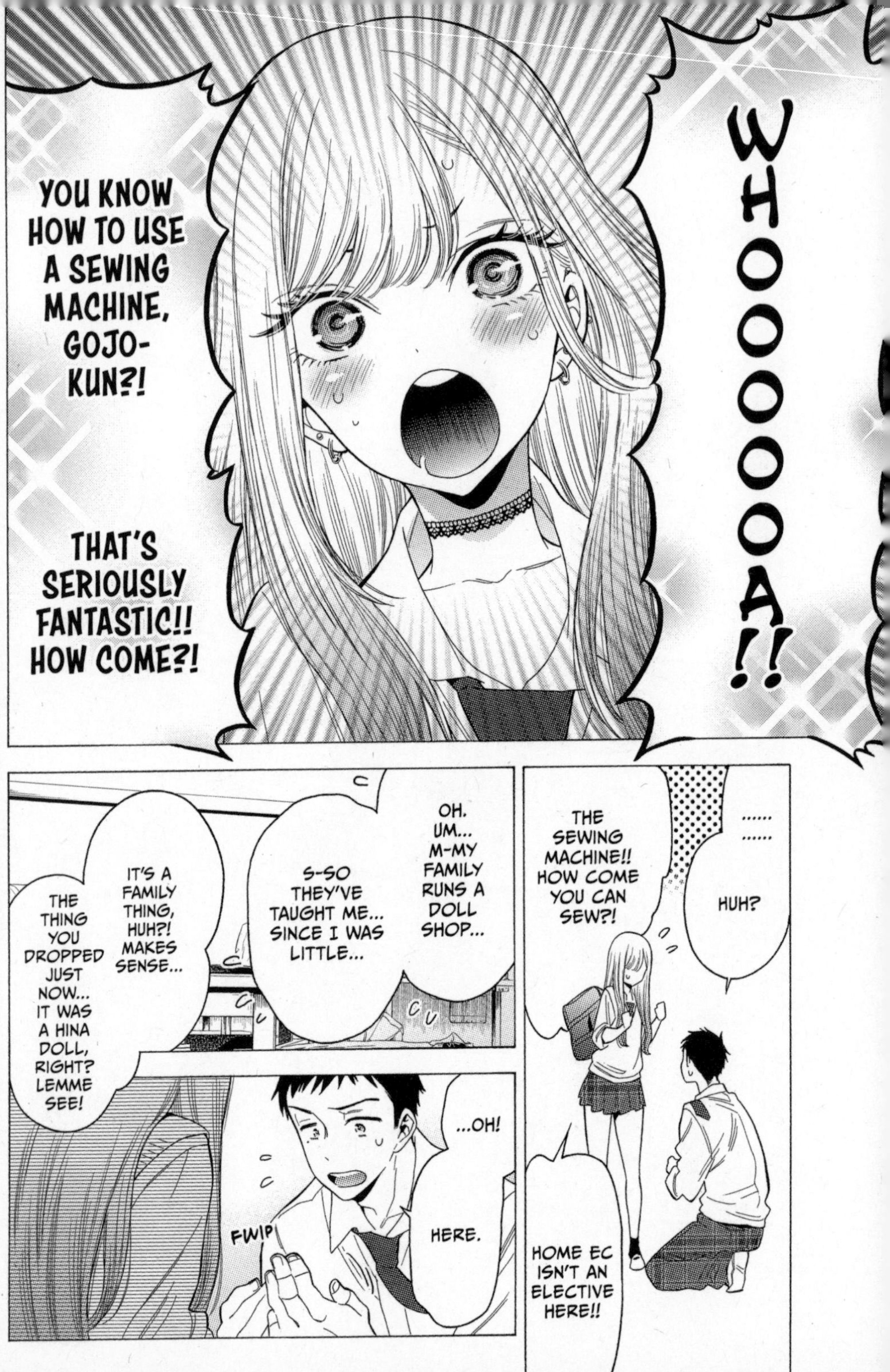
WHOOOOOA!!
YOU KNOW HOW TO USE A SEWING MACHINE, GOJO-KUN?!
THAT'S SERIOUSLY FANTASTIC!! HOW COME?!
.... HUH?
THE SEWING MACHINE!! HOW COME YOU CAN SEW?!
HOME EC ISN'T AN ELECTIVE HERE!!
OH. UM... M-MY FAMILY RUNS A DOLL SHOP...
S-SO THEY'VE TAUGHT ME... SINCE I WAS LITTLE...
IT'S A FAMILY THING, HUH?! MAKES SENSE...
THE THING YOU DROPPED JUST NOW... IT WAS A HINA DOLL, RIGHT? LEMME SEE!
...OH!
HERE.
FWIP

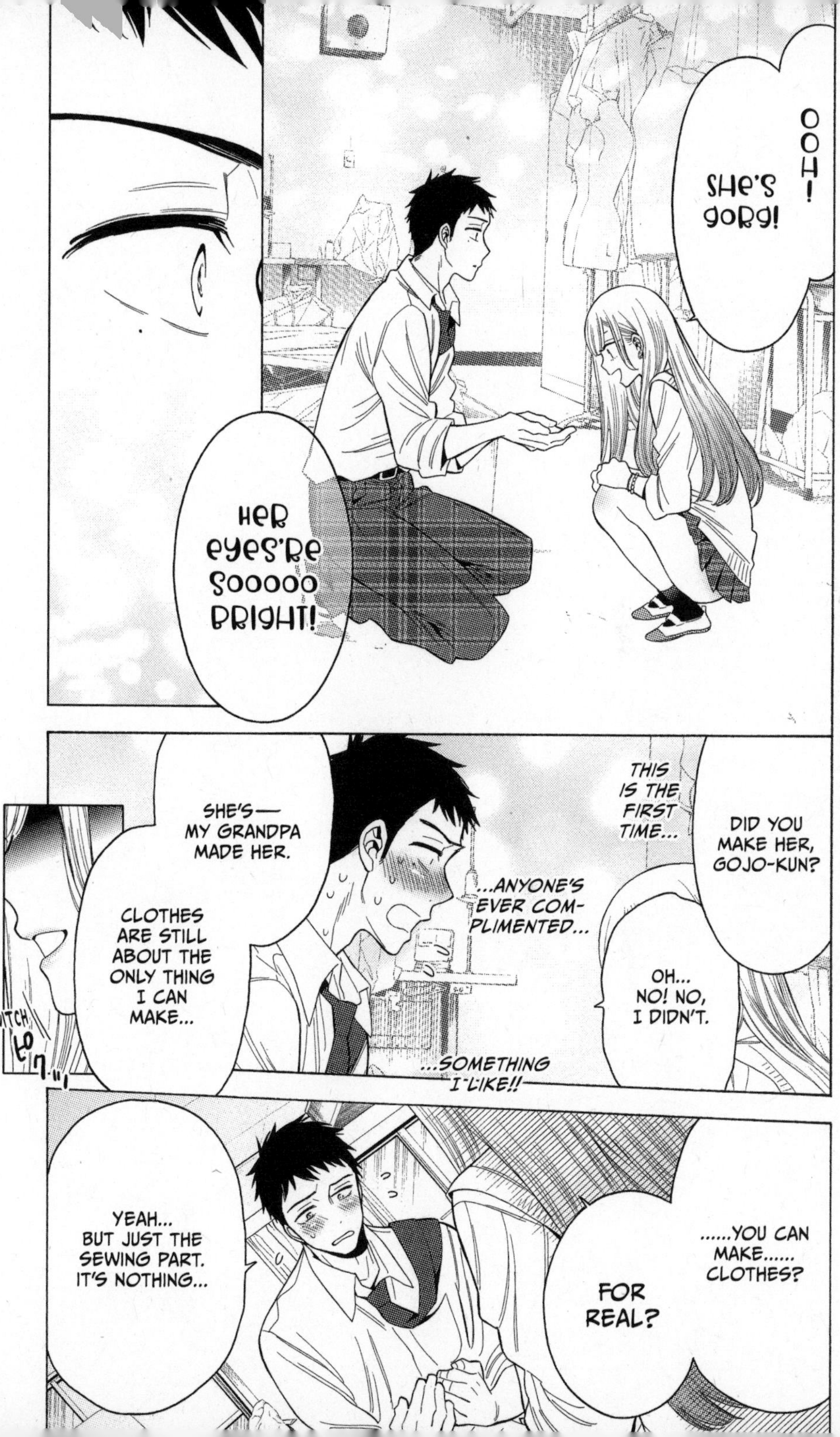
OOH! SHE'S GORG!
HER EYES'RE SOOOOO BRIGHT!
DID YOU MAKE HER, GOJO-KUN?
OH... NO! NO, I DIDN'T.
THIS IS THE FIRST TIME...
...ANYONE'S EVER COMPLIMENTED...
...SOMETHING I LIKE!!
SHE'S— MY GRANDPA MADE HER.
CLOTHES ARE STILL ABOUT THE ONLY THING I CAN MAKE...
TWITCH
......YOU CAN MAKE...... CLOTHES?
FOR REAL?
YEAH... BUT JUST THE SEWING PART. IT'S NOTHING...

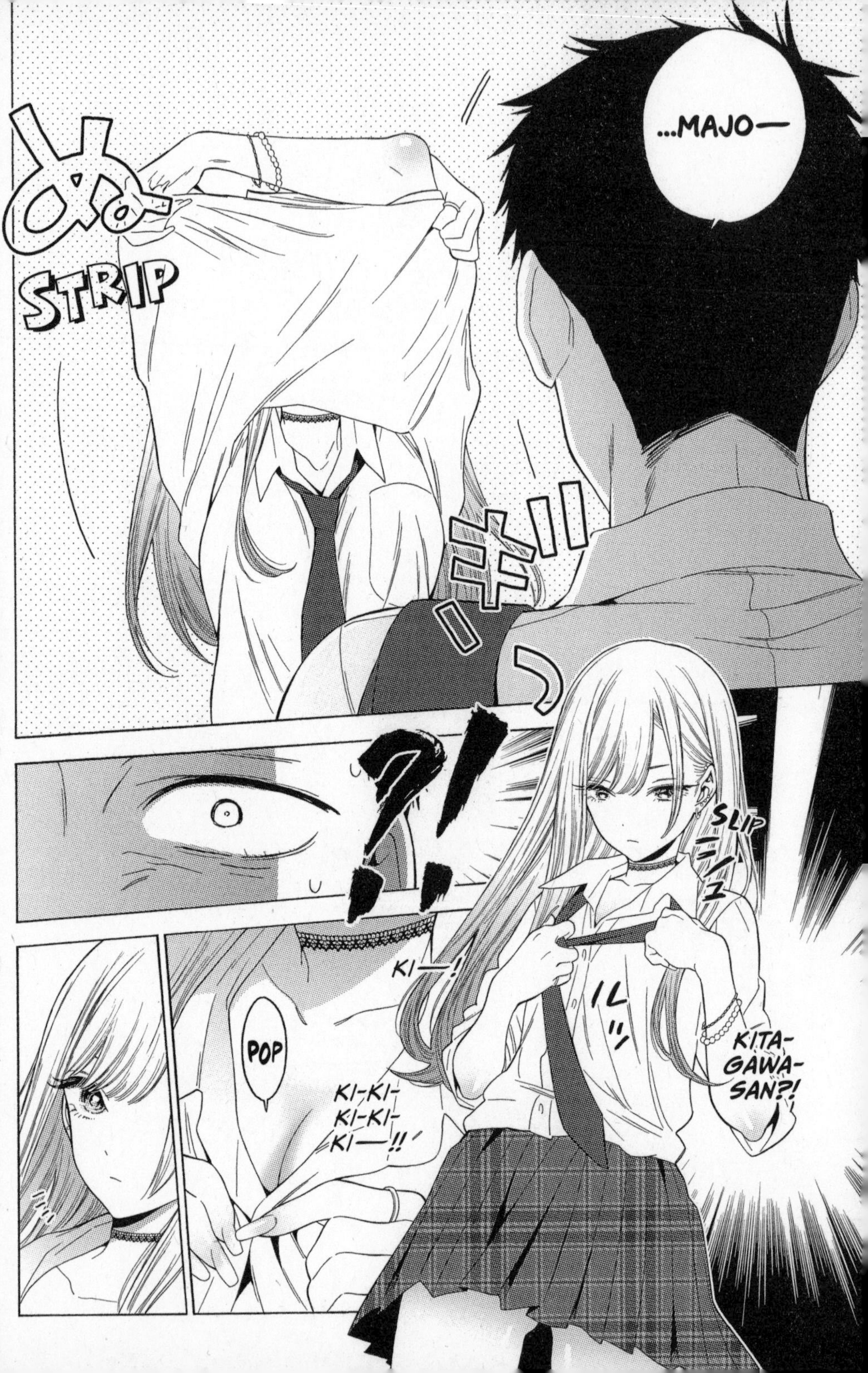
...MAJO—
STRIP
?!
SLIP
KITA-GAWA-SAN?!
KI—!
KI-KI-KI-KI-KI—!!
POP

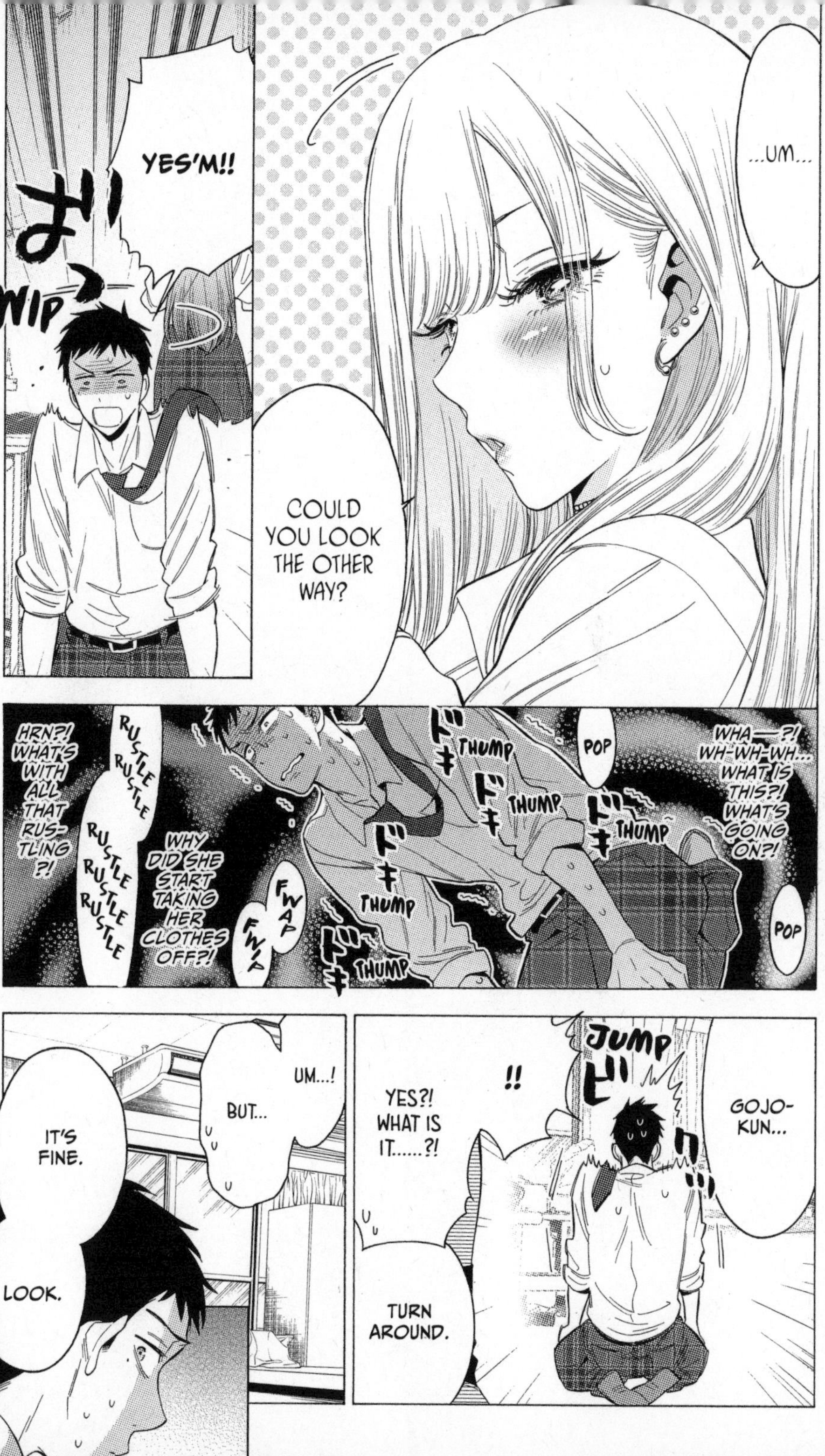
...UM...
COULD YOU LOOK THE OTHER WAY?
YES'M!!
はい
VWIP
WHA—?! WH-WH-WH... WHAT IS THIS?! WHAT'S GOING ON?!
POP
POP
ドキ THUMP
ドキ THUMP
ドキ THUMP
ドキ THUMP
ドキ THUMP
FWAP
FWAP
WHY DID SHE START TAKING HER CLOTHES OFF?!
RUSTLE RUSTLE
RUSTLE RUSTLE RUSTLE
HRN?! WHAT'S WITH ALL THAT RUS-TLING?!
GOJO-KUN...
JUMP
ビ
!!
YES?! WHAT IS IT......?!
TURN AROUND.
UM...!
BUT...
IT'S FINE.
LOOK.

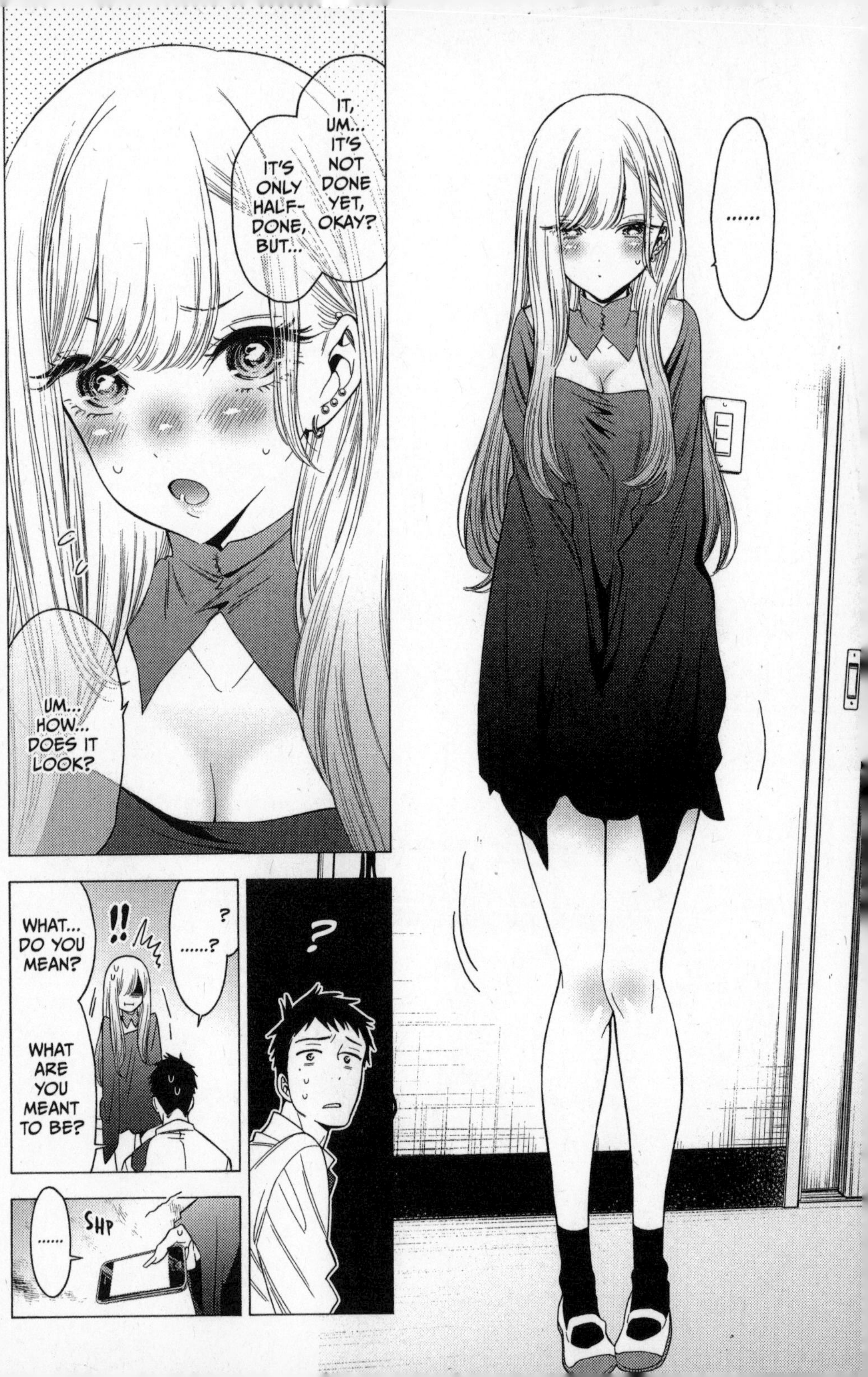
......
IT, UM... IT'S NOT DONE YET, OKAY?
IT'S ONLY HALF-DONE, BUT...
UM... HOW... DOES IT LOOK?
?
?
!!
......?
WHAT... DO YOU MEAN?
WHAT ARE YOU MEANT TO BE?
......
SHP

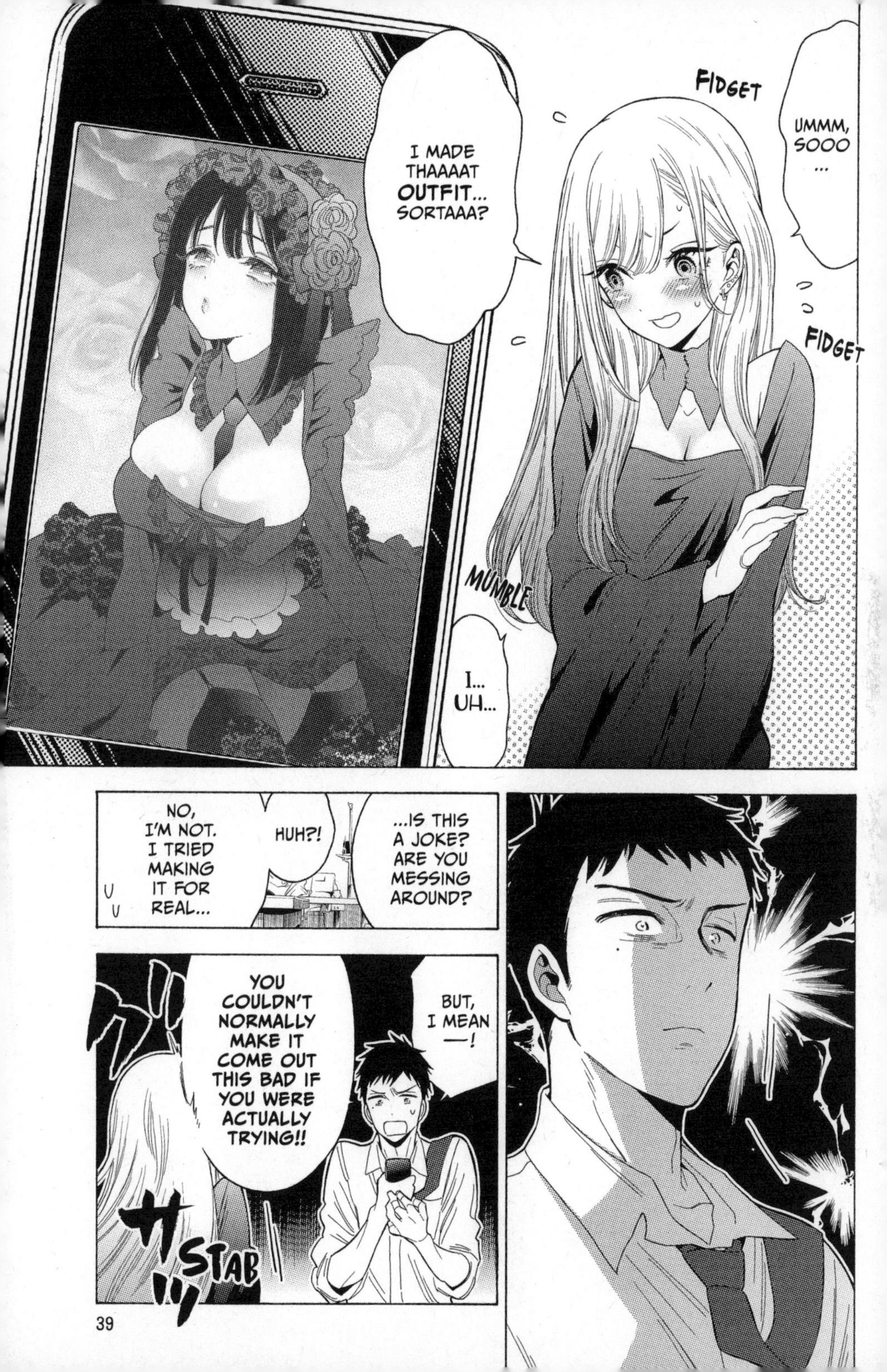
FIDGET
UMMM, SOOO ...
FIDGET
I MADE THAAAAT OUTFIT... SORTAAA?
MUMBLE
I... UH...
...IS THIS A JOKE? ARE YOU MESSING AROUND?
HUH?!
NO, I'M NOT. I TRIED MAKING IT FOR REAL...
BUT, I MEAN—!
YOU COULDN'T NORMALLY MAKE IT COME OUT THIS BAD IF YOU WERE ACTUALLY TRYING!!
STAB

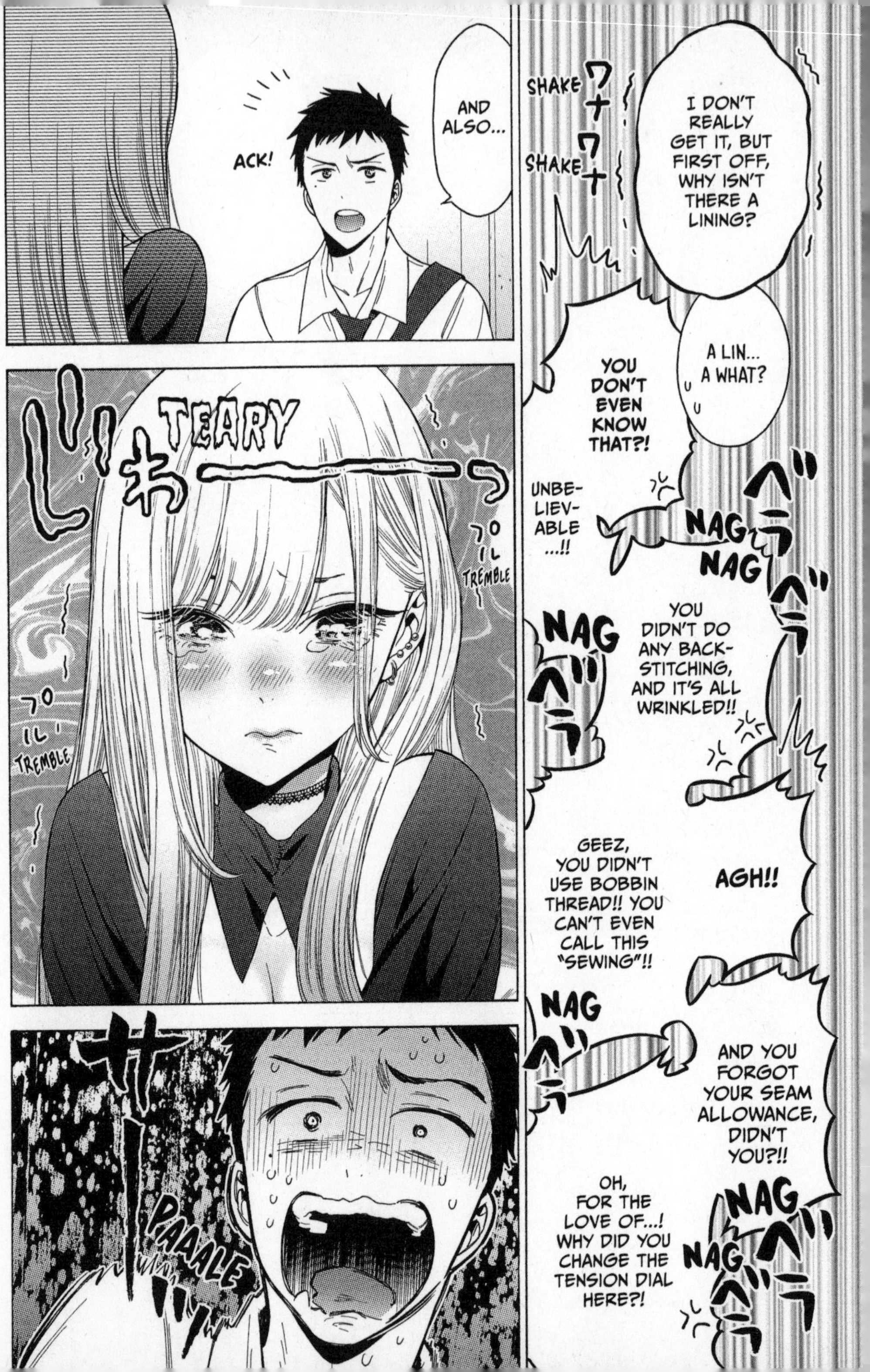
I DON'T REALLY GET IT, BUT FIRST OFF, WHY ISN'T THERE A LINING?
SHAKE
SHAKE
A LIN... A WHAT?
YOU DON'T EVEN KNOW THAT?!
UNBE-LIEV-ABLE...!!
NAG
NAG
YOU DIDN'T DO ANY BACK-STITCHING, AND IT'S ALL WRINKLED!!
NAG
AGH!!
GEEZ, YOU DIDN'T USE BOBBIN THREAD!! YOU CAN'T EVEN CALL THIS "SEWING"!!
NAG
AND YOU FORGOT YOUR SEAM ALLOWANCE, DIDN'T YOU?!!
NAG
NAG
OH, FOR THE LOVE OF...! WHY DID YOU CHANGE THE TENSION DIAL HERE?!
AND ALSO...
ACK!
TEARY
TREMBLE
TREMBLE
PAAAALE

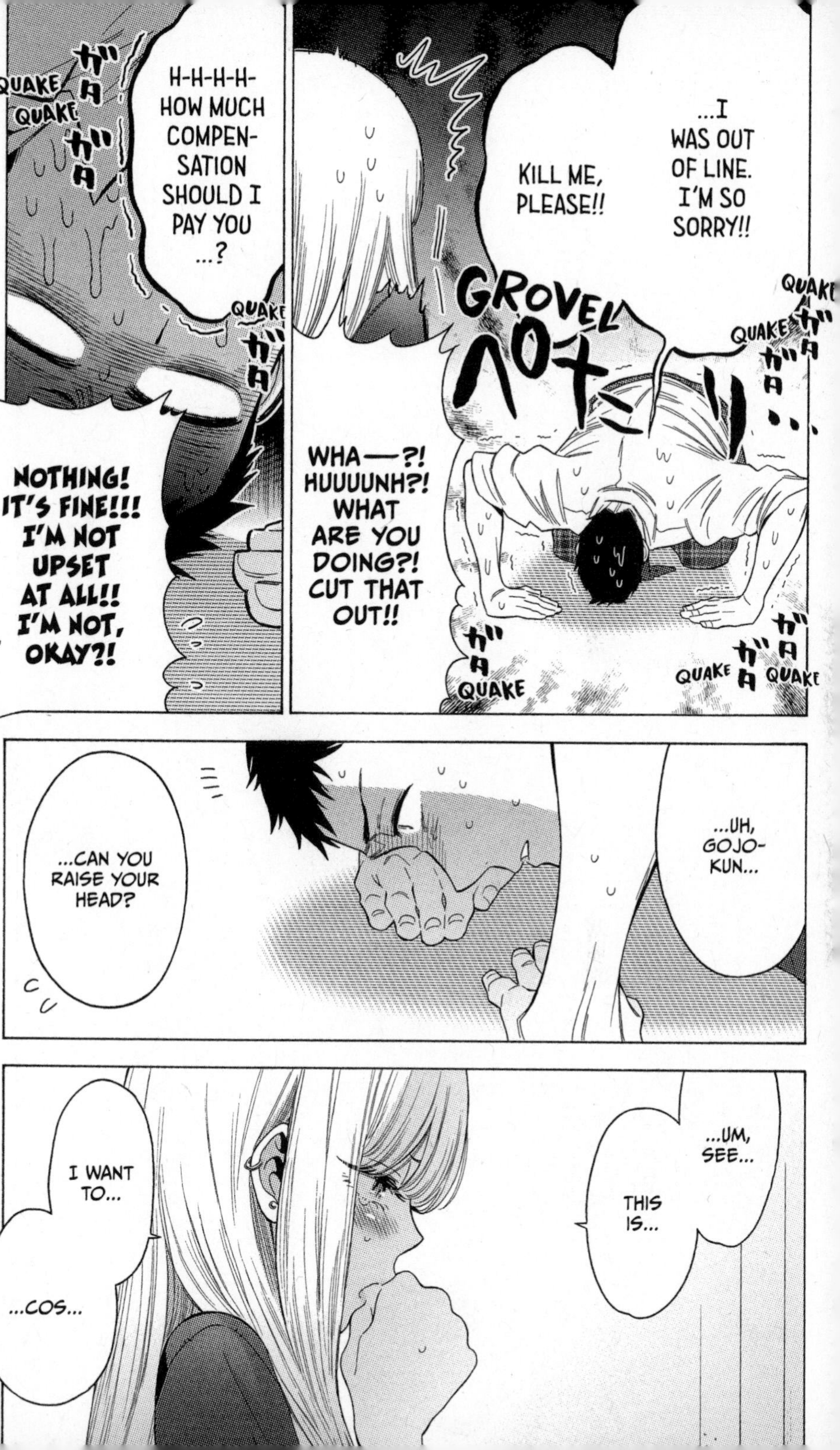
...I WAS OUT OF LINE. I'M SO SORRY!!
KILL ME, PLEASE!!
QUAKE
QUAKE
GROVEL
QUAKE
QUAKE
QUAKE
WHA—?! HUUUUNH?! WHAT ARE YOU DOING?! CUT THAT OUT!!
QUAKE
QUAKE
H-H-H-H-HOW MUCH COMPEN-SATION SHOULD I PAY YOU ...?
QUAKE
NOTHING! IT'S FINE!!! I'M NOT UPSET AT ALL!! I'M NOT, OKAY?!
...UH, GOJO-KUN...
...CAN YOU RAISE YOUR HEAD?
...UM, SEE...
THIS IS...
I WANT TO...
...COS...

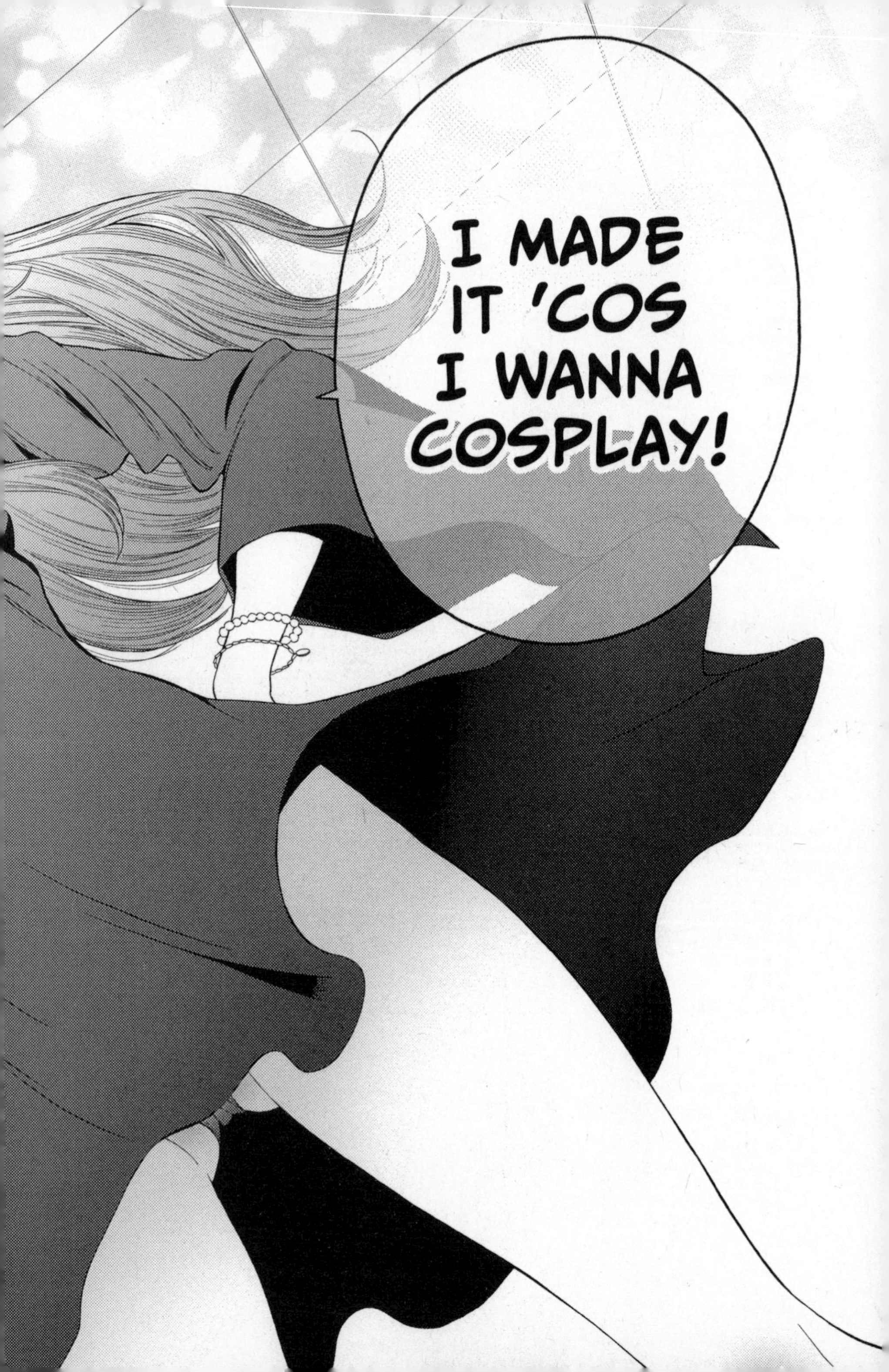
I MADE IT 'COS I WANNA COSPLAY!

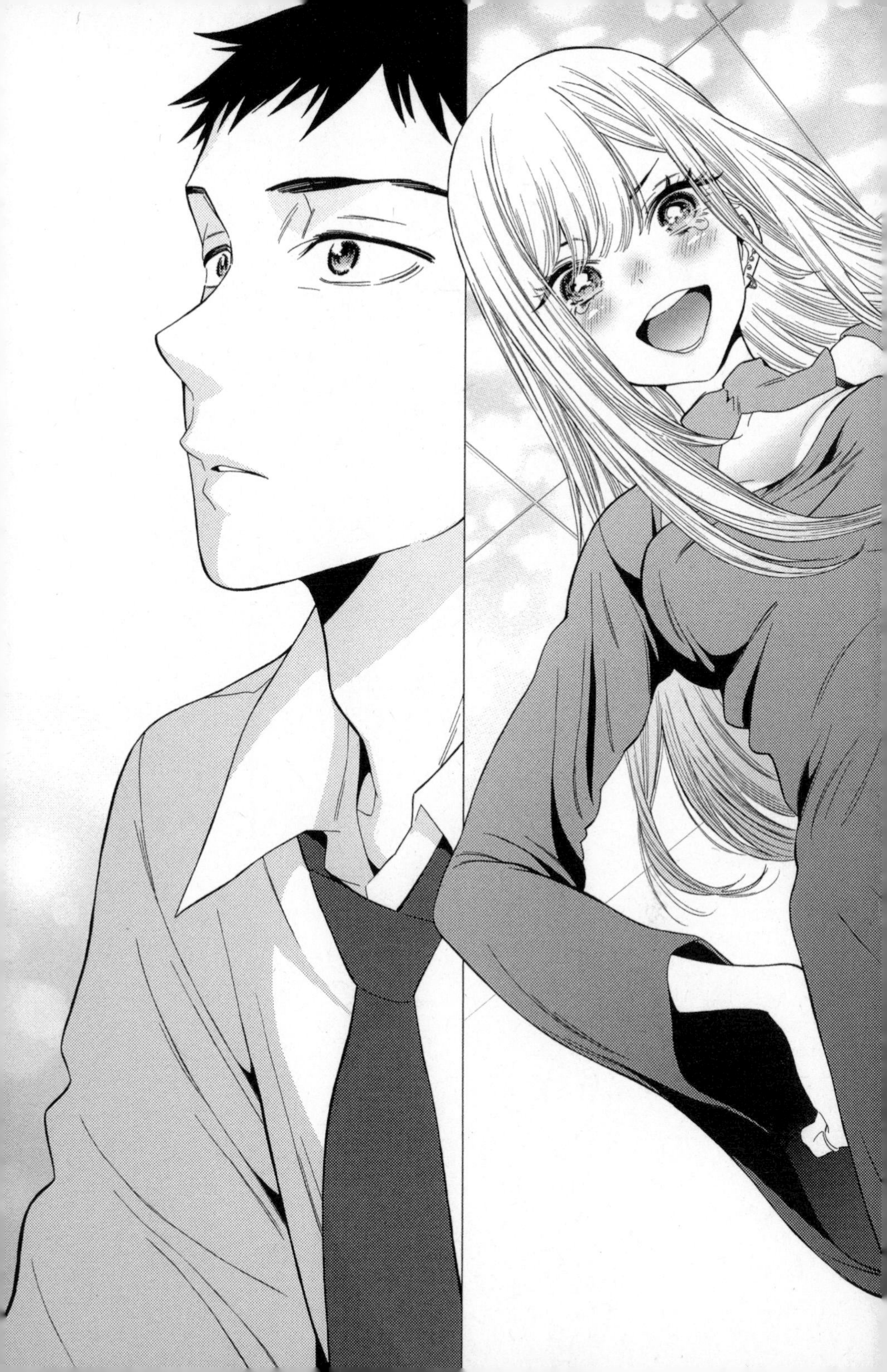

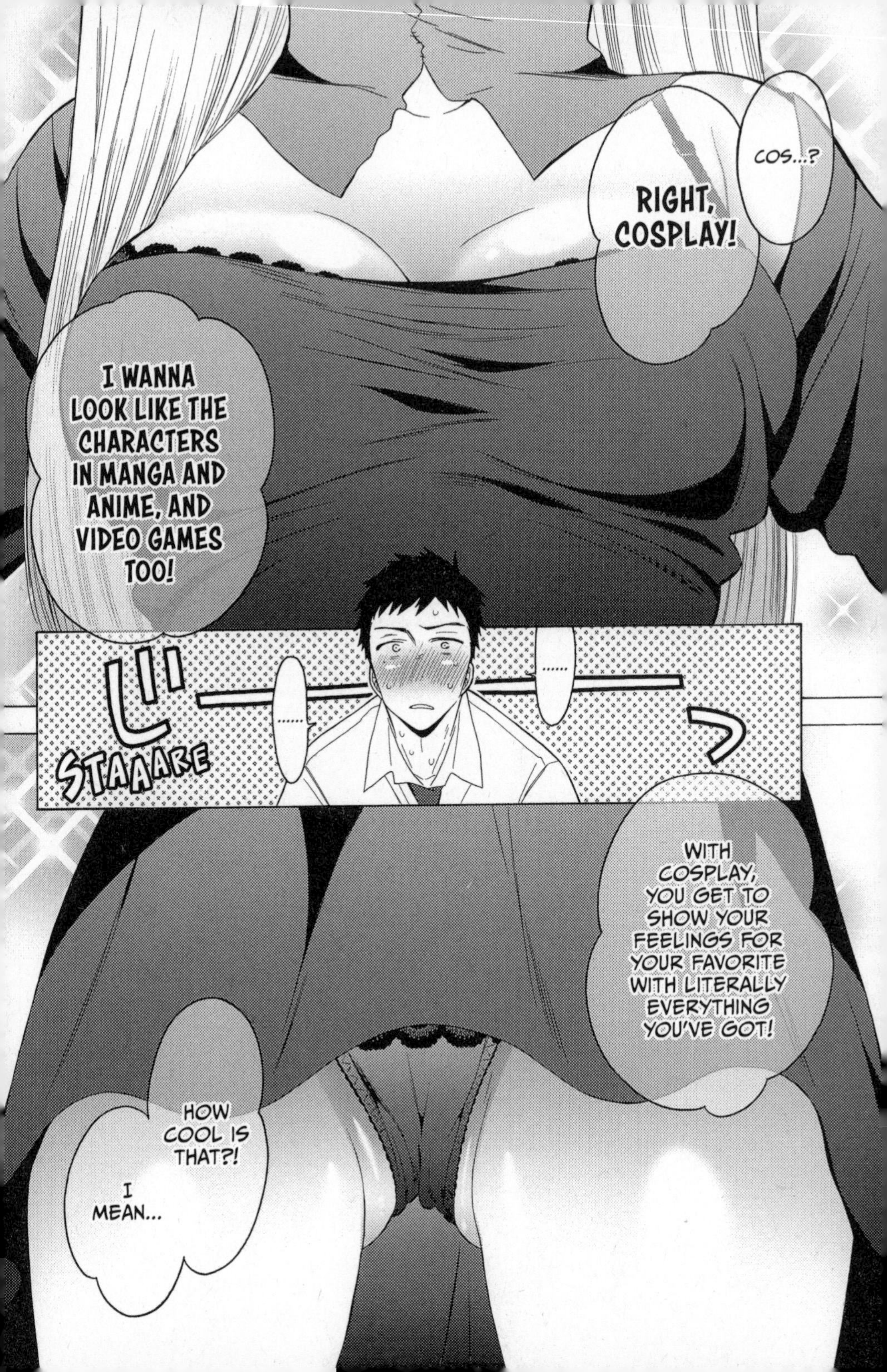
COS...?
RIGHT, COSPLAY!
I WANNA LOOK LIKE THE CHARACTERS IN MANGA AND ANIME, AND VIDEO GAMES TOO!
......
......
じー
STAAARE
WITH COSPLAY, YOU GET TO SHOW YOUR FEELINGS FOR YOUR FAVORITE WITH LITERALLY EVERYTHING YOU'VE GOT!
HOW COOL IS THAT?!
I MEAN...

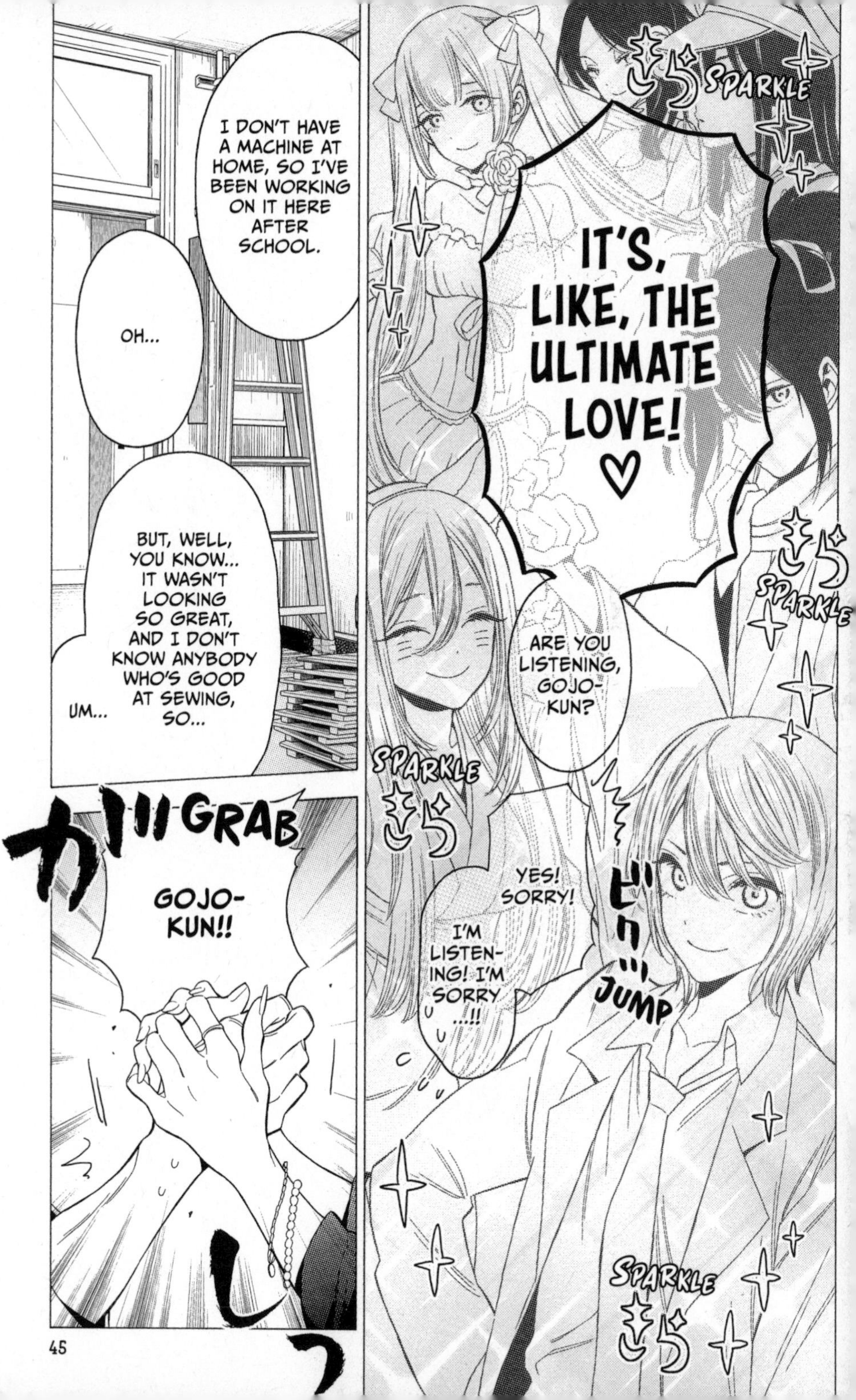
SPARKLE
IT'S, LIKE, THE ULTIMATE LOVE! ♥
SPARKLE
ARE YOU LISTENING, GOJO-KUN?
SPARKLE
JUMP
YES! SORRY!
I'M LISTENING! I'M SORRY...!!
SPARKLE
I DON'T HAVE A MACHINE AT HOME, SO I'VE BEEN WORKING ON IT HERE AFTER SCHOOL.
OH...
BUT, WELL, YOU KNOW... IT WASN'T LOOKING SO GREAT, AND I DON'T KNOW ANYBODY WHO'S GOOD AT SEWING, SO...
UM...
GRAB
GOJO-KUN!!

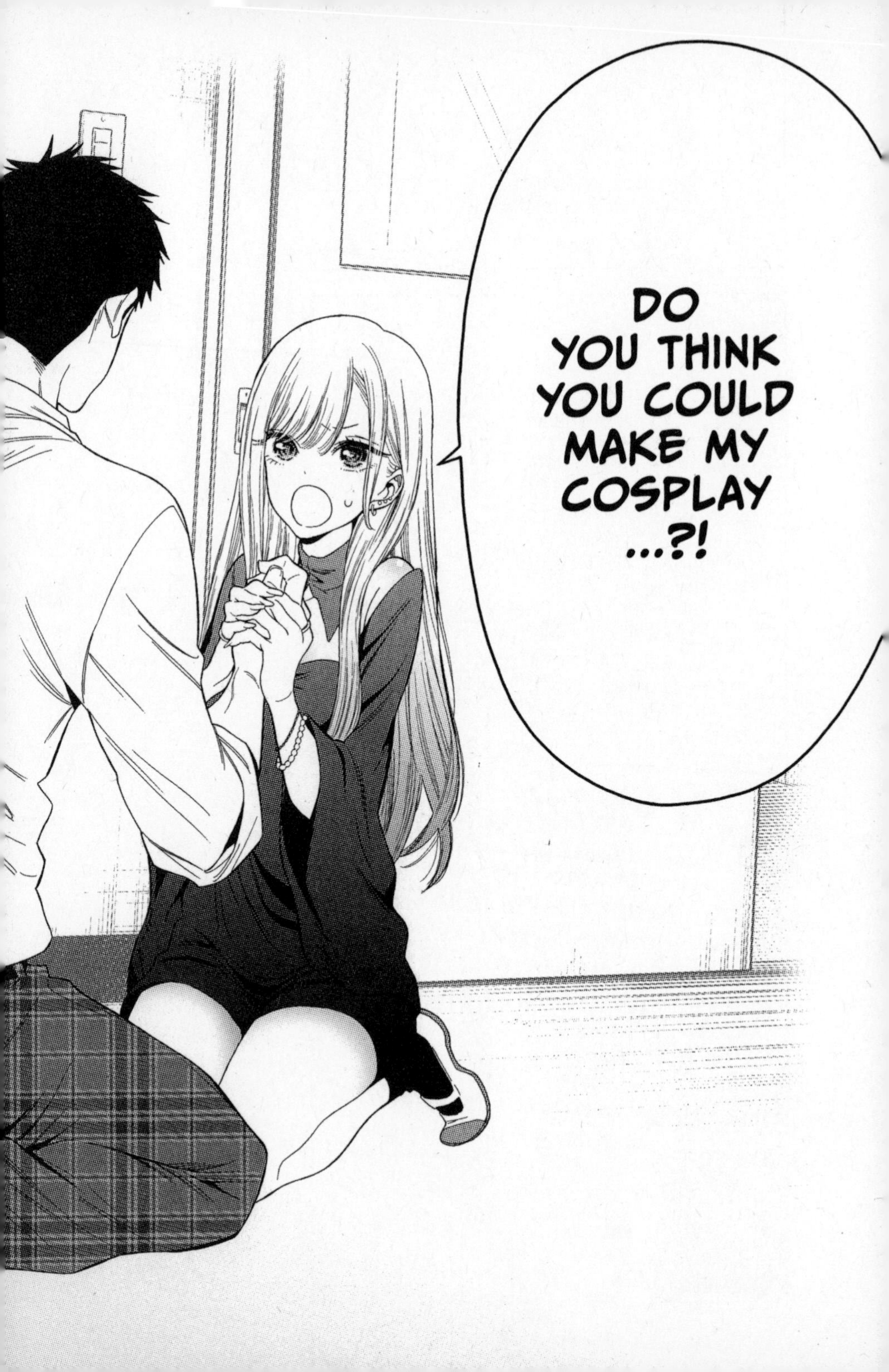
DO YOU THINK YOU COULD MAKE MY COSPLAY ...?!

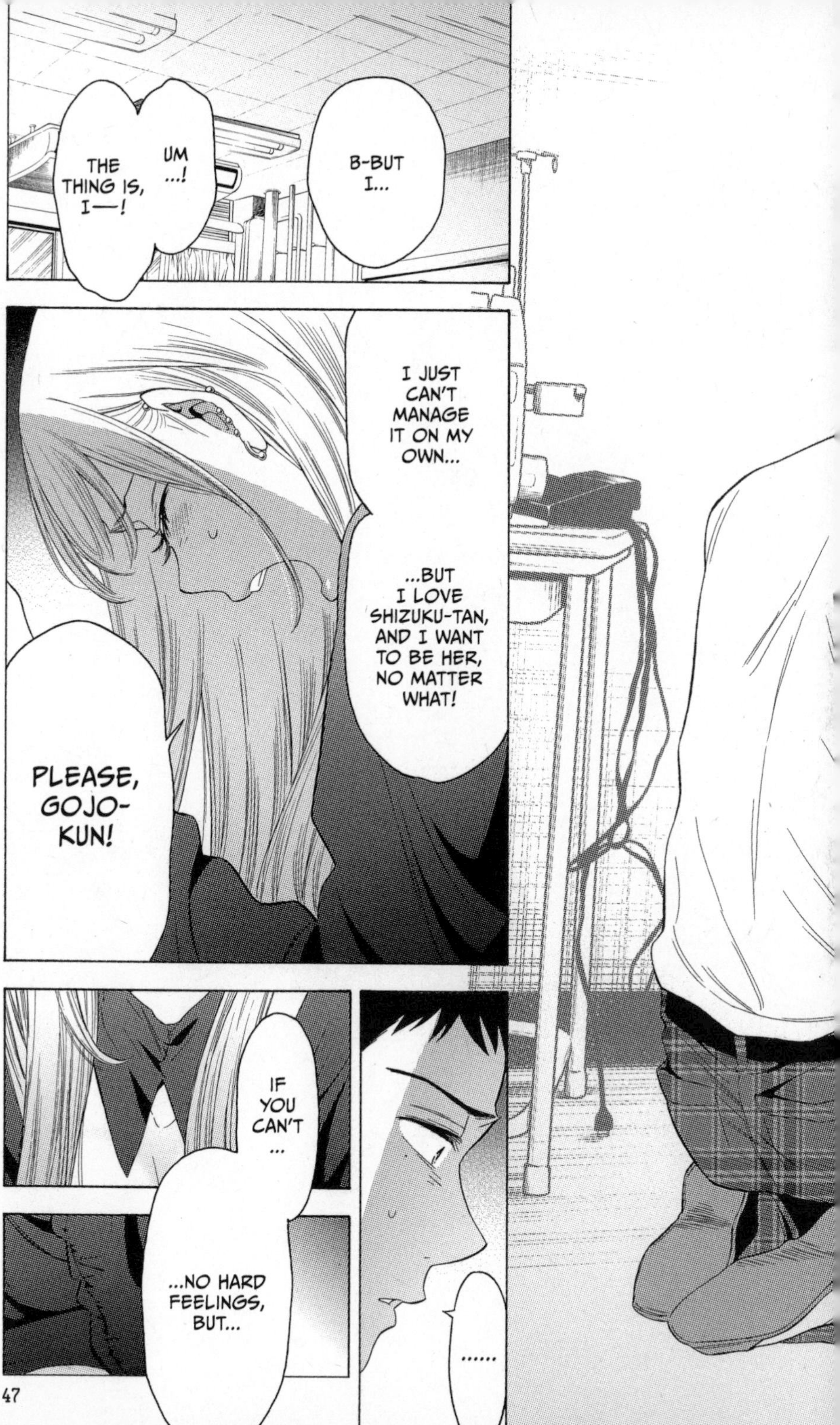
B-BUT I...
UM ...!
THE THING IS, I—!
I JUST CAN'T MANAGE IT ON MY OWN...
...BUT I LOVE SHIZUKU-TAN, AND I WANT TO BE HER, NO MATTER WHAT!
PLEASE, GOJO-KUN!
IF YOU CAN'T ...
...NO HARD FEELINGS, BUT...
......

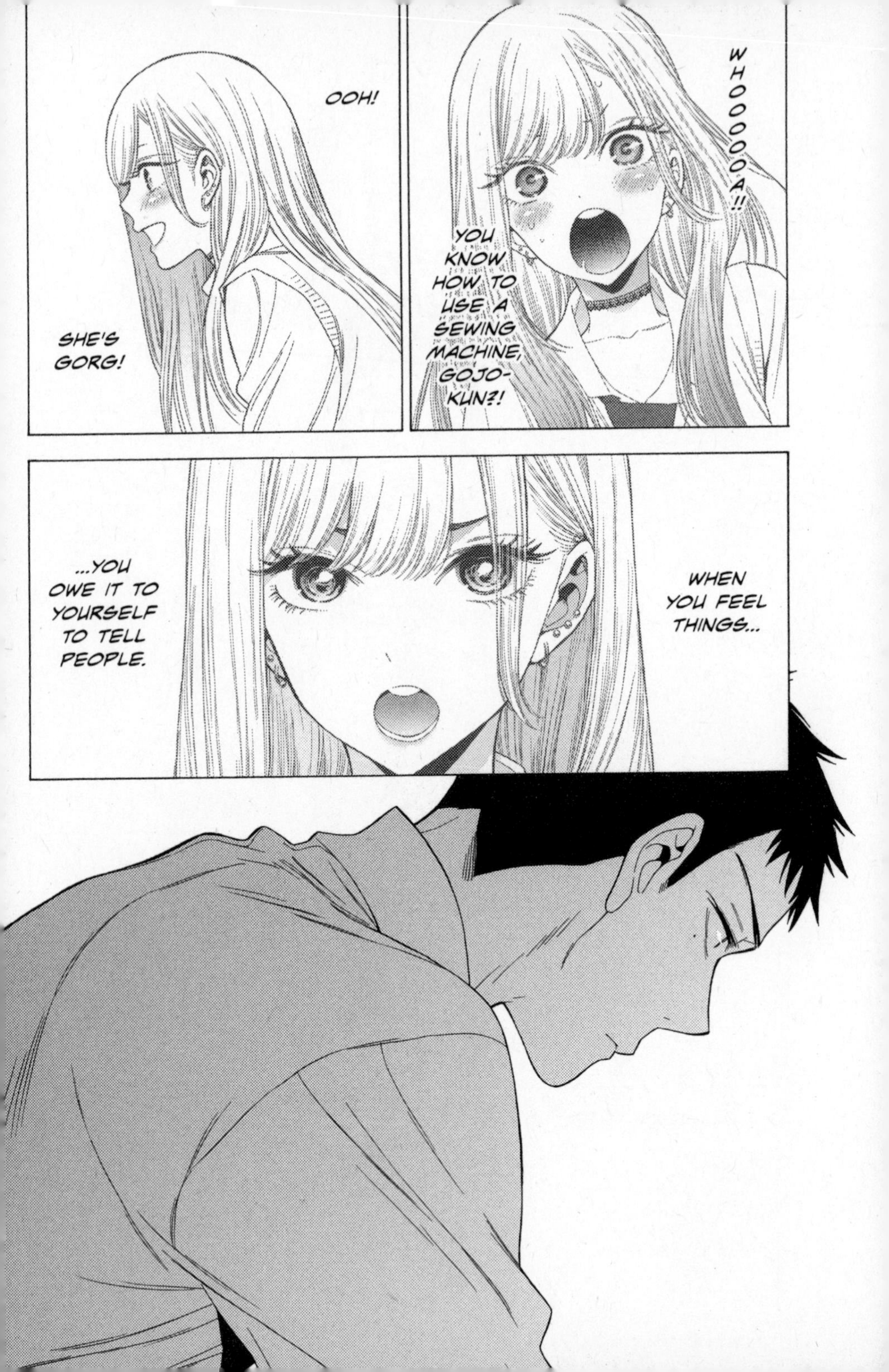
WHOOOOOA!!
YOU KNOW HOW TO USE A SEWING MACHINE, GOJO-KUN?!
OOH!
SHE'S GORG!
WHEN YOU FEEL THINGS...
...YOU OWE IT TO YOURSELF TO TELL PEOPLE.

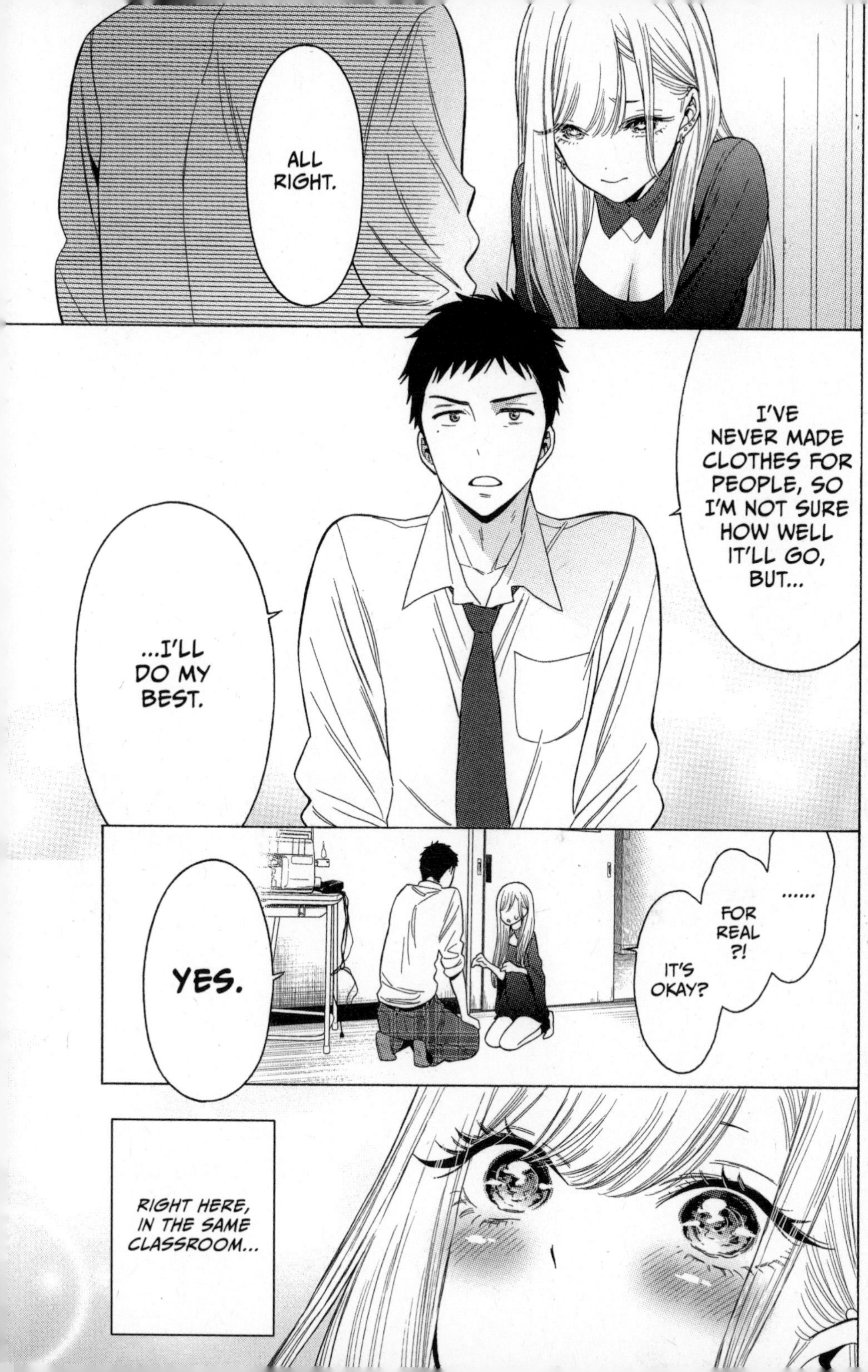
ALL RIGHT.
I'VE NEVER MADE CLOTHES FOR PEOPLE, SO I'M NOT SURE HOW WELL IT'LL GO, BUT...
...I'LL DO MY BEST.
......
FOR REAL?!
IT'S OKAY?
YES.
RIGHT HERE, IN THE SAME CLASSROOM...

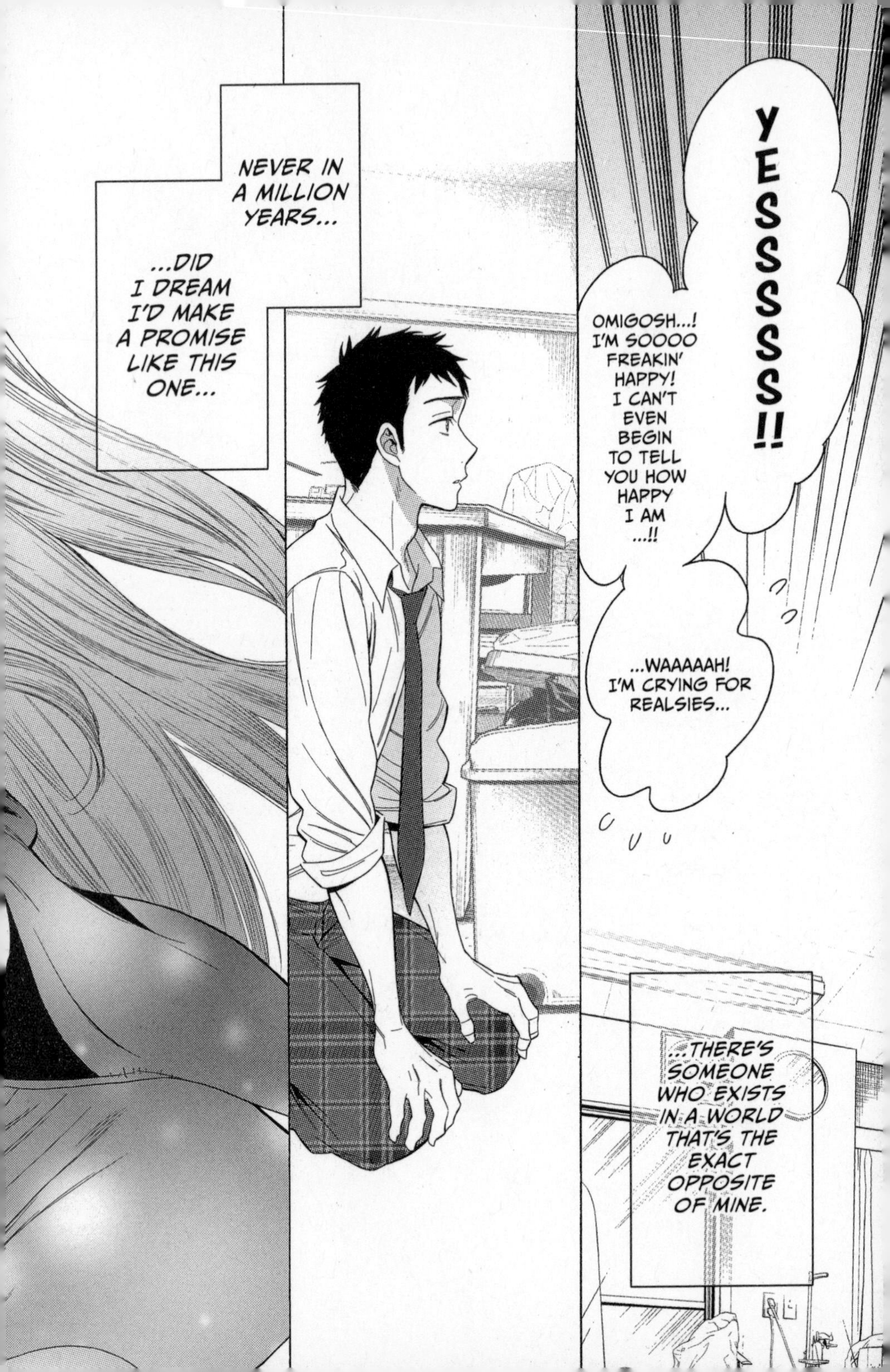
YESSSSS!!
OMIGOSH...! I'M SOOOO FREAKIN' HAPPY! I CAN'T EVEN BEGIN TO TELL YOU HOW HAPPY I AM ...!!
...WAAAAAH! I'M CRYING FOR REALSIES...
...THERE'S SOMEONE WHO EXISTS IN A WORLD THAT'S THE EXACT OPPOSITE OF MINE.
NEVER IN A MILLION YEARS...
...DID I DREAM I'D MAKE A PROMISE LIKE THIS ONE...

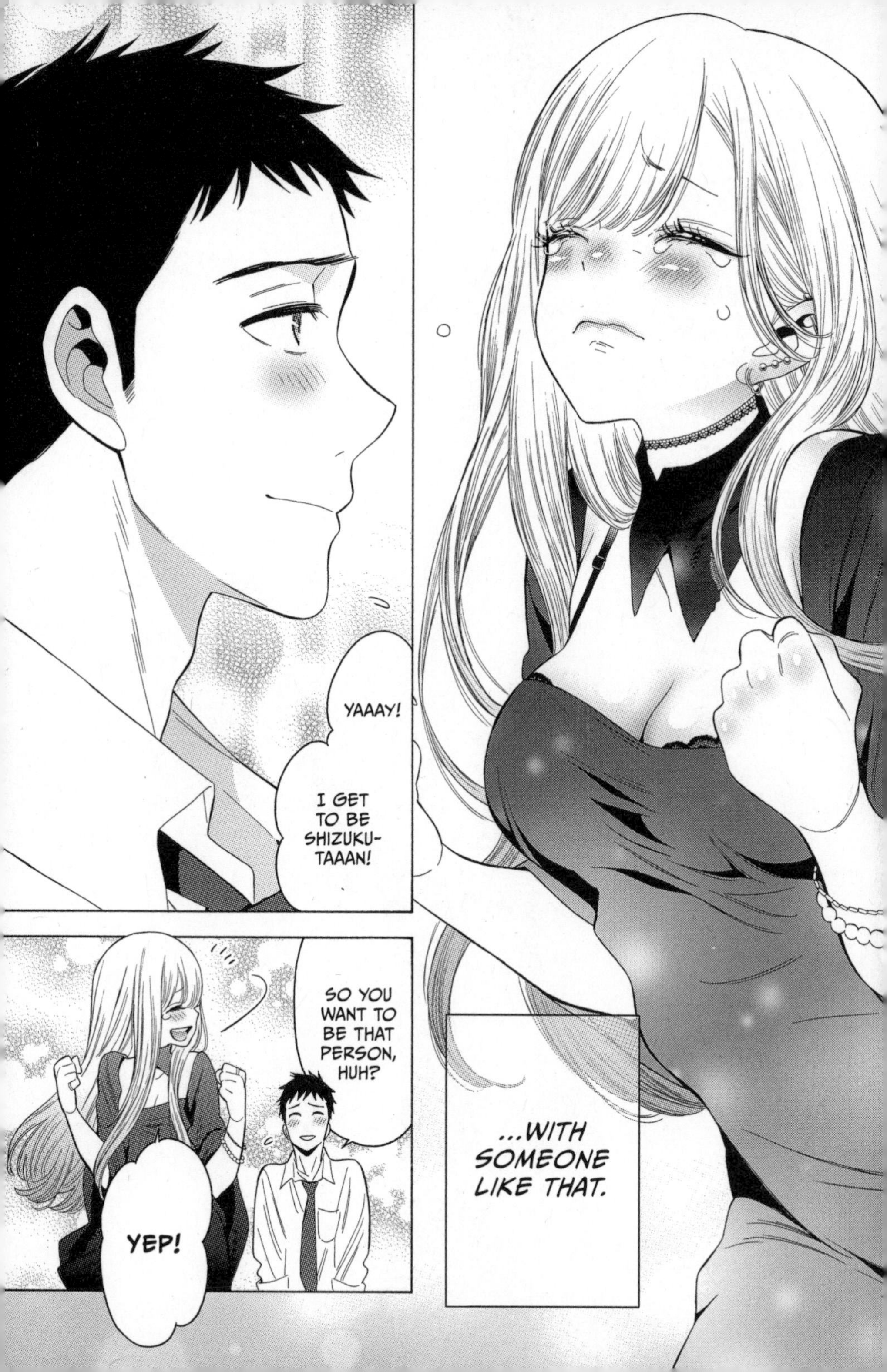
...WITH SOMEONE LIKE THAT.
YAAAY!
I GET TO BE SHIZUKU-TAAAN!
SO YOU WANT TO BE THAT PERSON, HUH?
YEP!

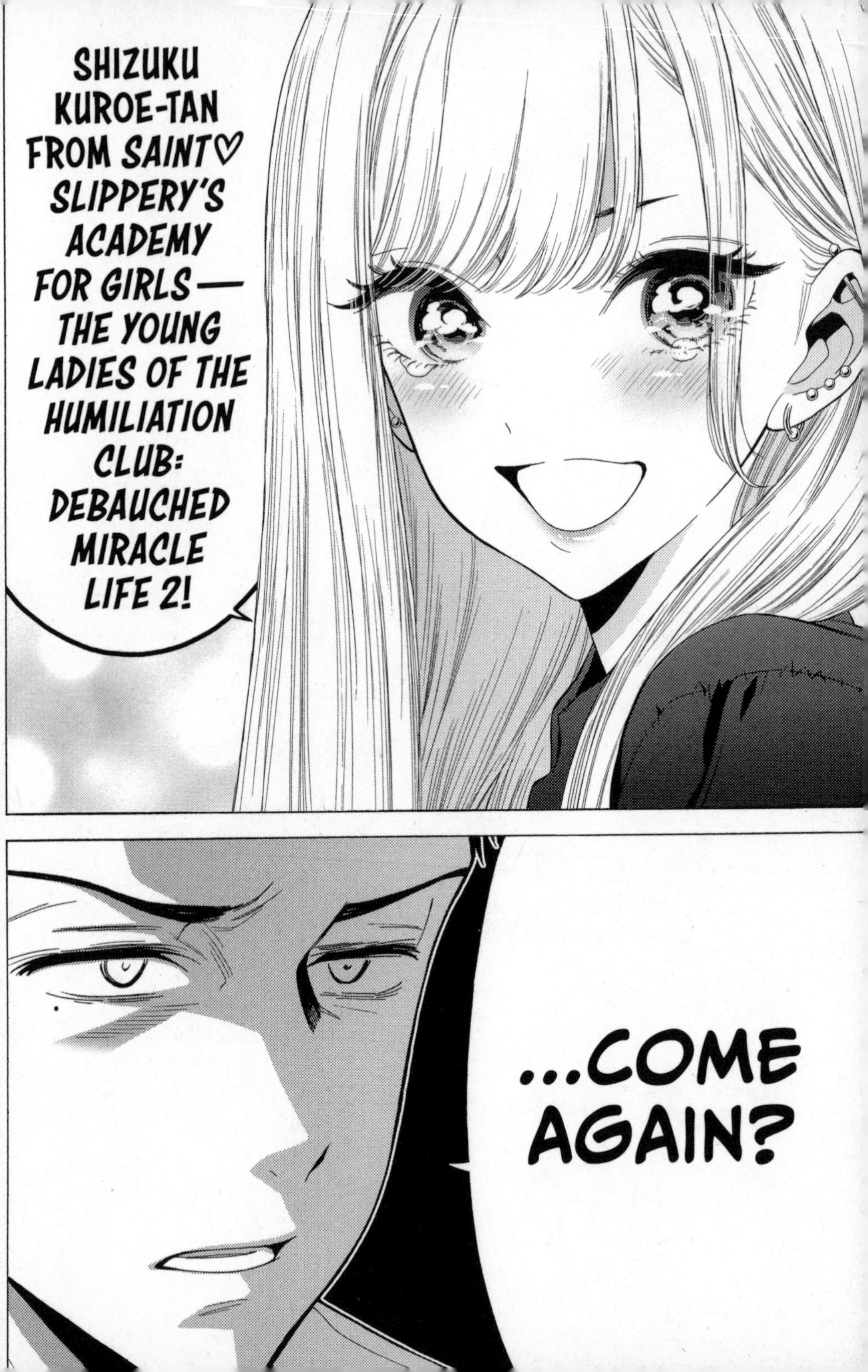
SHIZUKU KUROE-TAN FROM SAINT♡ SLIPPERY'S ACADEMY FOR GIRLS—THE YOUNG LADIES OF THE HUMILIATION CLUB: DEBAUCHED MIRACLE LIFE 2!
...COME AGAIN?

My
DRESS-UP
Darling

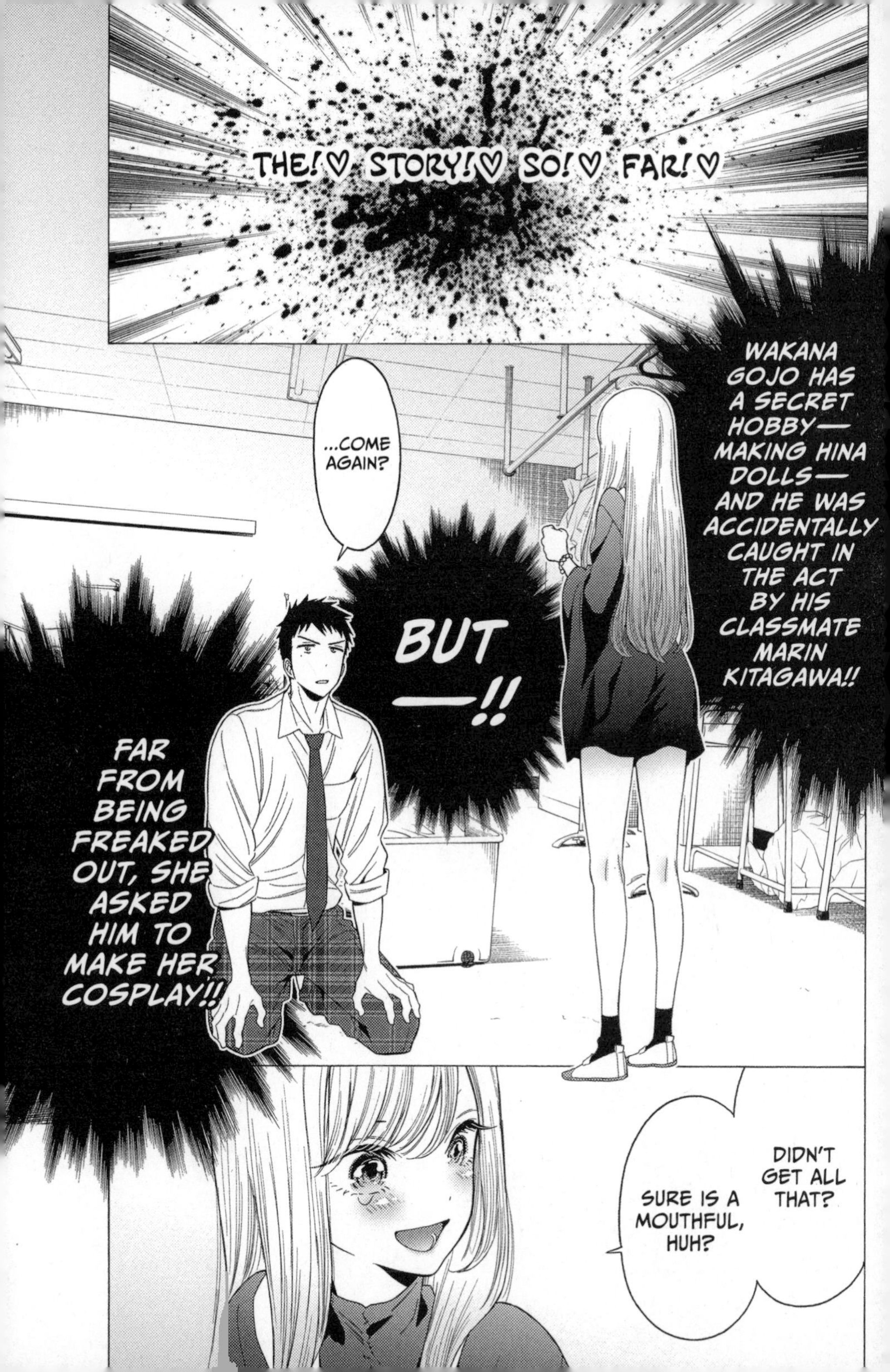
THE!♡ STORY!♡ SO!♡ FAR!♡
WAKANA GOJO HAS A SECRET HOBBY—MAKING HINA DOLLS—AND HE WAS ACCIDENTALLY CAUGHT IN THE ACT BY HIS CLASSMATE MARIN KITAGAWA!!
...COME AGAIN?
BUT—!!
FAR FROM BEING FREAKED OUT, SHE ASKED HIM TO MAKE HER COSPLAY!!
DIDN'T GET ALL THAT?
SURE IS A MOUTHFUL, HUH?

CHAPTER 2

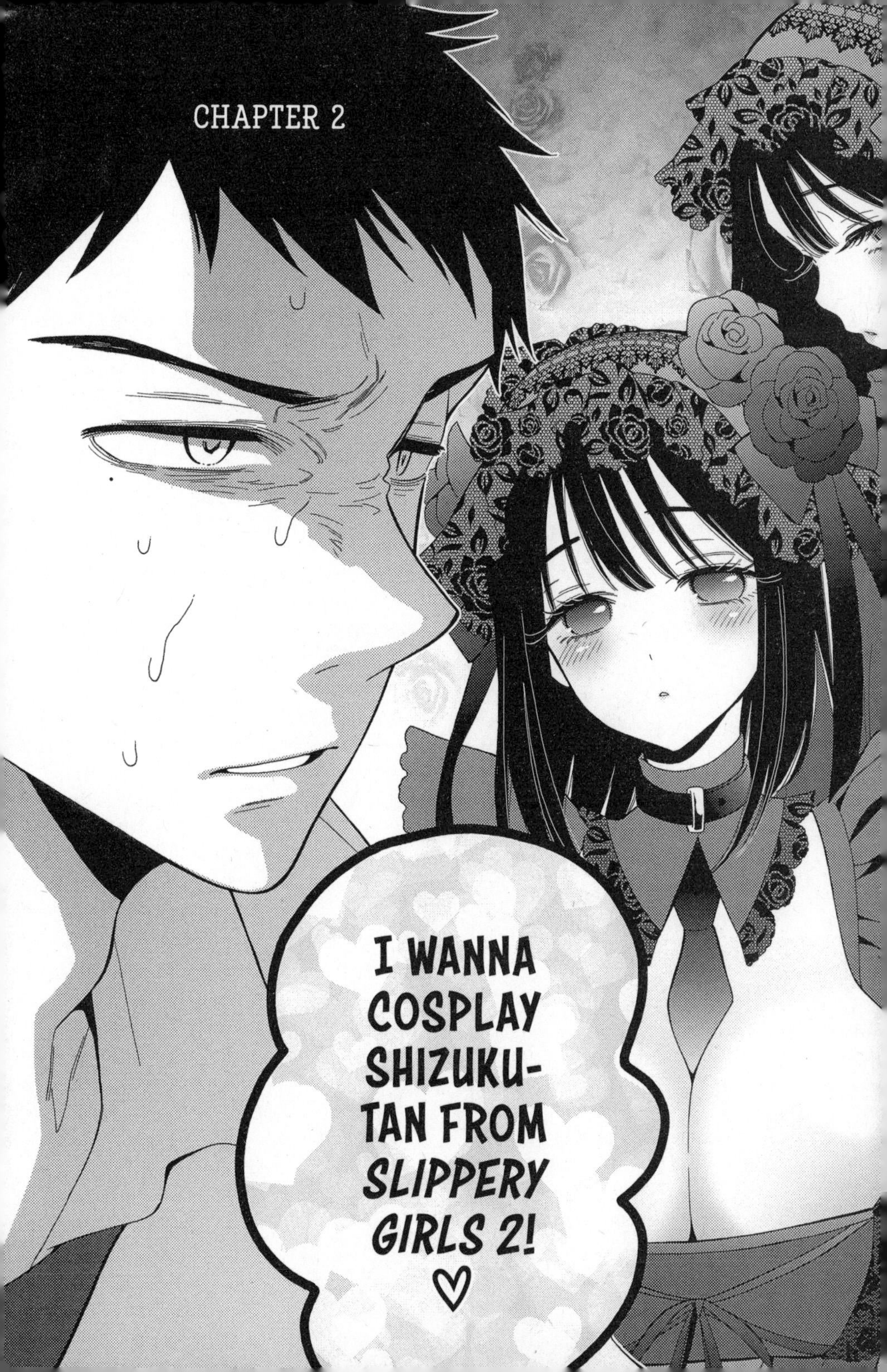
I WANNA COSPLAY SHIZUKU-TAN FROM *SLIPPERY GIRLS 2!* ♡

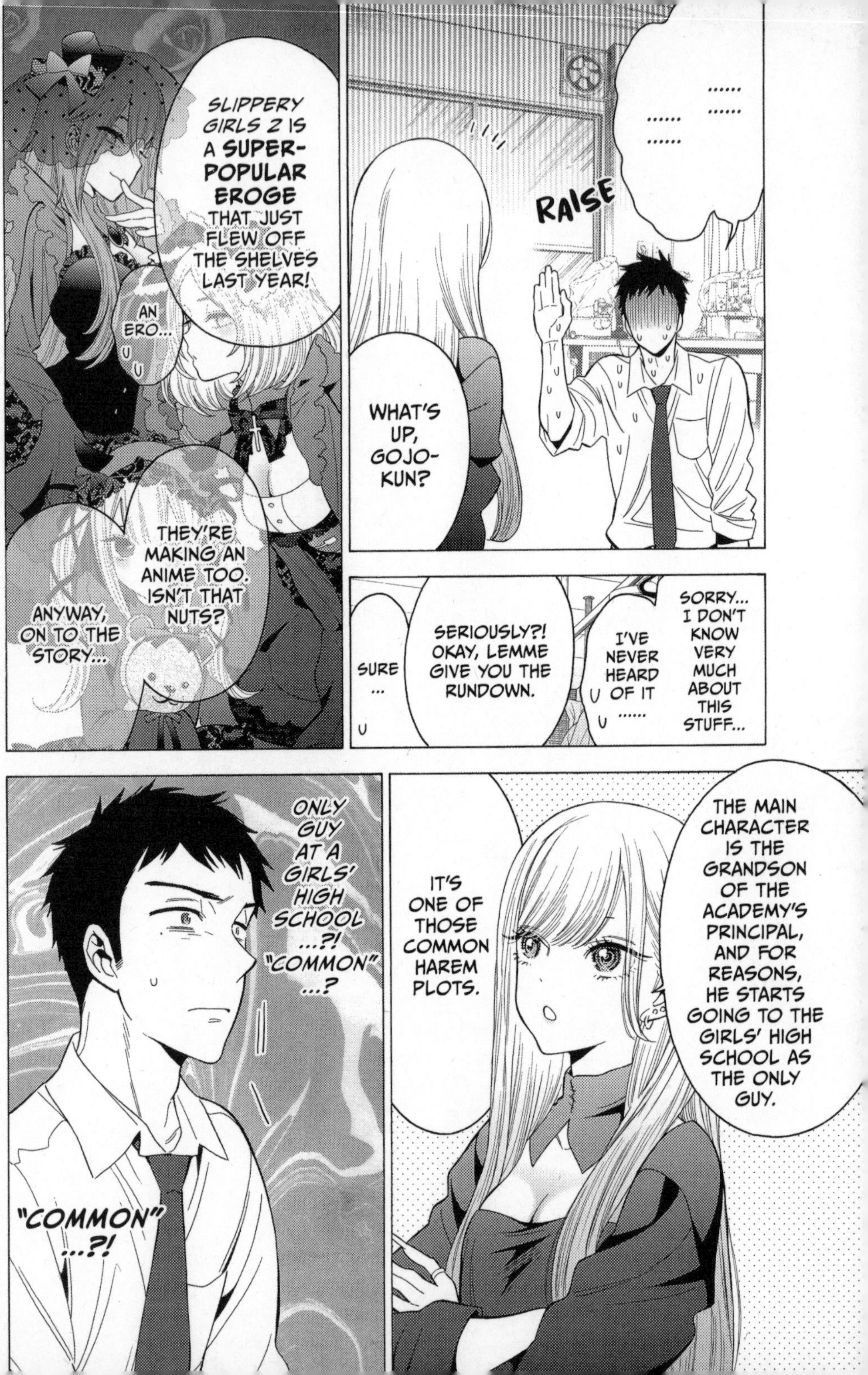

....
RAISE
WHAT'S UP, GOJO-KUN?
SORRY... I DON'T KNOW VERY MUCH ABOUT THIS STUFF...
I'VE NEVER HEARD OF IT ......
SERIOUSLY?! OKAY, LEMME GIVE YOU THE RUNDOWN.
SURE ...
SLIPPERY GIRLS 2 IS A SUPER-POPULAR EROGE THAT JUST FLEW OFF THE SHELVES LAST YEAR!
AN ERO...
THEY'RE MAKING AN ANIME TOO. ISN'T THAT NUTS?
ANYWAY, ON TO THE STORY...
THE MAIN CHARACTER IS THE GRANDSON OF THE ACADEMY'S PRINCIPAL, AND FOR REASONS, HE STARTS GOING TO THE GIRLS' HIGH SCHOOL AS THE ONLY GUY.
IT'S ONE OF THOSE COMMON HAREM PLOTS.
ONLY GUY AT A GIRLS' HIGH SCHOOL ...?! "COMMON" ...?
"COMMON" ...?!

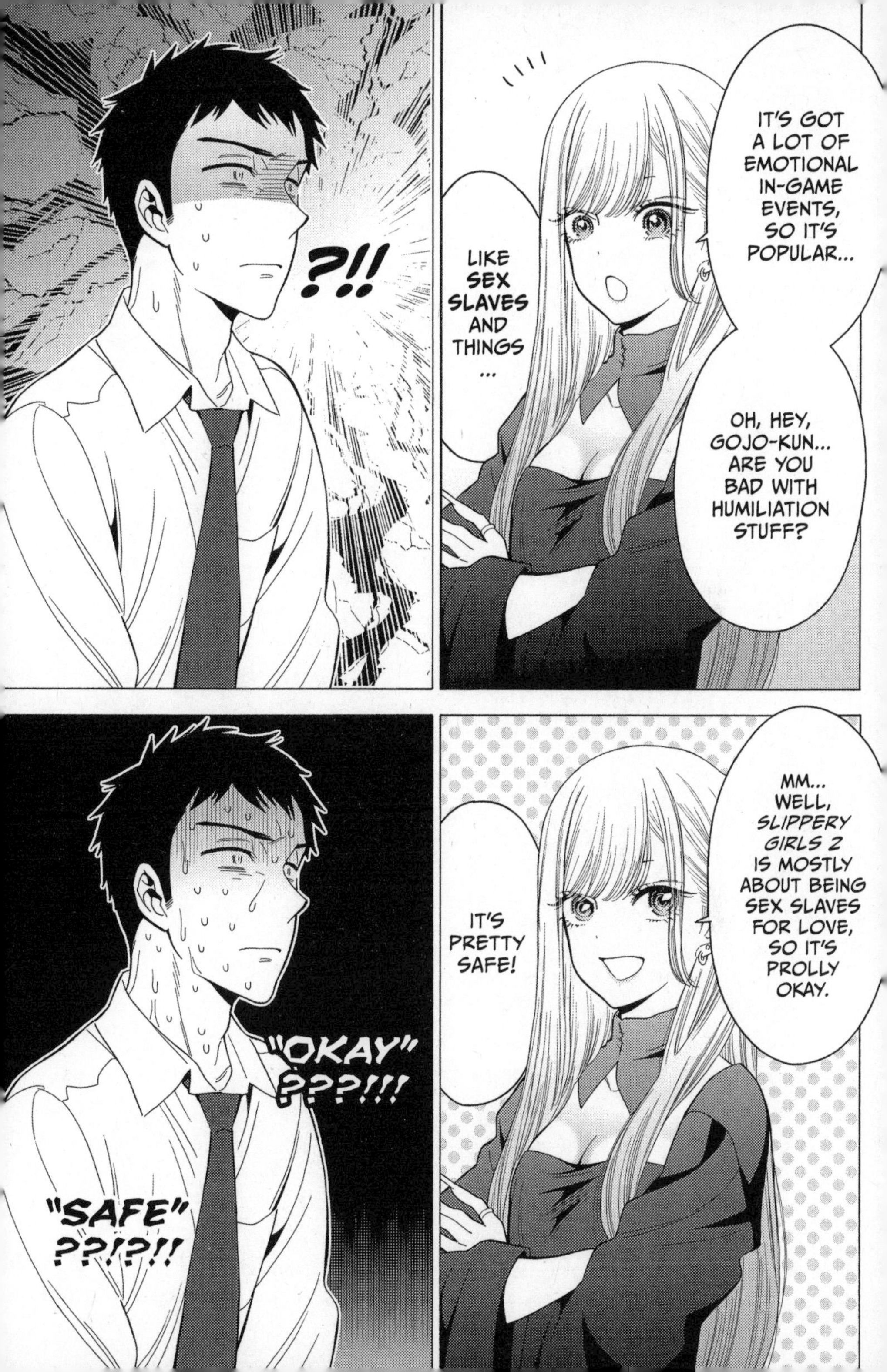
IT'S GOT A LOT OF EMOTIONAL IN-GAME EVENTS, SO IT'S POPULAR...
LIKE SEX SLAVES AND THINGS ...
OH, HEY, GOJO-KUN... ARE YOU BAD WITH HUMILIATION STUFF?
?!!
MM... WELL, *SLIPPERY GIRLS 2* IS MOSTLY ABOUT BEING SEX SLAVES FOR LOVE, SO IT'S PROLLY OKAY.
IT'S PRETTY SAFE!
"OKAY" ???!!!
"SAFE" ??!?!!

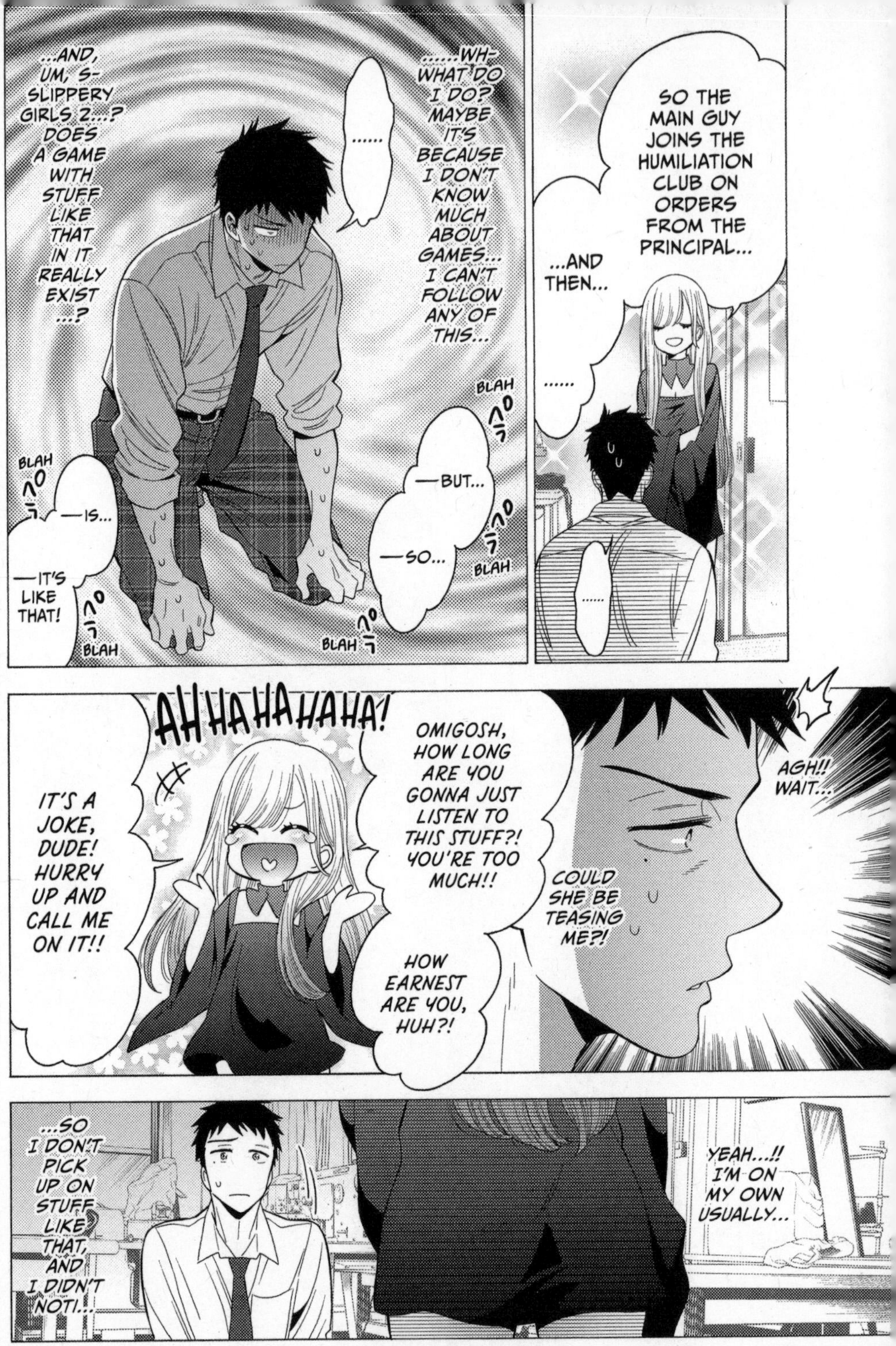
SO THE MAIN GUY JOINS THE HUMILIATION CLUB ON ORDERS FROM THE PRINCIPAL...
...AND THEN...
......
......
......WH-WHAT DO I DO? MAYBE IT'S BECAUSE I DON'T KNOW MUCH ABOUT GAMES... I CAN'T FOLLOW ANY OF THIS...
......
...AND, UM, S-SLIPPERY GIRLS 2...? DOES A GAME WITH STUFF LIKE THAT IN IT REALLY EXIST...?
BLAH
—BUT...
BLAH
—SO...
BLAH
—IS...
BLAH
—IT'S LIKE THAT!
BLAH
BLAH
AGH!! WAIT...
COULD SHE BE TEASING ME?!
AH HAHAHAHA!
OMIGOSH, HOW LONG ARE YOU GONNA JUST LISTEN TO THIS STUFF?! YOU'RE TOO MUCH!!
HOW EARNEST ARE YOU, HUH?!
IT'S A JOKE, DUDE! HURRY UP AND CALL ME ON IT!!
YEAH...!! I'M ON MY OWN USUALLY...
...SO I DON'T PICK UP ON STUFF LIKE THAT, AND I DIDN'T NOTI...

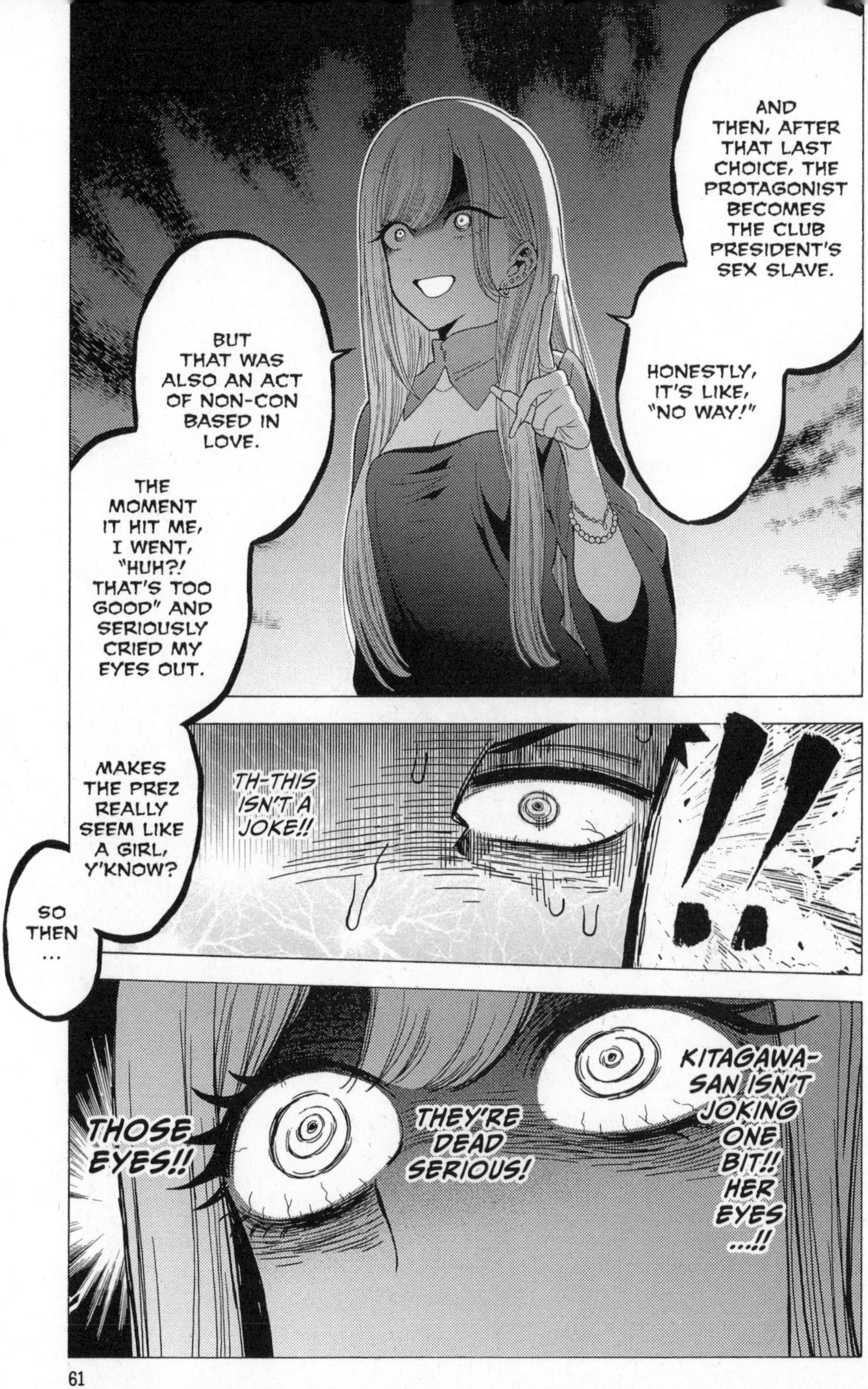
AND THEN, AFTER THAT LAST CHOICE, THE PROTAGONIST BECOMES THE CLUB PRESIDENT'S SEX SLAVE.
HONESTLY, IT'S LIKE, "NO WAY!"
BUT THAT WAS ALSO AN ACT OF NON-CON BASED IN LOVE.
THE MOMENT IT HIT ME, I WENT, "HUH?! THAT'S TOO GOOD" AND SERIOUSLY CRIED MY EYES OUT.
TH-THIS ISN'T A JOKE!!
MAKES THE PREZ REALLY SEEM LIKE A GIRL, Y'KNOW?
SO THEN ...
KITAGAWA-SAN ISN'T JOKING ONE BIT!! HER EYES ...!!
THEY'RE DEAD SERIOUS!
THOSE EYES!!

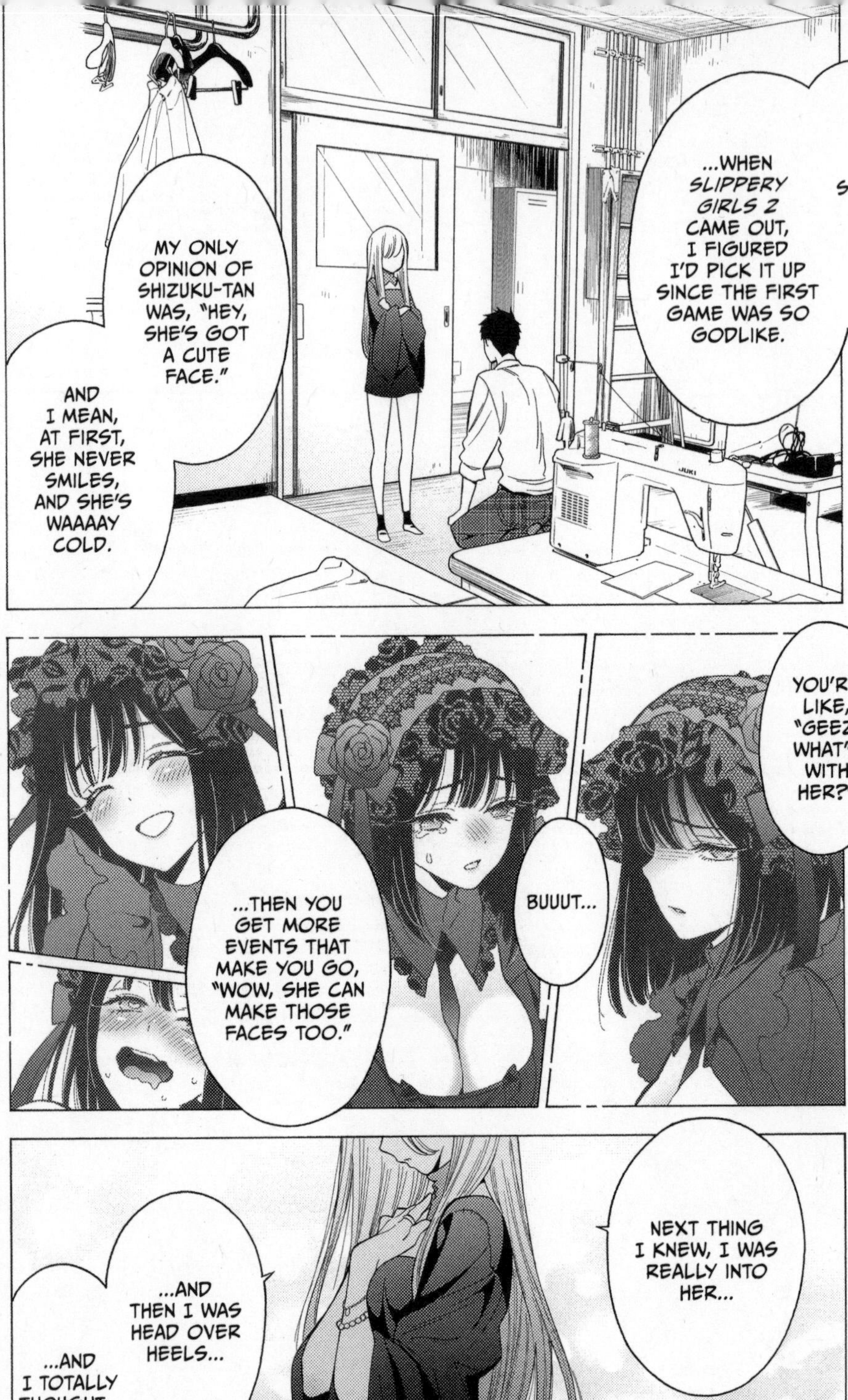
SO...
...WHEN SLIPPERY GIRLS 2 CAME OUT, I FIGURED I'D PICK IT UP SINCE THE FIRST GAME WAS SO GODLIKE.
MY ONLY OPINION OF SHIZUKU-TAN WAS, "HEY, SHE'S GOT A CUTE FACE."
AND I MEAN, AT FIRST, SHE NEVER SMILES, AND SHE'S WAAAAY COLD.
YOU'RE LIKE, "GEEZ, WHAT'S WITH HER?"
BUUUT...
...THEN YOU GET MORE EVENTS THAT MAKE YOU GO, "WOW, SHE CAN MAKE THOSE FACES TOO."
NEXT THING I KNEW, I WAS REALLY INTO HER...
...AND THEN I WAS HEAD OVER HEELS...
...AND I TOTALLY THOUGHT...

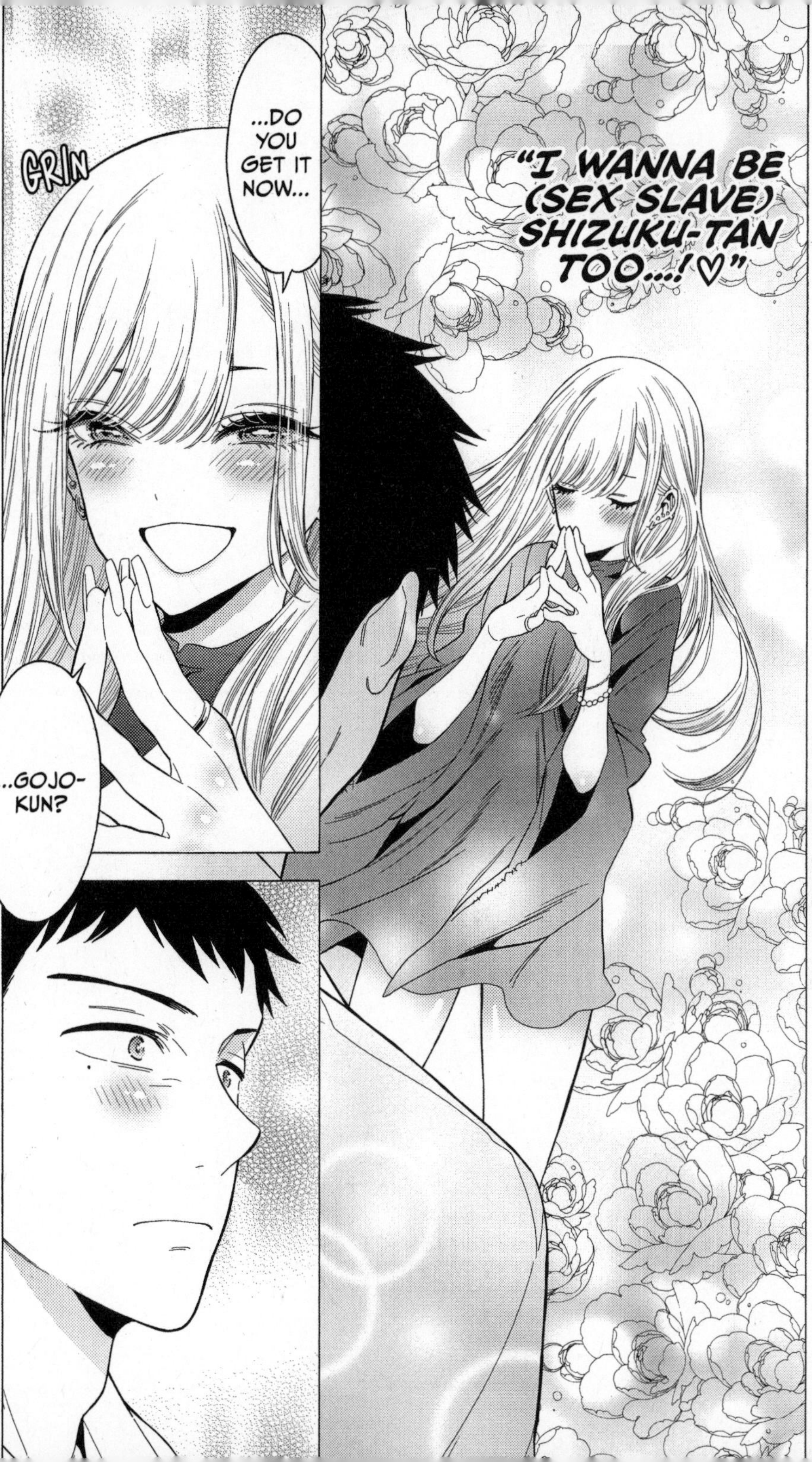
"I WANNA BE (SEX SLAVE) SHIZUKU-TAN TOO...! ♡"
...DO YOU GET IT NOW...
GRIN
...GOJO-KUN?

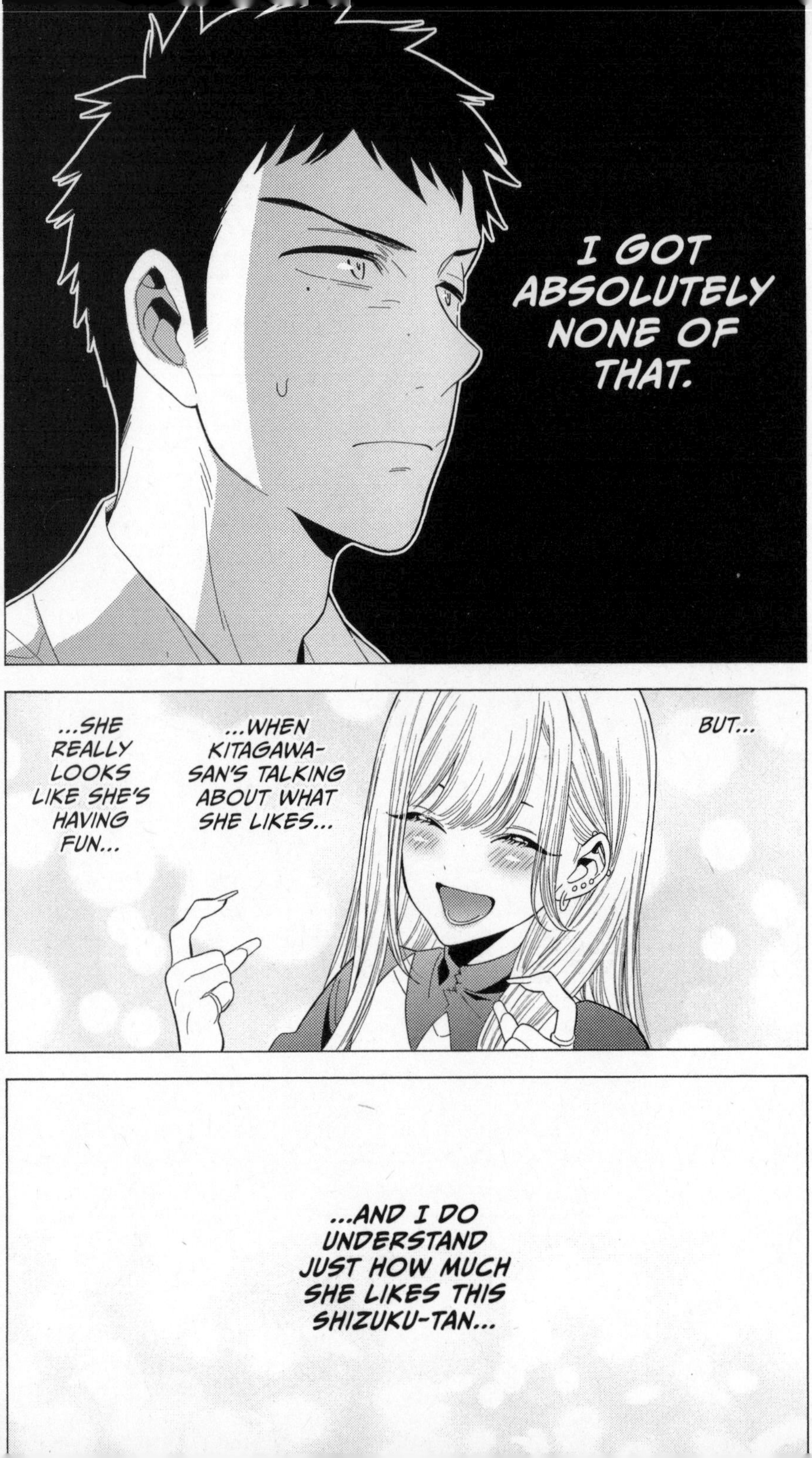
I GOT ABSOLUTELY NONE OF THAT.
BUT...
...WHEN KITAGAWA-SAN'S TALKING ABOUT WHAT SHE LIKES...
...SHE REALLY LOOKS LIKE SHE'S HAVING FUN...
...AND I DO UNDERSTAND JUST HOW MUCH SHE LIKES THIS SHIZUKU-TAN...

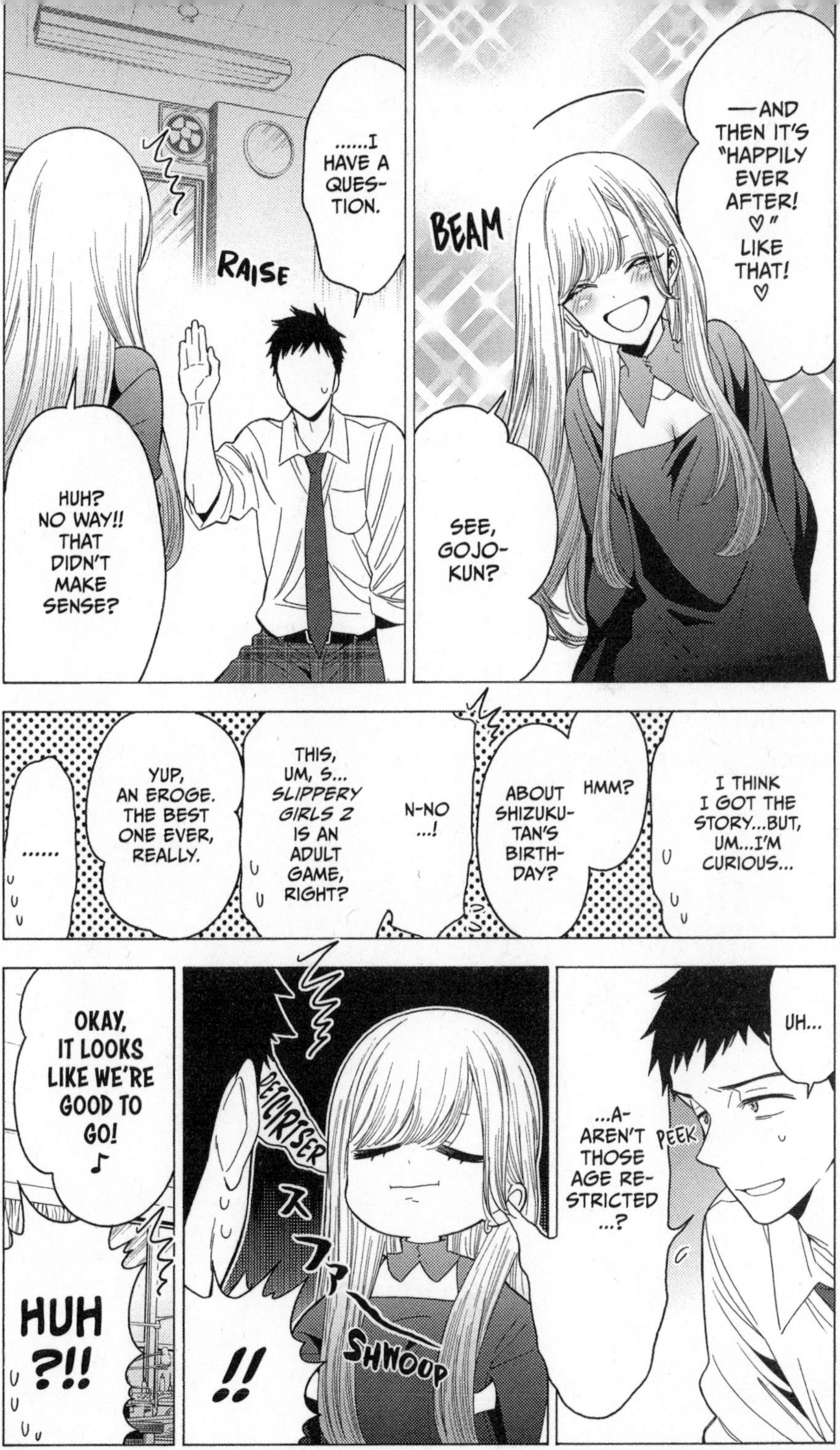
—AND THEN IT'S "HAPPILY EVER AFTER! ♡" LIKE THAT! ♡
BEAM
SEE, GOJO-KUN?
......I HAVE A QUES-TION.
RAISE
HUH? NO WAY!! THAT DIDN'T MAKE SENSE?
I THINK I GOT THE STORY...BUT, UM...I'M CURIOUS...
HMM?
ABOUT SHIZUKU-TAN'S BIRTH-DAY?
N-NO ...!
THIS, UM, S... *SLIPPERY GIRLS 2* IS AN ADULT GAME, RIGHT?
YUP, AN EROGE. THE BEST ONE EVER, REALLY.
......
UH...
...A-AREN'T THOSE AGE RE-STRICTED ...?
PEEK
スファ
SHWOOP
!!
OKAY, IT LOOKS LIKE WE'RE GOOD TO GO! ♪
HUH ?!!

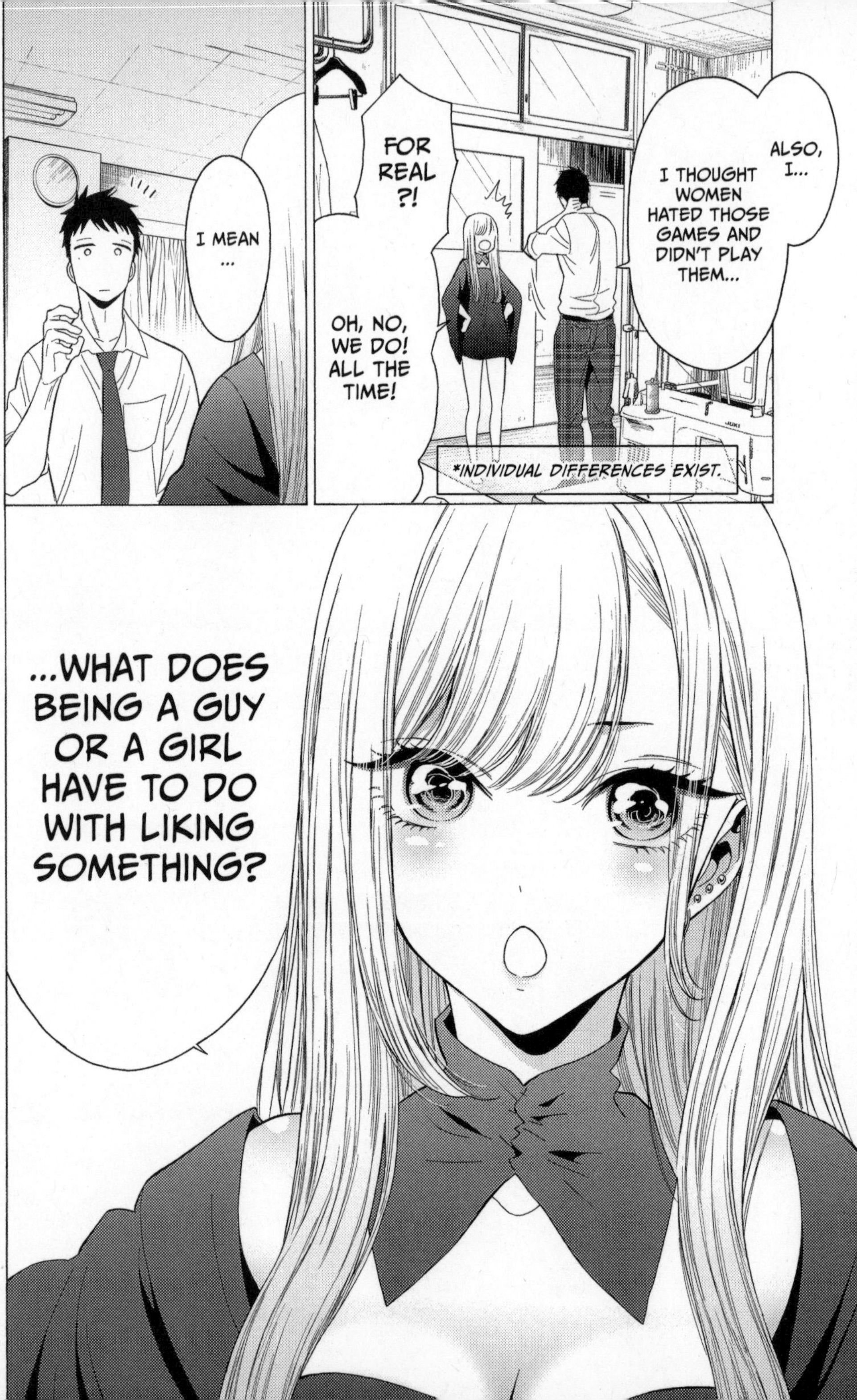
ALSO, I...
I THOUGHT WOMEN HATED THOSE GAMES AND DIDN'T PLAY THEM...
FOR REAL ?!
OH, NO, WE DO! ALL THE TIME!
*INDIVIDUAL DIFFERENCES EXIST.
I MEAN ...
...WHAT DOES BEING A GUY OR A GIRL HAVE TO DO WITH LIKING SOMETHING?

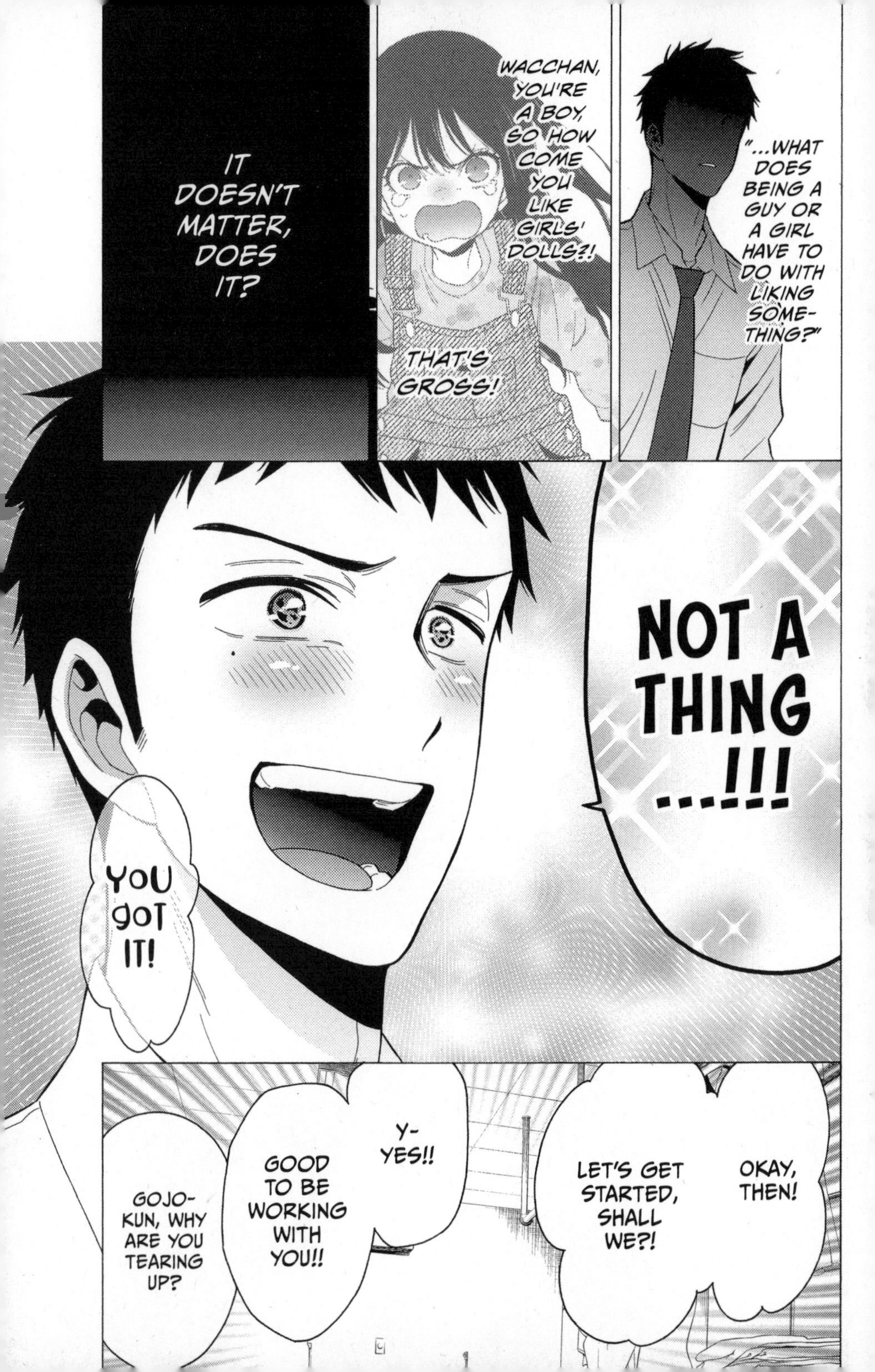
"...WHAT DOES BEING A GUY OR A GIRL HAVE TO DO WITH LIKING SOME-THING?"
WACCHAN, YOU'RE A BOY, SO HOW COME YOU LIKE GIRLS' DOLLS?!
THAT'S GROSS!
IT DOESN'T MATTER, DOES IT?
NOT A THING ...!!!
YOU GOT IT!
OKAY, THEN!
LET'S GET STARTED, SHALL WE?!
Y-YES!!
GOOD TO BE WORKING WITH YOU!!
GOJO-KUN, WHY ARE YOU TEARING UP?

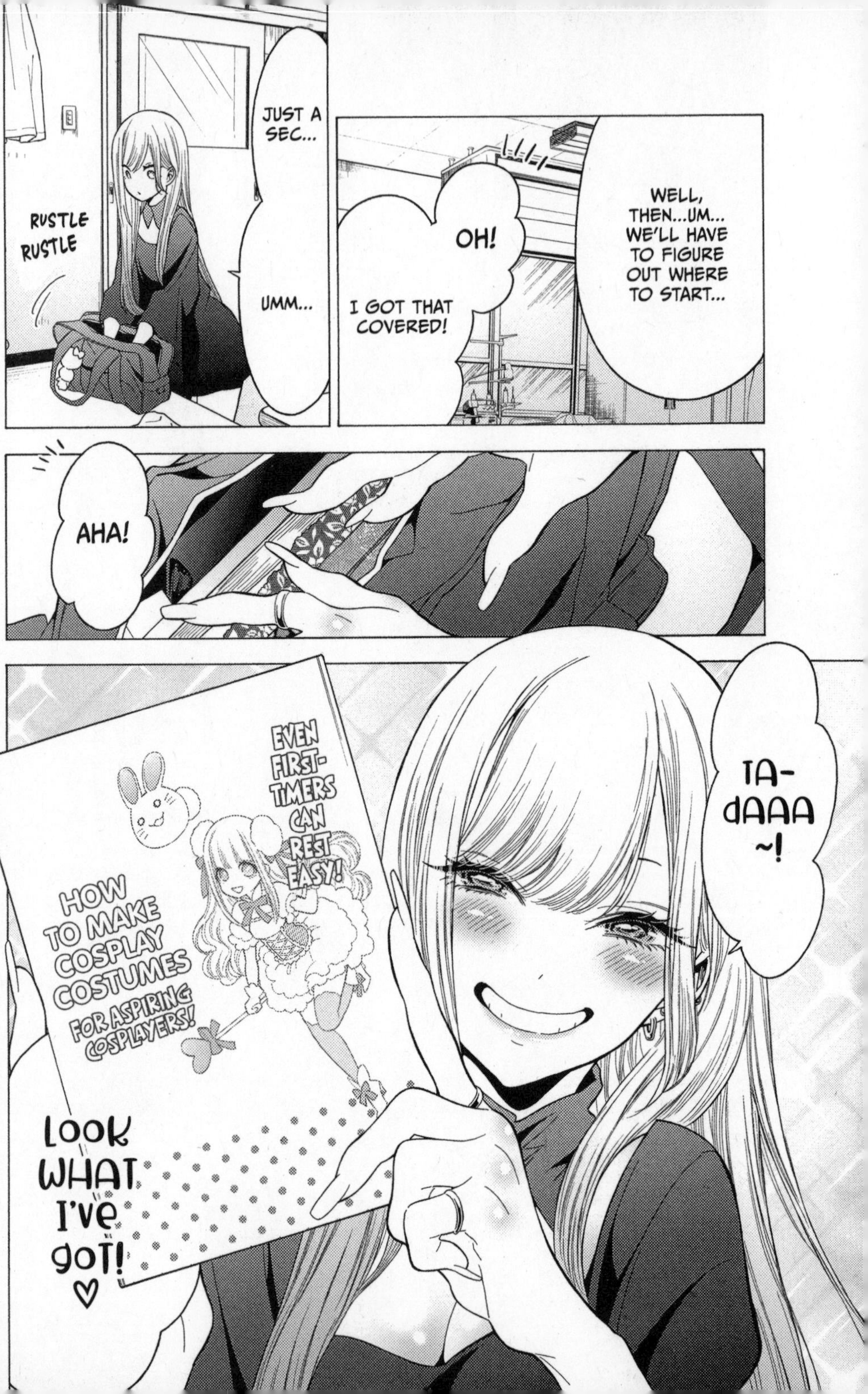
WELL, THEN...UM... WE'LL HAVE TO FIGURE OUT WHERE TO START...
OH!
I GOT THAT COVERED!
JUST A SEC...
UMM...
RUSTLE RUSTLE
AHA!
TA-DAAA~!
EVEN FIRST-TIMERS CAN REST EASY!
HOW TO MAKE COSPLAY COSTUMES
FOR ASPIRING COSPLAYERS!
LOOK WHAT I'VE GOT! ♡

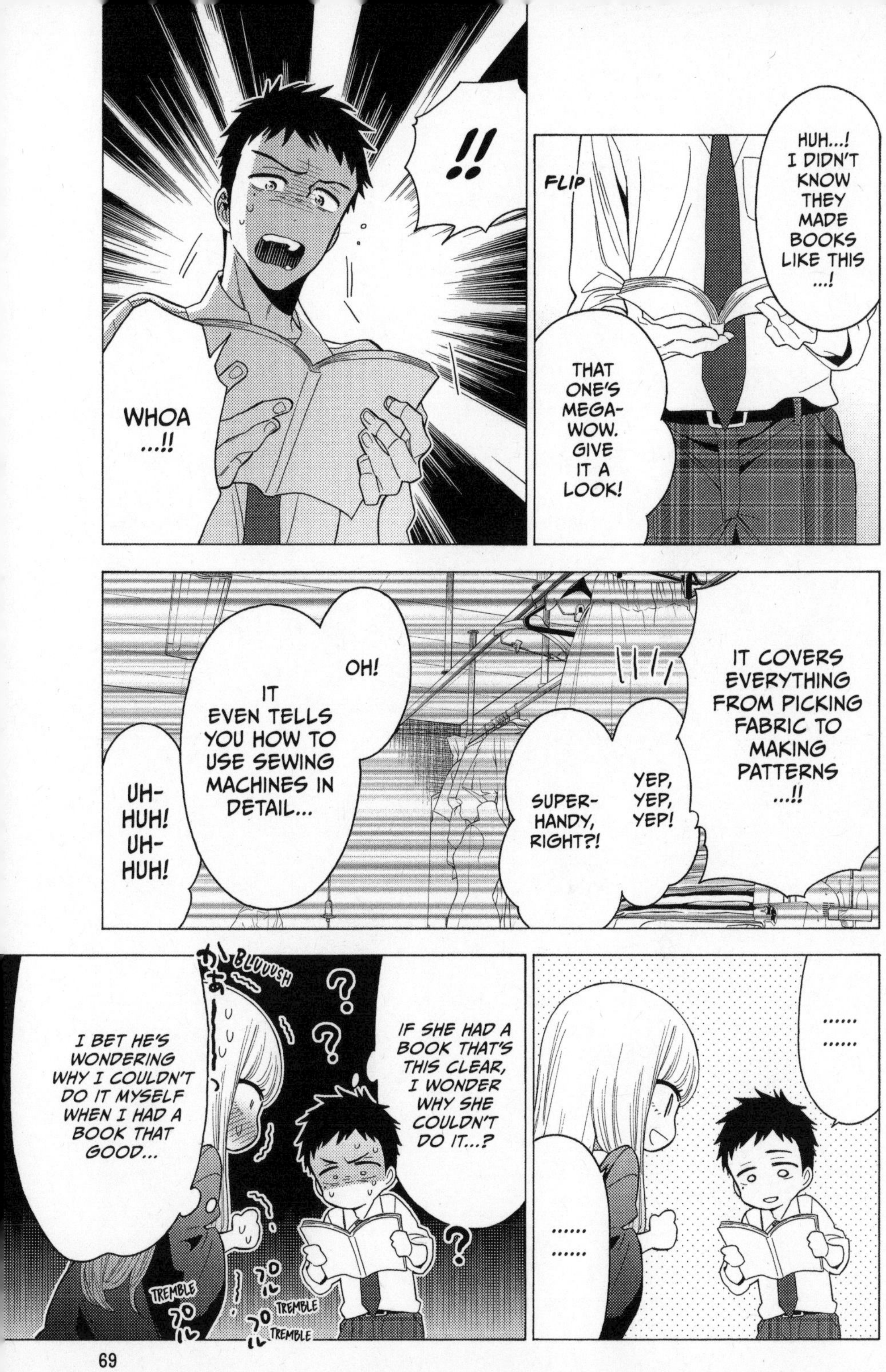
HUH...! I DIDN'T KNOW THEY MADE BOOKS LIKE THIS ...!
FLIP
THAT ONE'S MEGA-WOW. GIVE IT A LOOK!
!!
WHOA ...!!
IT COVERS EVERYTHING FROM PICKING FABRIC TO MAKING PATTERNS ...!!
YEP, YEP, YEP!
SUPER-HANDY, RIGHT?!
OH!
IT EVEN TELLS YOU HOW TO USE SEWING MACHINES IN DETAIL...
UH-HUH! UH-HUH!
....
....
IF SHE HAD A BOOK THAT'S THIS CLEAR, I WONDER WHY SHE COULDN'T DO IT...?
BLUUUSH
I BET HE'S WONDERING WHY I COULDN'T DO IT MYSELF WHEN I HAD A BOOK THAT GOOD...
TREMBLE
TREMBLE
TREMBLE

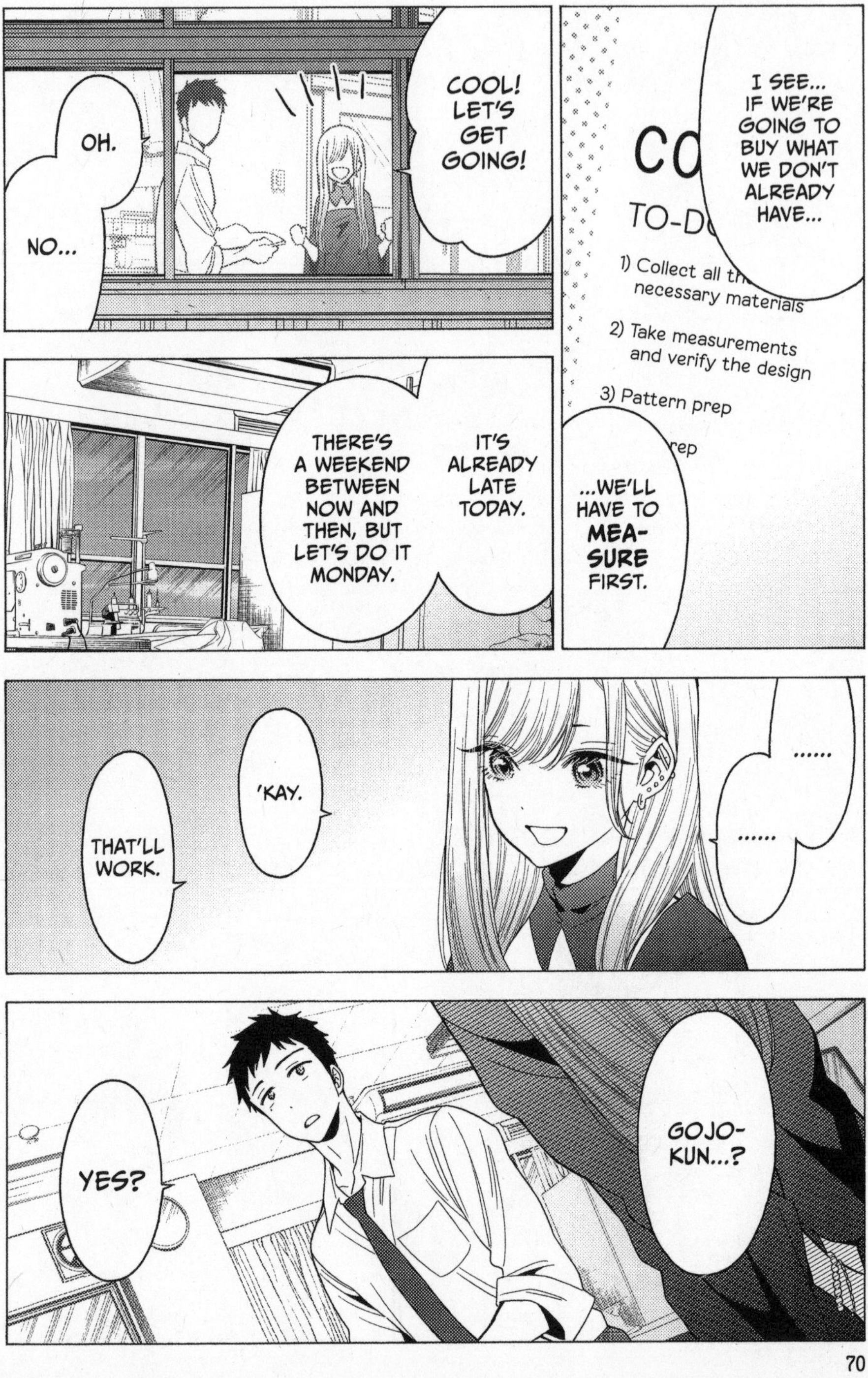
I SEE... IF WE'RE GOING TO BUY WHAT WE DON'T ALREADY HAVE...
1) Collect all th
necessary materials
2) Take measurements and verify the design
3) Pattern prep
...WE'LL HAVE TO MEA-SURE FIRST.
COOL! LET'S GET GOING!
OH.
NO...
IT'S ALREADY LATE TODAY.
THERE'S A WEEKEND BETWEEN NOW AND THEN, BUT LET'S DO IT MONDAY.
......
......
'KAY.
THAT'LL WORK.
GOJO-KUN...?
YES?

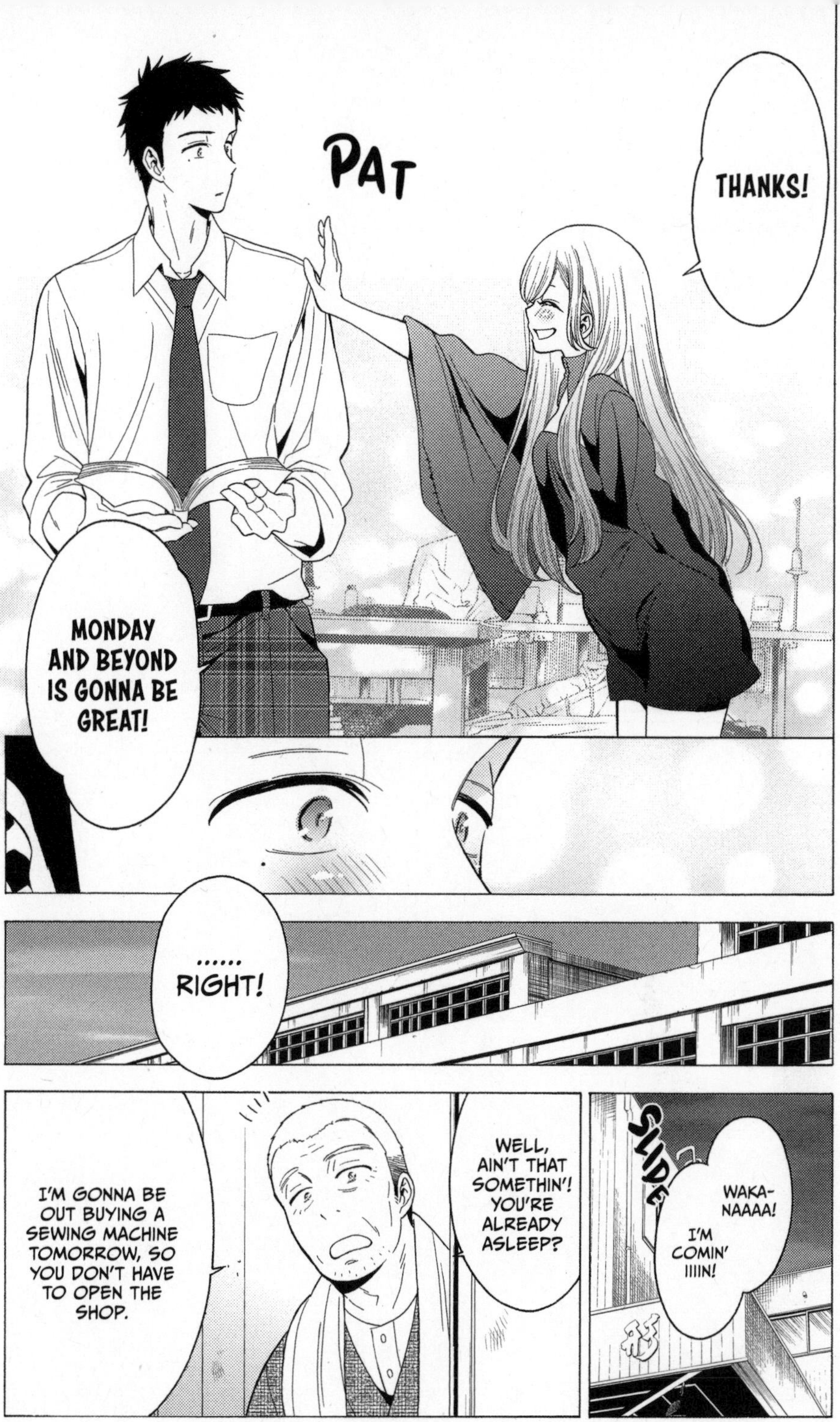
THANKS!
PAT
MONDAY AND BEYOND IS GONNA BE GREAT!
...... RIGHT!
SLIDE
WAKA-NAAAA!
I'M COMIN' IIIIN!
WELL, AIN'T THAT SOMETHIN'! YOU'RE ALREADY ASLEEP?
I'M GONNA BE OUT BUYING A SEWING MACHINE TOMORROW, SO YOU DON'T HAVE TO OPEN THE SHOP.

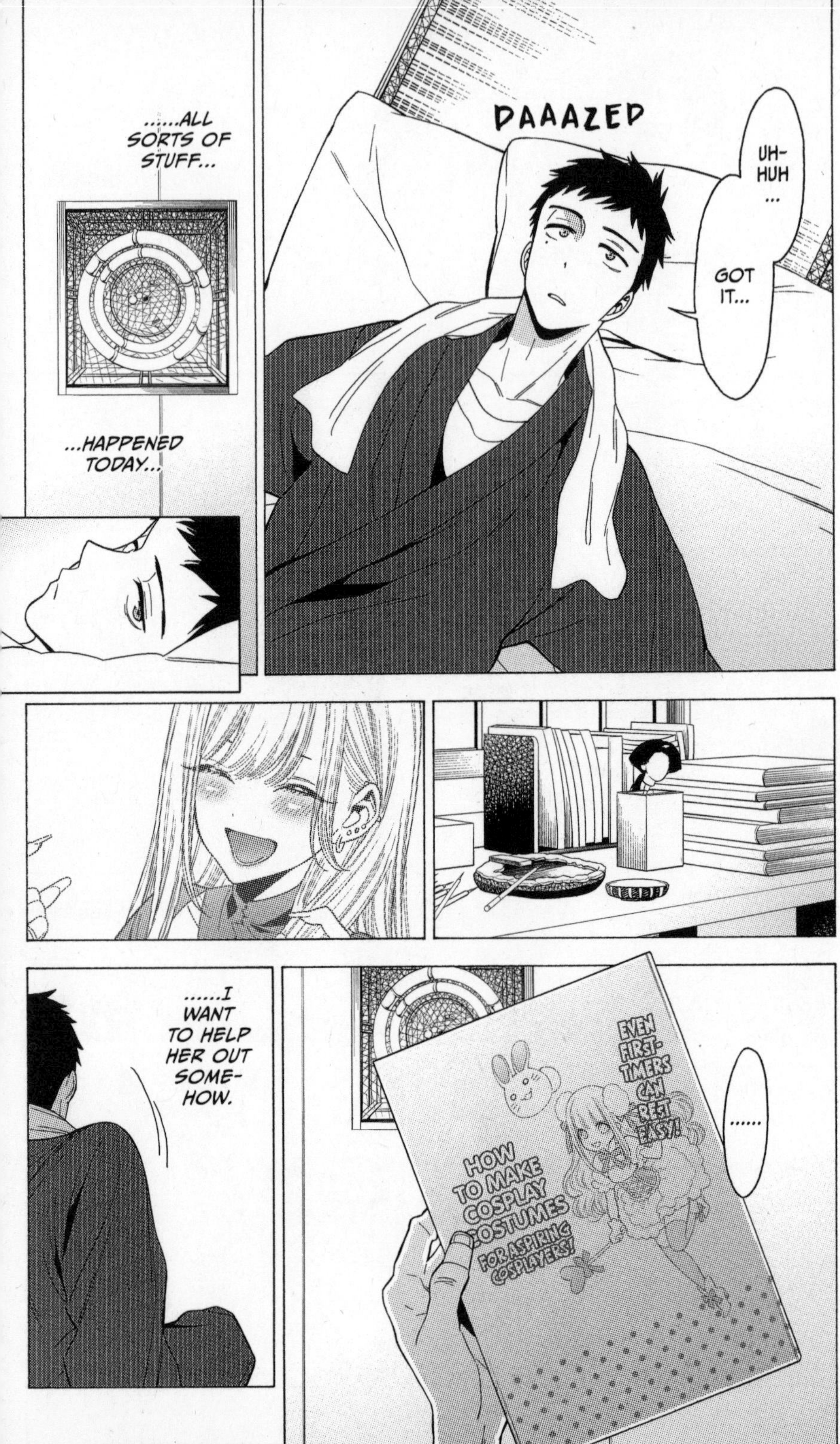
DAAAZED
UH-HUH...
GOT IT...
......ALL SORTS OF STUFF...
...HAPPENED TODAY...
......
EVEN FIRST-TIMERS CAN REST EASY!
HOW TO MAKE COSPLAY COSTUMES
FOR ASPIRING COSPLAYERS!
......I WANT TO HELP HER OUT SOME-HOW.

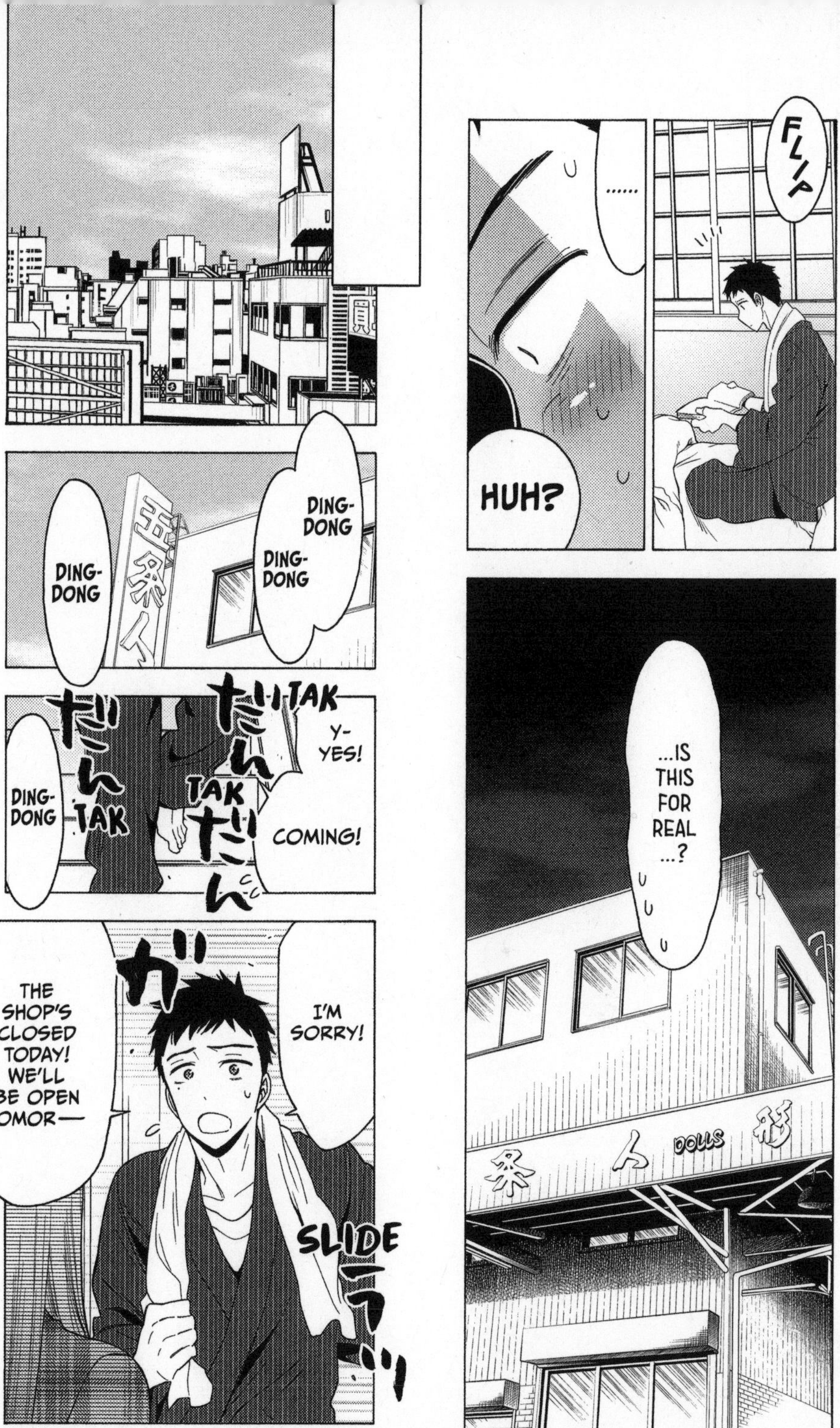
FLIP
......
HUH?
...IS THIS FOR REAL ...?
DING-DONG
DING-DONG
DING-DONG
TAK
Y-YES!
COMING!
TAK
TAK
DING-DONG
I'M SORRY!
THE SHOP'S CLOSED TODAY! WE'LL BE OPEN TOMOR—
SLIDE

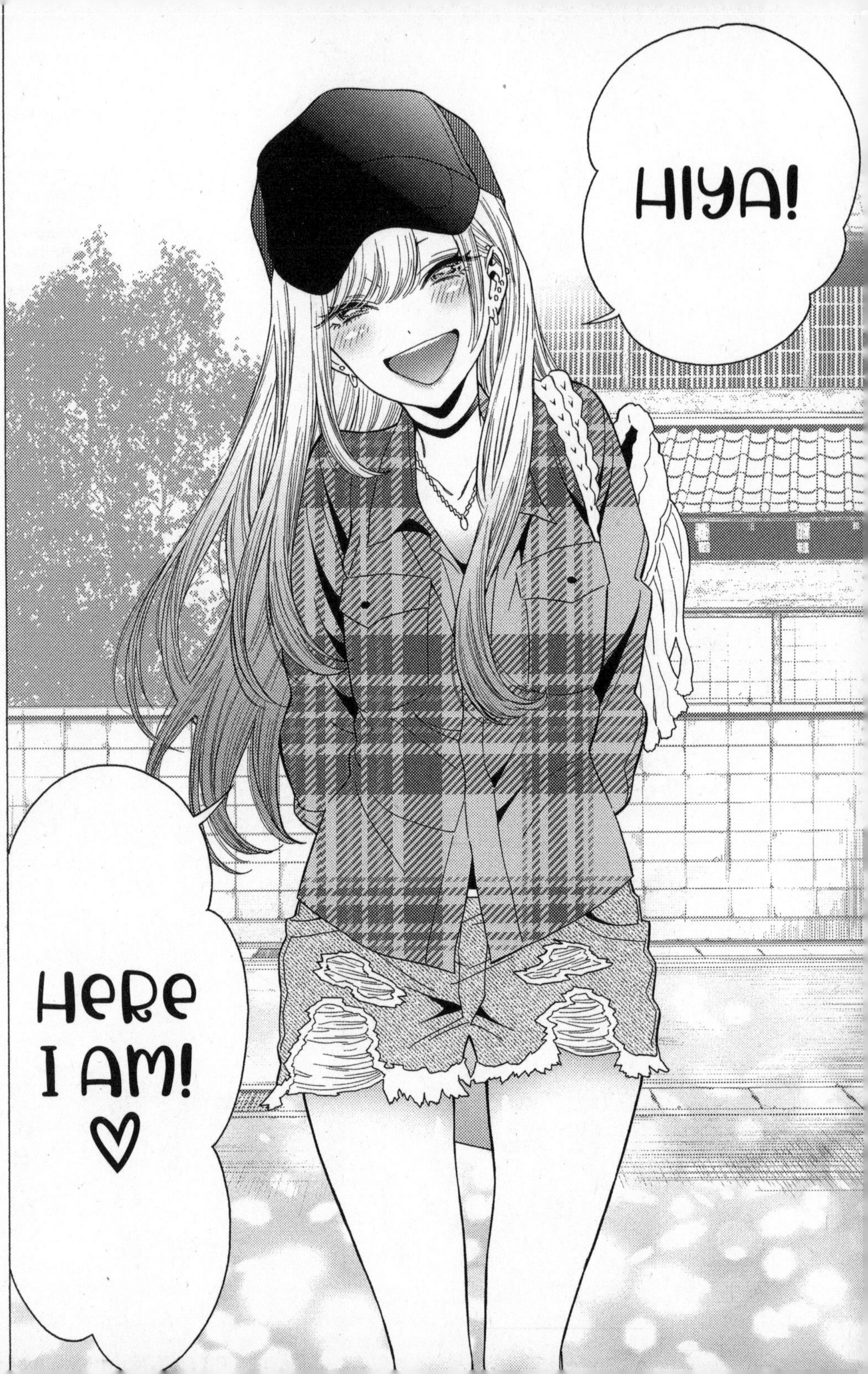
HIYA!
HERE I AM! ♥

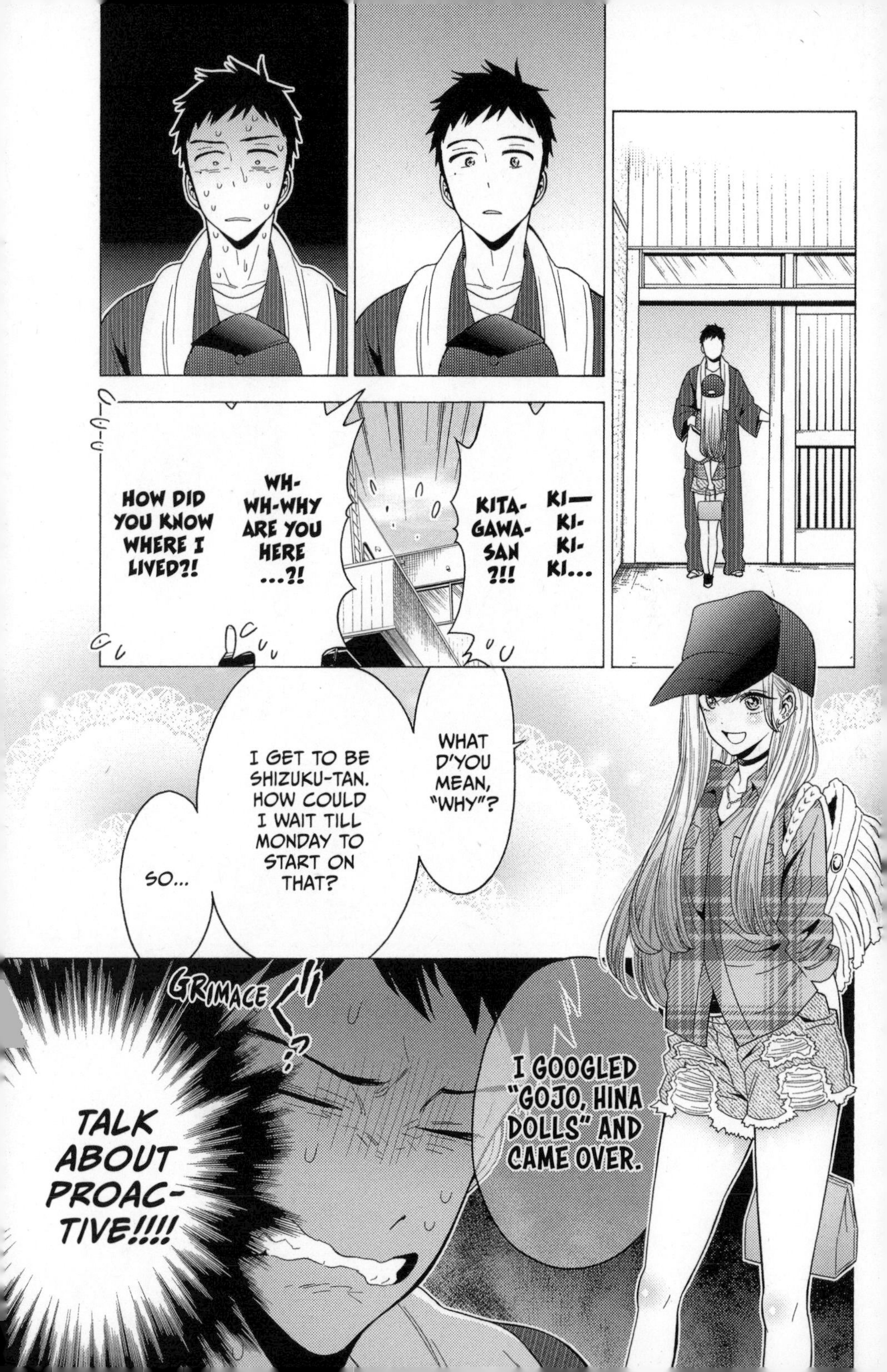
KI— KI- KI- KI...
KITA-GAWA-SAN?!!
WH-WH-WHY ARE YOU HERE...?!
HOW DID YOU KNOW WHERE I LIVED?!
WHAT D'YOU MEAN, "WHY"?
I GET TO BE SHIZUKU-TAN. HOW COULD I WAIT TILL MONDAY TO START ON THAT?
SO...
I GOOGLED "GOJO, HINA DOLLS" AND CAME OVER.
GRIMACE
TALK ABOUT PROAC-TIVE!!!!

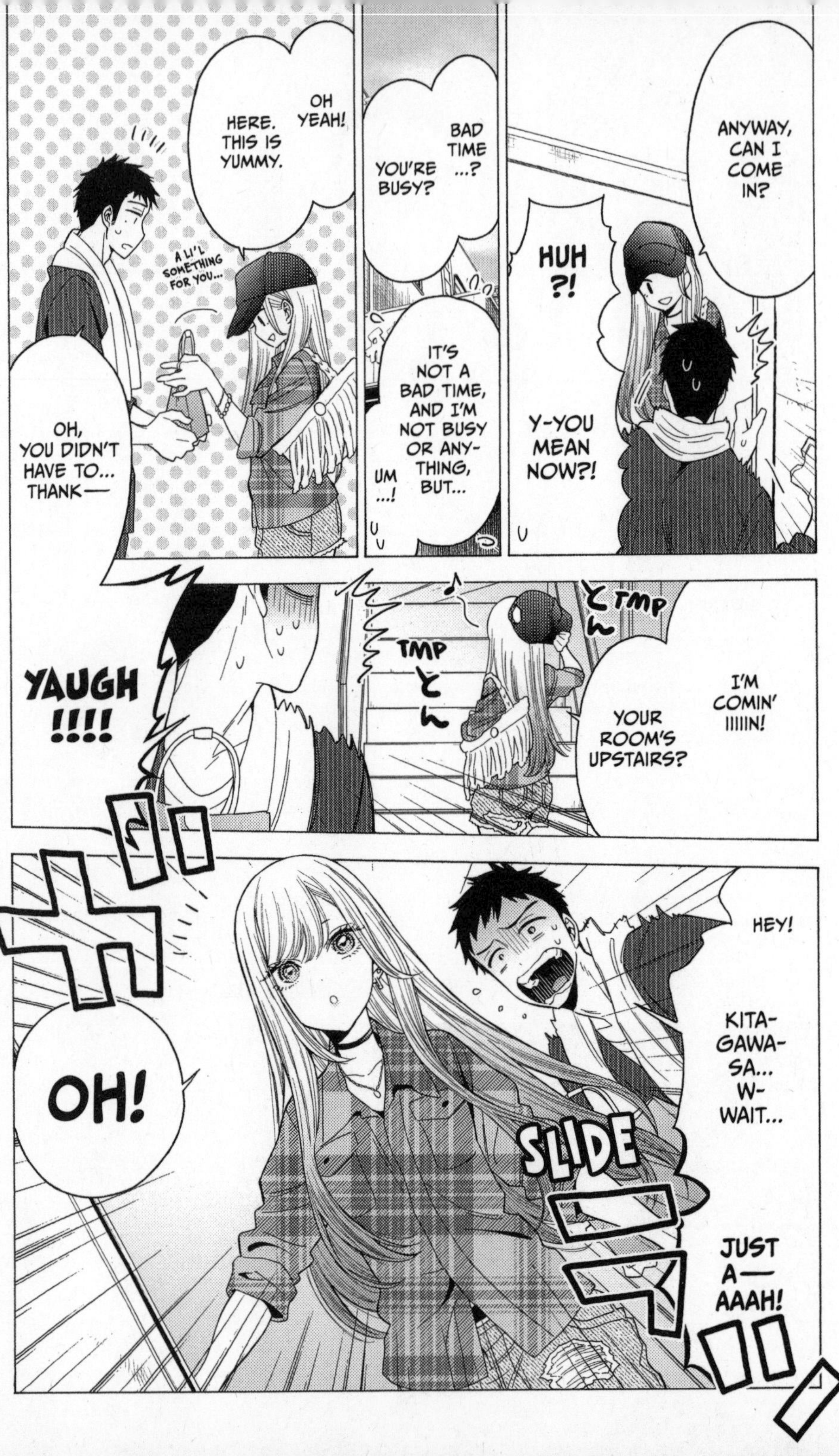
ANYWAY, CAN I COME IN?
HUH ?!
Y-YOU MEAN NOW?!
BAD TIME ...?
YOU'RE BUSY?
IT'S NOT A BAD TIME, AND I'M NOT BUSY OR ANY-THING, BUT...
UM ...!
OH YEAH!
HERE. THIS IS YUMMY.
A LI'L SOMETHING FOR YOU...
OH, YOU DIDN'T HAVE TO... THANK—
I'M COMIN' IIIIIN!
YOUR ROOM'S UPSTAIRS?
TMP
TMP
YAUGH !!!!
HEY!
KITA-GAWA-SA... W-WAIT...
JUST A— AAAH!
SLIDE
OH!

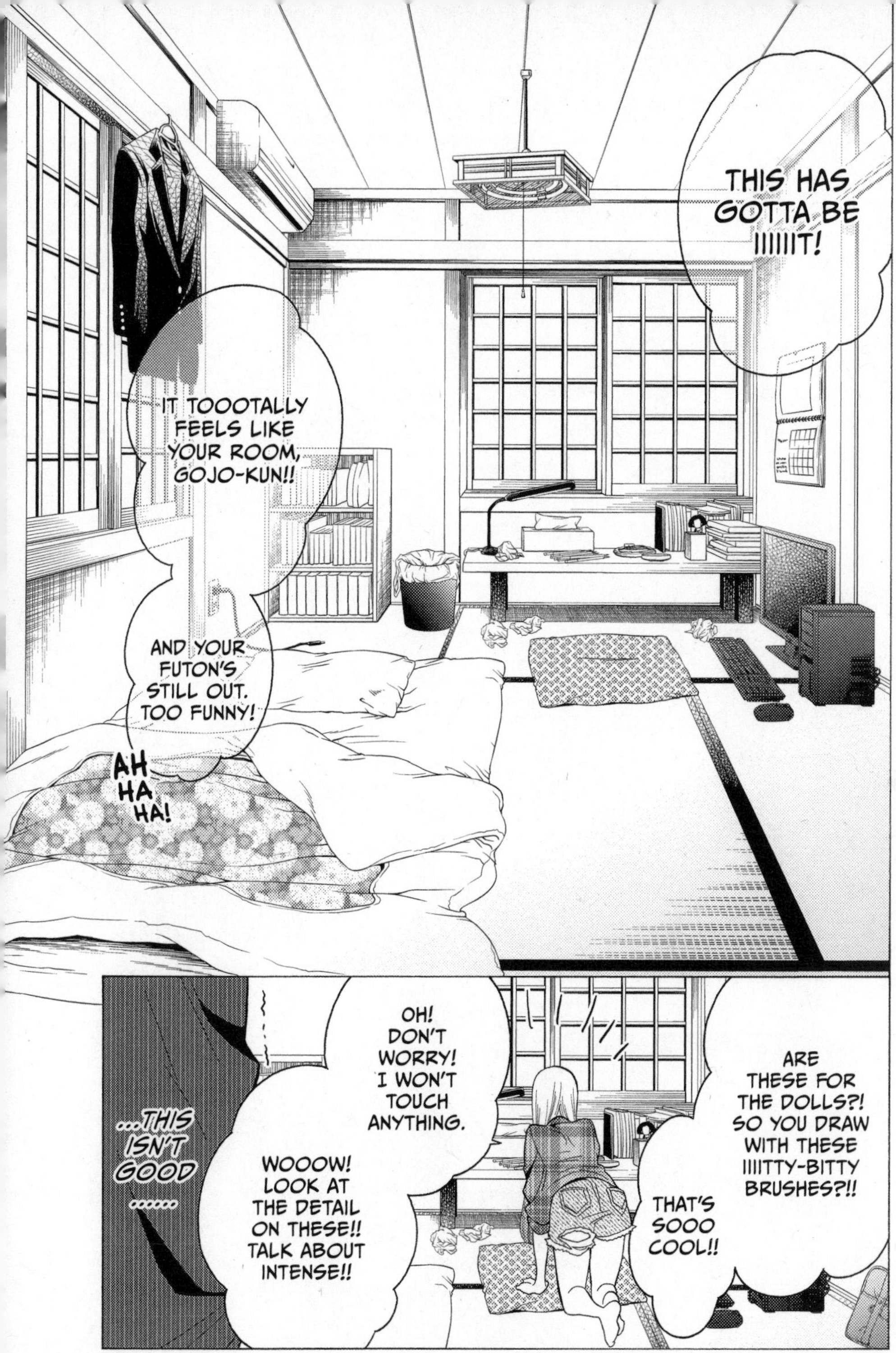
THIS HAS GOTTA BE IIIIIIIT!
IT TOOOTALLY FEELS LIKE YOUR ROOM, GOJO-KUN!!
AND YOUR FUTON'S STILL OUT. TOO FUNNY!
AH HA HA!
ARE THESE FOR THE DOLLS?! SO YOU DRAW WITH THESE IIIIITTY-BITTY BRUSHES?!!
THAT'S SOOO COOL!!
OH! DON'T WORRY! I WON'T TOUCH ANYTHING.
WOOOW! LOOK AT THE DETAIL ON THESE!! TALK ABOUT INTENSE!!
...THIS ISN'T GOOD ......

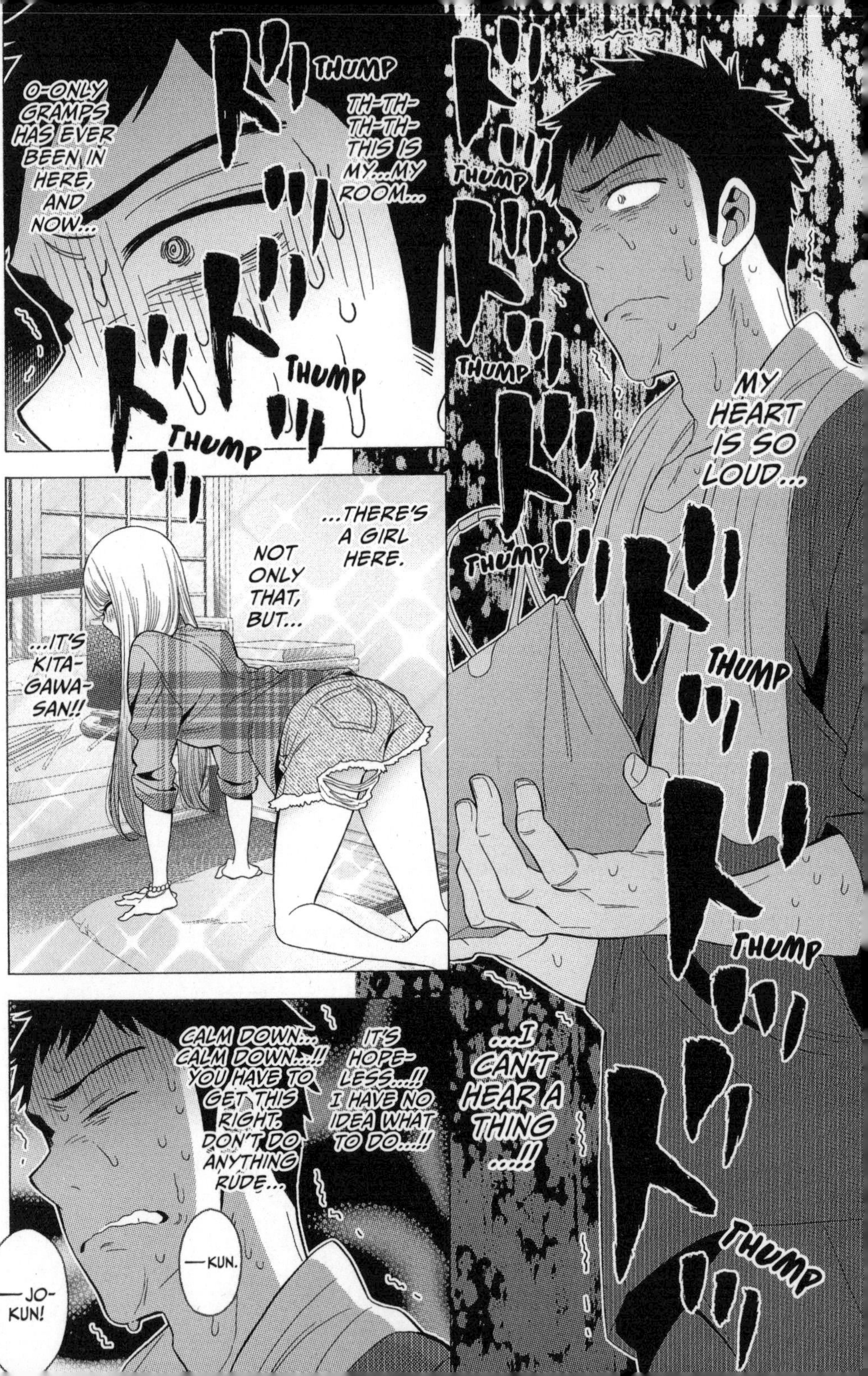
THUMP
THUMP
THUMP
MY HEART IS SO LOUD...
THUMP
THUMP
...I CAN'T HEAR A THING...!!
THUMP
THUMP
TH-TH-TH-TH-THIS IS MY...MY ROOM...
O-ONLY GRAMPS HAS EVER BEEN IN HERE, AND NOW...
THUMP
THUMP
...THERE'S A GIRL HERE.
NOT ONLY THAT, BUT...
...IT'S KITA-GAWA-SAN!!
IT'S HOPE-LESS...!! I HAVE NO IDEA WHAT TO DO...!!
CALM DOWN... CALM DOWN...!! YOU HAVE TO GET THIS RIGHT. DON'T DO ANYTHING RUDE...
—KUN.
—JO-KUN!

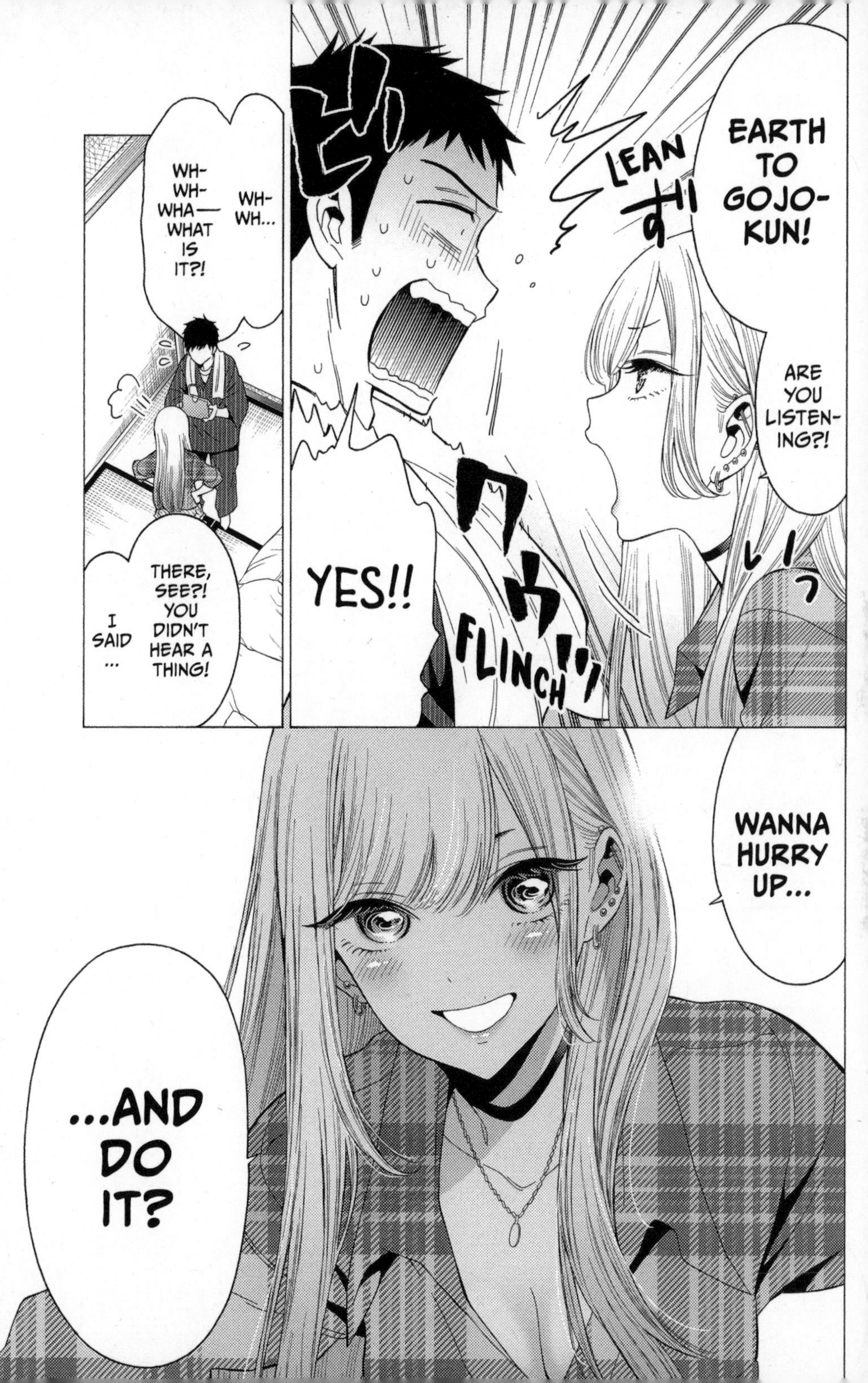
EARTH TO GOJO-KUN!
LEAN
ARE YOU LISTENING?!
YES!!
FLINCH!!
WH- WH...
WH- WH- WHA— WHAT IS IT?!
THERE, SEE?! YOU DIDN'T HEAR A THING!
I SAID ...
WANNA HURRY UP...
...AND DO IT?

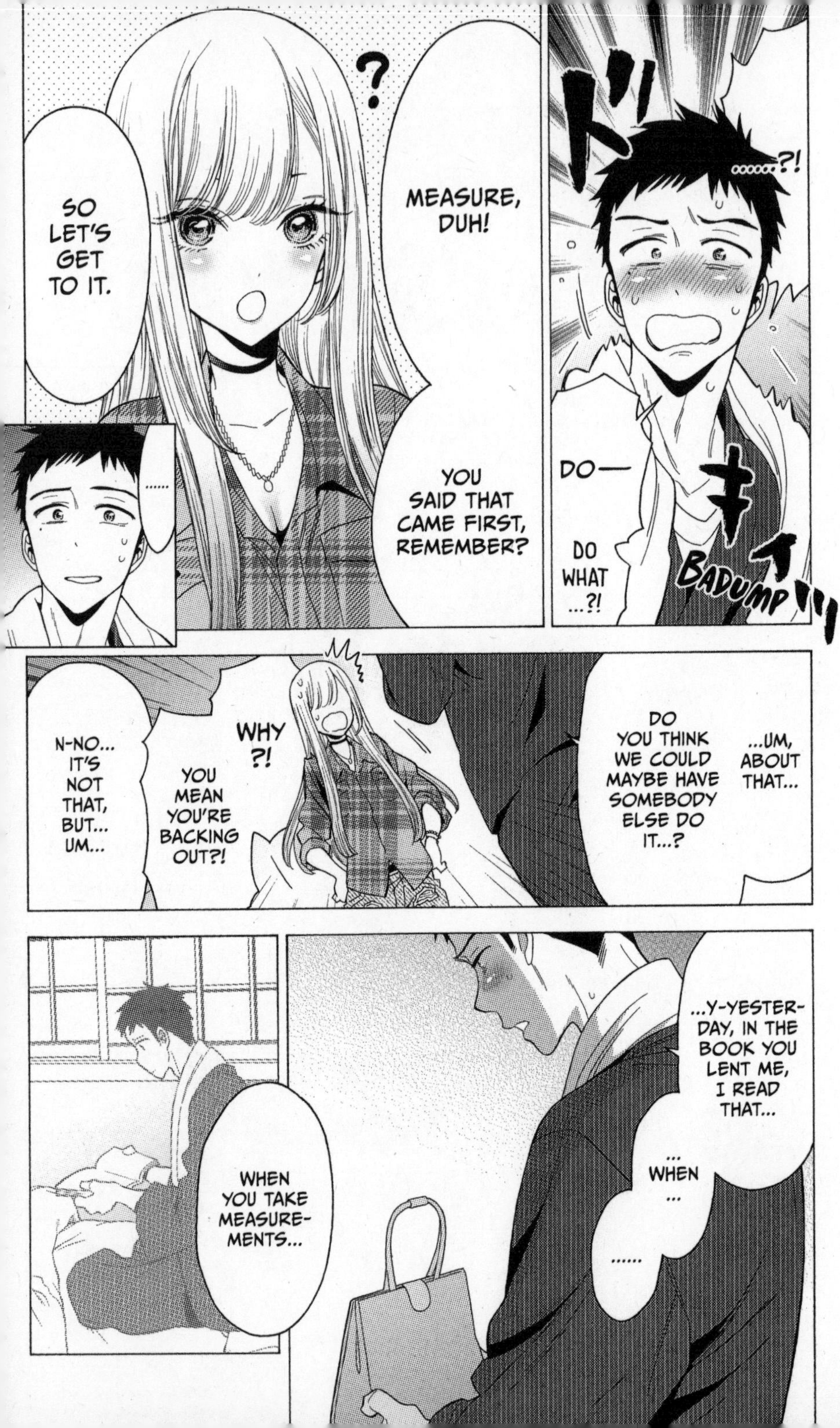
......?!
DO—
DO WHAT ...?!
BADUMP
?
MEASURE, DUH!
YOU SAID THAT CAME FIRST, REMEMBER?
SO LET'S GET TO IT.
......
...UM, ABOUT THAT...
DO YOU THINK WE COULD MAYBE HAVE SOMEBODY ELSE DO IT...?
WHY?!
YOU MEAN YOU'RE BACKING OUT?!
N-NO... IT'S NOT THAT, BUT... UM...
...Y-YESTERDAY, IN THE BOOK YOU LENT ME, I READ THAT...
... WHEN ...
......
WHEN YOU TAKE MEASUREMENTS...

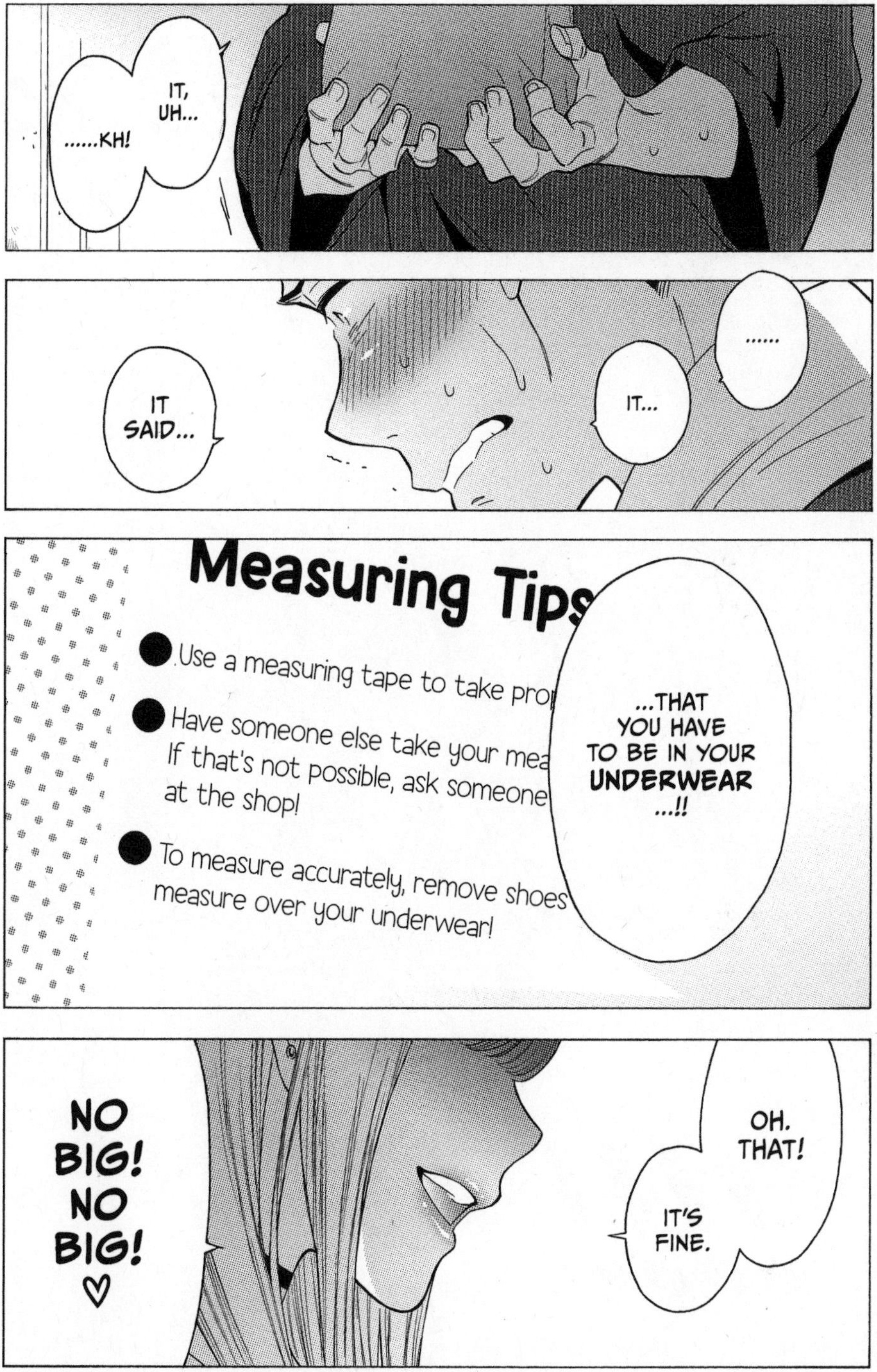
IT, UH...
......KH!
......
IT...
IT SAID...
Measuring Tips
Use a measuring tape to take prop
Have someone else take your mea
If that's not possible, ask someone
at the shop!
To measure accurately, remove shoes
measure over your underwear!
...THAT YOU HAVE TO BE IN YOUR UNDERWEAR ...!!
OH. THAT!
IT'S FINE.
NO BIG! NO BIG! ♡

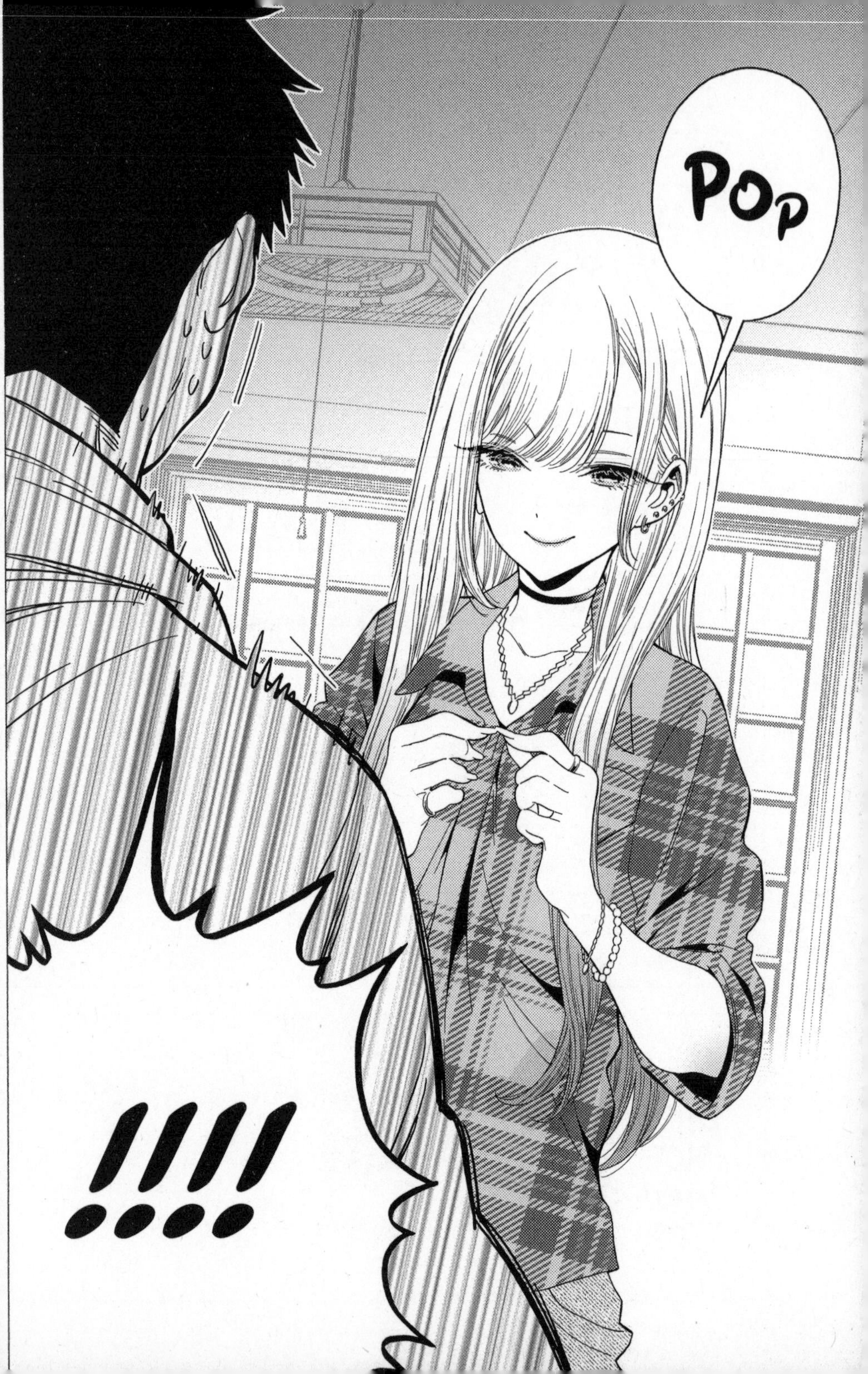
POP
!!!!

My DRESS-UP Darling

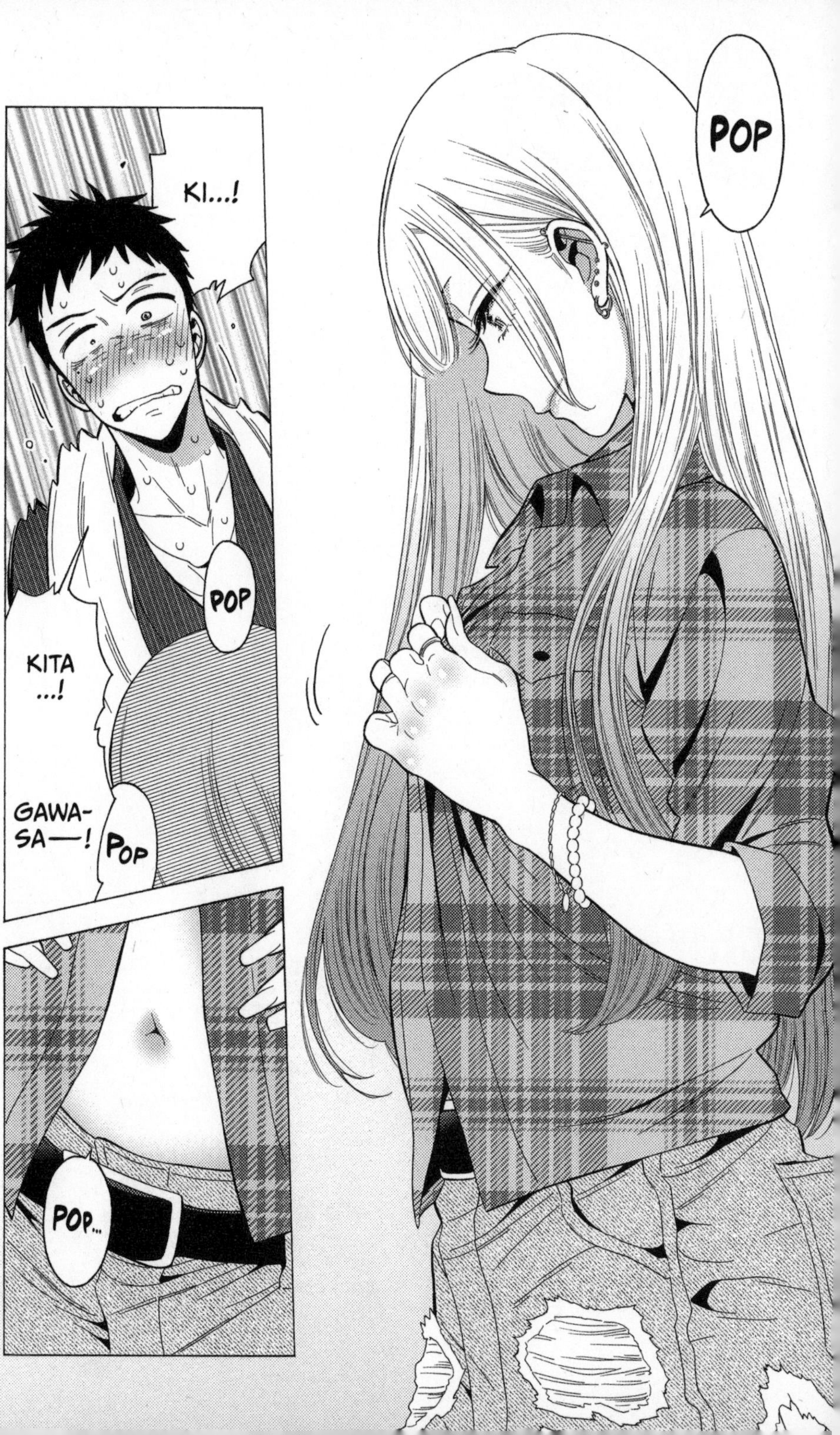
POP
KI...!
POP
KITA ...!
POP
GAWA-SA—!
POP...

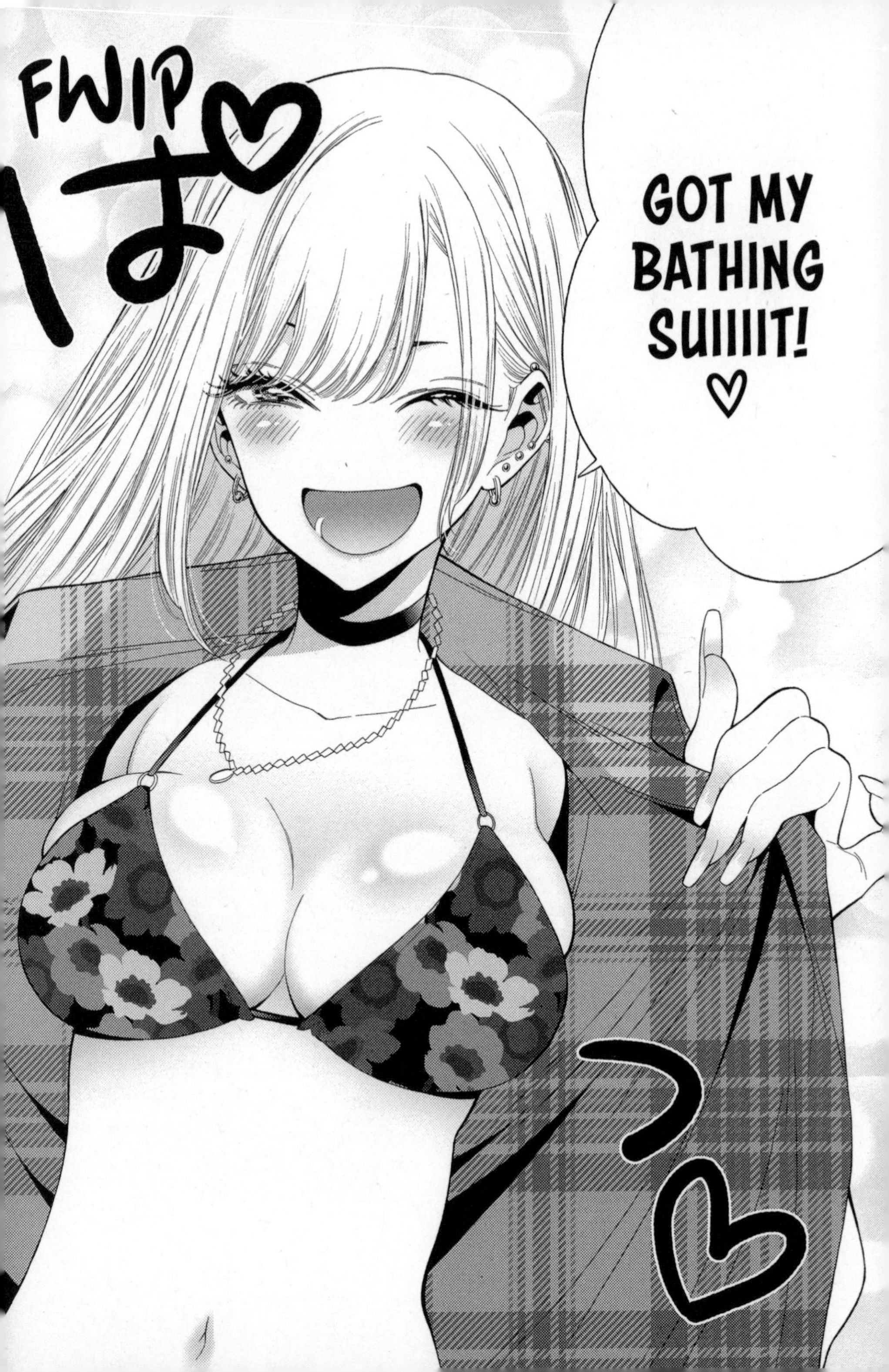
GOT MY BATHING SUIIIIT! ♡
FWIP
ぱ♡
つ♡

CHAPTER 3

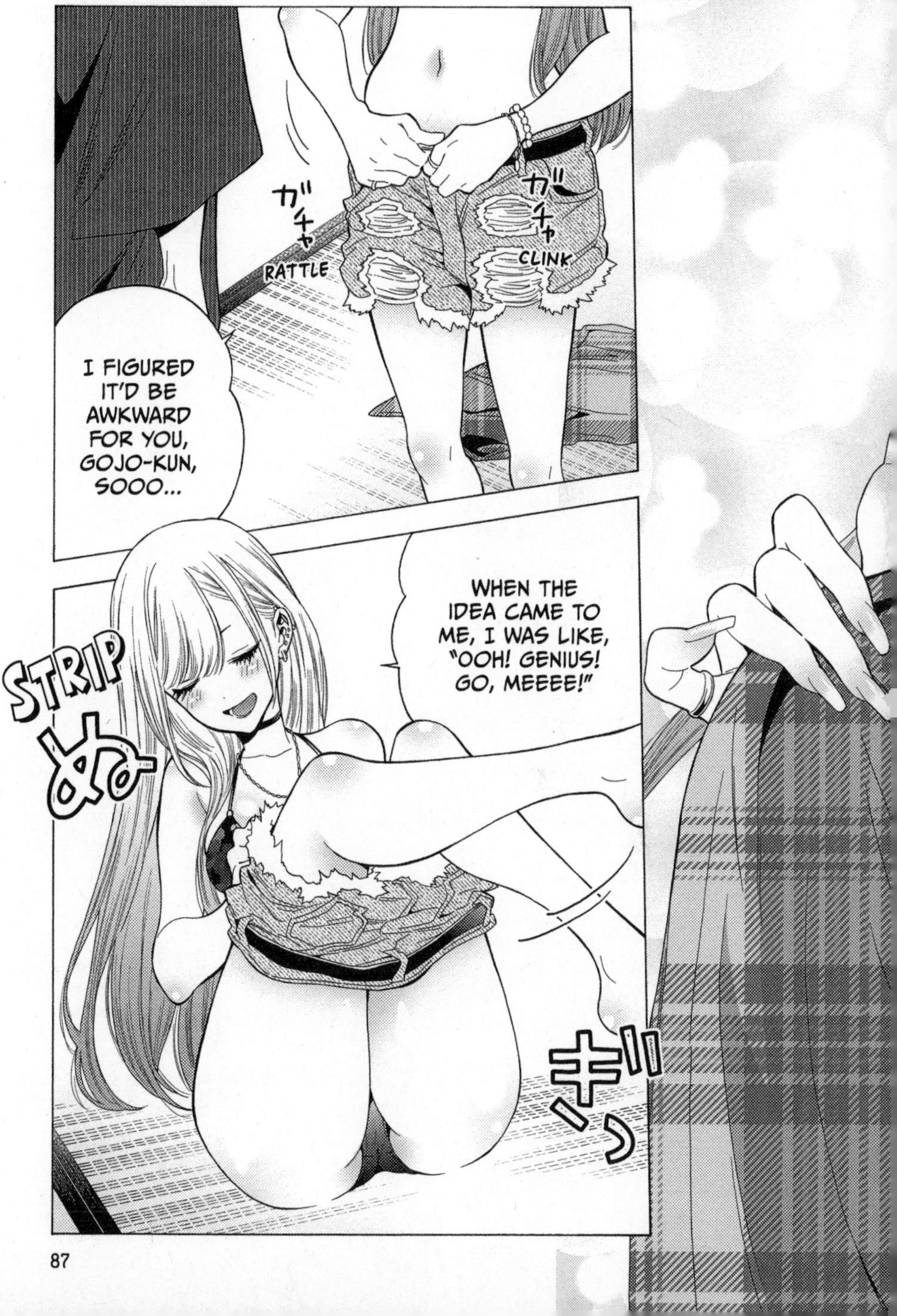

ガチャ
CLINK
ガチャ
RATTLE
I FIGURED IT'D BE AWKWARD FOR YOU, GOJO-KUN, SOOO...
WHEN THE IDEA CAME TO ME, I WAS LIKE, "OOH! GENIUS! GO, MEEEE!"
キュッ
STRIP
ぬ

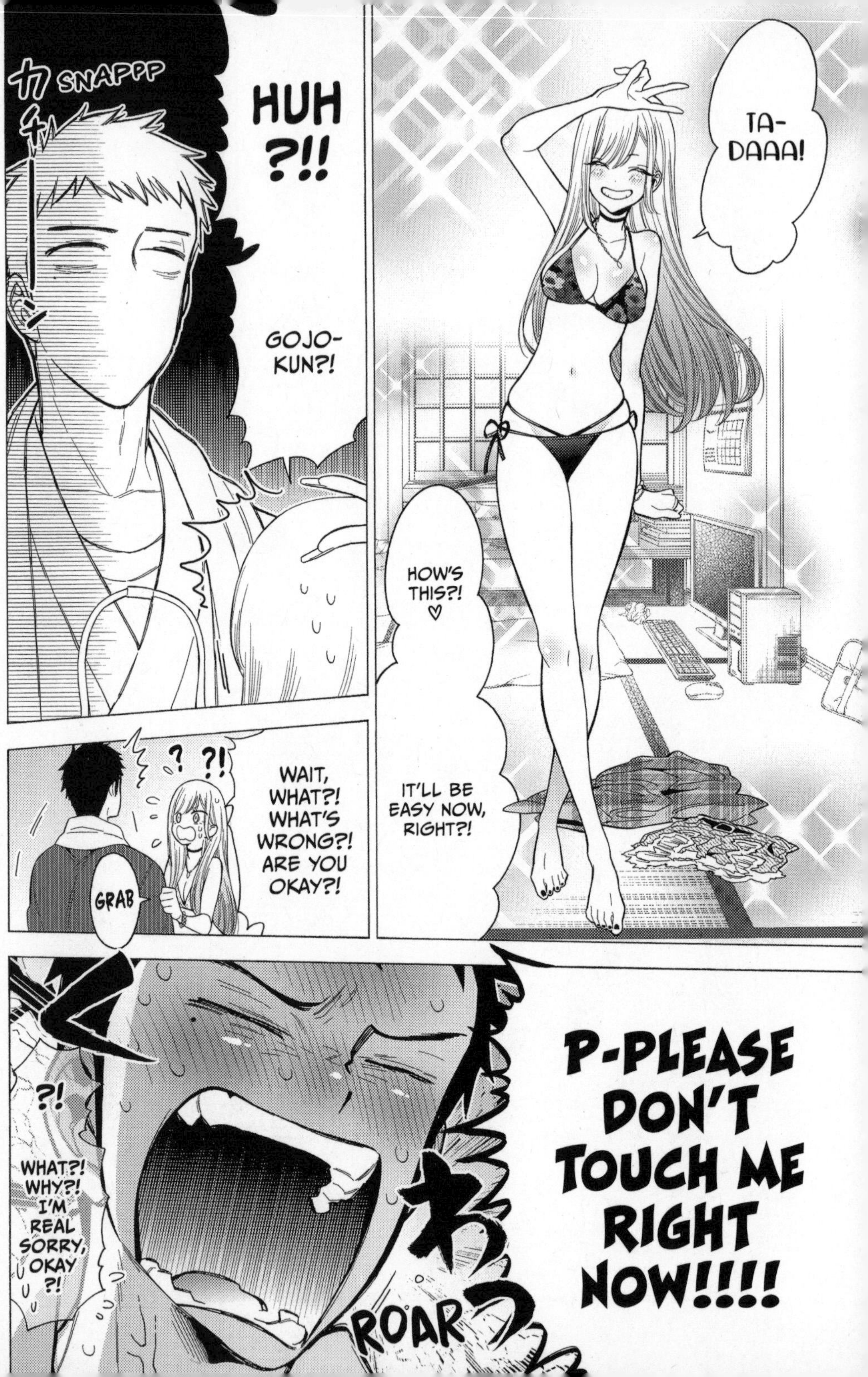
TA-DAAA!
HOW'S THIS?! ♡
IT'LL BE EASY NOW, RIGHT?!
SNAPPP
HUH?!!
GOJO-KUN?!
? ?!
WAIT, WHAT?! WHAT'S WRONG?! ARE YOU OKAY?!
GRAB
P-PLEASE DON'T TOUCH ME RIGHT NOW!!!!
ROAR
?!
WHAT?! WHY?! I'M REAL SORRY, OKAY?!

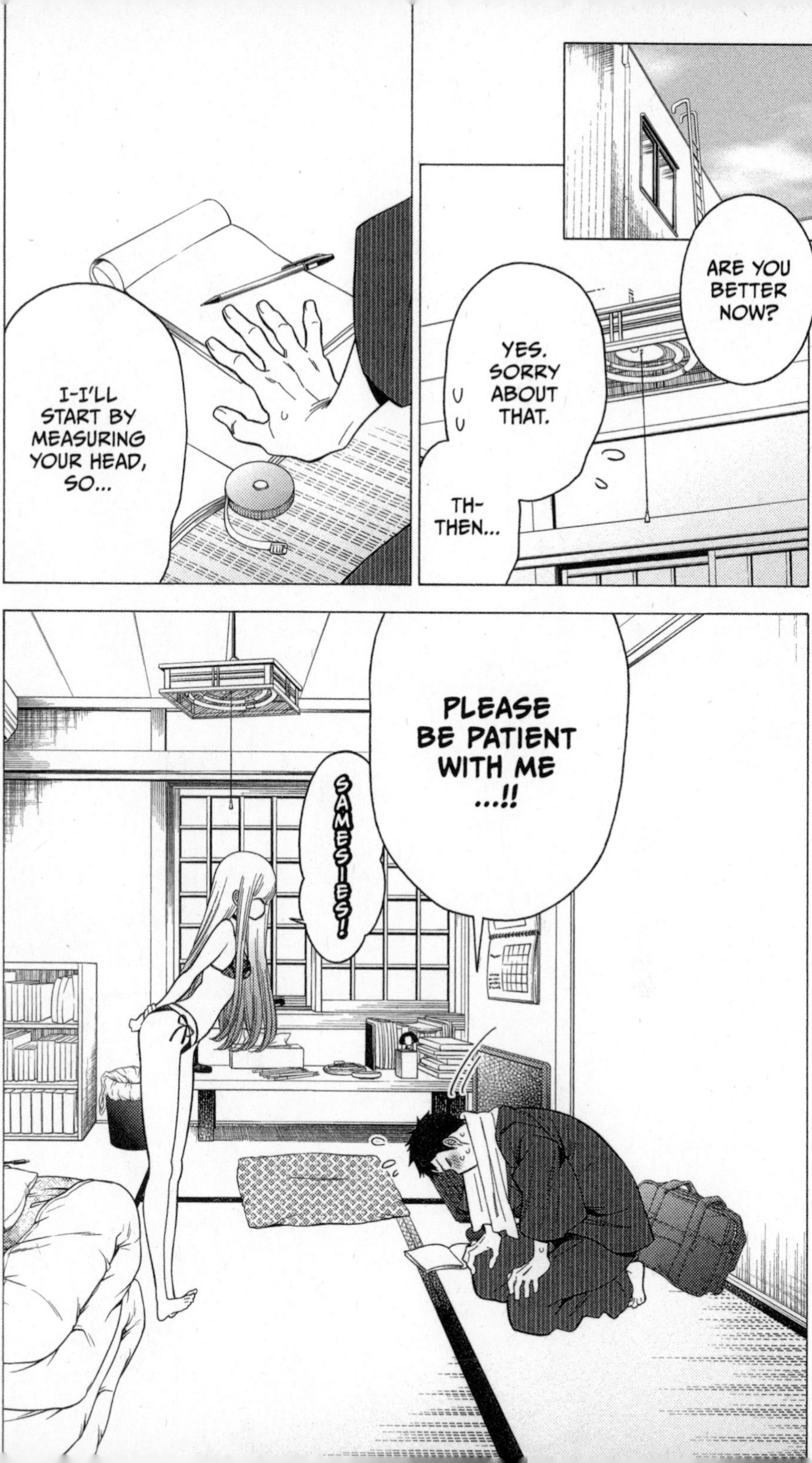
ARE YOU BETTER NOW?
YES. SORRY ABOUT THAT.
TH-THEN...
I-I'LL START BY MEASURING YOUR HEAD, SO...
PLEASE BE PATIENT WITH ME ...!!
SAMESIES!

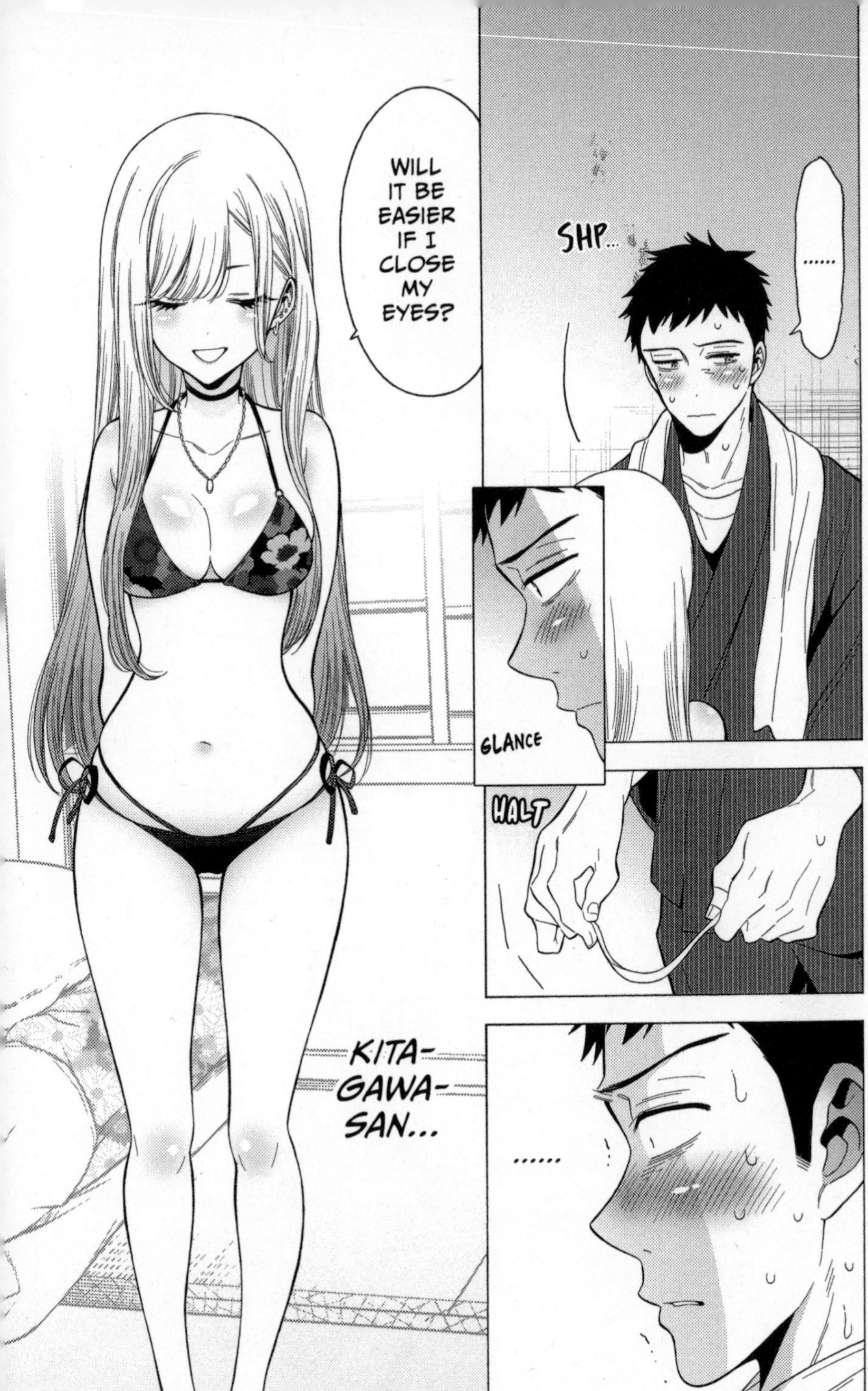
......
SHP...
GLANCE
HALT
......
WILL IT BE EASIER IF I CLOSE MY EYES?
KITA-GAWA-SAN...

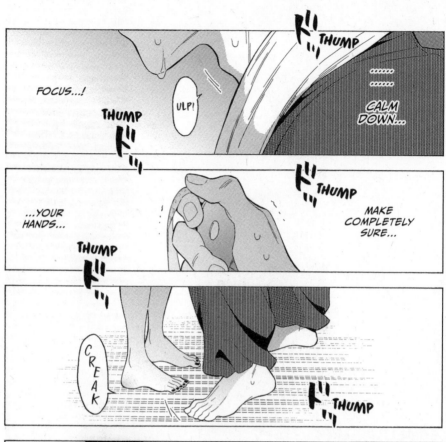

FOCUS...!

ULP!

THUMP

THUMP

CALM DOWN...

THUMP

...YOUR HANDS...

THUMP

MAKE COMPLETELY SURE...

CREAK

THUMP

...NEVER TOUCH KITAGAWA-SAN...

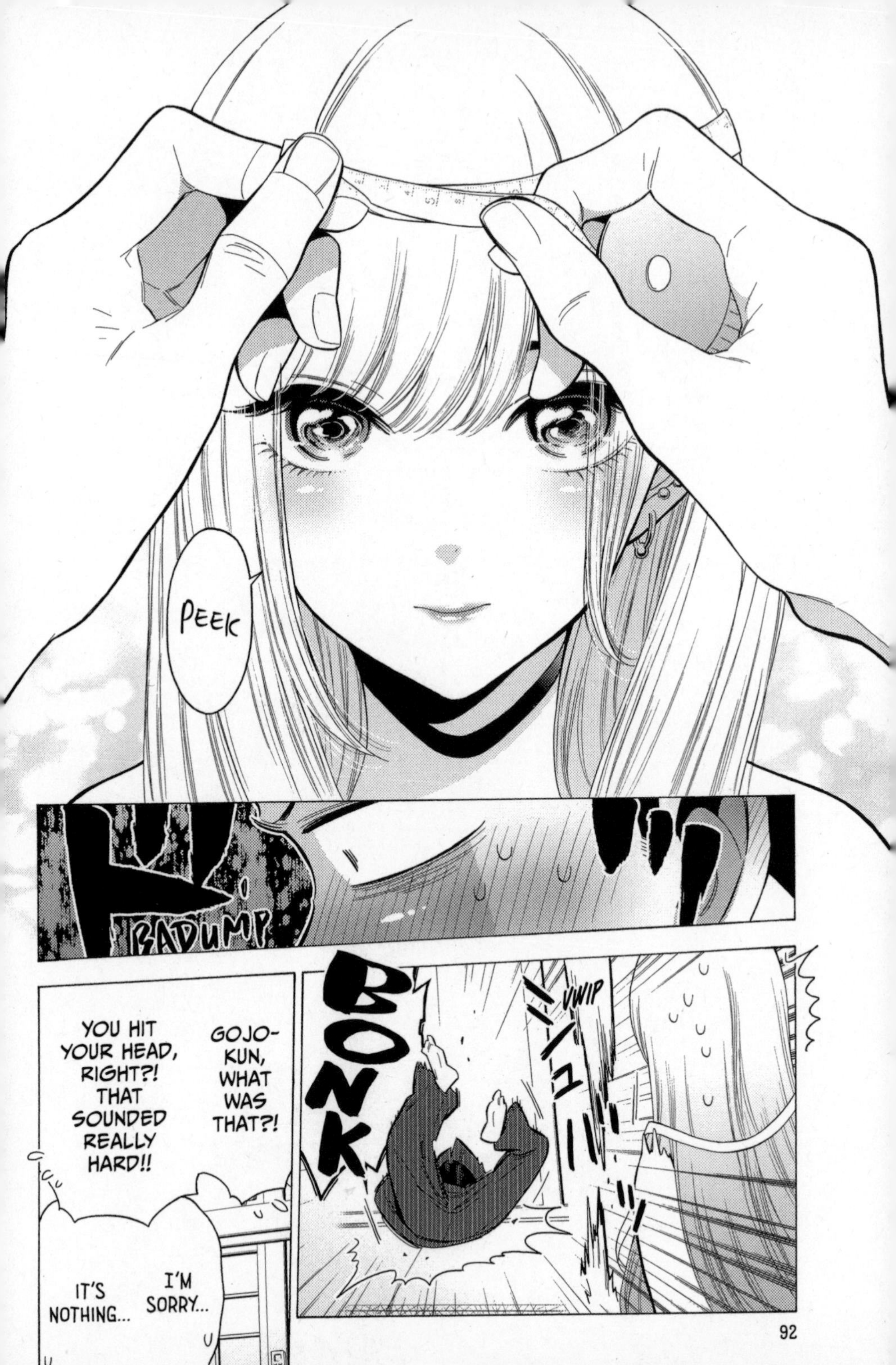
PEEK
BADUMP
BONK
VWIP
GOJO-KUN, WHAT WAS THAT?!
YOU HIT YOUR HEAD, RIGHT?! THAT SOUNDED REALLY HARD!!
I'M SORRY...
IT'S NOTHING...

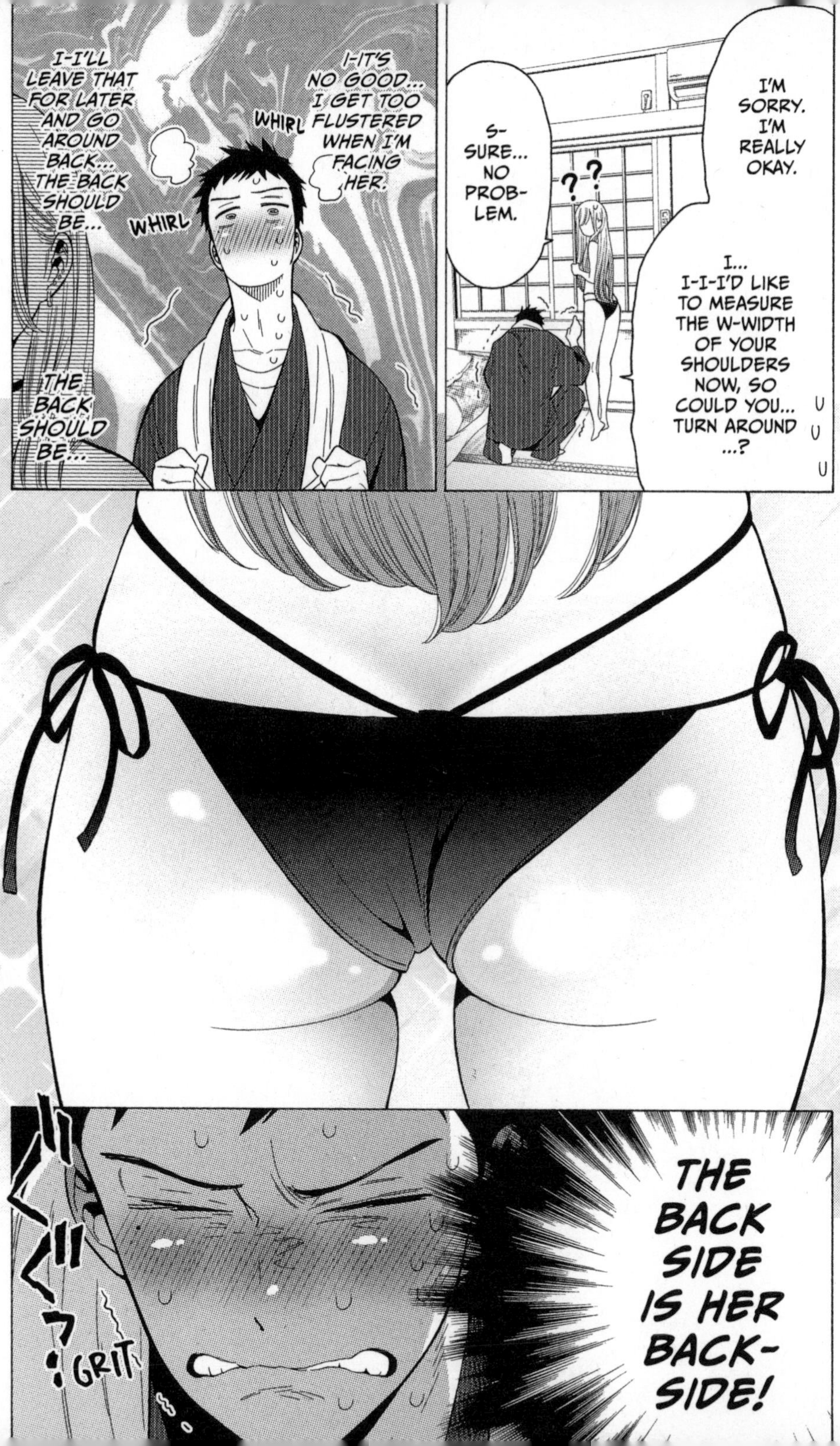
I'M SORRY. I'M REALLY OKAY.
S-SURE... NO PROBLEM.
I... I-I-I'D LIKE TO MEASURE THE W-WIDTH OF YOUR SHOULDERS NOW, SO COULD YOU... TURN AROUND ...?
U U U
I-IT'S NO GOOD... I GET TOO FLUSTERED WHEN I'M FACING HER.
WHIRL
I-I'LL LEAVE THAT FOR LATER AND GO AROUND BACK... THE BACK SHOULD BE...
WHIRL
THE BACK SHOULD BE...
THE BACK SIDE IS HER BACK-SIDE!
GRIT

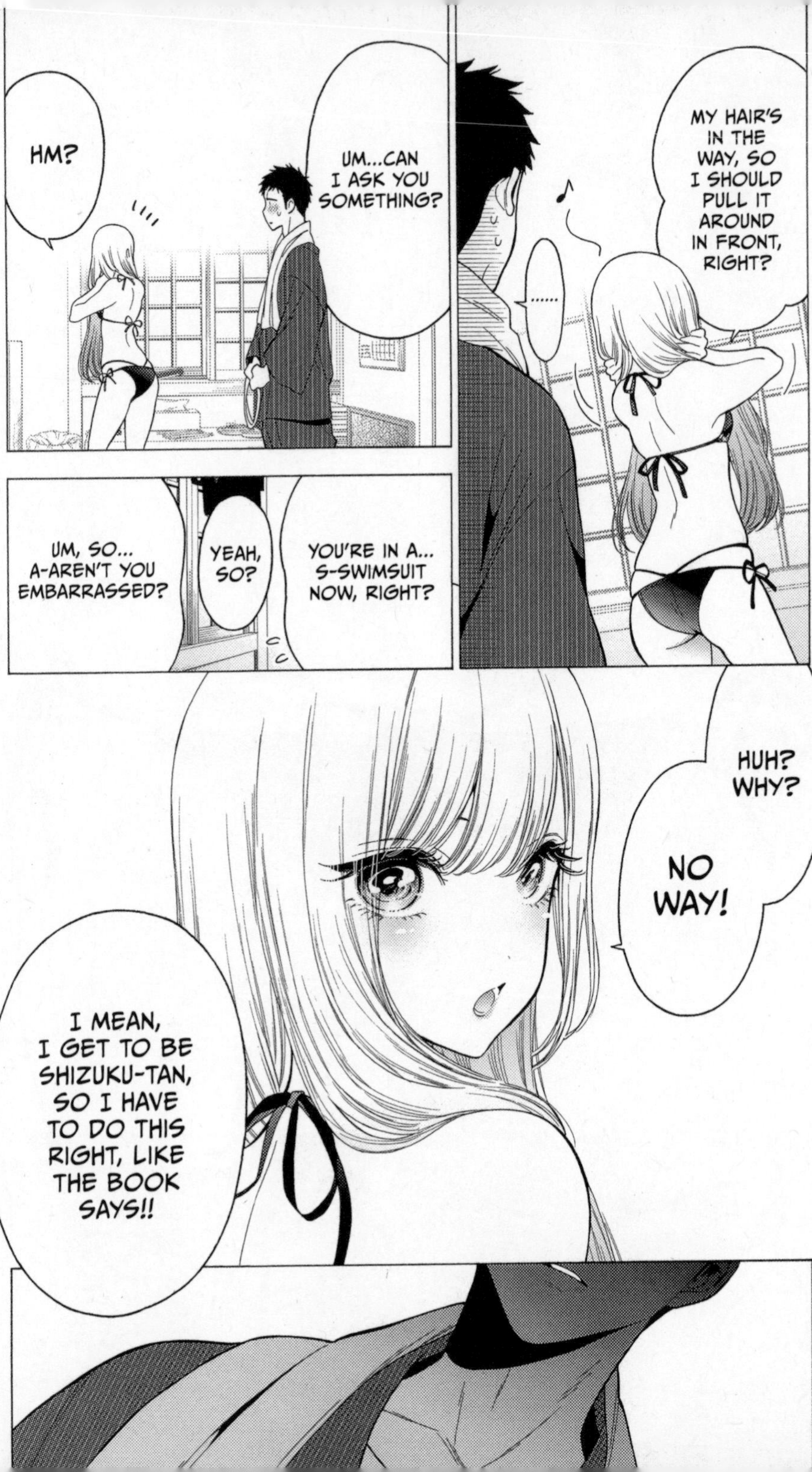
MY HAIR'S IN THE WAY, SO I SHOULD PULL IT AROUND IN FRONT, RIGHT?
......
UM...CAN I ASK YOU SOMETHING?
HM?
YOU'RE IN A... S-SWIMSUIT NOW, RIGHT?
YEAH, SO?
UM, SO... A-AREN'T YOU EMBARRASSED?
HUH? WHY?
NO WAY!
I MEAN, I GET TO BE SHIZUKU-TAN, SO I HAVE TO DO THIS RIGHT, LIKE THE BOOK SAYS!!

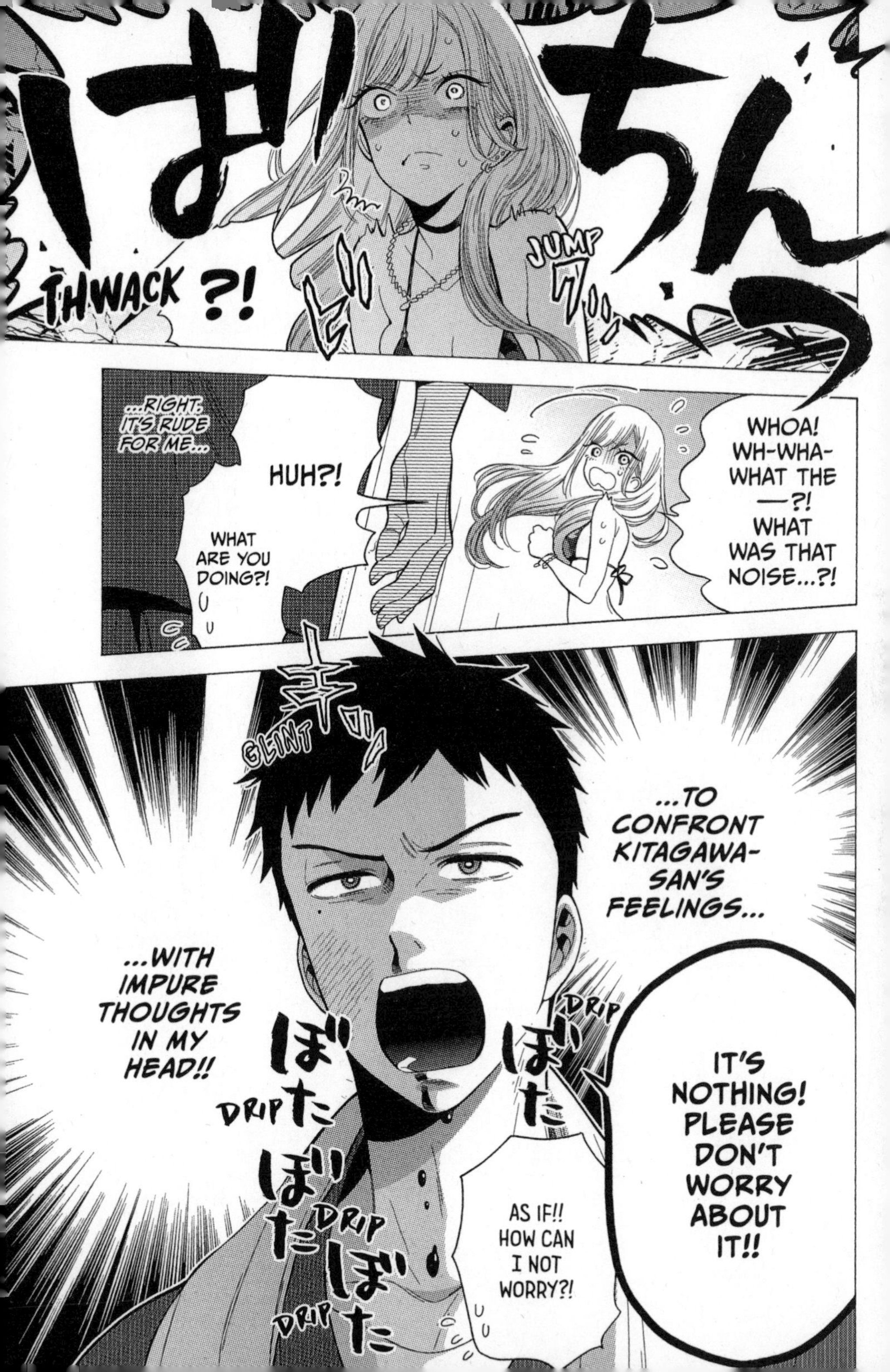
JUMP
THWACK ?!
WHOA! WH-WHA-WHAT THE—?! WHAT WAS THAT NOISE...?!
HUH?!
WHAT ARE YOU DOING?!
...RIGHT. IT'S RUDE FOR ME...
GLINT
...TO CONFRONT KITAGAWA-SAN'S FEELINGS...
IT'S NOTHING! PLEASE DON'T WORRY ABOUT IT!!
...WITH IMPURE THOUGHTS IN MY HEAD!!
DRIP
DRIP
AS IF!! HOW CAN I NOT WORRY?!
DRIP
DRIP

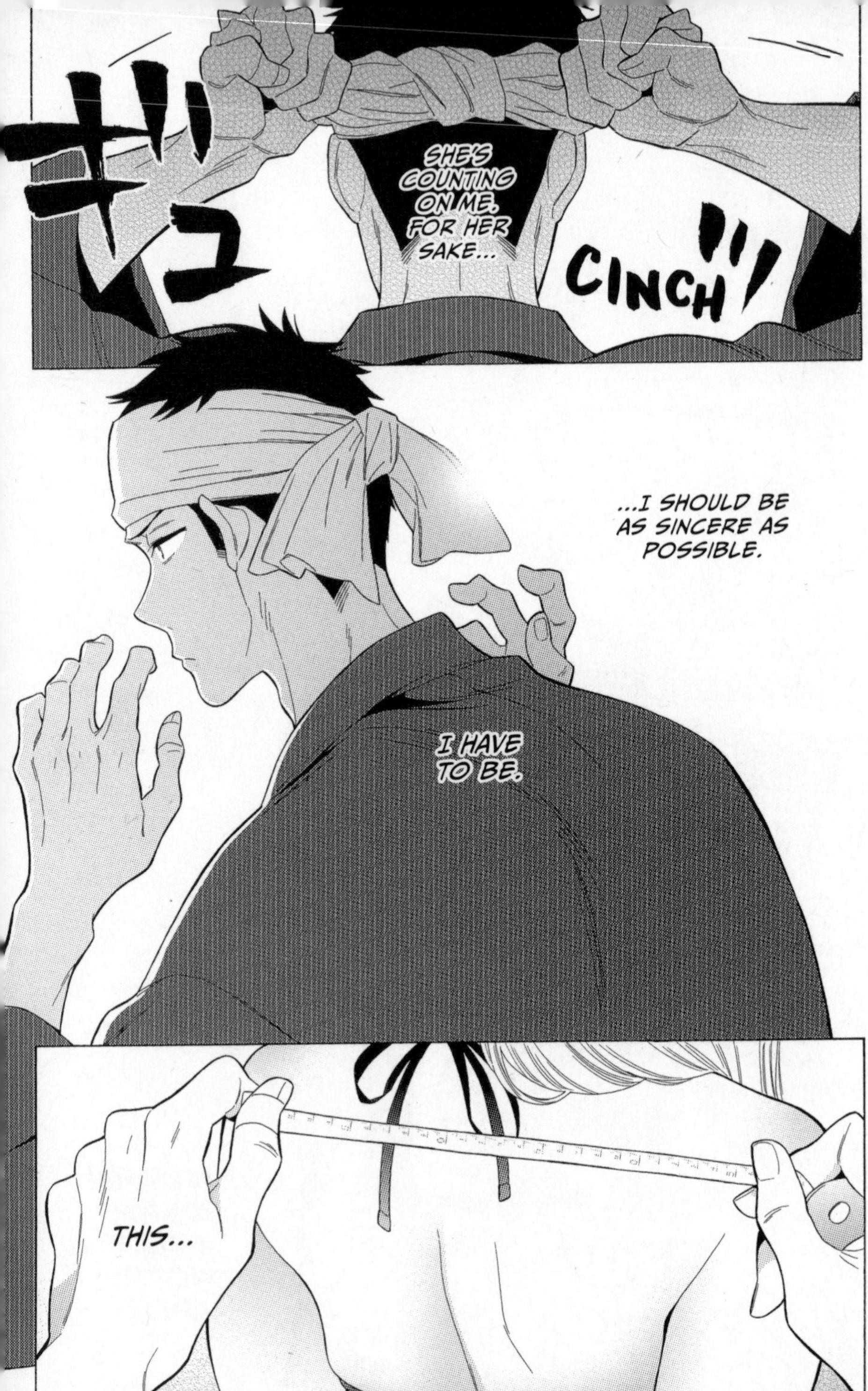
SHE'S COUNTING ON ME. FOR HER SAKE...
CINCH!!
ギュ
...I SHOULD BE AS SINCERE AS POSSIBLE.
I HAVE TO BE.
THIS...

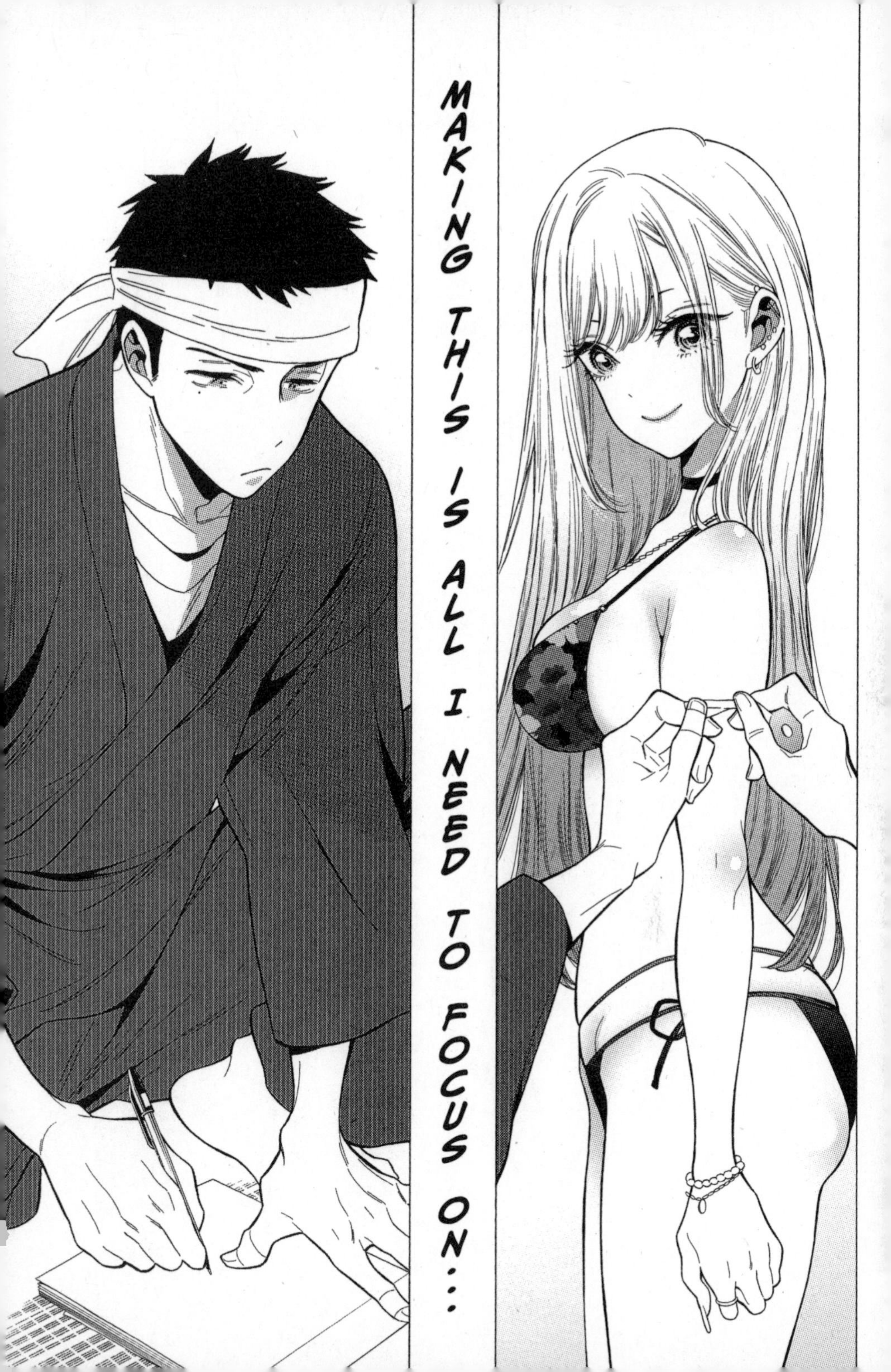
MAKING THIS IS ALL I NEED TO FOCUS ON...

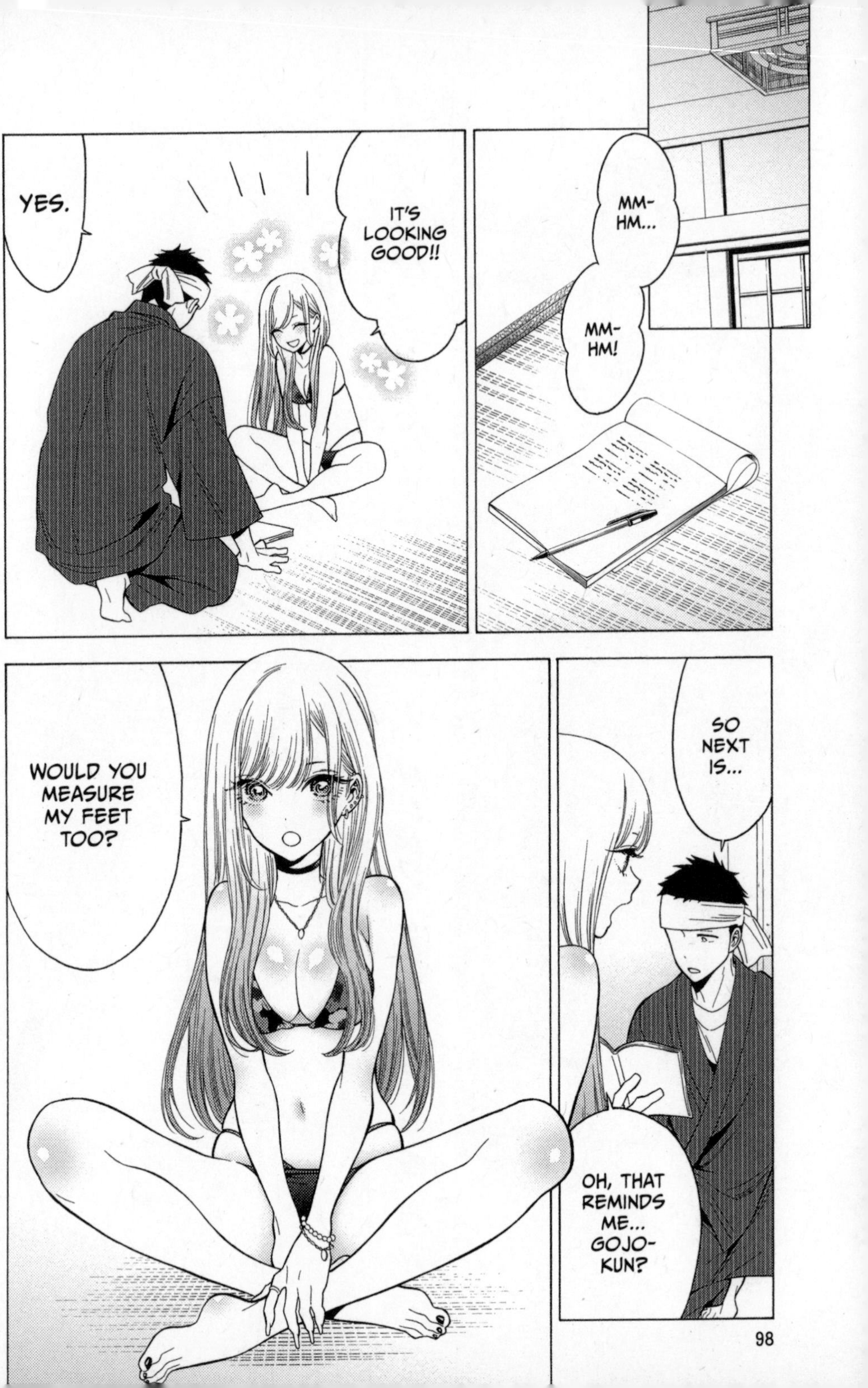
MM-HM...
MM-HM!
IT'S LOOKING GOOD!!
YES.
SO NEXT IS...
OH, THAT REMINDS ME... GOJO-KUN?
WOULD YOU MEASURE MY FEET TOO?

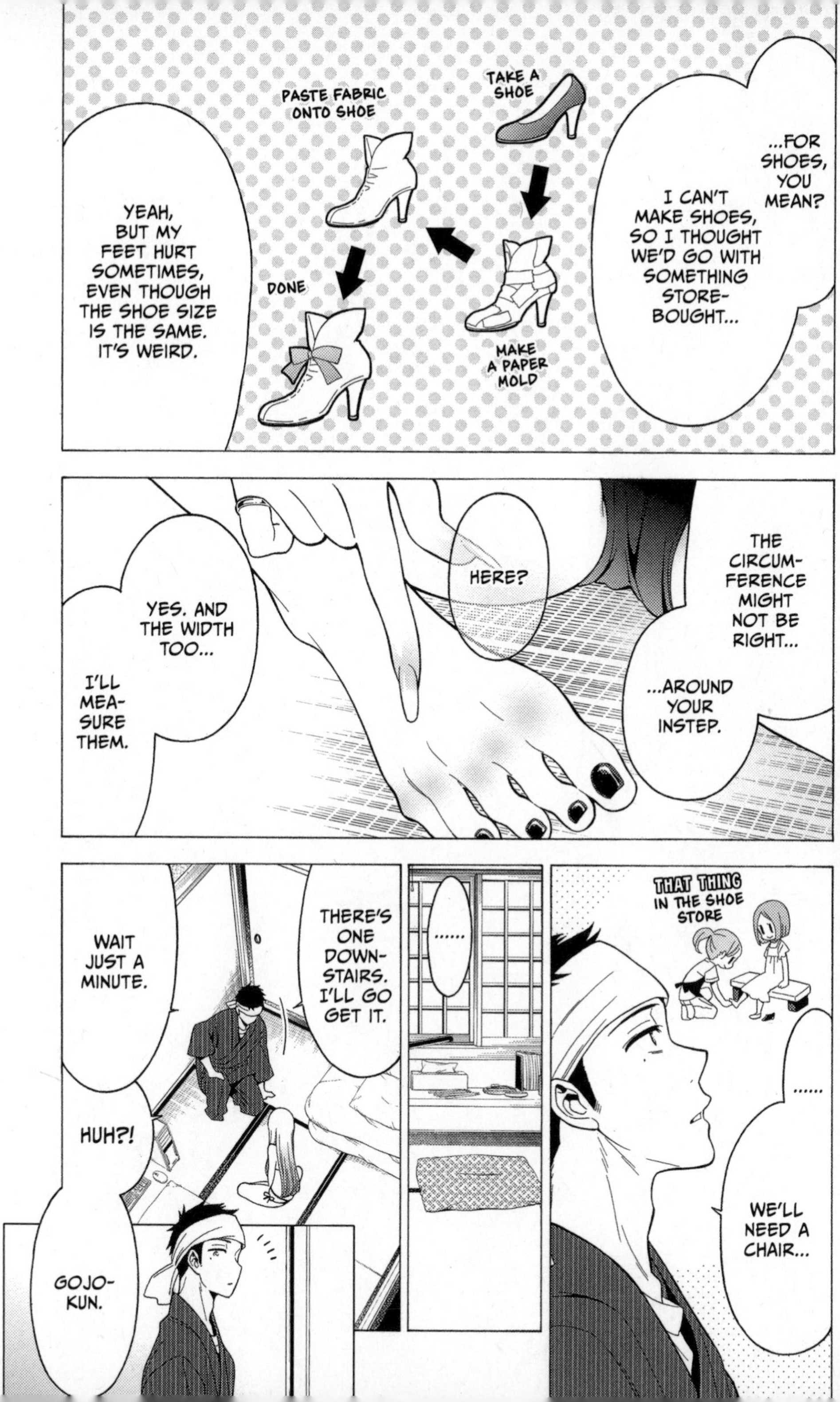
...FOR SHOES, YOU MEAN?
I CAN'T MAKE SHOES, SO I THOUGHT WE'D GO WITH SOMETHING STORE-BOUGHT...
TAKE A SHOE
MAKE A PAPER MOLD
PASTE FABRIC ONTO SHOE
DONE
YEAH, BUT MY FEET HURT SOMETIMES, EVEN THOUGH THE SHOE SIZE IS THE SAME. IT'S WEIRD.
THE CIRCUMFERENCE MIGHT NOT BE RIGHT...
...AROUND YOUR INSTEP.
HERE?
YES. AND THE WIDTH TOO...
I'LL MEASURE THEM.
THAT THING IN THE SHOE STORE
......
WE'LL NEED A CHAIR...
......
THERE'S ONE DOWNSTAIRS. I'LL GO GET IT.
WAIT JUST A MINUTE.
HUH?!
GOJO-KUN.

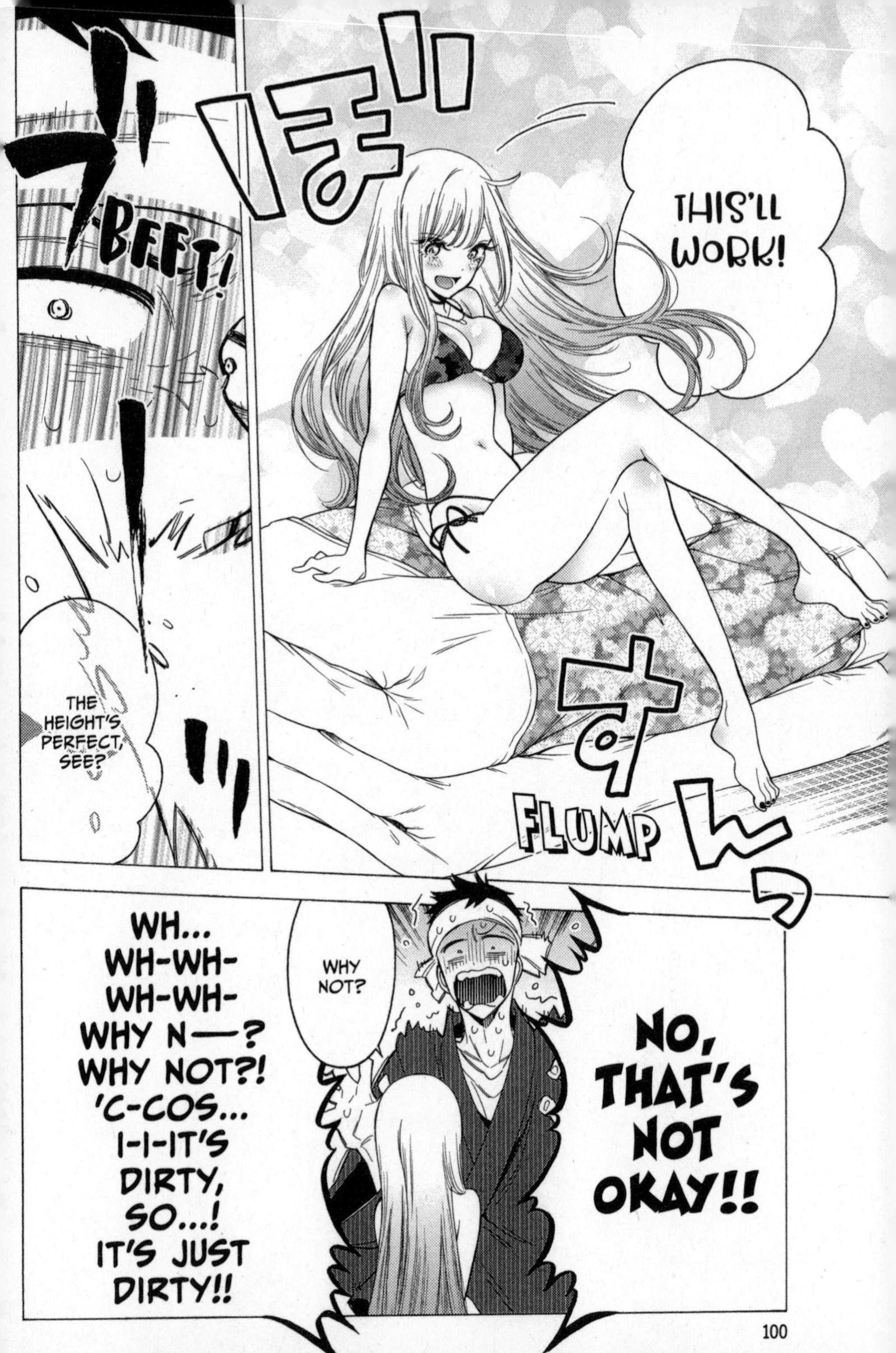
THIS'LL WORK!
FLUMP
BFFT!
THE HEIGHT'S PERFECT, SEE?
NO, THAT'S NOT OKAY!!
WHY NOT?
WH... WH-WH-WH-WH-WHY N—? WHY NOT?! 'C-COS... I-I-IT'S DIRTY, SO...! IT'S JUST DIRTY!!

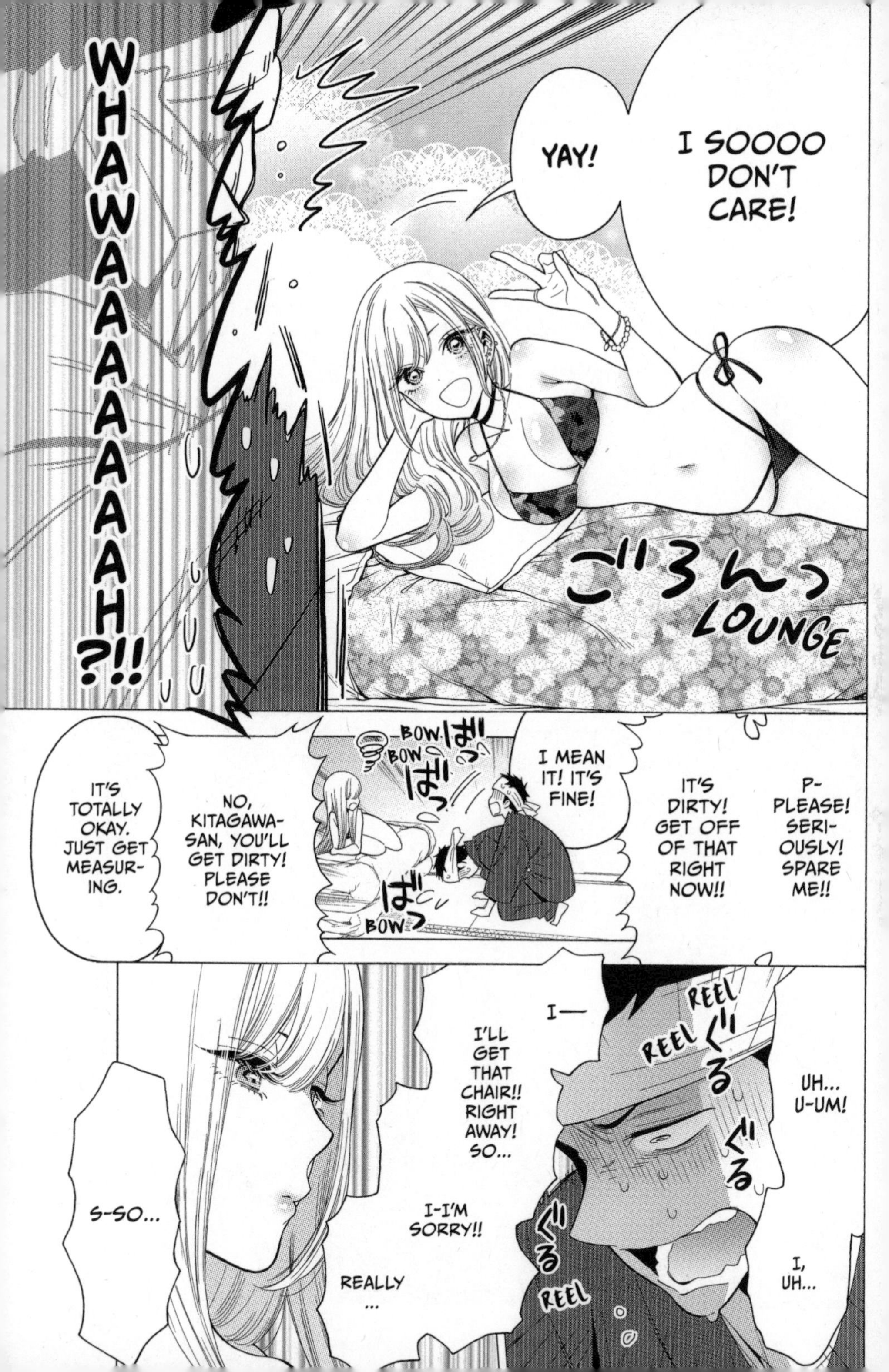
I SOOOO DON'T CARE!
YAY!
ごろんっ
LOUNGE
WHAAAAAAAAAAH?!!
P-PLEASE! SERIOUSLY! SPARE ME!!
IT'S DIRTY! GET OFF OF THAT RIGHT NOW!!
I MEAN IT! IT'S FINE!
BOW ぼっ
BOW ぼっ
ぼっ
BOW
NO, KITAGAWA-SAN, YOU'LL GET DIRTY! PLEASE DON'T!!
IT'S TOTALLY OKAY. JUST GET MEASURING.
REEL ぐる
REEL ぐる
ぐる
REEL ぐる
UH... U-UM!
I—
I'LL GET THAT CHAIR!! RIGHT AWAY! SO...
I, UH...
I-I'M SORRY!!
REALLY ...
S-SO...

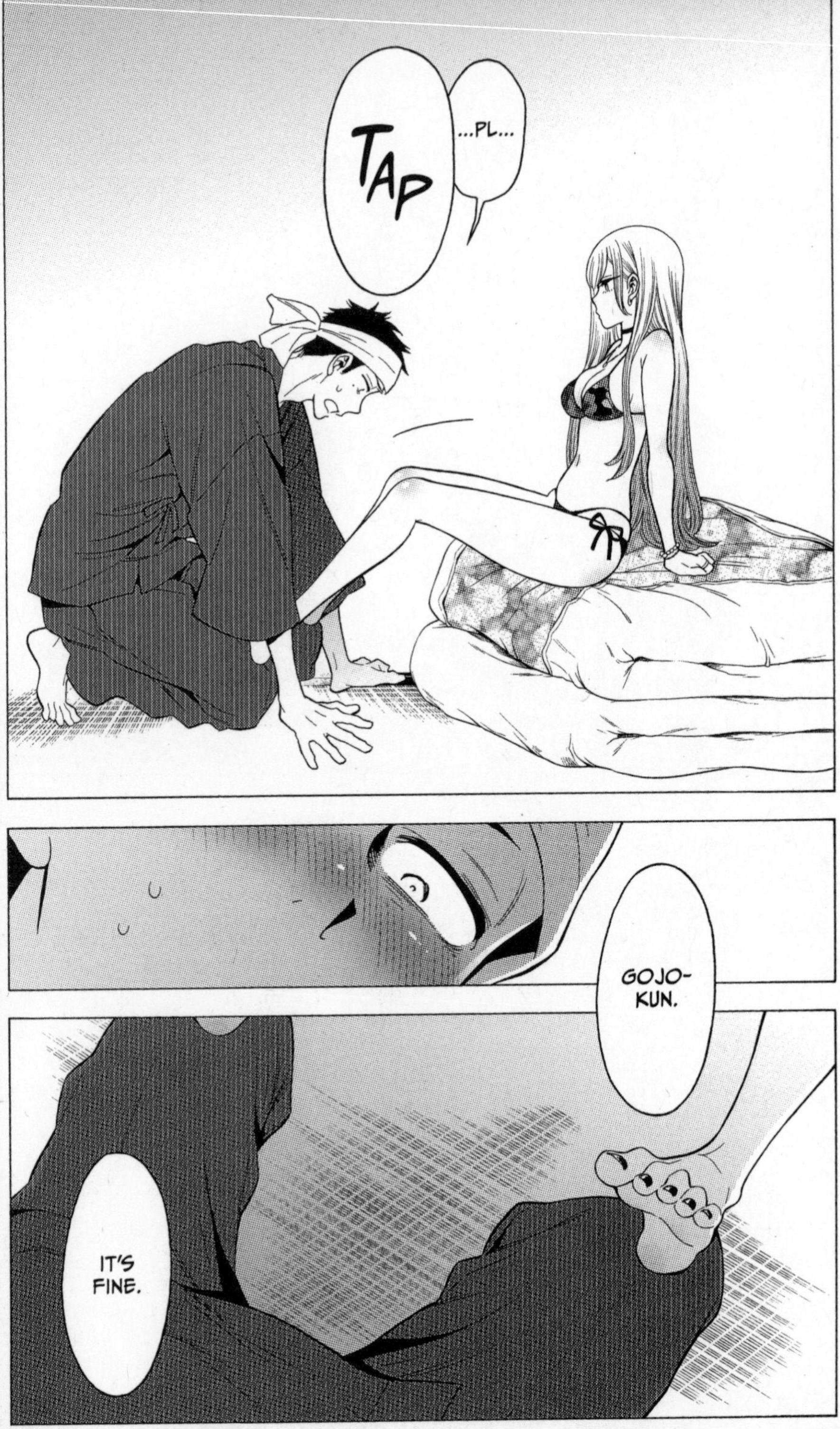
...PL...
TAP
GOJO-KUN.
IT'S FINE.

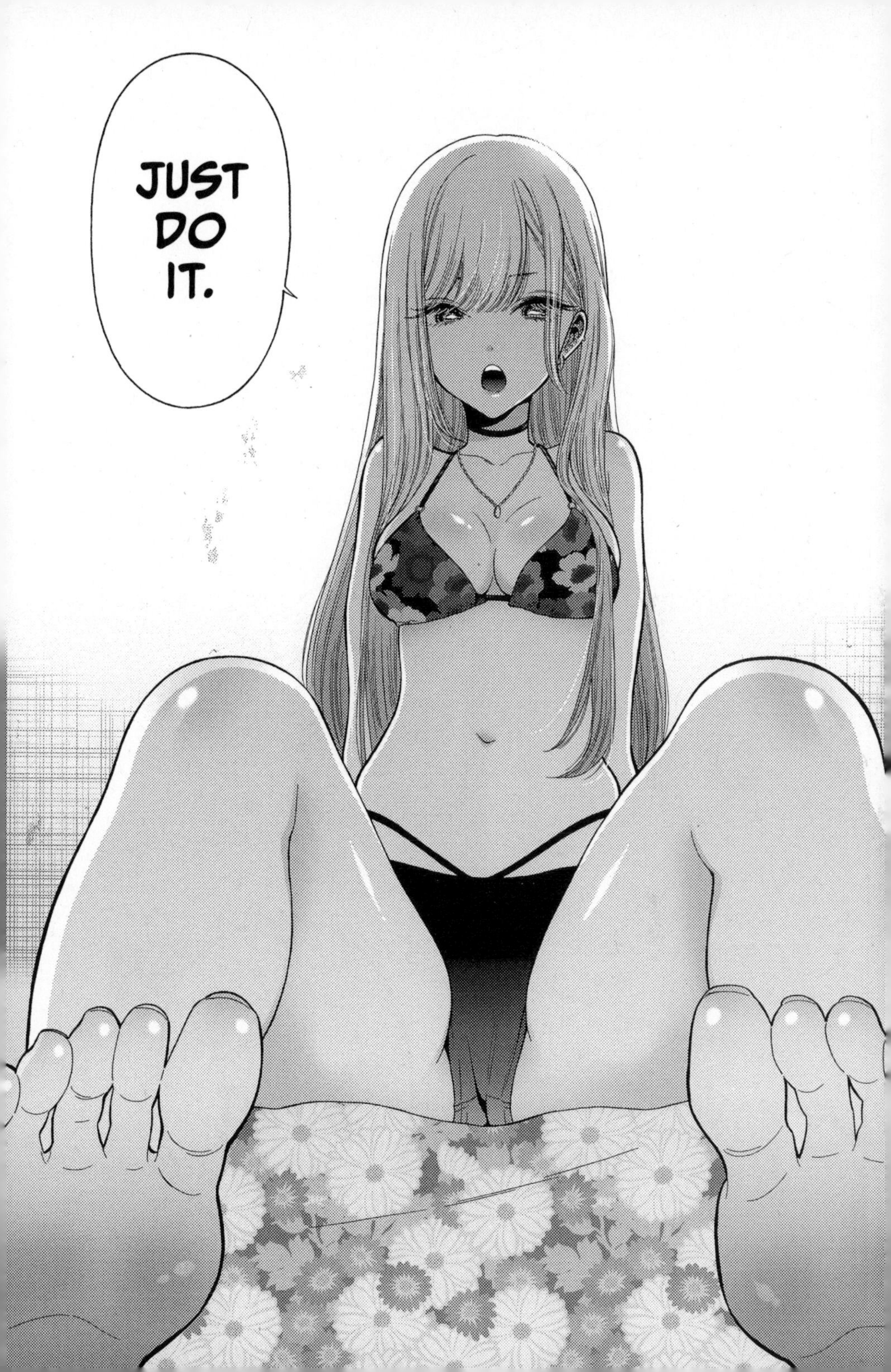
JUST DO IT.

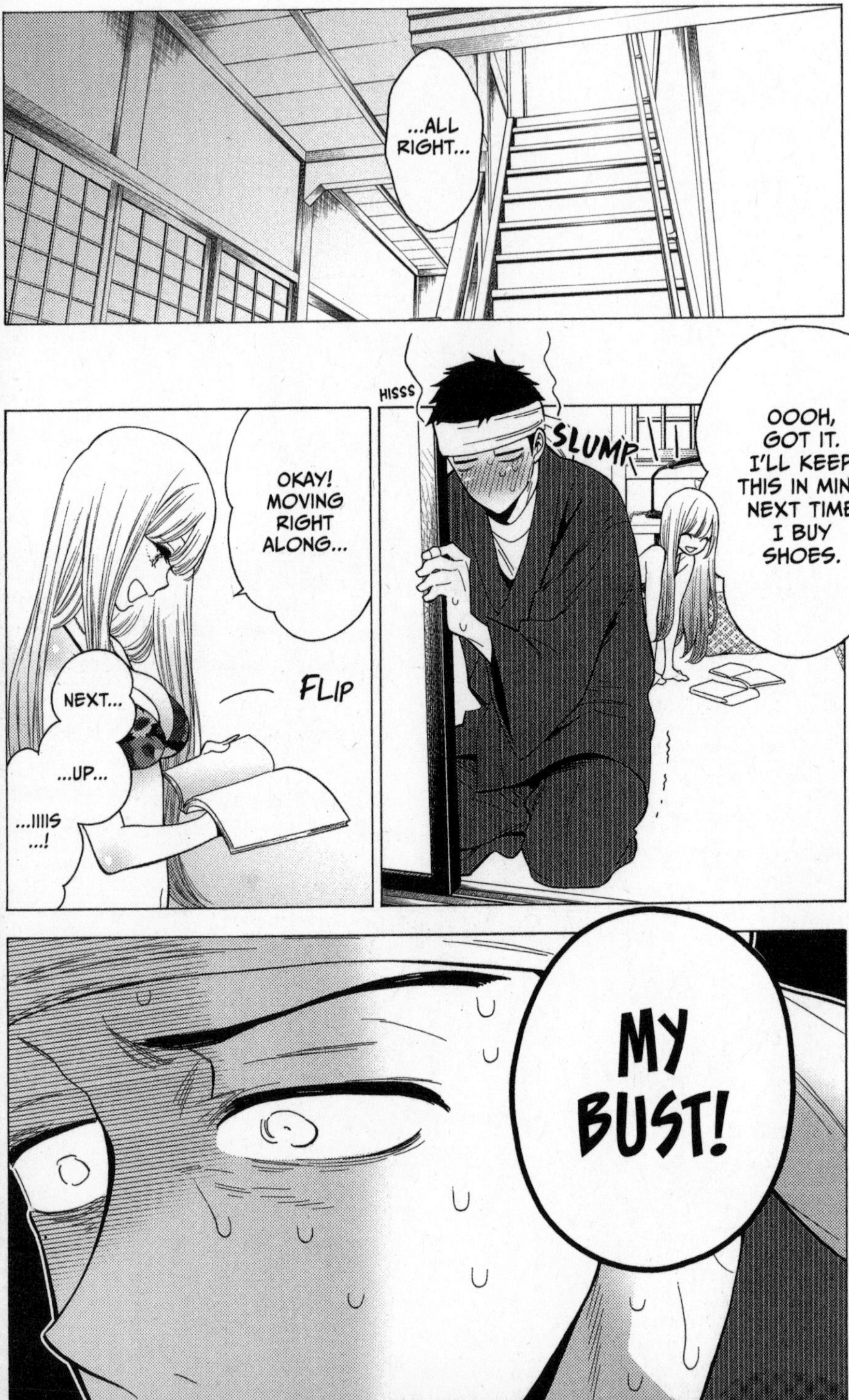
...ALL RIGHT...
OOOH, GOT IT. I'LL KEEP THIS IN MIND NEXT TIME I BUY SHOES.
SLUMP
HISSS
OKAY! MOVING RIGHT ALONG...
FLIP
NEXT...
...UP...
...IIIIS ...!
MY BUST!

My DRESS-UP Darling

CHAPTER 4

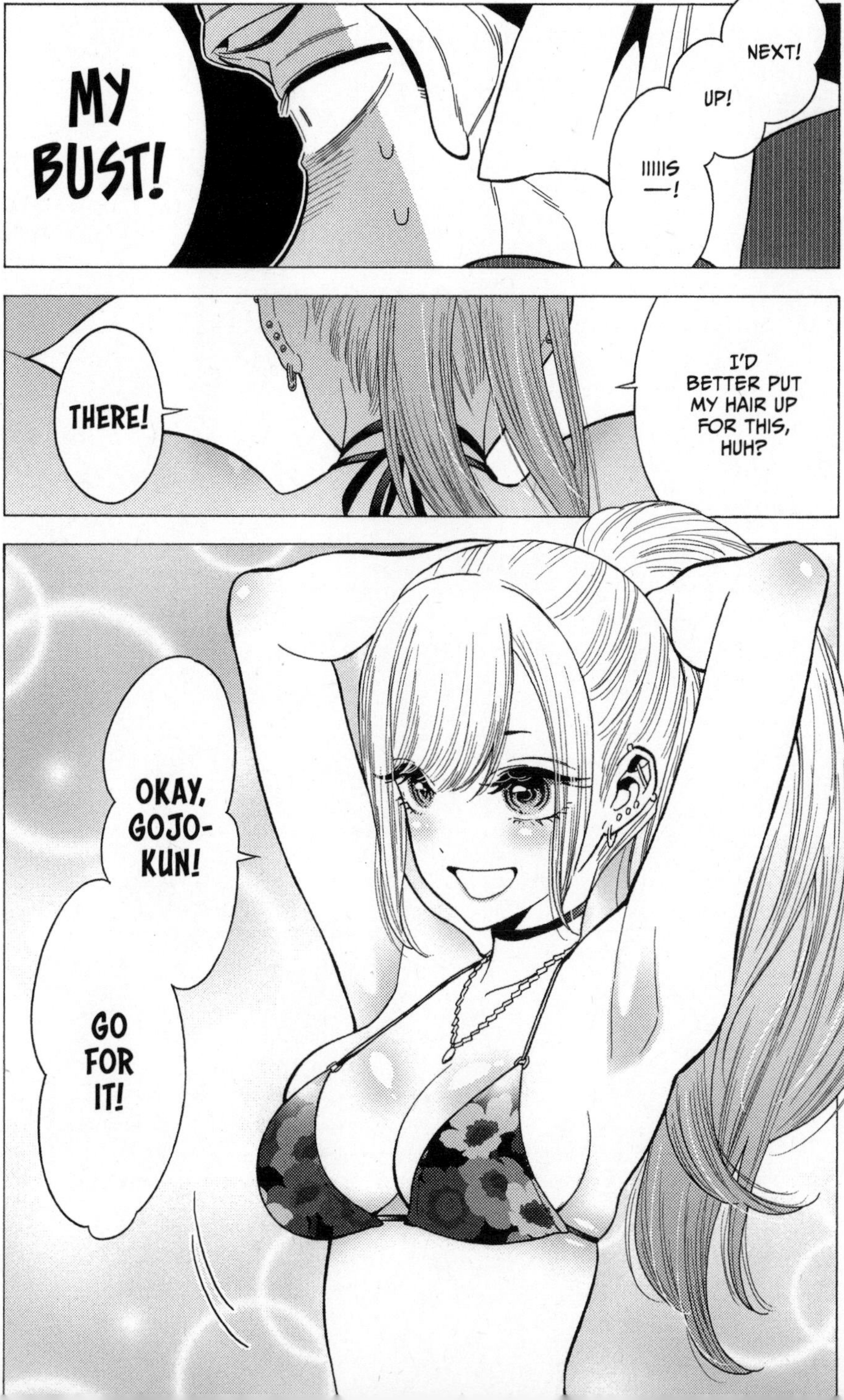
NEXT!
UP!
IIIIIS—!
MY BUST!
I'D BETTER PUT MY HAIR UP FOR THIS, HUH?
THERE!
OKAY, GOJO-KUN!
GO FOR IT!

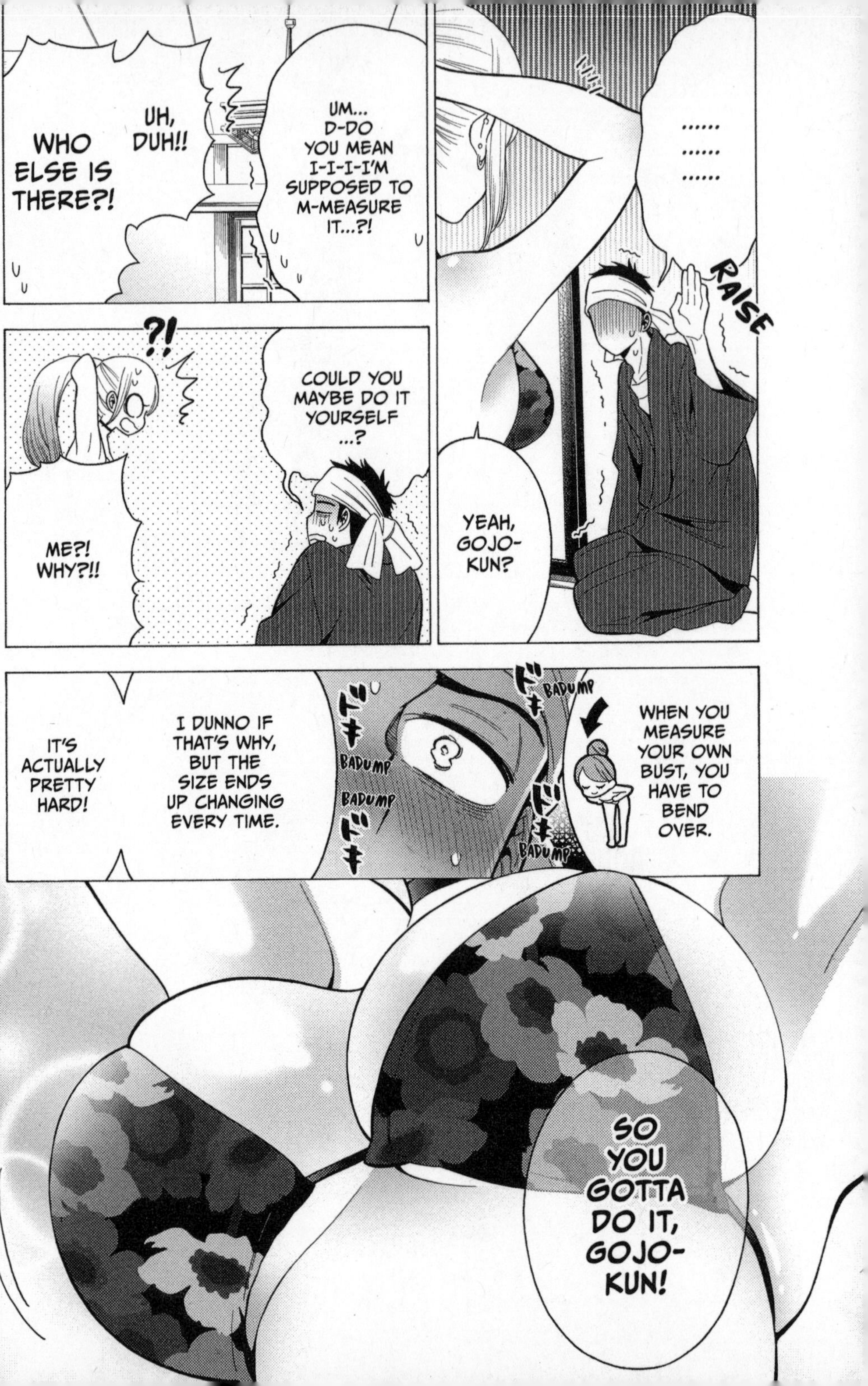

......
......
......
RAISE
YEAH, GOJO-KUN?
UM... D-DO YOU MEAN I-I-I-I'M SUPPOSED TO M-MEASURE IT...?!
UH, DUH!!
WHO ELSE IS THERE?!
COULD YOU MAYBE DO IT YOURSELF ...?
?!
ME?! WHY?!!
WHEN YOU MEASURE YOUR OWN BUST, YOU HAVE TO BEND OVER.
ドキ BADUMP
ドキ BADUMP
ドキ BADUMP
ドキ BADUMP
I DUNNO IF THAT'S WHY, BUT THE SIZE ENDS UP CHANGING EVERY TIME.
IT'S ACTUALLY PRETTY HARD!
SO YOU GOTTA DO IT, GOJO-KUN!

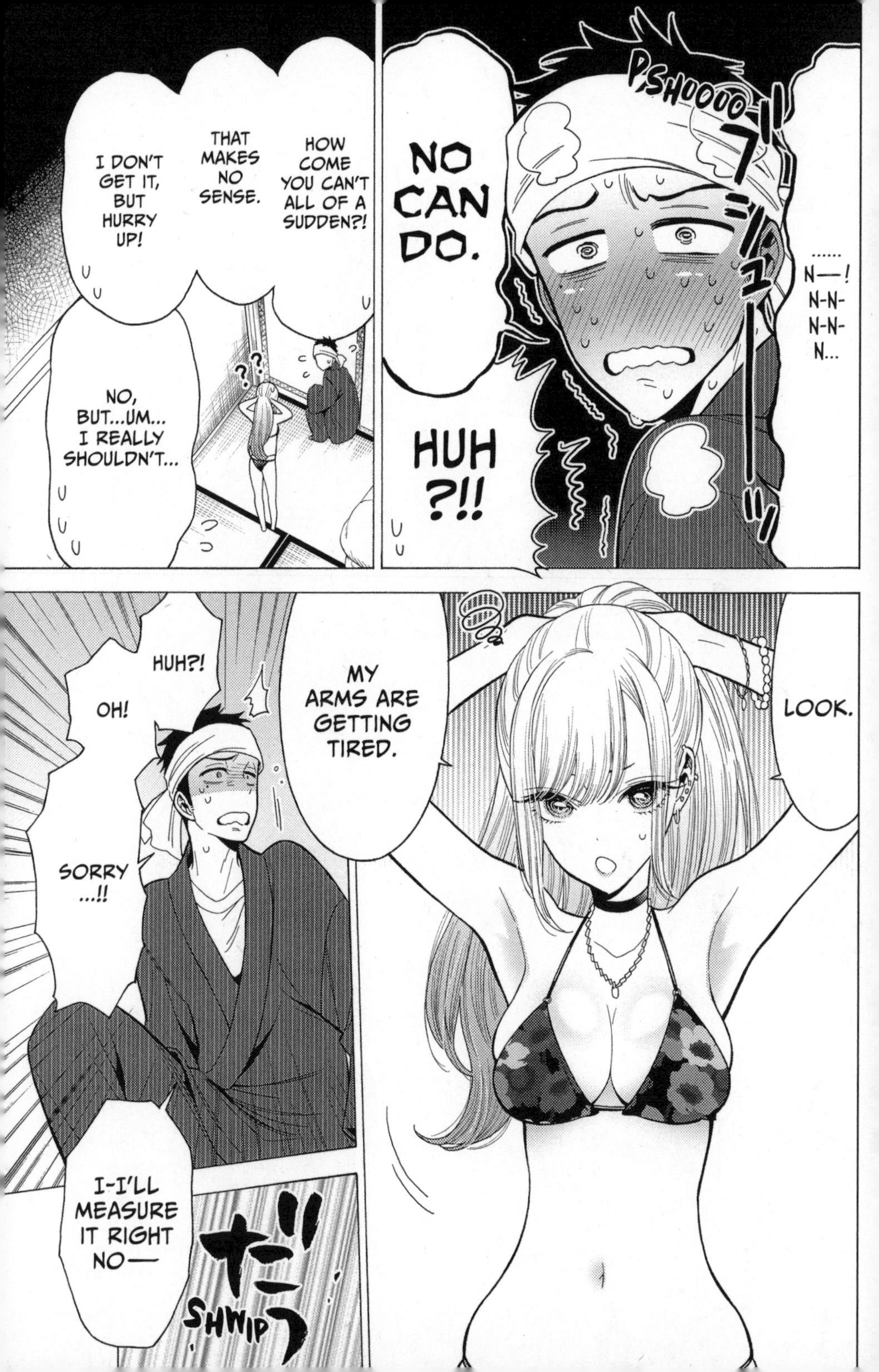
PSHOOOO
...... N—! N-N-N-N-N...
NO CAN DO.
HUH?!!
HOW COME YOU CAN'T ALL OF A SUDDEN?!
THAT MAKES NO SENSE.
I DON'T GET IT, BUT HURRY UP!
NO, BUT...UM... I REALLY SHOULDN'T...
LOOK.
MY ARMS ARE GETTING TIRED.
HUH?!
OH!
SORRY ...!!
I-I'LL MEASURE IT RIGHT NO—
SHWIP

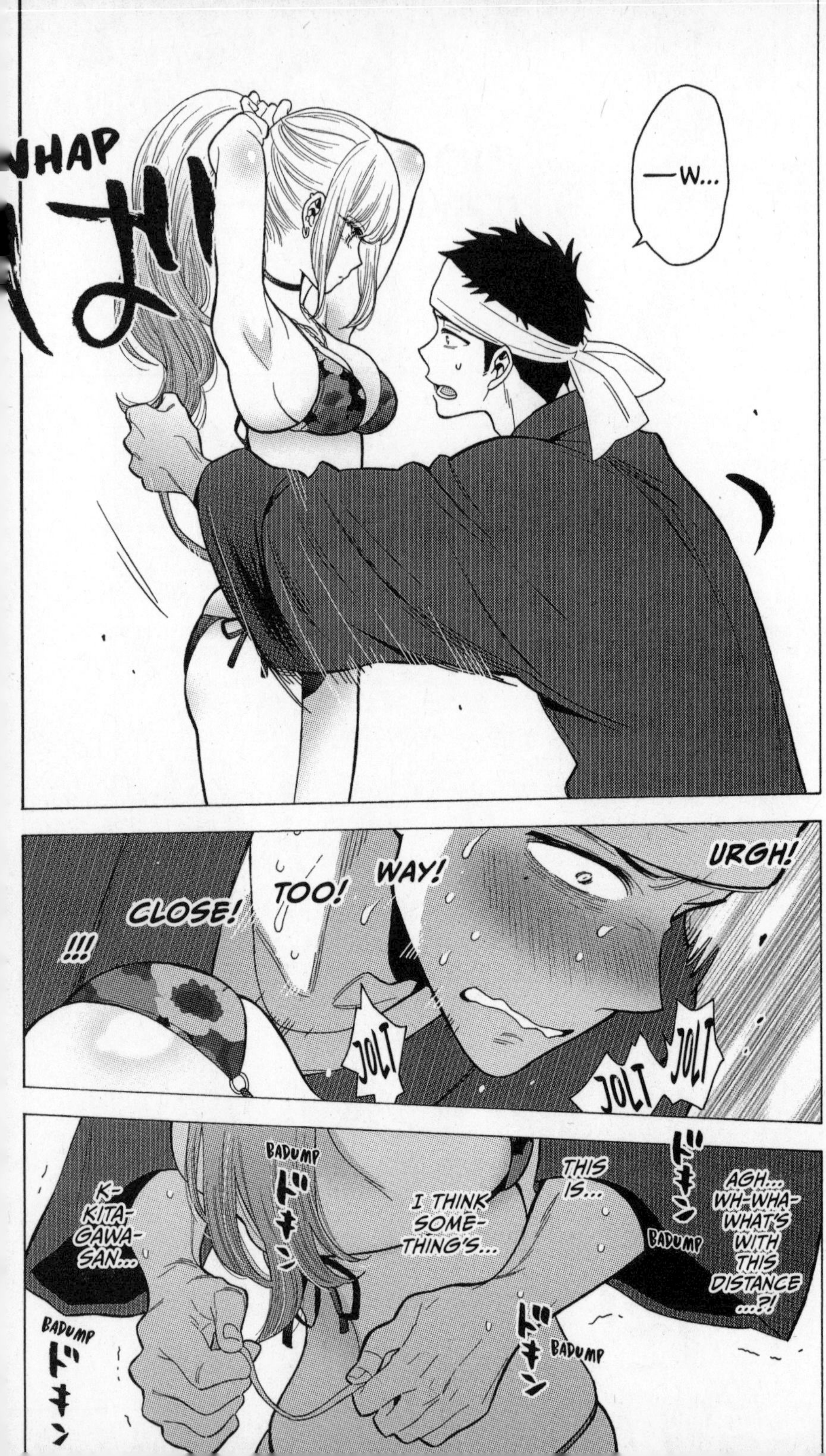
—W...
WHAP
URGH!
JOLT
JOLT
JOLT
WAY!
TOO!
CLOSE!
!!!
AGH... WH-WHA-WHAT'S WITH THIS DISTANCE...?!
BADUMP
ドキン
THIS IS...
I THINK SOME-THING'S...
BADUMP
ドキン
BADUMP
ドキン
K-KITA-GAWA-SAN...
BADUMP
ドキン

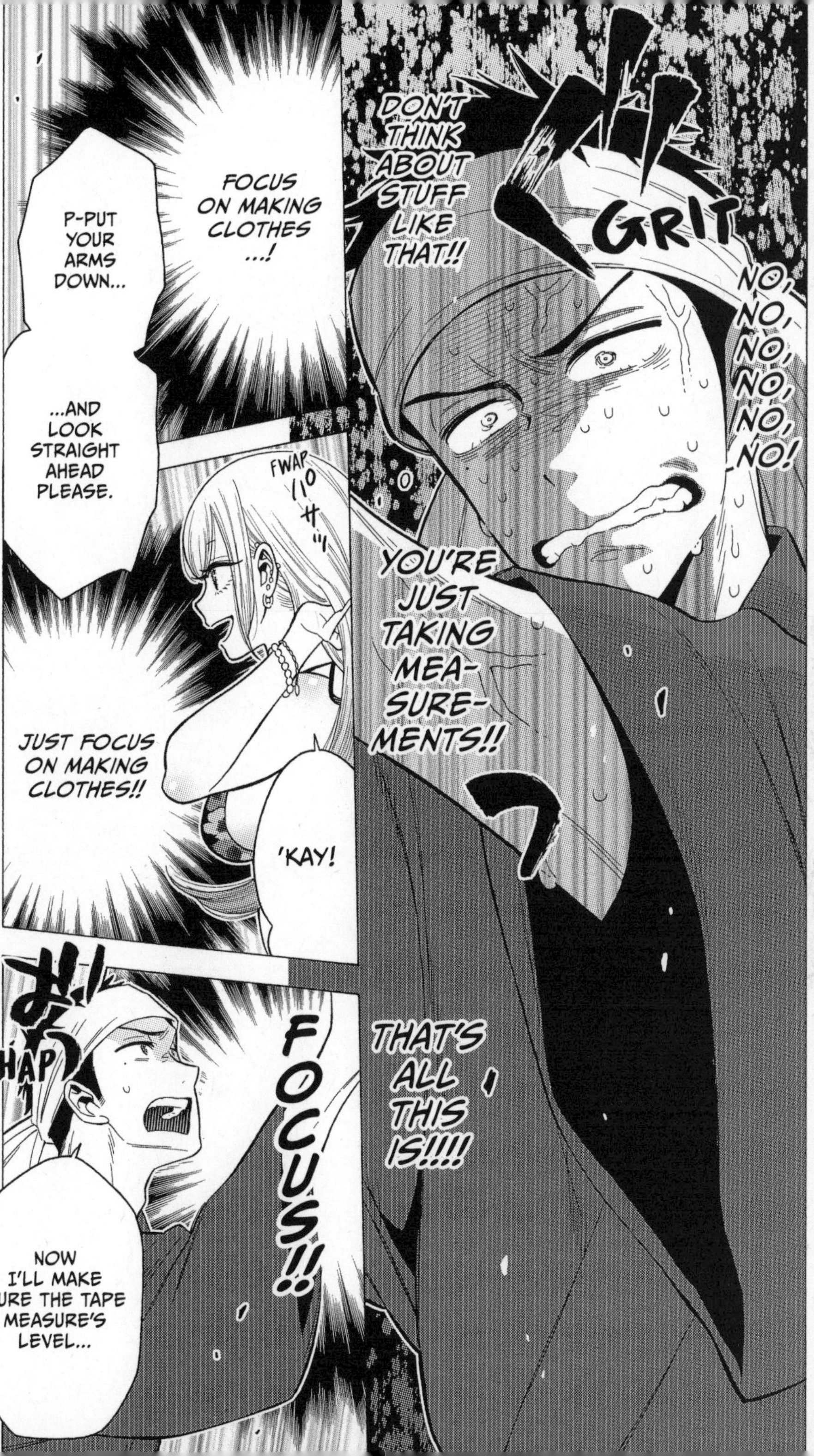

DON'T THINK ABOUT STUFF LIKE THAT!!
GRIT
NO, NO, NO, NO, NO, NO!
YOU'RE JUST TAKING MEA-SURE-MENTS!!
THAT'S ALL THIS IS!!!!
FOCUS ON MAKING CLOTHES ...!
P-PUT YOUR ARMS DOWN...
...AND LOOK STRAIGHT AHEAD PLEASE.
FWAP
JUST FOCUS ON MAKING CLOTHES!!
'KAY!
FOCUS!!
WHAP
NOW I'LL MAKE SURE THE TAPE MEASURE'S LEVEL...

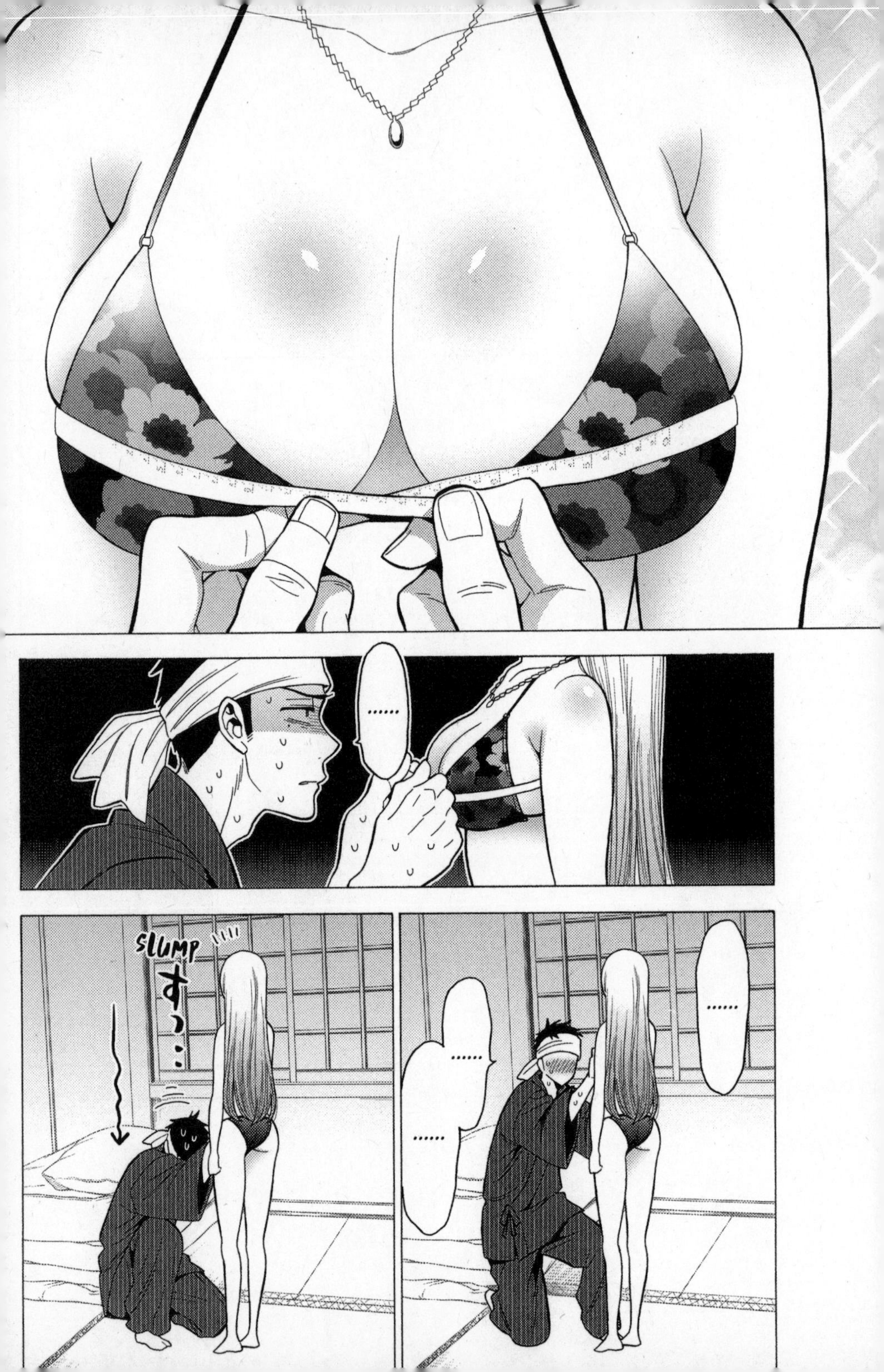
......
......
......
......
SLUMP
すっ‥

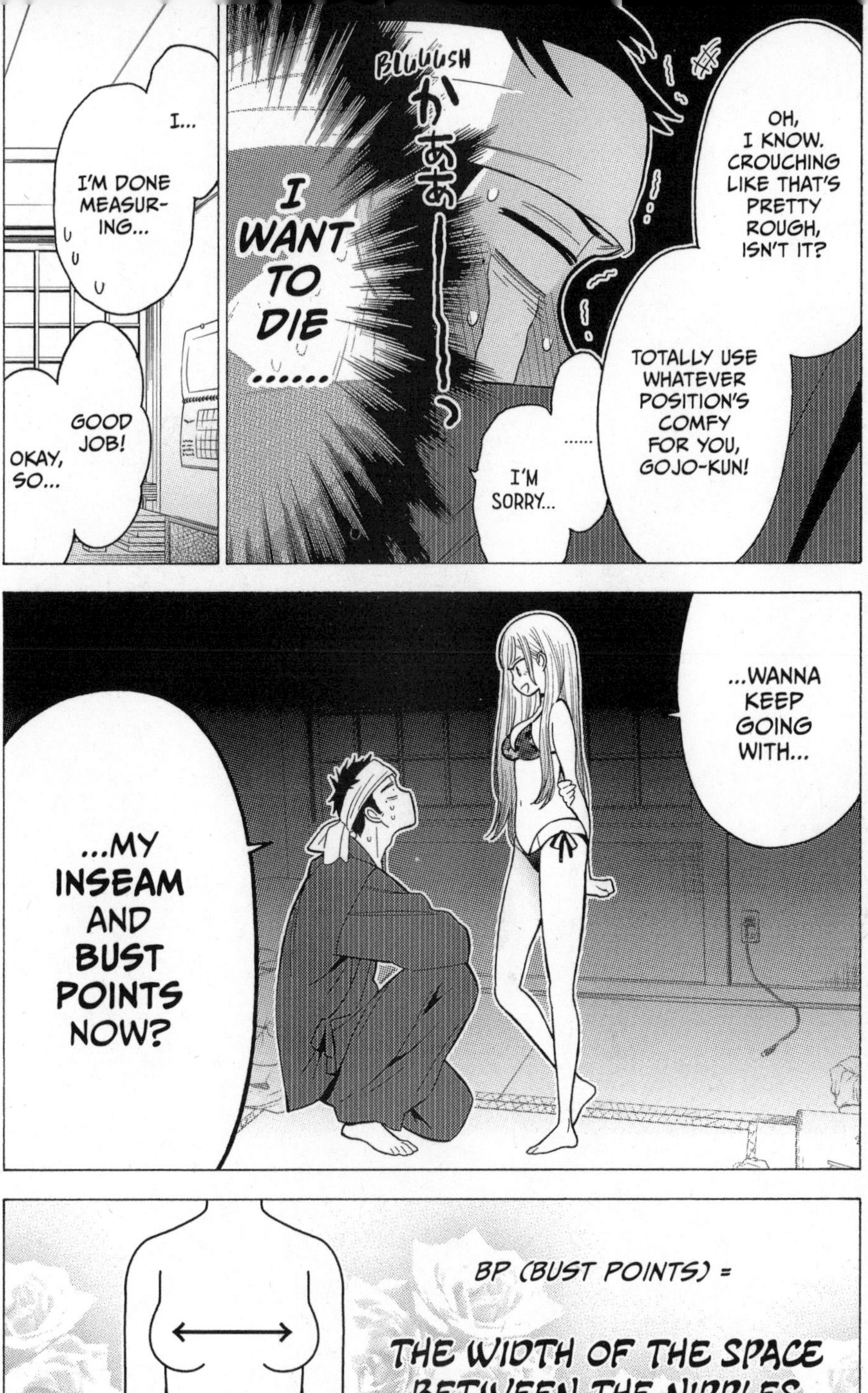
OH, I KNOW. CROUCHING LIKE THAT'S PRETTY ROUGH, ISN'T IT?
TOTALLY USE WHATEVER POSITION'S COMFY FOR YOU, GOJO-KUN!
......
I'M SORRY...
BLUUUSH
かあぁーっ
I WANT TO DIE ......
I...
I'M DONE MEASUR-ING...
GOOD JOB!
OKAY, SO...
...WANNA KEEP GOING WITH...
...MY INSEAM AND BUST POINTS NOW?
BP (BUST POINTS) =
THE WIDTH OF THE SPACE BETWEEN THE NIPPLES

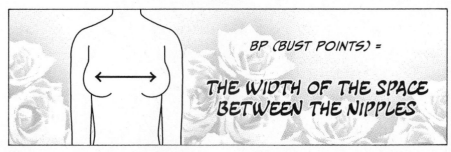

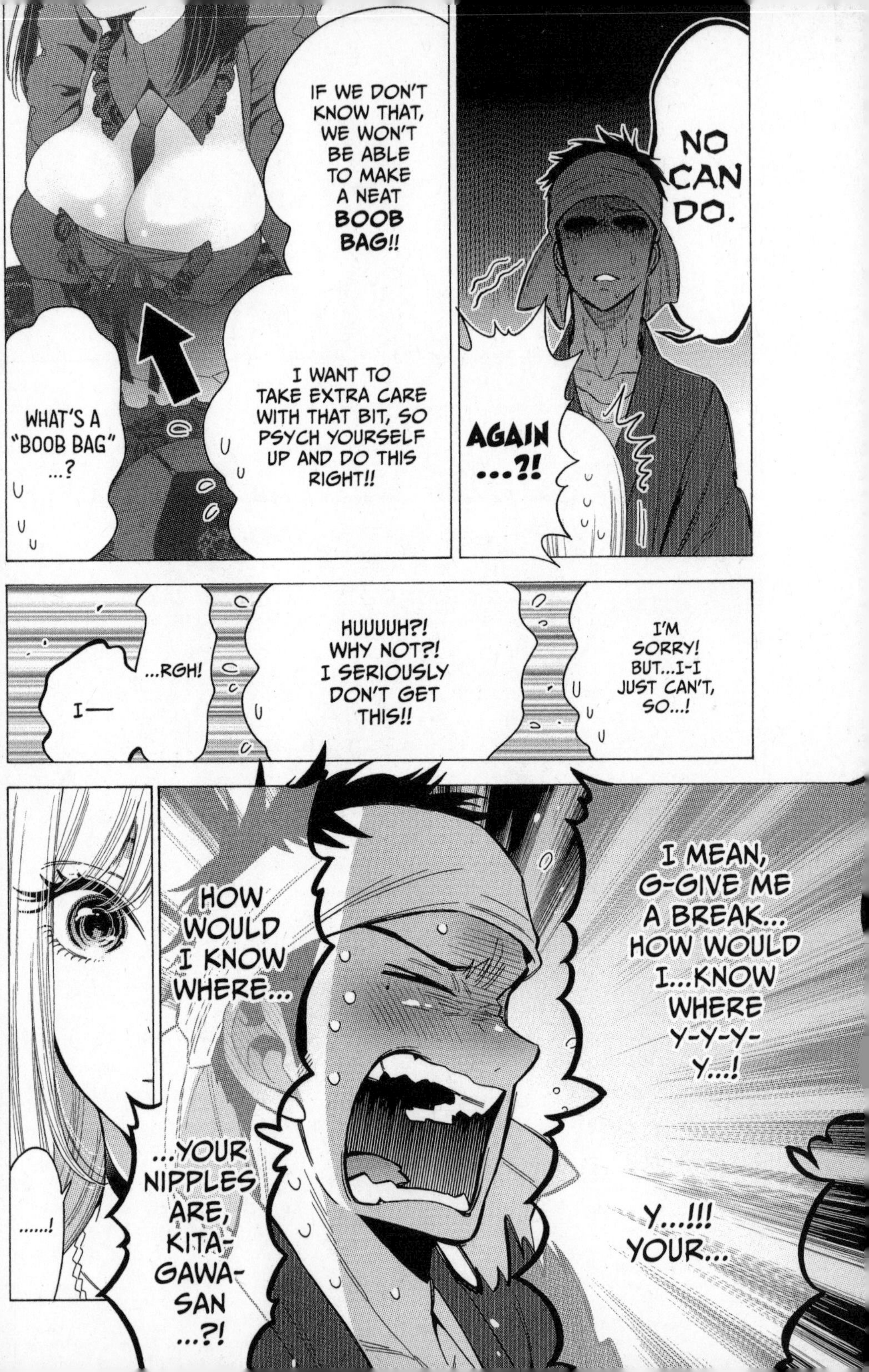
NO CAN DO.
AGAIN ...?!
IF WE DON'T KNOW THAT, WE WON'T BE ABLE TO MAKE A NEAT BOOB BAG!!
I WANT TO TAKE EXTRA CARE WITH THAT BIT, SO PSYCH YOURSELF UP AND DO THIS RIGHT!!
WHAT'S A "BOOB BAG" ...?
I'M SORRY! BUT...I-I JUST CAN'T, SO...!
HUUUUH?! WHY NOT?! I SERIOUSLY DON'T GET THIS!!
...RGH!
I—
I MEAN, G-GIVE ME A BREAK... HOW WOULD I...KNOW WHERE Y-Y-Y-Y...!
Y...!!! YOUR...
HOW WOULD I KNOW WHERE...
...YOUR NIPPLES ARE, KITA-GAWA-SAN ...?!
......!

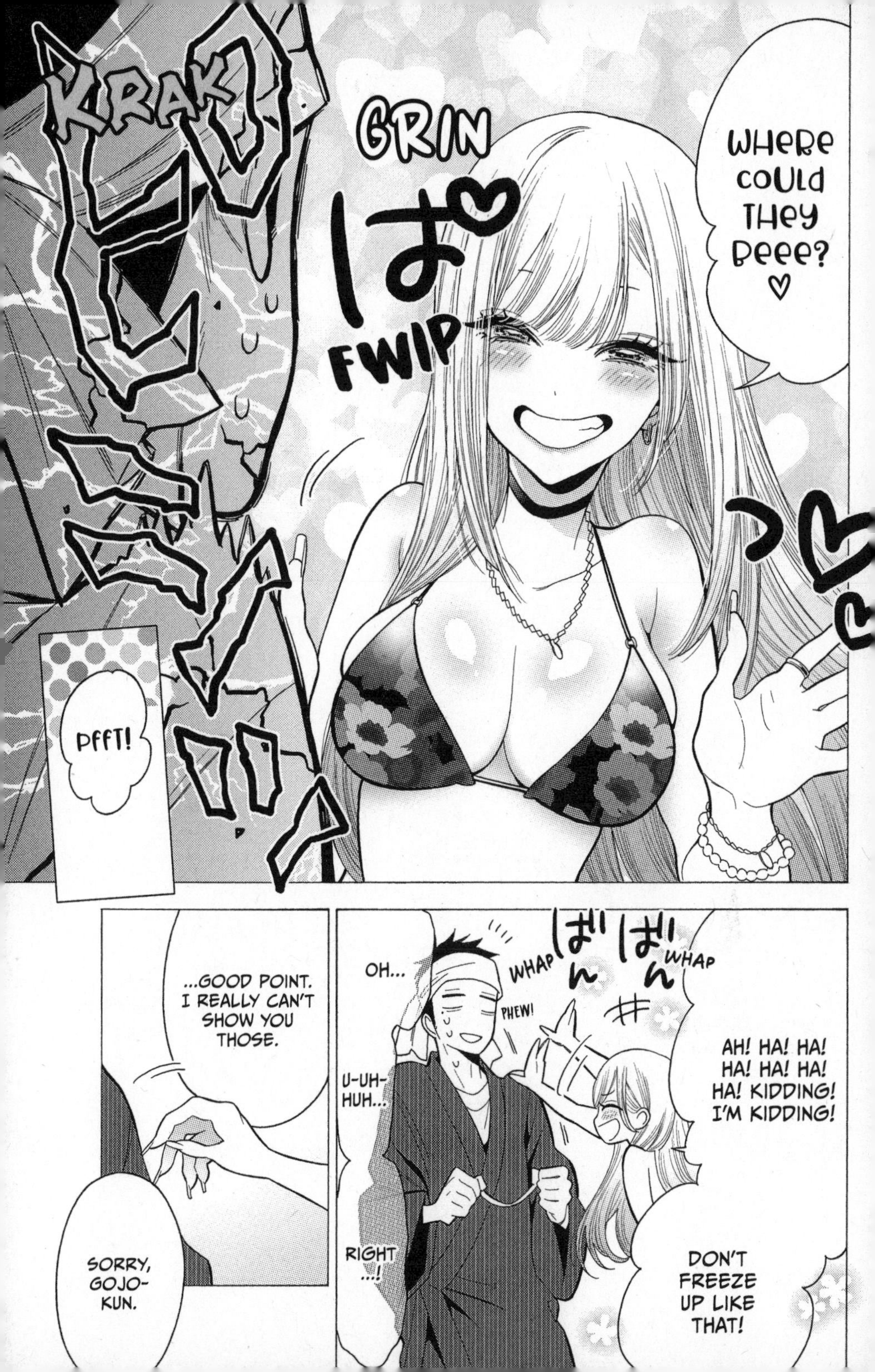
WHERE COULD THEY BEEE? ♡
つ♡
GRIN
ぱ♡
FWIP
KRAK
PFFT!
WHAP
ばん ばん
WHAP
AH! HA! HA! HA! HA! HA! HA! KIDDING! I'M KIDDING!
DON'T FREEZE UP LIKE THAT!
OH...
PHEW!
U-UH-HUH...
RIGHT ...!
...GOOD POINT. I REALLY CAN'T SHOW YOU THOSE.
SORRY, GOJO-KUN.

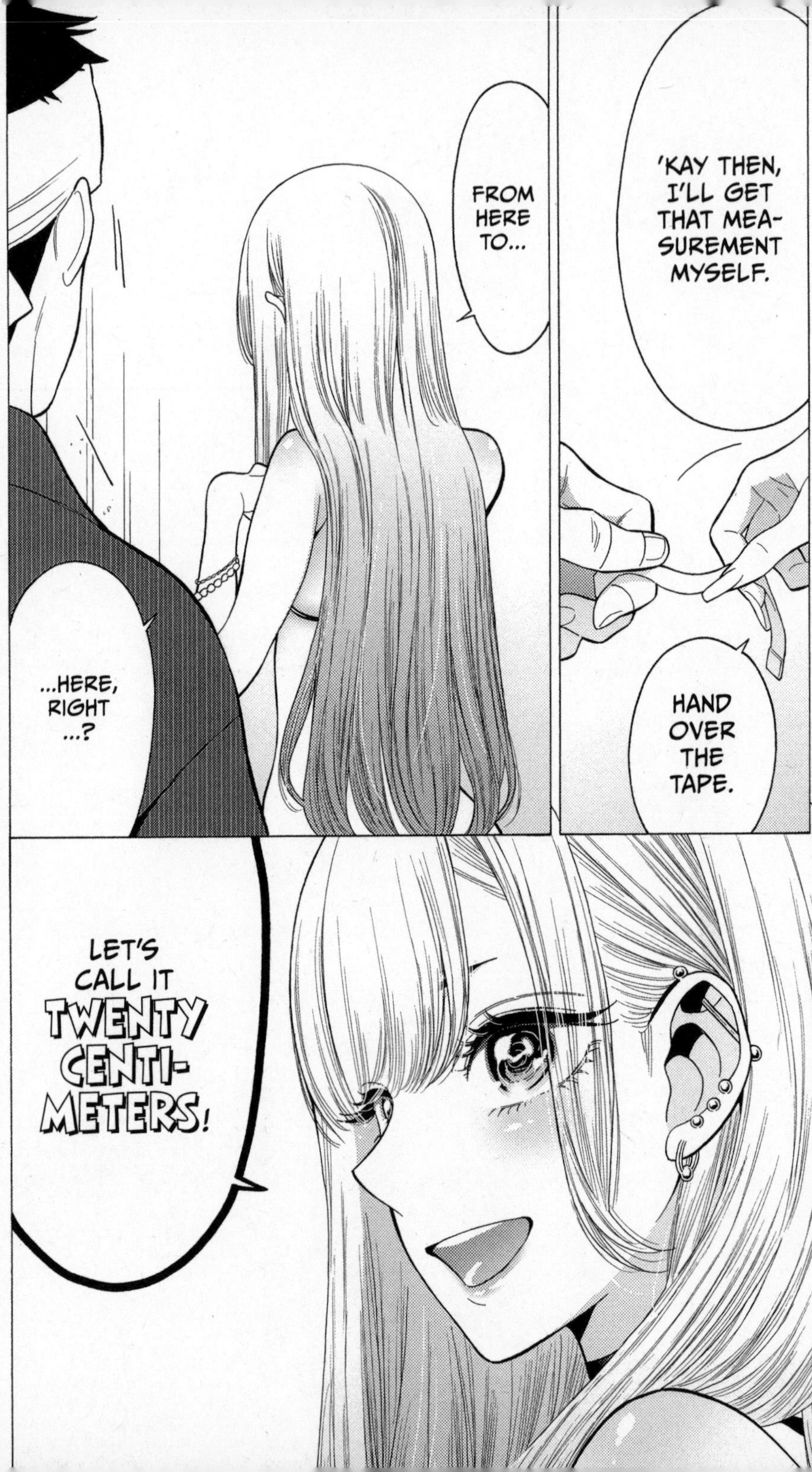
'KAY THEN, I'LL GET THAT MEA- SUREMENT MYSELF.
HAND OVER THE TAPE.
FROM HERE TO...
...HERE, RIGHT ...?
LET'S CALL IT TWENTY CENTI- METERS!

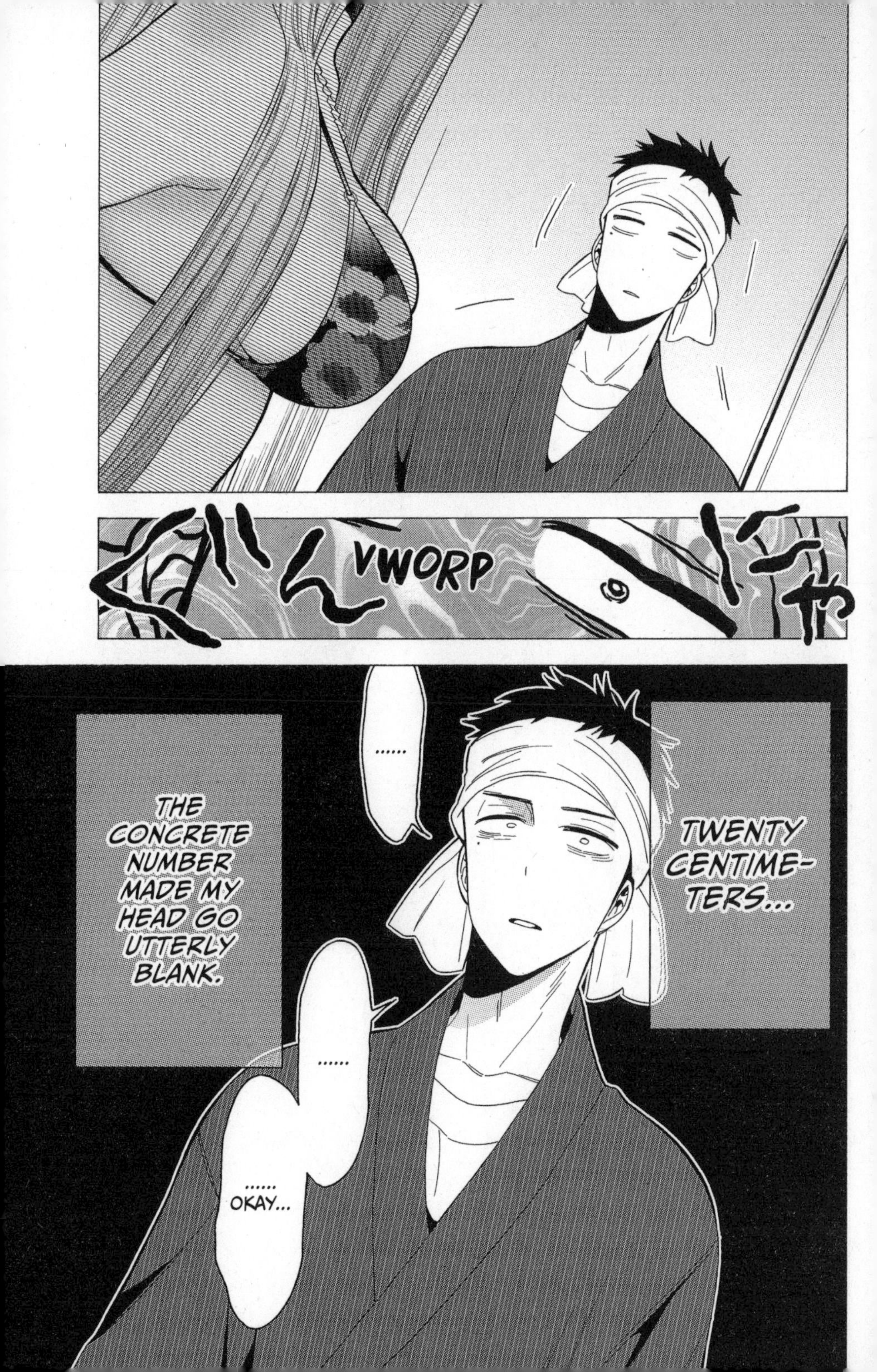
VWORP
TWENTY CENTIME- TERS...
......
THE CONCRETE NUMBER MADE MY HEAD GO UTTERLY BLANK.
......
...... OKAY...

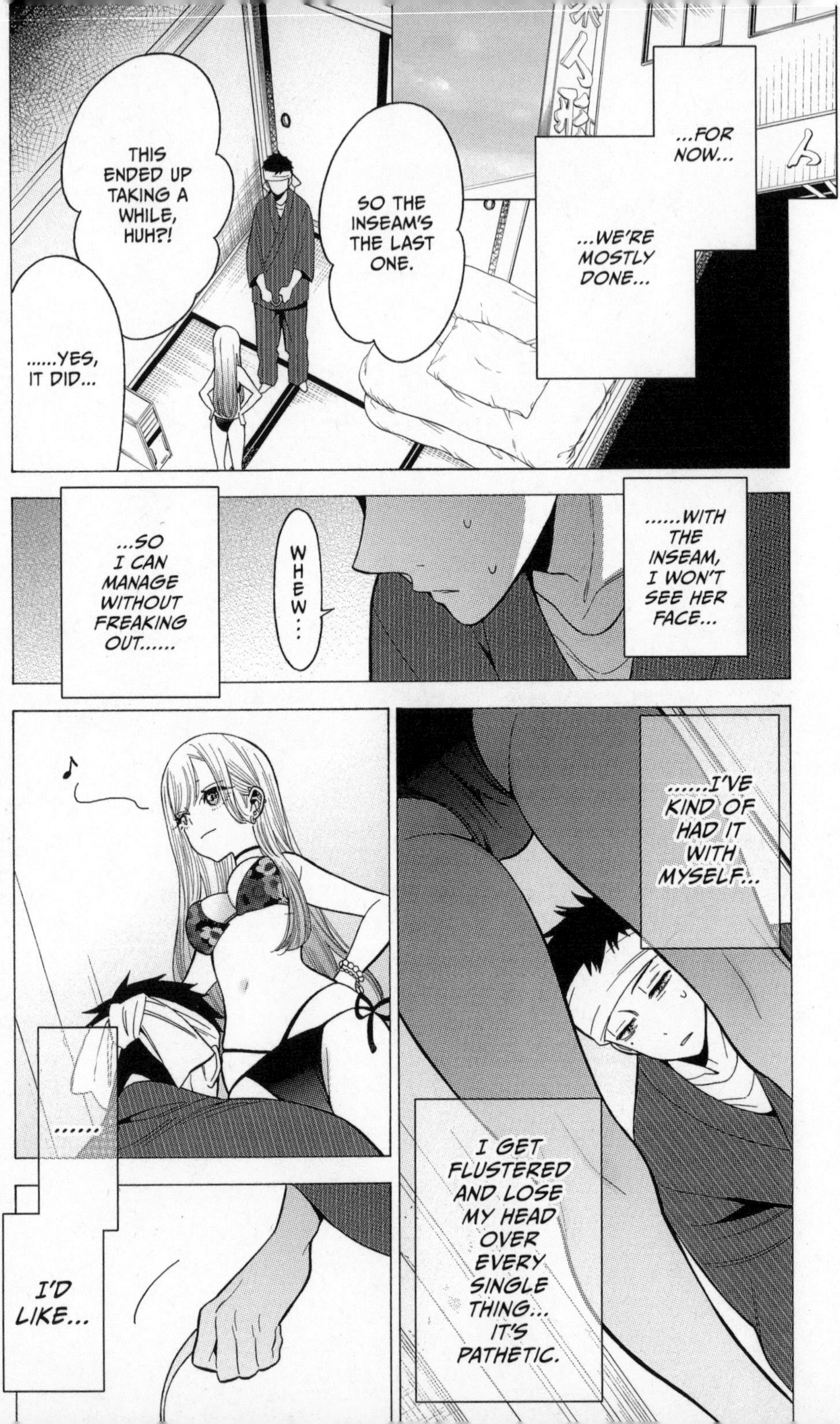

...FOR NOW...
...WE'RE MOSTLY DONE...
SO THE INSEAM'S THE LAST ONE.
THIS ENDED UP TAKING A WHILE, HUH?!
......YES, IT DID...
......WITH THE INSEAM, I WON'T SEE HER FACE...
WHEW...
...SO I CAN MANAGE WITHOUT FREAKING OUT......
......I'VE KIND OF HAD IT WITH MYSELF...
I GET FLUSTERED AND LOSE MY HEAD OVER EVERY SINGLE THING... IT'S PATHETIC.
♪
......
I'D LIKE...

...TO BE LIKE KITAGAWA-SAN.

PULL

SWF

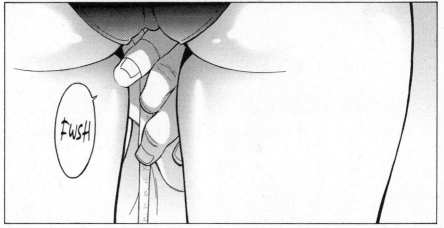

FWSH

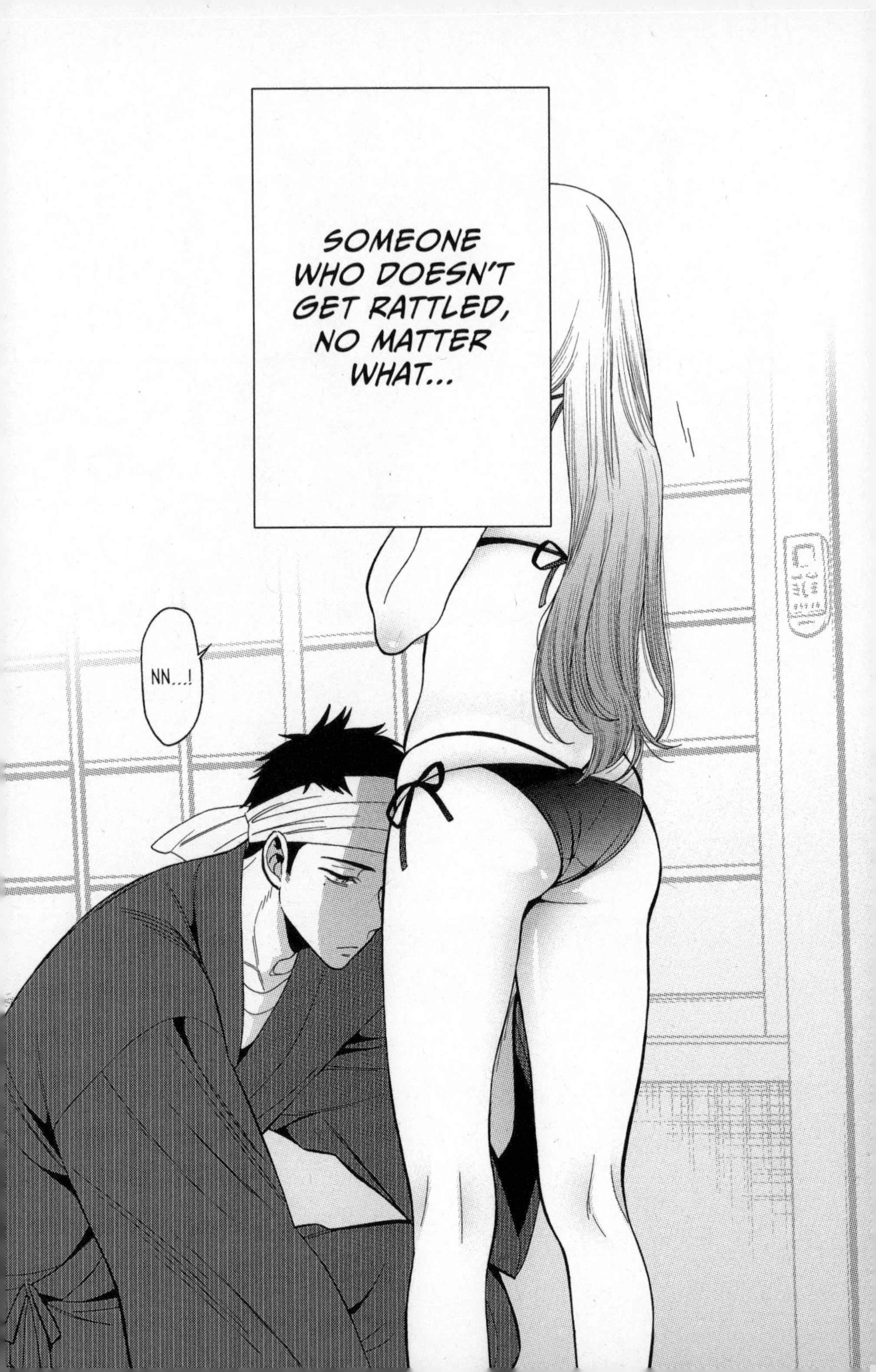
SOMEONE WHO DOESN'T GET RATTLED, NO MATTER WHAT...
NN...!

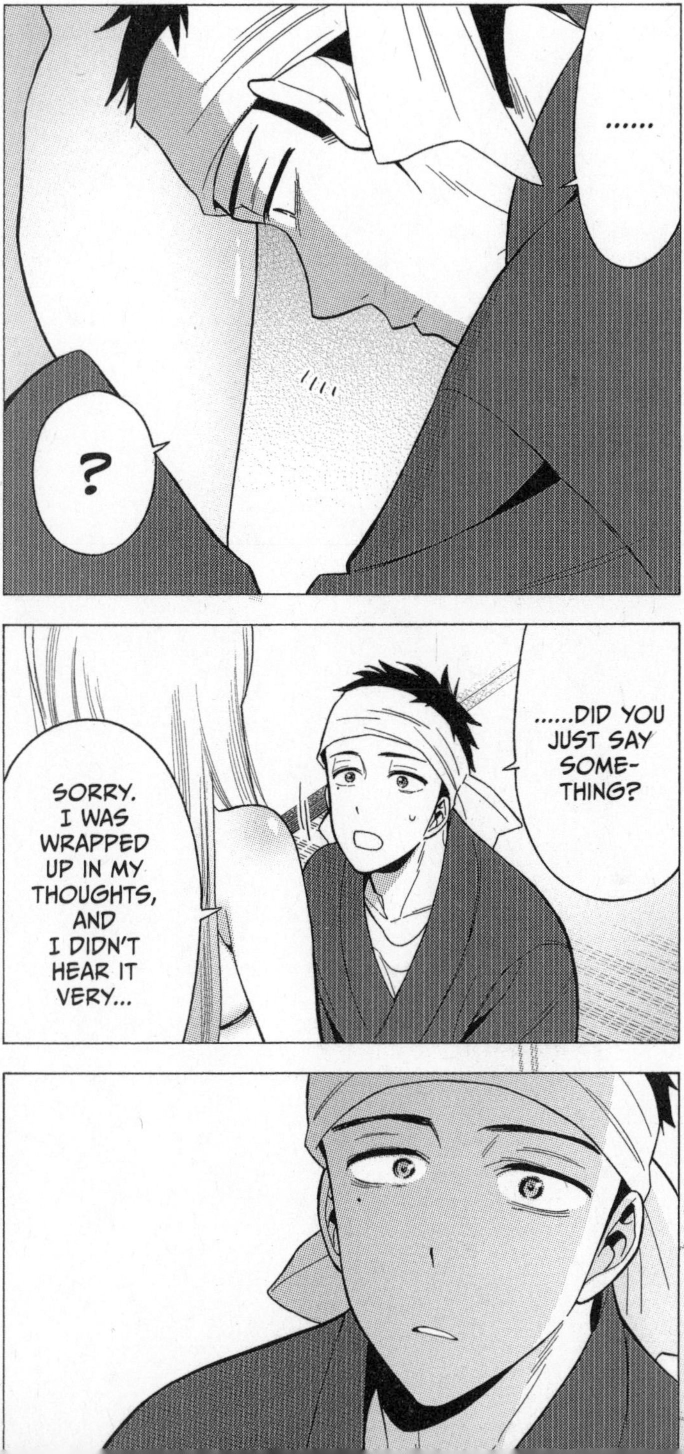
......
?
......DID YOU JUST SAY SOME-THING?
SORRY. I WAS WRAPPED UP IN MY THOUGHTS, AND I DIDN'T HEAR IT VERY...

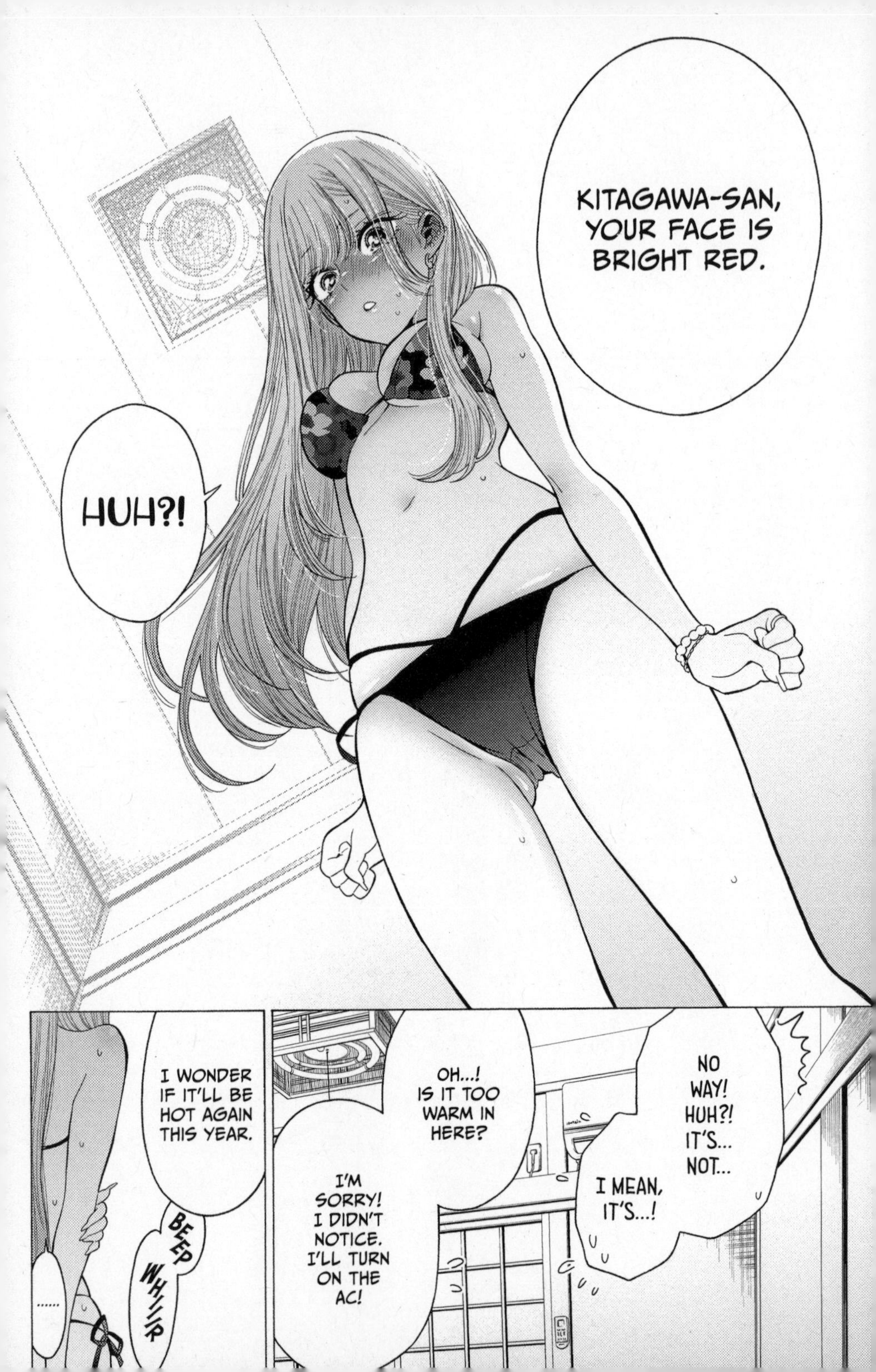
KITAGAWA-SAN, YOUR FACE IS BRIGHT RED.
HUH?!
NO WAY! HUH?! IT'S... NOT...
I MEAN, IT'S...!
OH...! IS IT TOO WARM IN HERE?
I'M SORRY! I DIDN'T NOTICE. I'LL TURN ON THE AC!
I WONDER IF IT'LL BE HOT AGAIN THIS YEAR.
BEEP
WHIIIR
......

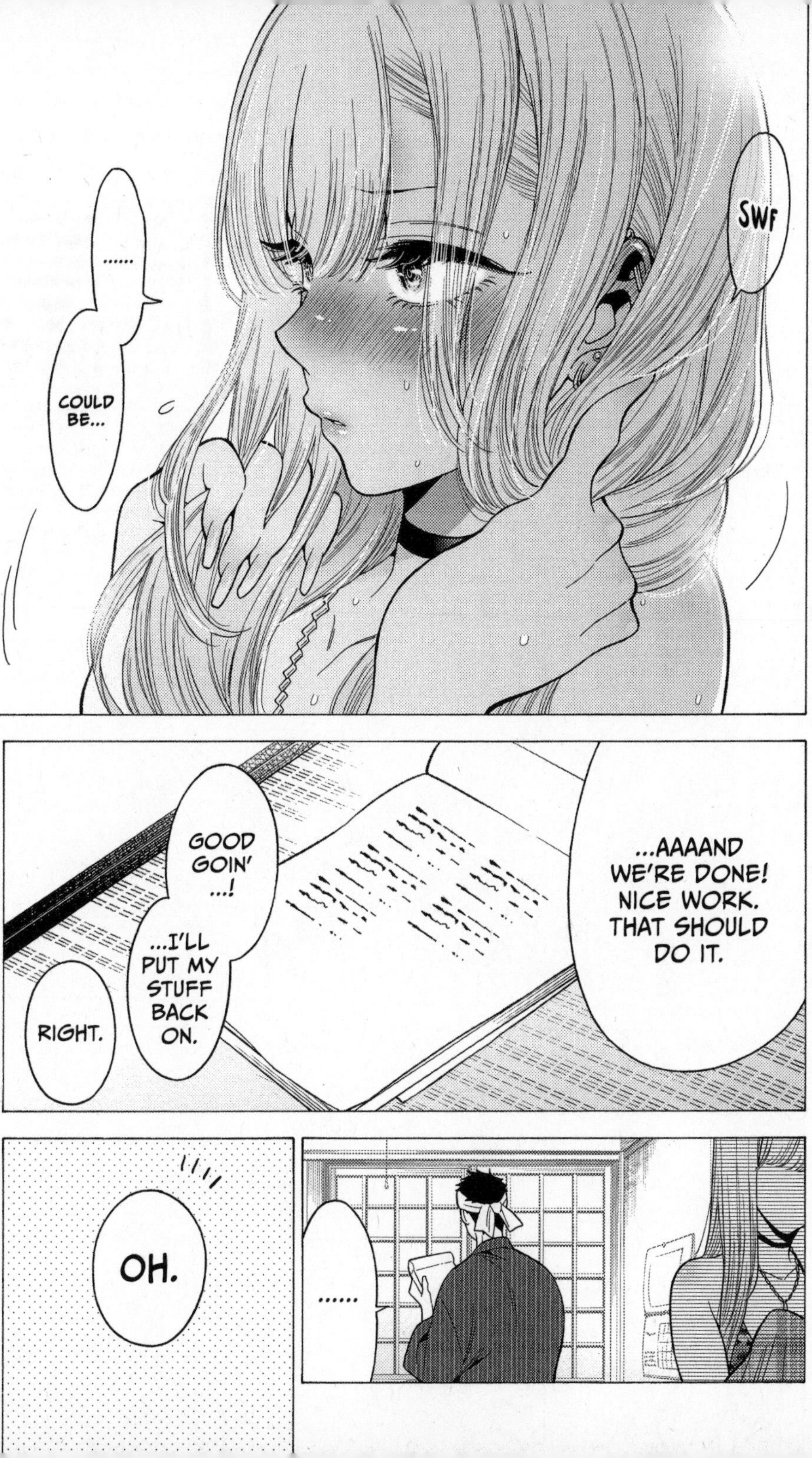
SWF
......
COULD BE...
...AAAAND WE'RE DONE! NICE WORK. THAT SHOULD DO IT.
GOOD GOIN' ...!
...I'LL PUT MY STUFF BACK ON.
RIGHT.
......
OH.

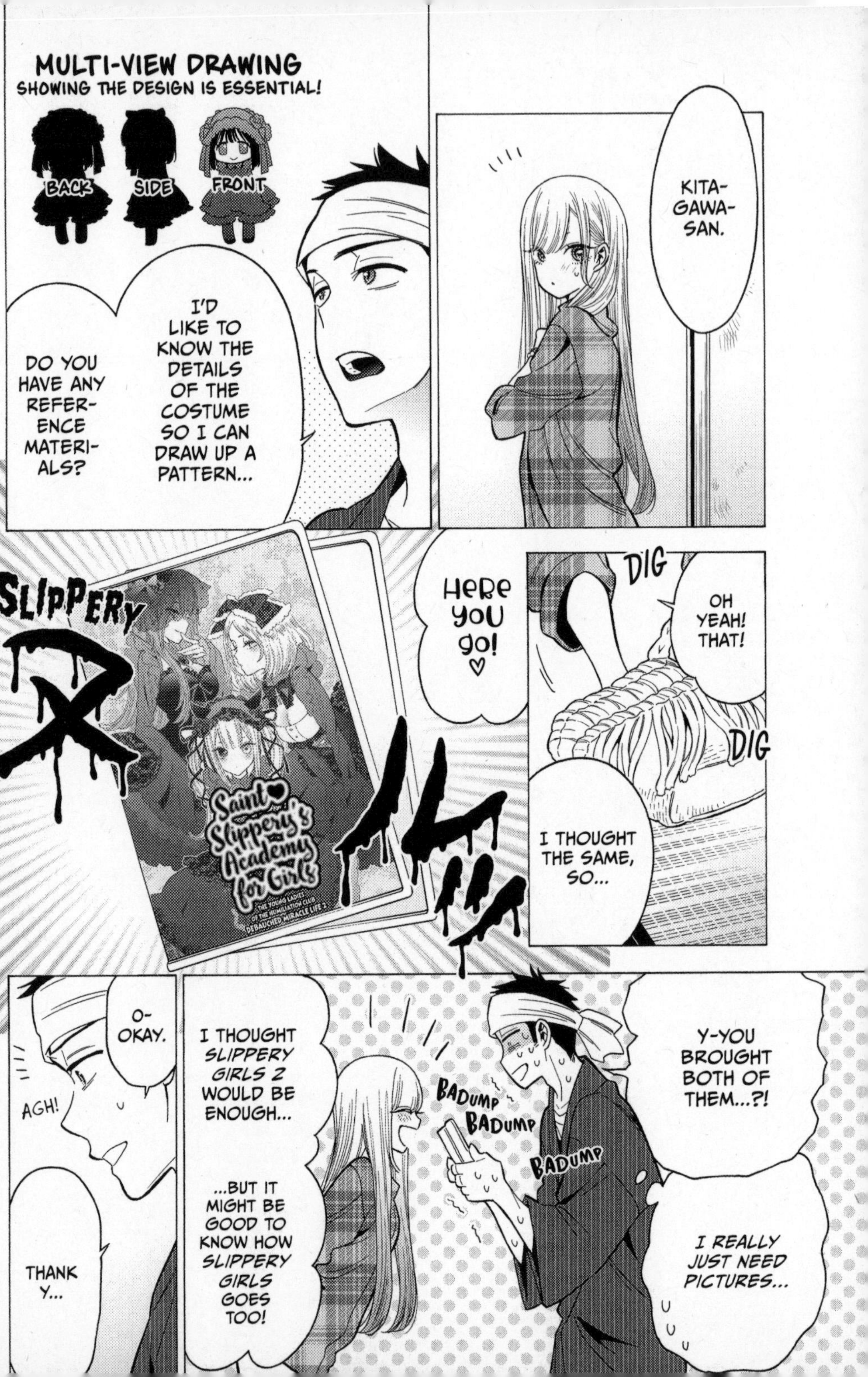
KITA-GAWA-SAN.
MULTI-VIEW DRAWING
SHOWING THE DESIGN IS ESSENTIAL!
BACK
SIDE
FRONT
I'D LIKE TO KNOW THE DETAILS OF THE COSTUME SO I CAN DRAW UP A PATTERN...
DO YOU HAVE ANY REFER-ENCE MATERI-ALS?
DIG
OH YEAH! THAT!
DIG
I THOUGHT THE SAME, SO...
Here you go! ♡
SLIPPERY
Saint Slippery's Academy for Girls
THE YOUNG LADIES OF THE HUMILIATION CLUB
DEBAUCHED MIRACLE LIFE 2
Y-YOU BROUGHT BOTH OF THEM...?!
I REALLY JUST NEED PICTURES...
BADUMP
BADUMP
BADUMP
I THOUGHT SLIPPERY GIRLS 2 WOULD BE ENOUGH...
...BUT IT MIGHT BE GOOD TO KNOW HOW SLIPPERY GIRLS GOES TOO!
O-OKAY.
AGH!
THANK Y...

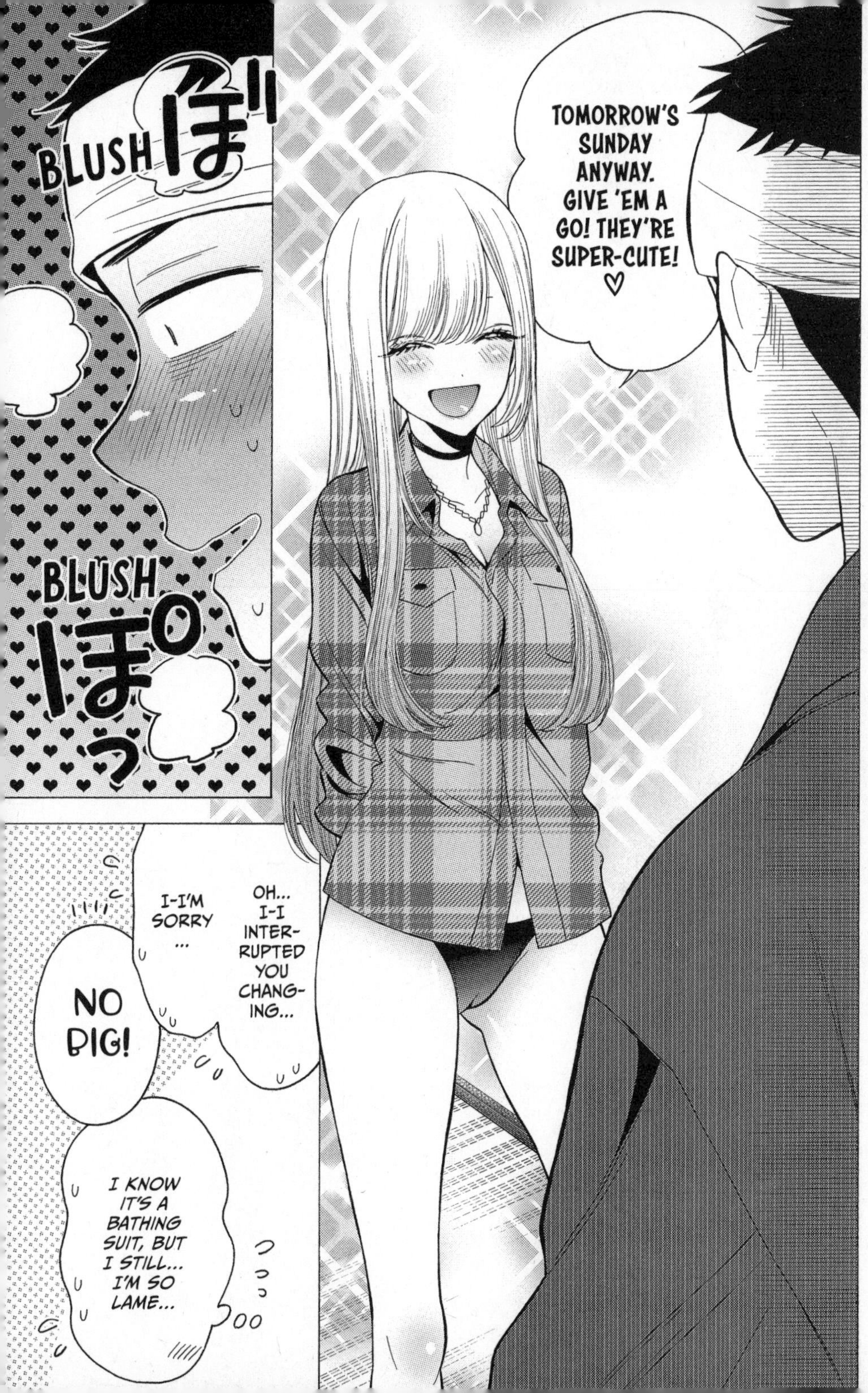
TOMORROW'S SUNDAY ANYWAY. GIVE 'EM A GO! THEY'RE SUPER-CUTE! ♡
BLUSH ぼ
BLUSH ぽっ
OH... I-I INTER-RUPTED YOU CHANG-ING...
I-I'M SORRY ...
NO BIG!
I KNOW IT'S A BATHING SUIT, BUT I STILL... I'M SO LAME...

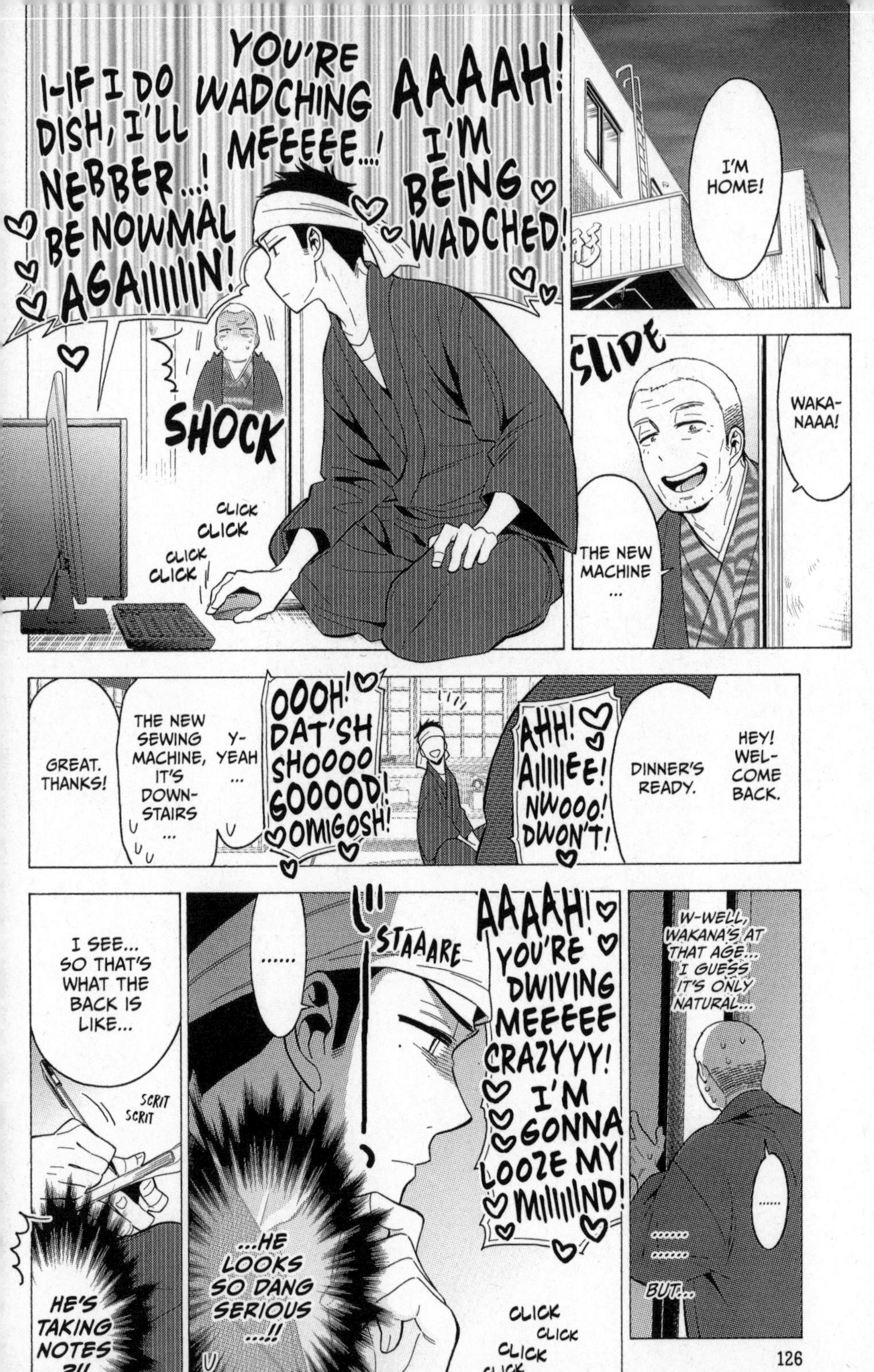
I'M HOME!
SLIDE
WAKA-NAAA!
THE NEW MACHINE ...
AAAAH! I'M BEING WADCHED!
YOU'RE WADCHING MEEEEE...!
I-IF I DO DISH, I'LL NEBBER...! BE NOWMAL AGAIIIIIIN!
SHOCK
CLICK CLICK CLICK CLICK
HEY! WEL-COME BACK.
DINNER'S READY.
AHH! AIIIIEE! NWOOO! DWON'T!
OOOH! DAT'SH SHOOOO GOOOOD! OMIGOSH!
Y-YEAH ...
THE NEW SEWING MACHINE, IT'S DOWN-STAIRS ...
GREAT. THANKS!
W-WELL, WAKANA'S AT THAT AGE... I GUESS IT'S ONLY NATURAL...
......
......
......
BUT...
STAAARE
......
AAAAH! YOU'RE DWIVING MEEEEE CRAZYYY! I'M GONNA LOOZE MY MIIIIIND!
...HE LOOKS SO DANG SERIOUS...!!
CLICK CLICK CLICK CLICK
I SEE... SO THAT'S WHAT THE BACK IS LIKE...
SCRIT SCRIT
HE'S TAKING NOTES?!!

My DRESS-UP Darling

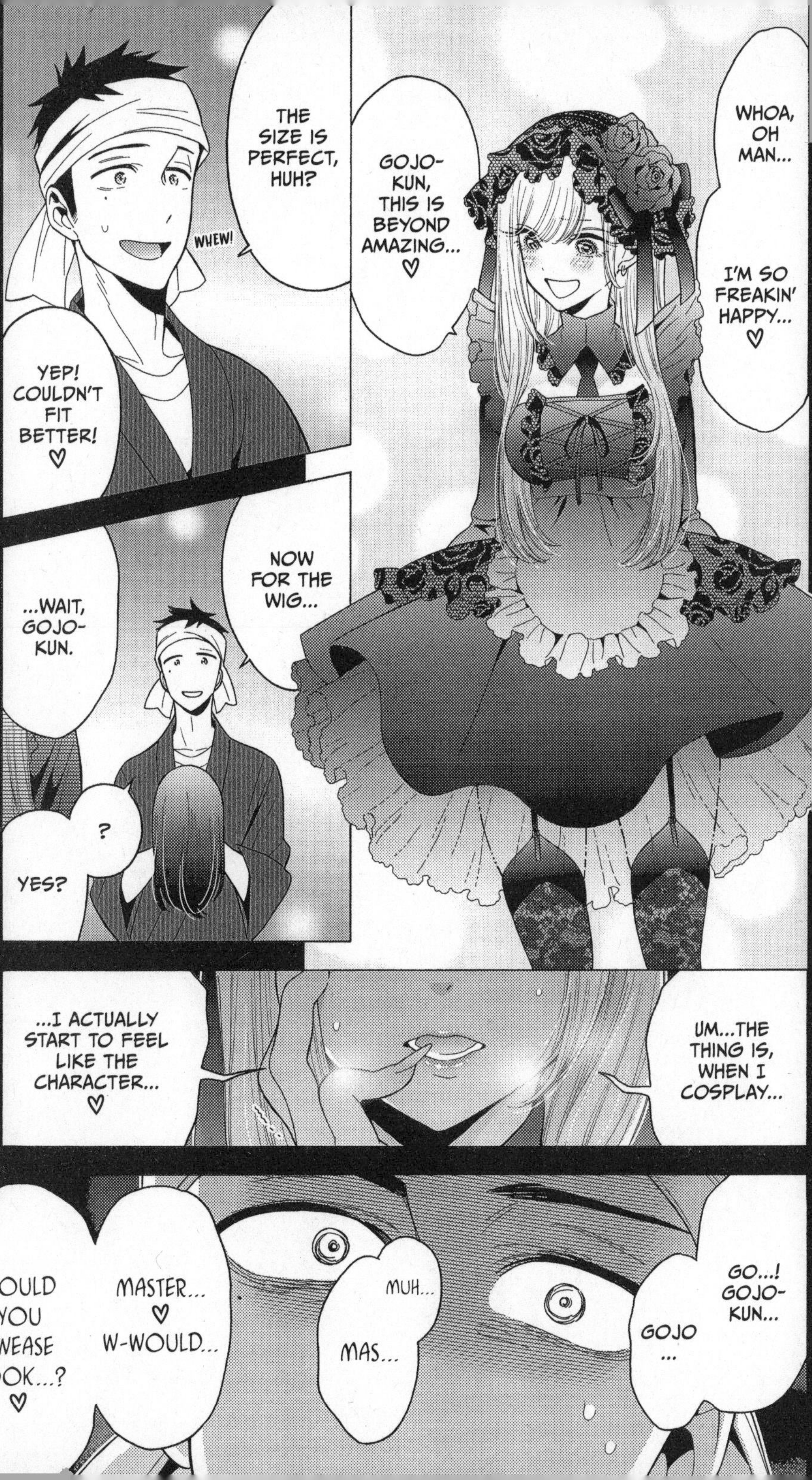
WHOA, OH MAN...
I'M SO FREAKIN' HAPPY... ♡
GOJO-KUN, THIS IS BEYOND AMAZING... ♡
THE SIZE IS PERFECT, HUH?
WHEW!
YEP! COULDN'T FIT BETTER! ♡
NOW FOR THE WIG...
...WAIT, GOJO-KUN.
?
YES?
UM...THE THING IS, WHEN I COSPLAY...
...I ACTUALLY START TO FEEL LIKE THE CHARACTER... ♡
GO...! GOJO-KUN...
GOJO ...
MUH...
MAS...
MASTER... ♡ W-WOULD...
WOULD YOU PWEASE LOOK...? ♡

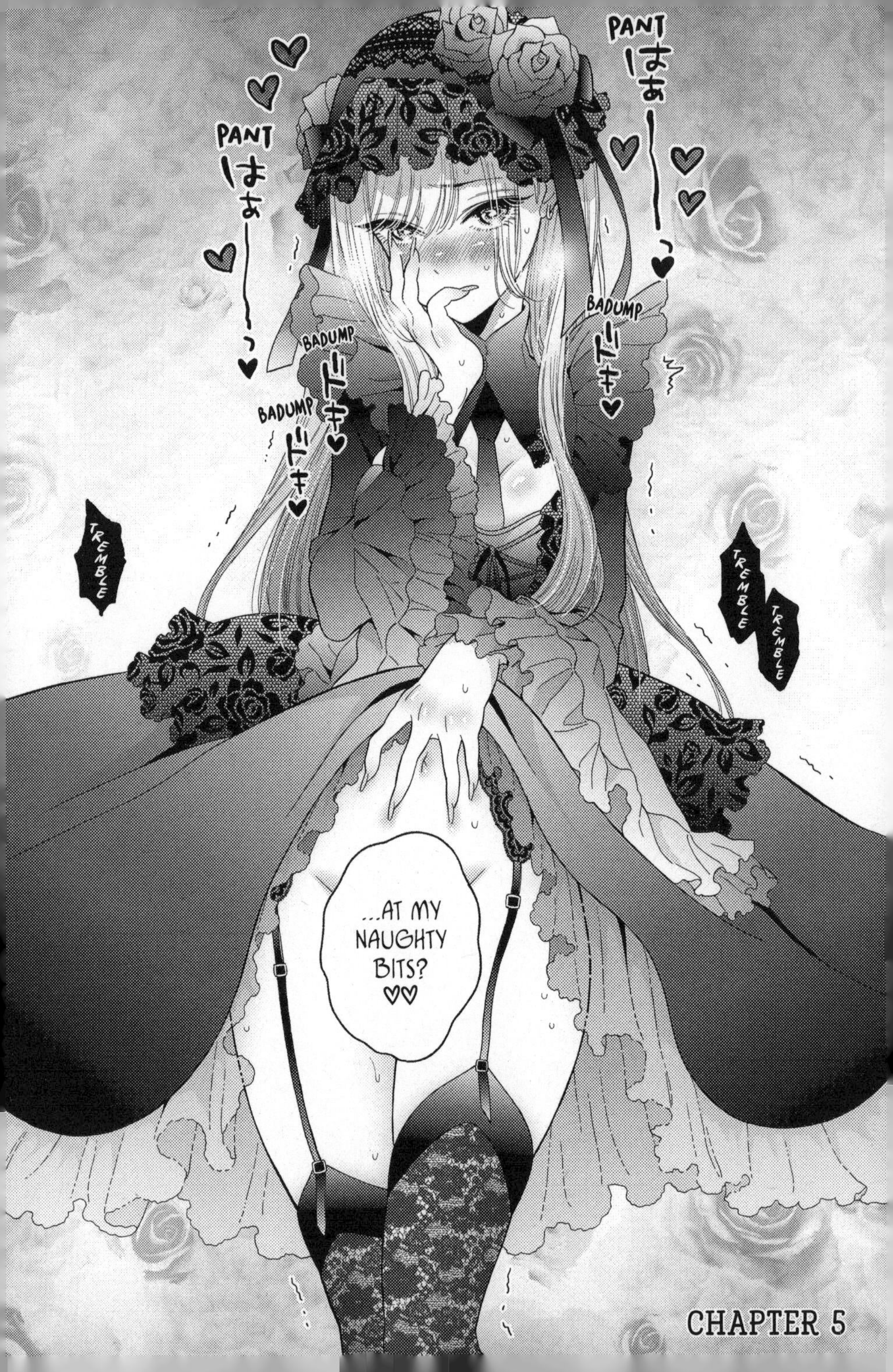
PANT
はぁ〜っ
BADUMP
ドキ
TREMBLE
TREMBLE
PANT
はぁ〜っ
BADUMP
ドキ
BADUMP
ドキ
TREMBLE
...AT MY NAUGHTY BITS? ♡♡

CHAPTER 5

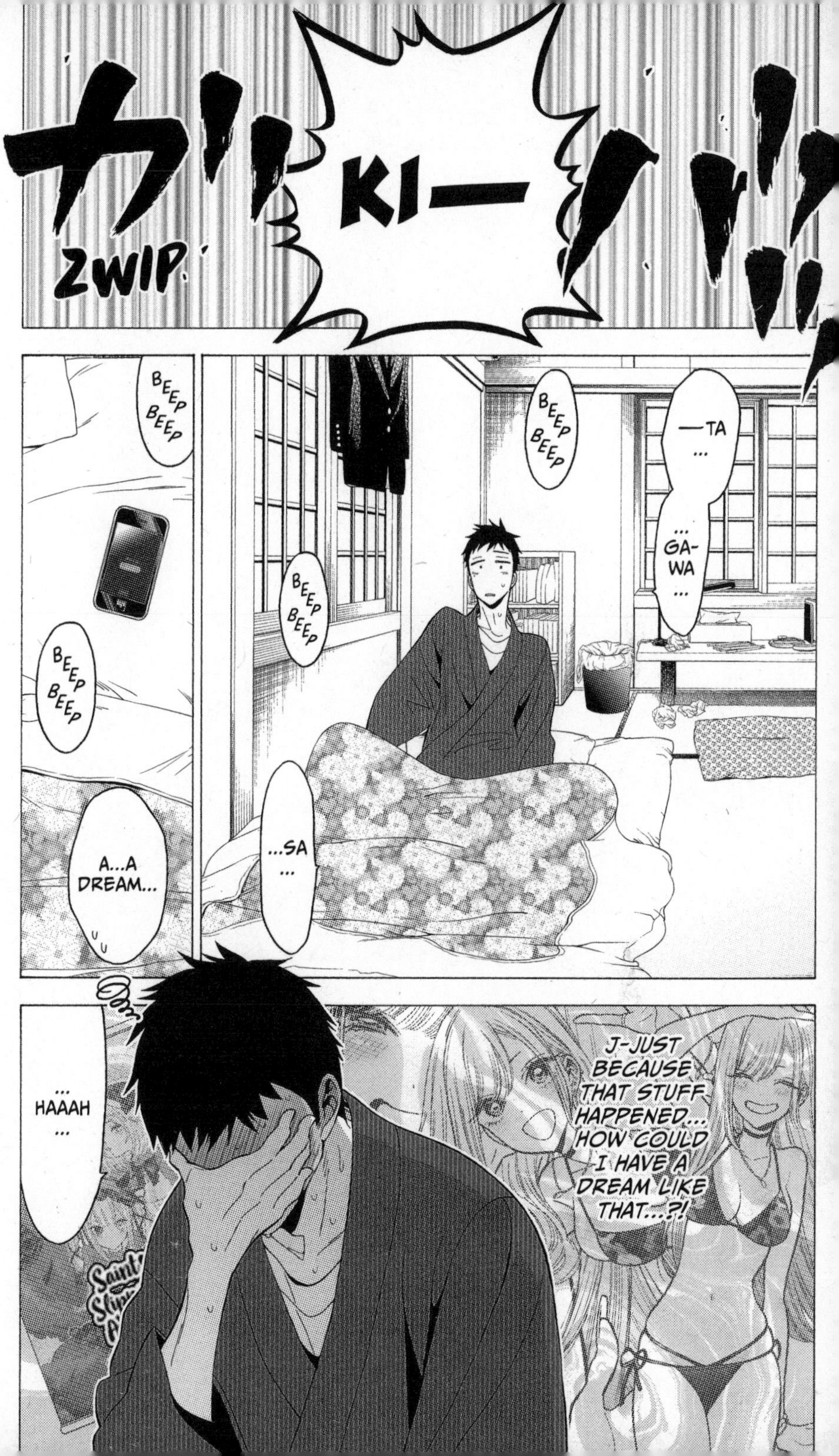
KI—
ZWIP.
—TA ... ... GA-WA ...
BEEP BEEP
BEEP BEEP
...SA ...
BEEP BEEP
BEEP BEEP
A...A DREAM...
J-JUST BECAUSE THAT STUFF HAPPENED... HOW COULD I HAVE A DREAM LIKE THAT...?!
... HAAAH ...

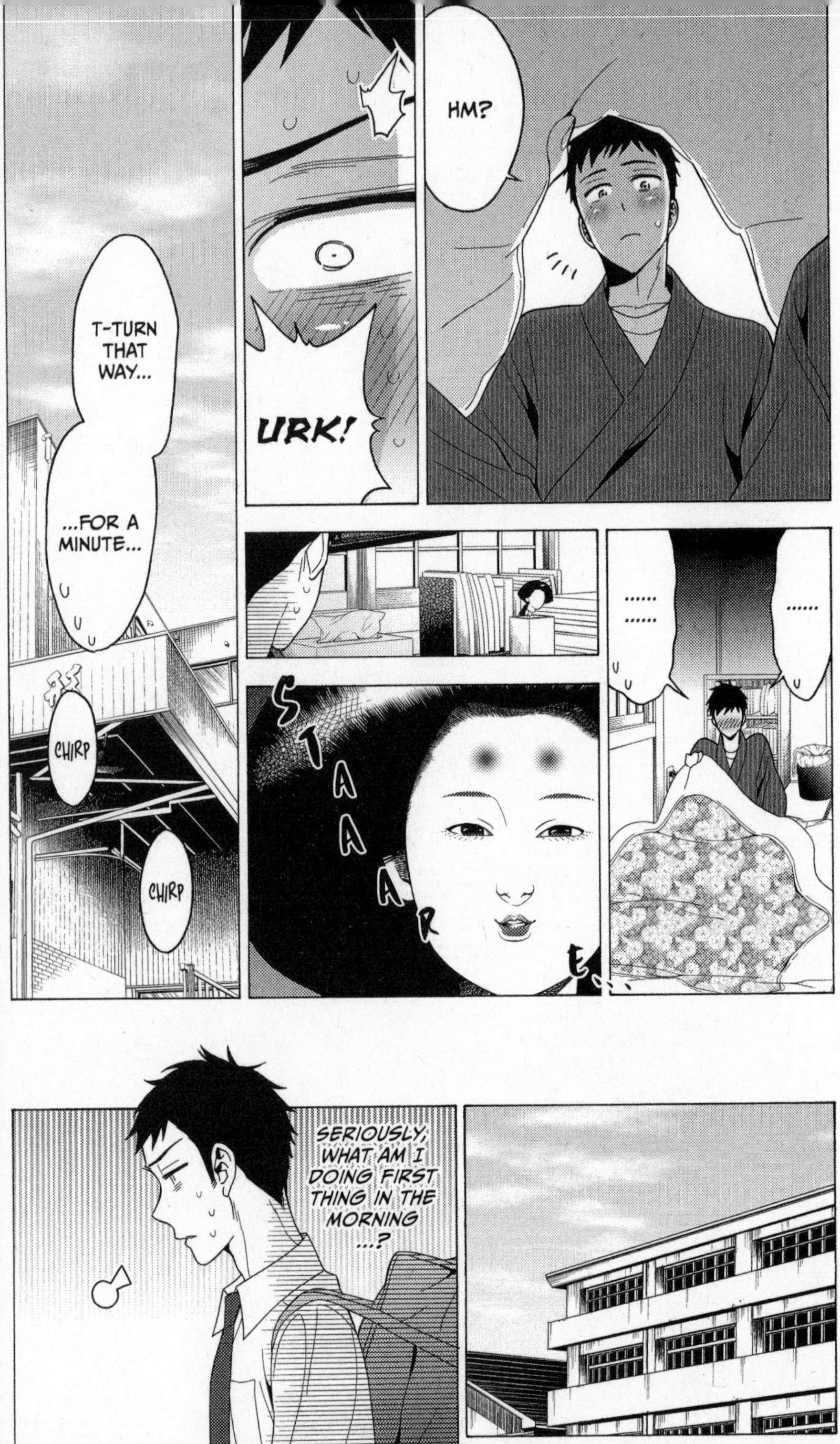
HM?
URK!
......
......
......
STAAARE...
T-TURN THAT WAY...
...FOR A MINUTE...
CHIRP
CHIRP
SERIOUSLY, WHAT AM I DOING FIRST THING IN THE MORNING...?

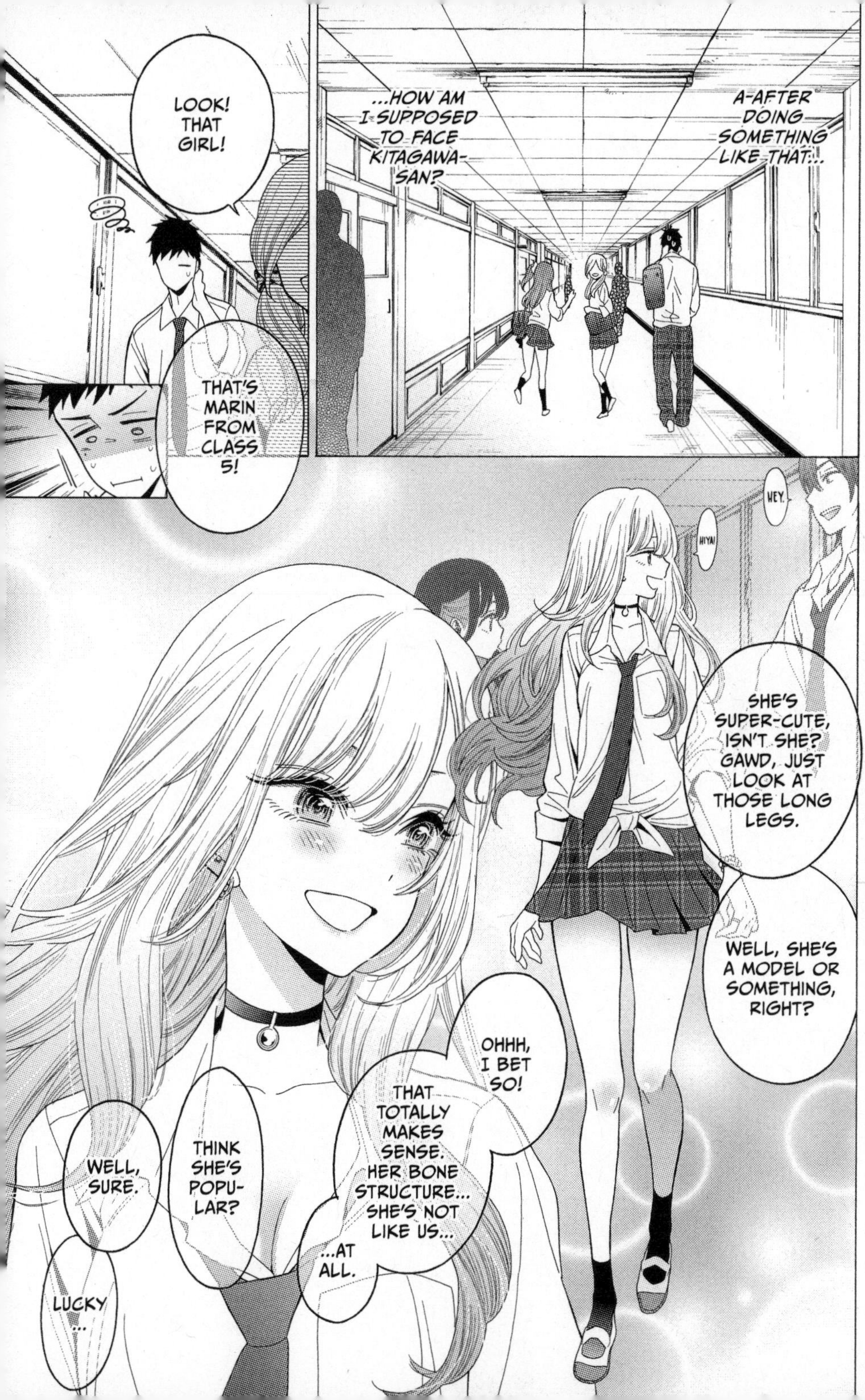
A-AFTER DOING SOMETHING LIKE THAT...
...HOW AM I SUPPOSED TO FACE KITAGAWA-SAN?
LOOK! THAT GIRL!
THAT'S MARIN FROM CLASS 5!
HEY.
HIYA!
SHE'S SUPER-CUTE, ISN'T SHE? GAWD, JUST LOOK AT THOSE LONG LEGS.
WELL, SHE'S A MODEL OR SOMETHING, RIGHT?
OHHH, I BET SO!
THAT TOTALLY MAKES SENSE. HER BONE STRUCTURE... SHE'S NOT LIKE US...
...AT ALL.
THINK SHE'S POPULAR?
WELL, SURE.
LUCKY...

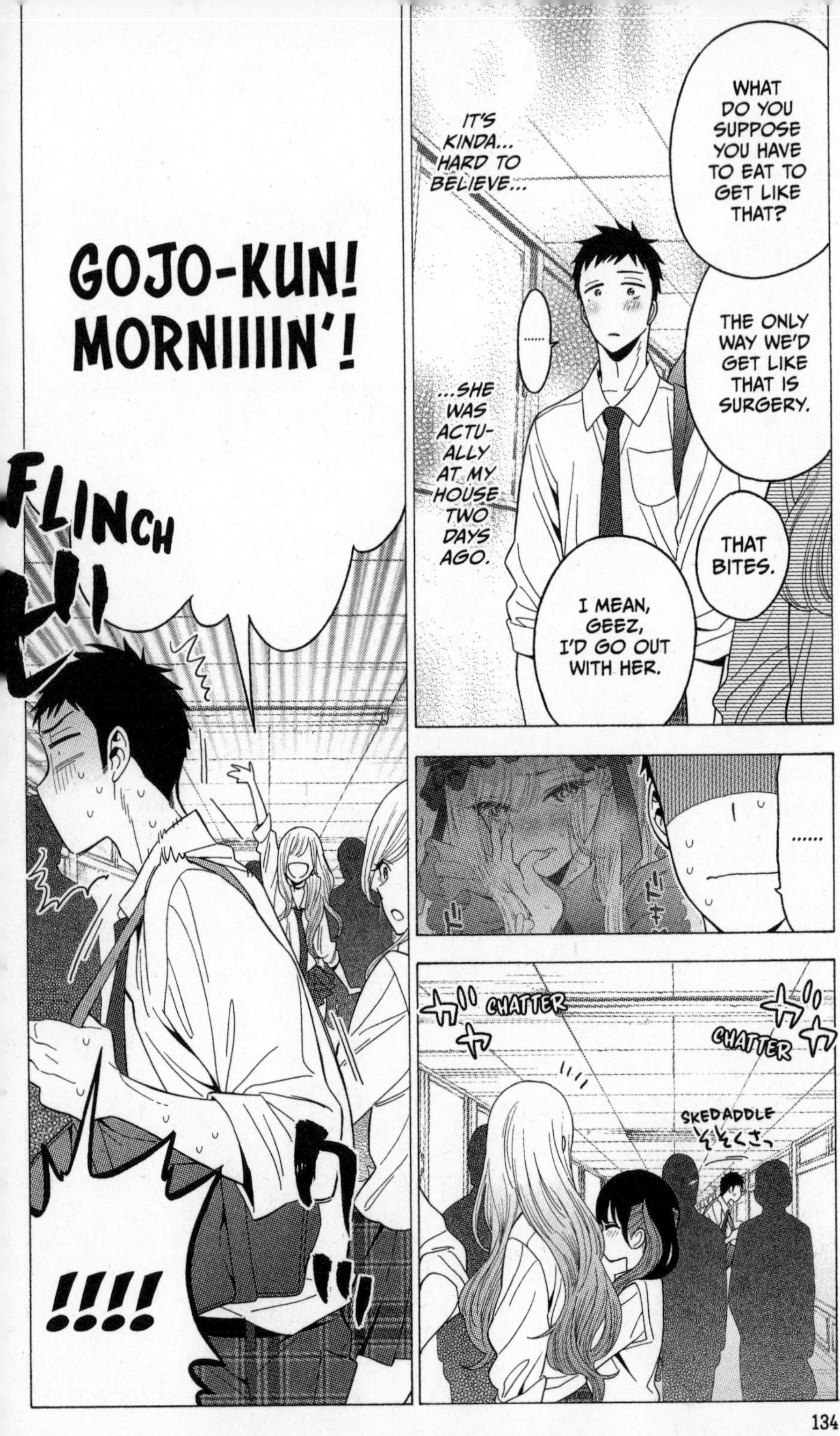
WHAT DO YOU SUPPOSE YOU HAVE TO EAT TO GET LIKE THAT?
IT'S KINDA... HARD TO BELIEVE...
THE ONLY WAY WE'D GET LIKE THAT IS SURGERY.
......
...SHE WAS ACTU-ALLY AT MY HOUSE TWO DAYS AGO.
THAT BITES.
I MEAN, GEEZ, I'D GO OUT WITH HER.
......
CHATTER
CHATTER
SKEDADDLE
そそくさ
GOJO-KUN! MORNIIIIN'!
FLINCH
!!!!

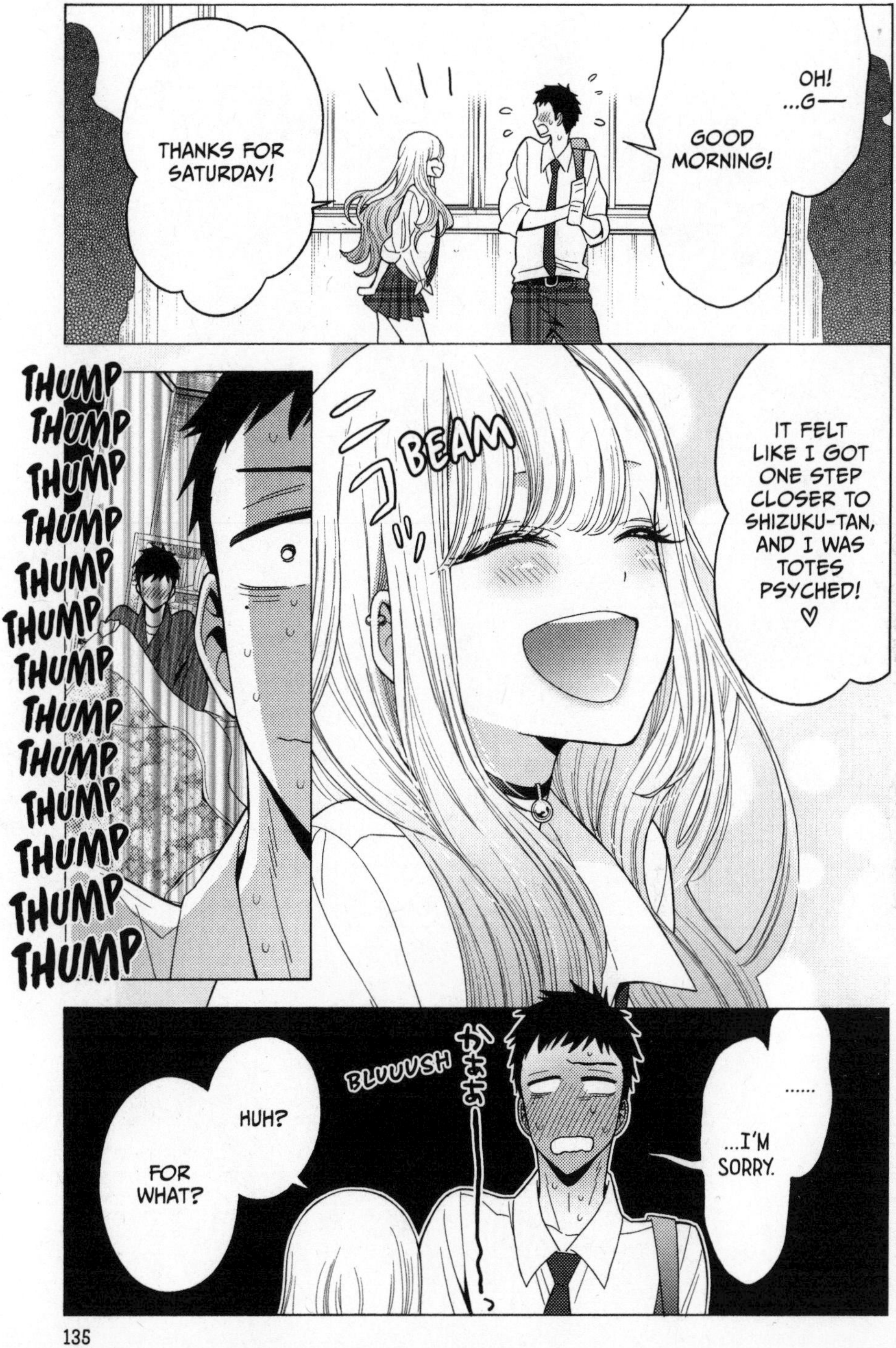
OH! ...G— GOOD MORNING!
THANKS FOR SATURDAY!
BEAM
...IT FELT LIKE I GOT ONE STEP CLOSER TO SHIZUKU-TAN, AND I WAS TOTES PSYCHED! ♡
THUMP THUMP THUMP THUMP THUMP THUMP THUMP THUMP THUMP THUMP THUMP THUMP THUMP
....I'M SORRY.
BLUUUSH
HUH? FOR WHAT?

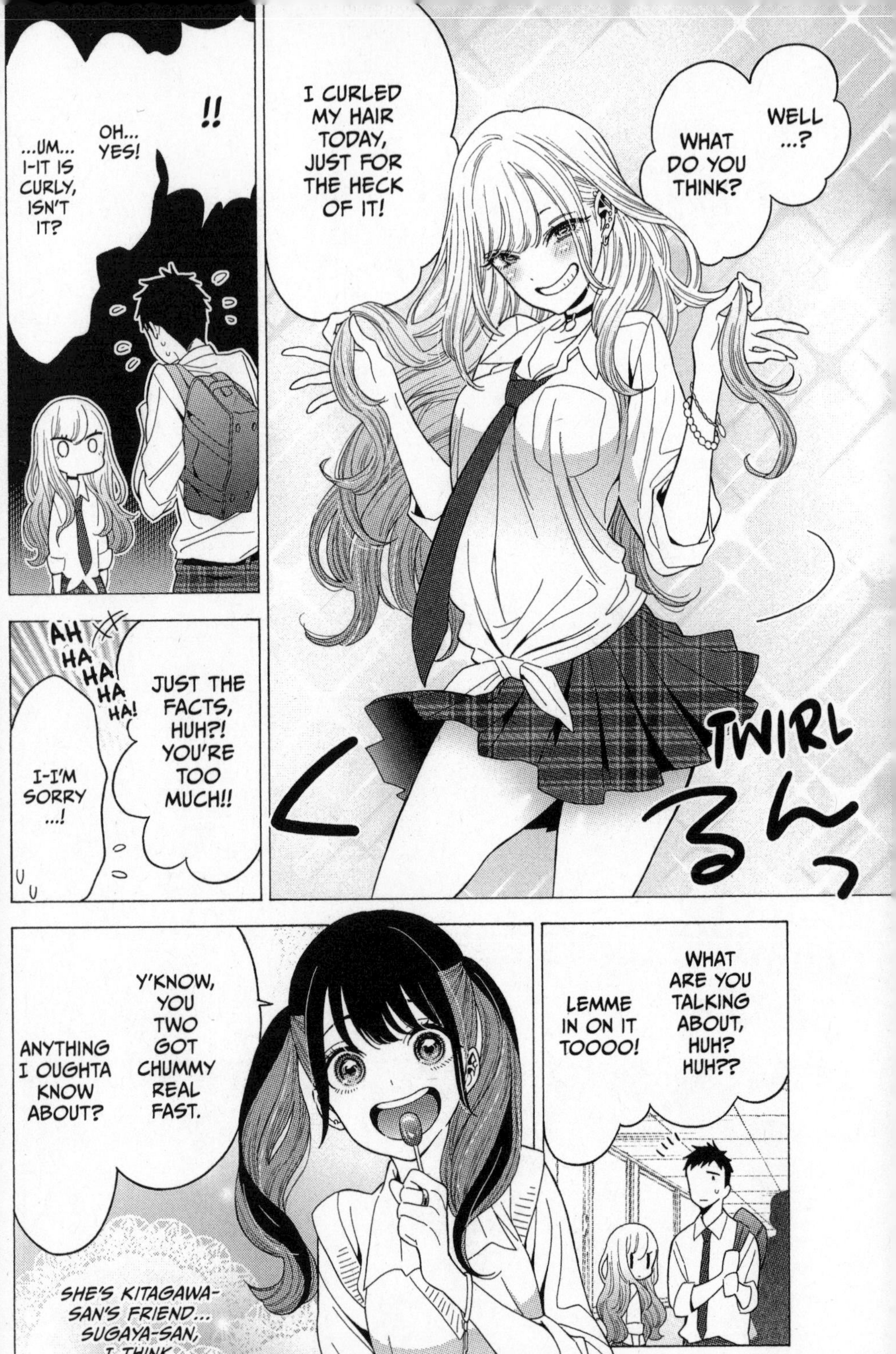
WELL ...? WHAT DO YOU THINK?
I CURLED MY HAIR TODAY, JUST FOR THE HECK OF IT!
TWIRL
!!
OH... YES!
...UM... I-IT IS CURLY, ISN'T IT?
AH HA HA HA HA!
JUST THE FACTS, HUH?! YOU'RE TOO MUCH!!
I-I'M SORRY ...!
WHAT ARE YOU TALKING ABOUT, HUH? HUH??
LEMME IN ON IT TOOOO!
Y'KNOW, YOU TWO GOT CHUMMY REAL FAST.
ANYTHING I OUGHTA KNOW ABOUT?
SHE'S KITAGAWA-SAN'S FRIEND... SUGAYA-SAN, I THINK.

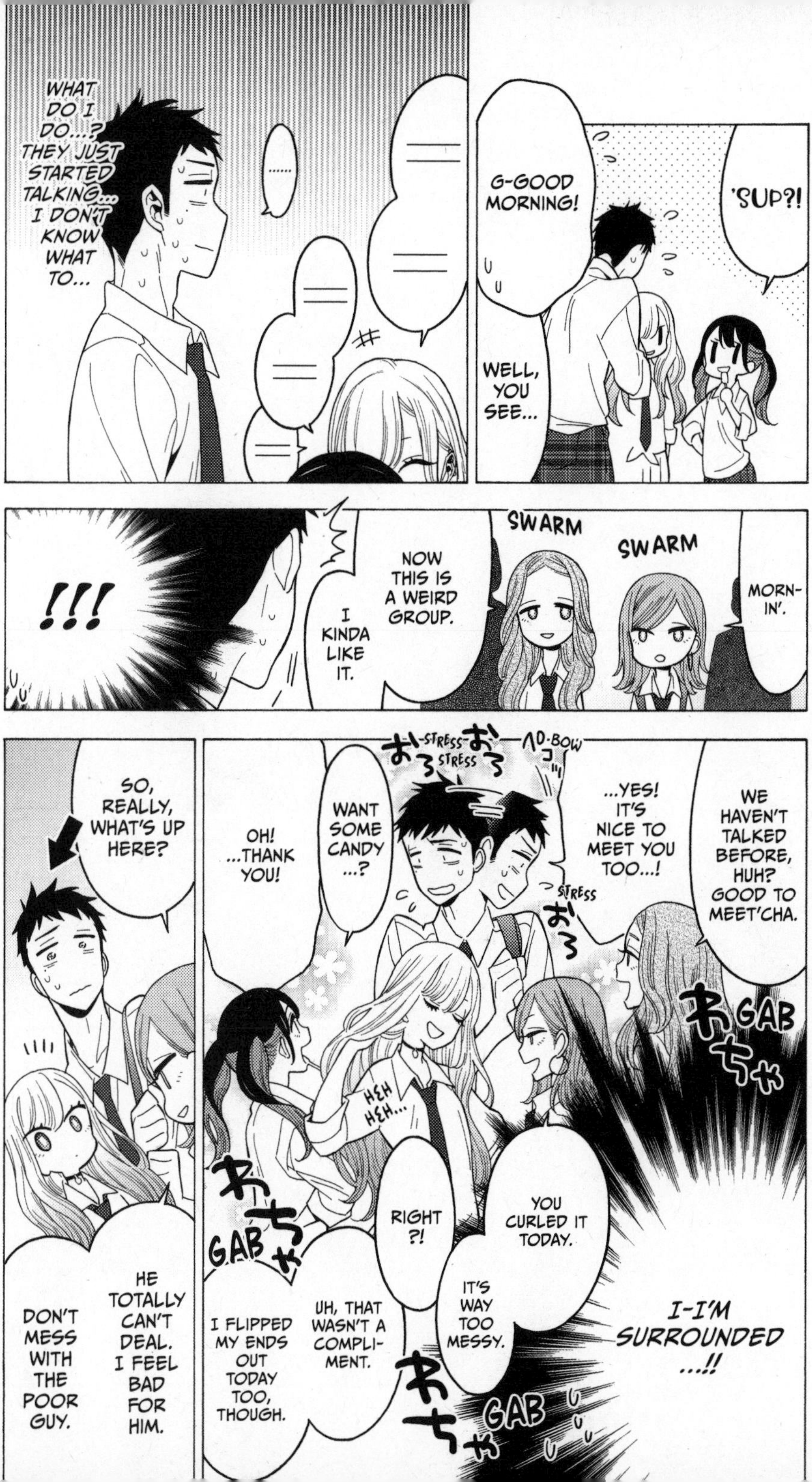
'SUP?!
G-GOOD MORNING!
WELL, YOU SEE...
WHAT DO I DO...? THEY JUST STARTED TALKING... I DON'T KNOW WHAT TO...
......
MORN-IN'.
SWARM
SWARM
NOW THIS IS A WEIRD GROUP.
I KINDA LIKE IT.
!!!
WE HAVEN'T TALKED BEFORE, HUH? GOOD TO MEET'CHA.
...YES! IT'S NICE TO MEET YOU TOO...!
BOW
STRESS
STRESS
WANT SOME CANDY...?
OH! ...THANK YOU!
STRESS
GAB
HEH HEH...
YOU CURLED IT TODAY.
RIGHT?!
IT'S WAY TOO MESSY.
UH, THAT WASN'T A COMPLIMENT.
I FLIPPED MY ENDS OUT TODAY TOO, THOUGH.
GAB
I-I'M SURROUNDED...!!
GAB
SO, REALLY, WHAT'S UP HERE?
HE TOTALLY CAN'T DEAL. I FEEL BAD FOR HIM.
DON'T MESS WITH THE POOR GUY.

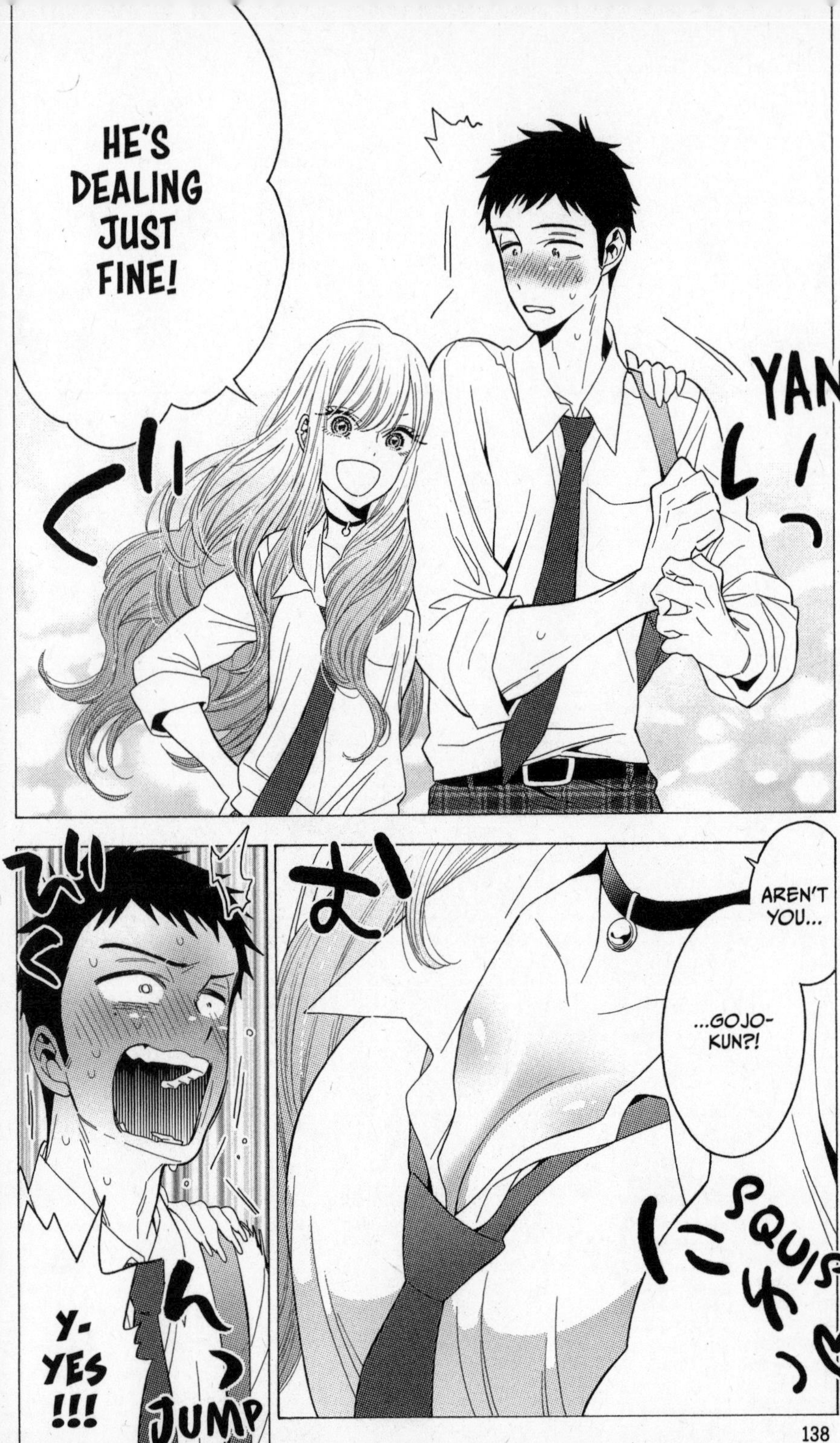
HE'S DEALING JUST FINE!
YANK
AREN'T YOU...
...GOJO-KUN?!
SQUISH
Y-YES!!!
JUMP

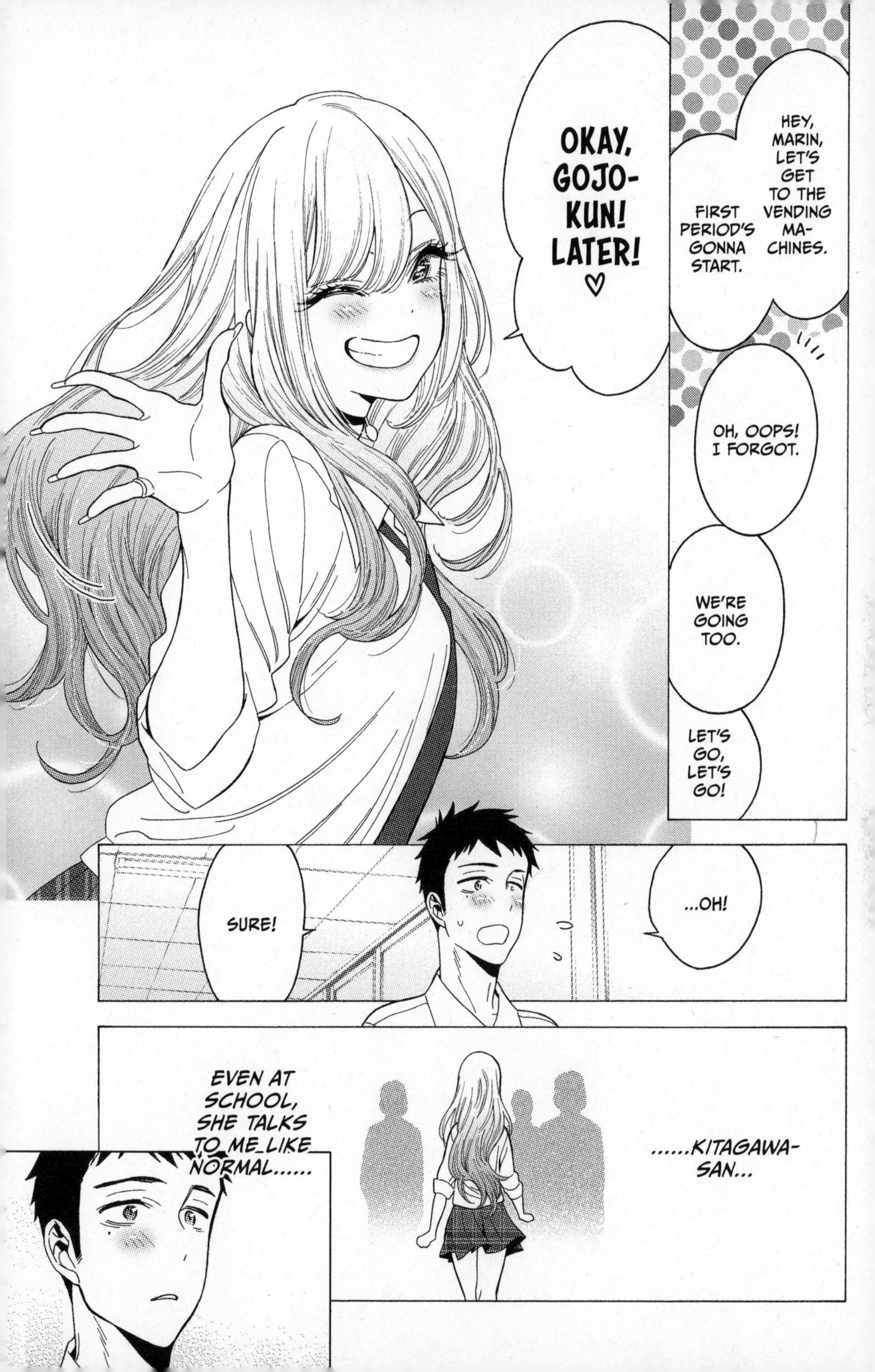
HEY, MARIN, LET'S GET TO THE VENDING MA-CHINES.
FIRST PERIOD'S GONNA START.
OH, OOPS! I FORGOT.
WE'RE GOING TOO.
LET'S GO, LET'S GO!
OKAY, GOJO-KUN! LATER! ♡
...OH!
SURE!
......KITAGAWA-SAN...
EVEN AT SCHOOL, SHE TALKS TO ME LIKE NORMAL......

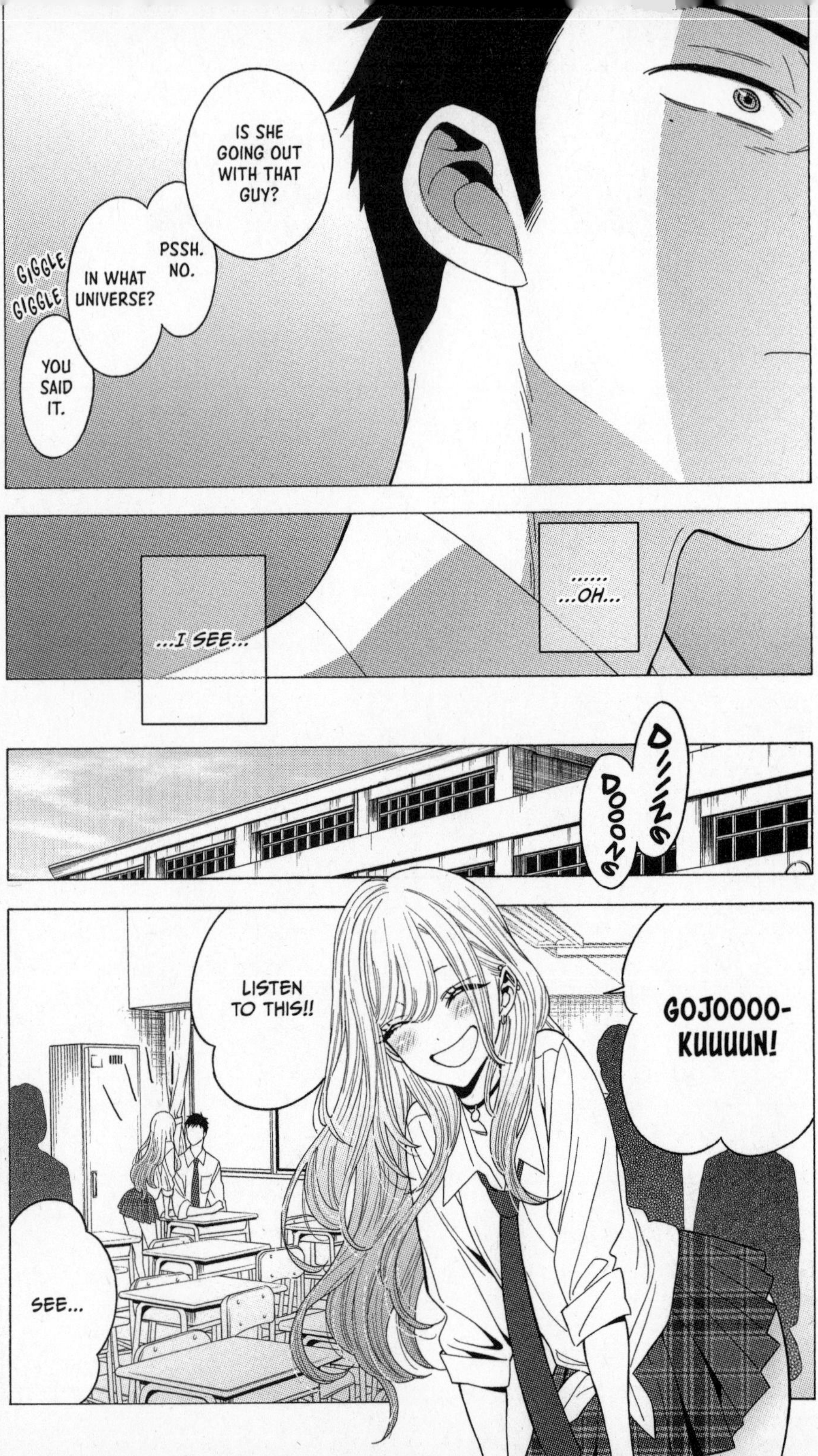
IS SHE GOING OUT WITH THAT GUY?
PSSH. NO.
IN WHAT UNIVERSE?
GIGGLE GIGGLE
YOU SAID IT.
......
...OH...
...I SEE...
DIIING DOOONG
GOJOOOO-KUUUUN!
LISTEN TO THIS!!
SEE...

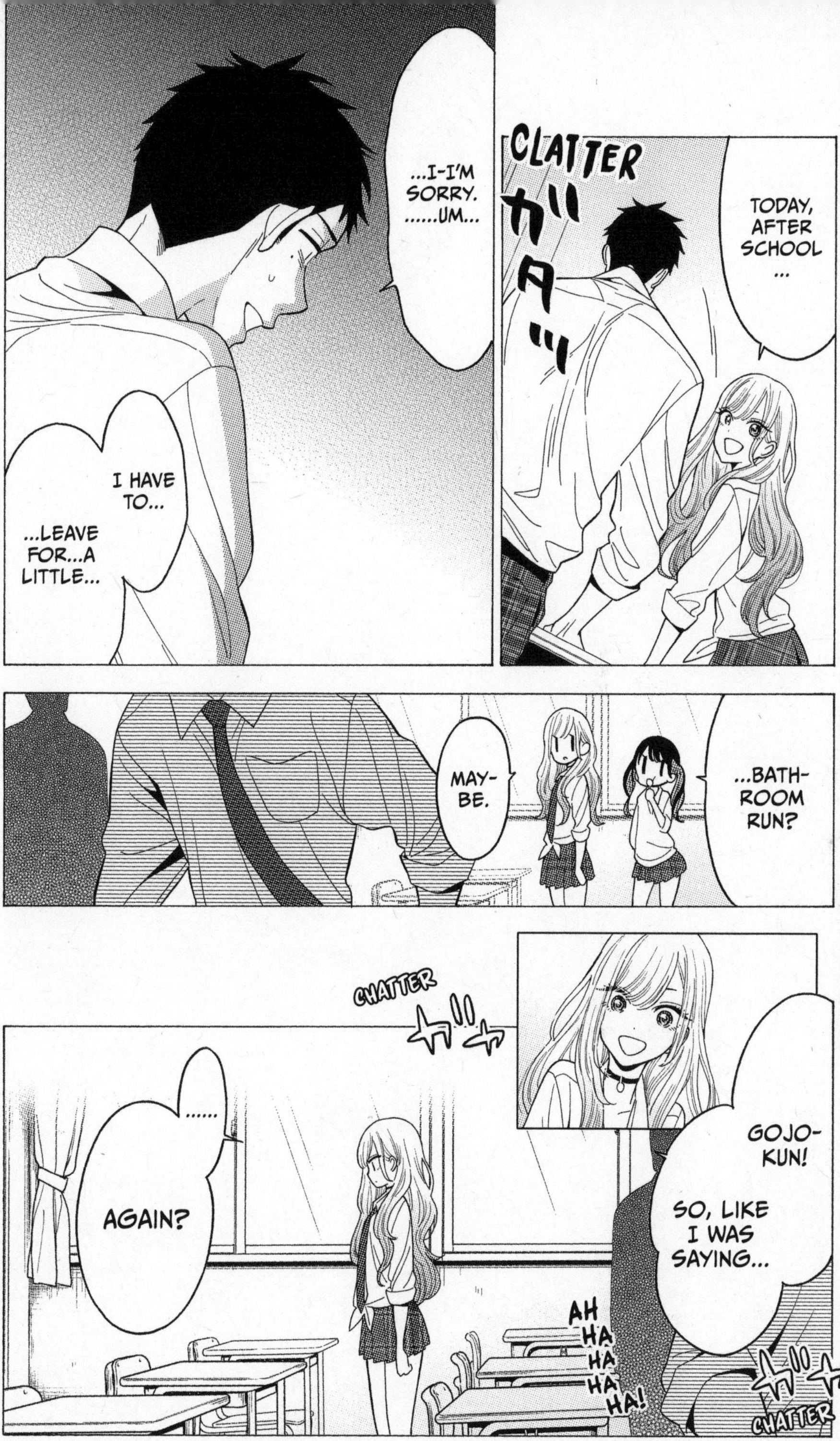
CLATTER
TODAY, AFTER SCHOOL ...
...I-I'M SORRY. ......UM...
I HAVE TO...
...LEAVE FOR...A LITTLE...
...BATH-ROOM RUN?
MAY-BE.
GOJO-KUN!
SO, LIKE I WAS SAYING...
CHATTER
CHATTER
......
AGAIN?
AH HA HA HA HA!

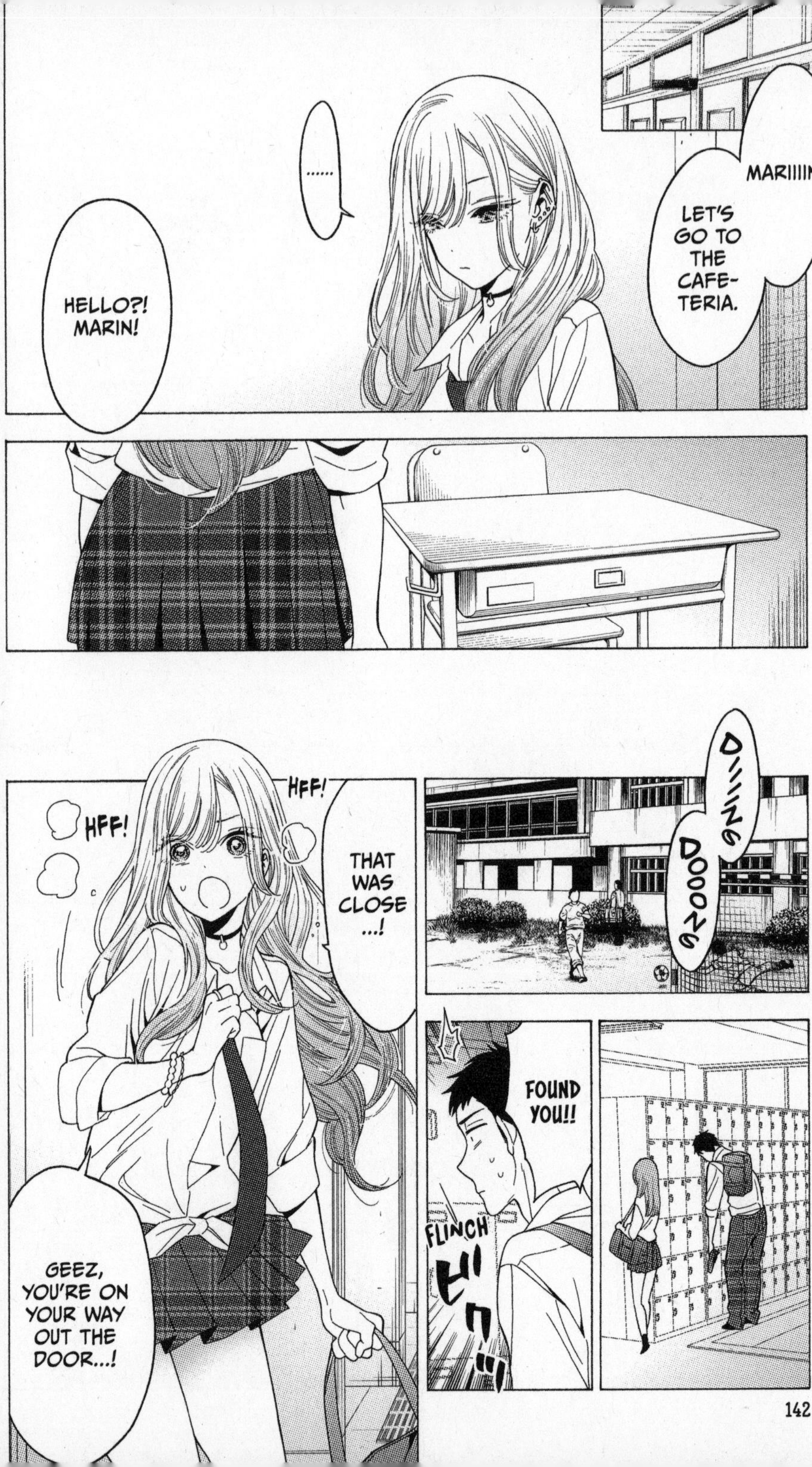
MARIIIIN!
LET'S GO TO THE CAFE-TERIA.
......
HELLO?! MARIN!
DIIING DOOONG
FOUND YOU!!
FLINCH
HFF!
HFF!
THAT WAS CLOSE ...!
GEEZ, YOU'RE ON YOUR WAY OUT THE DOOR...!

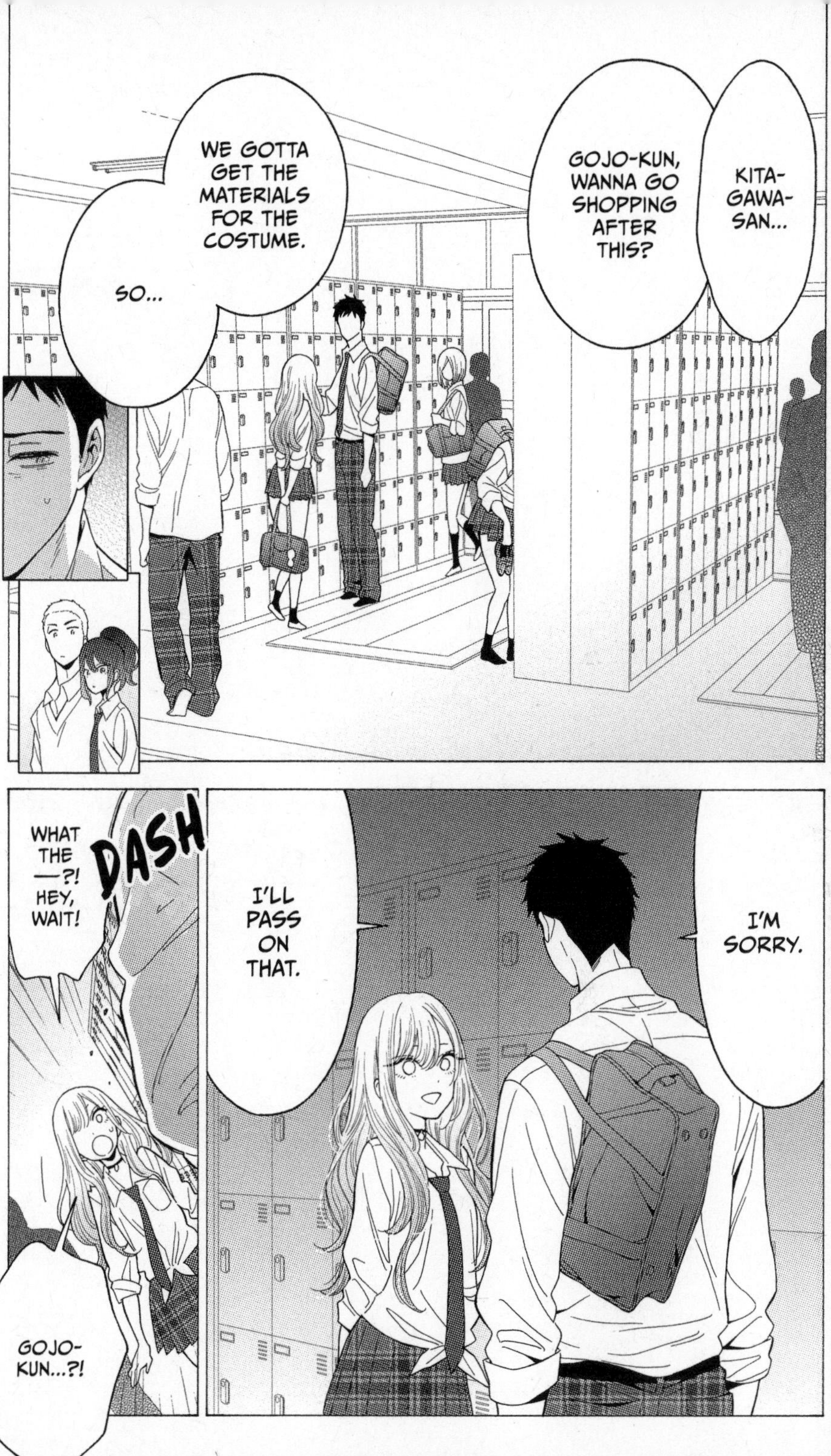
KITA-GAWA-SAN...
GOJO-KUN, WANNA GO SHOPPING AFTER THIS?
WE GOTTA GET THE MATERIALS FOR THE COSTUME.
SO...
I'M SORRY.
I'LL PASS ON THAT.
DASH
WHAT THE—?! HEY, WAIT!
GOJO-KUN...?!

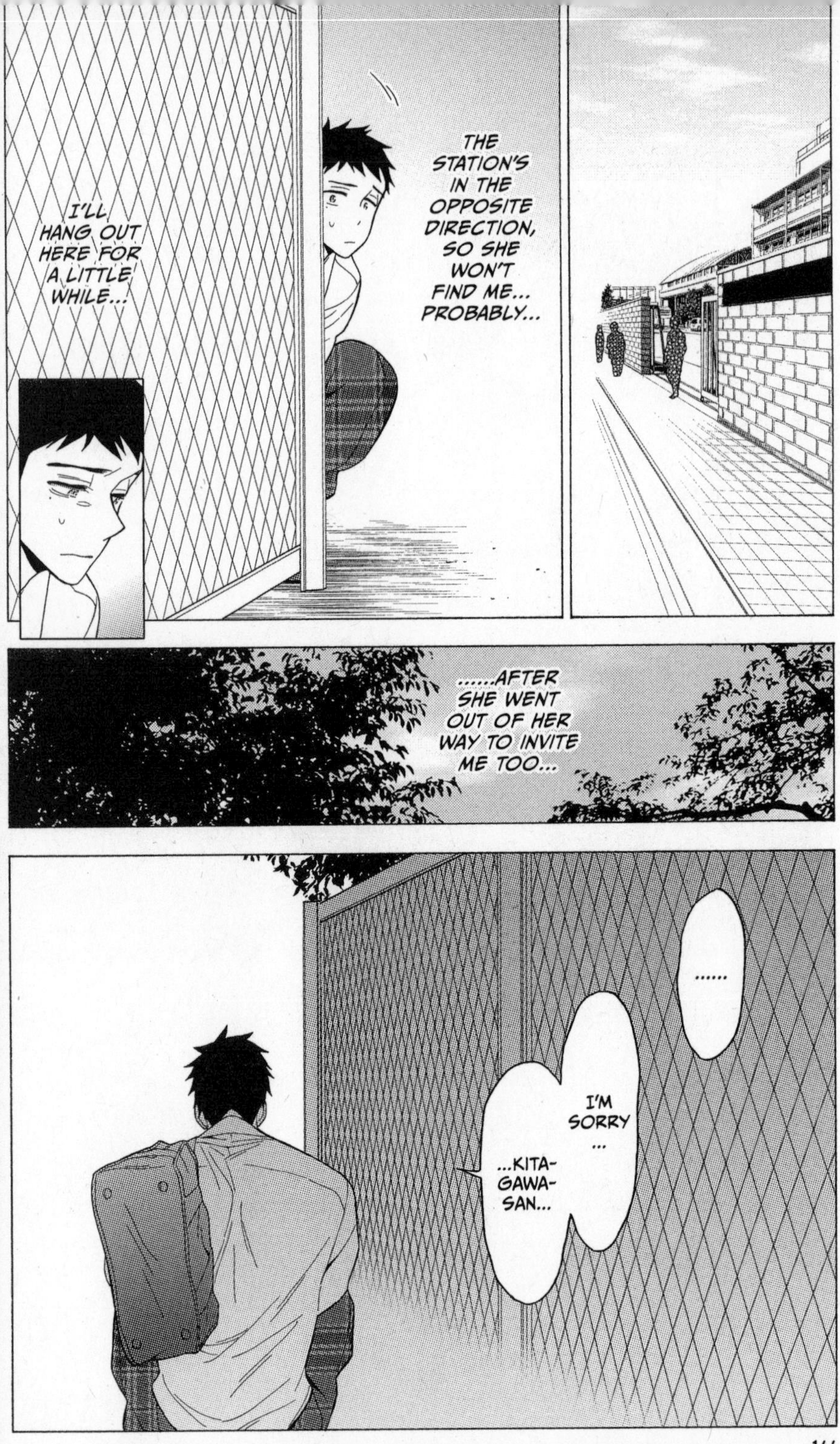
THE STATION'S IN THE OPPOSITE DIRECTION, SO SHE WON'T FIND ME... PROBABLY...
I'LL HANG OUT HERE FOR A LITTLE WHILE...
......AFTER SHE WENT OUT OF HER WAY TO INVITE ME TOO...
......
I'M SORRY ...
...KITA-GAWA-SAN...

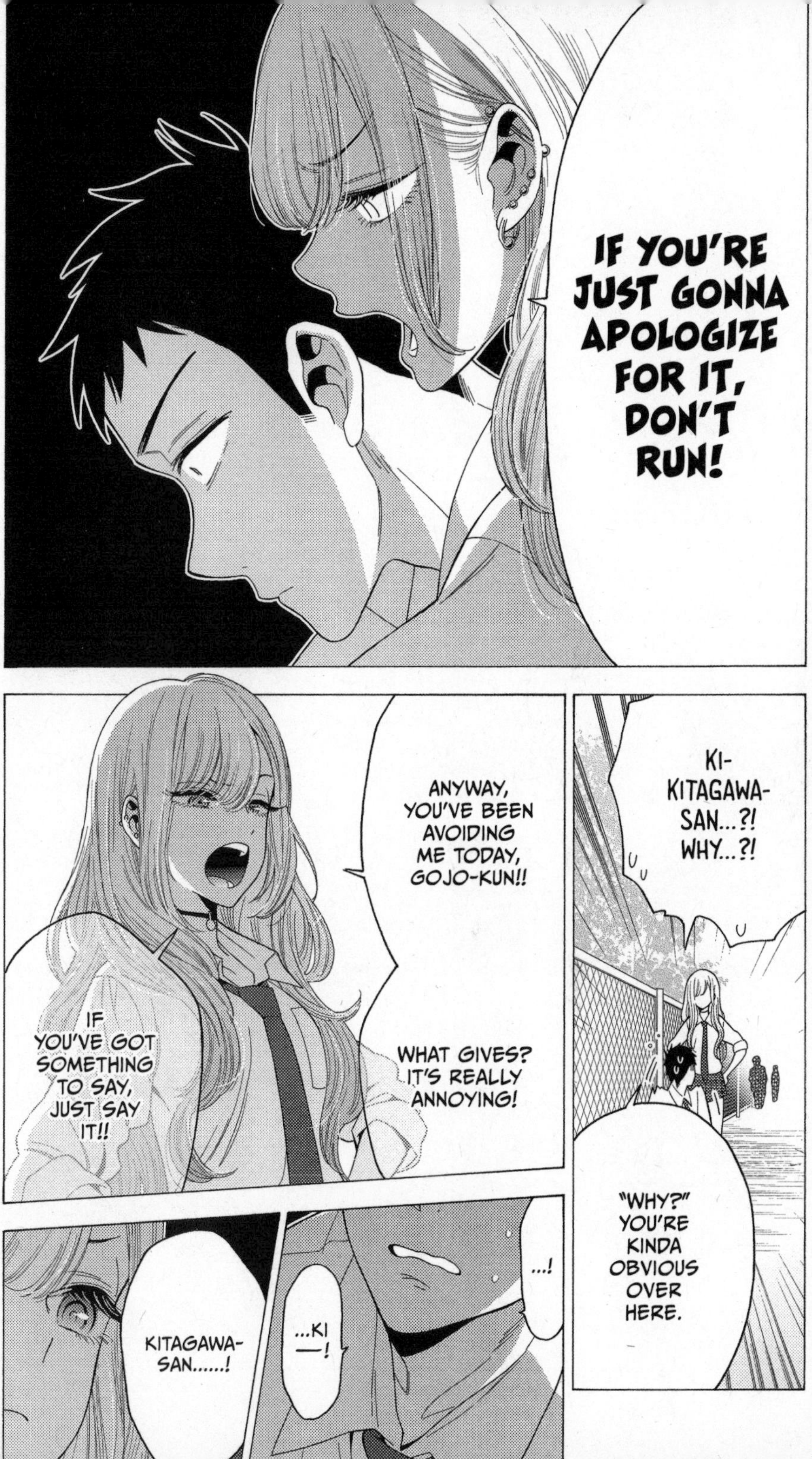
IF YOU'RE JUST GONNA APOLOGIZE FOR IT, DON'T RUN!
KI- KITAGAWA-SAN...?! WHY...?!
"WHY?" YOU'RE KINDA OBVIOUS OVER HERE.
ANYWAY, YOU'VE BEEN AVOIDING ME TODAY, GOJO-KUN!!
WHAT GIVES? IT'S REALLY ANNOYING!
IF YOU'VE GOT SOMETHING TO SAY, JUST SAY IT!!
...!
...KI —!
KITAGAWA-SAN......!

PEOPLE... ARE STARTING TO THINK YOU KNOW ME...

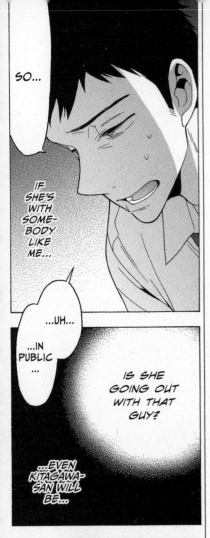

SO...

IF SHE'S WITH SOME-BODY LIKE ME...

...UH...

...IN PUBLIC...

IS SHE GOING OUT WITH THAT GUY?

...EVEN KITAGAWA-SAN WILL BE...

SQUEEZE

...YOU SHOULD PRETEND YOU DON'T...

HUH?

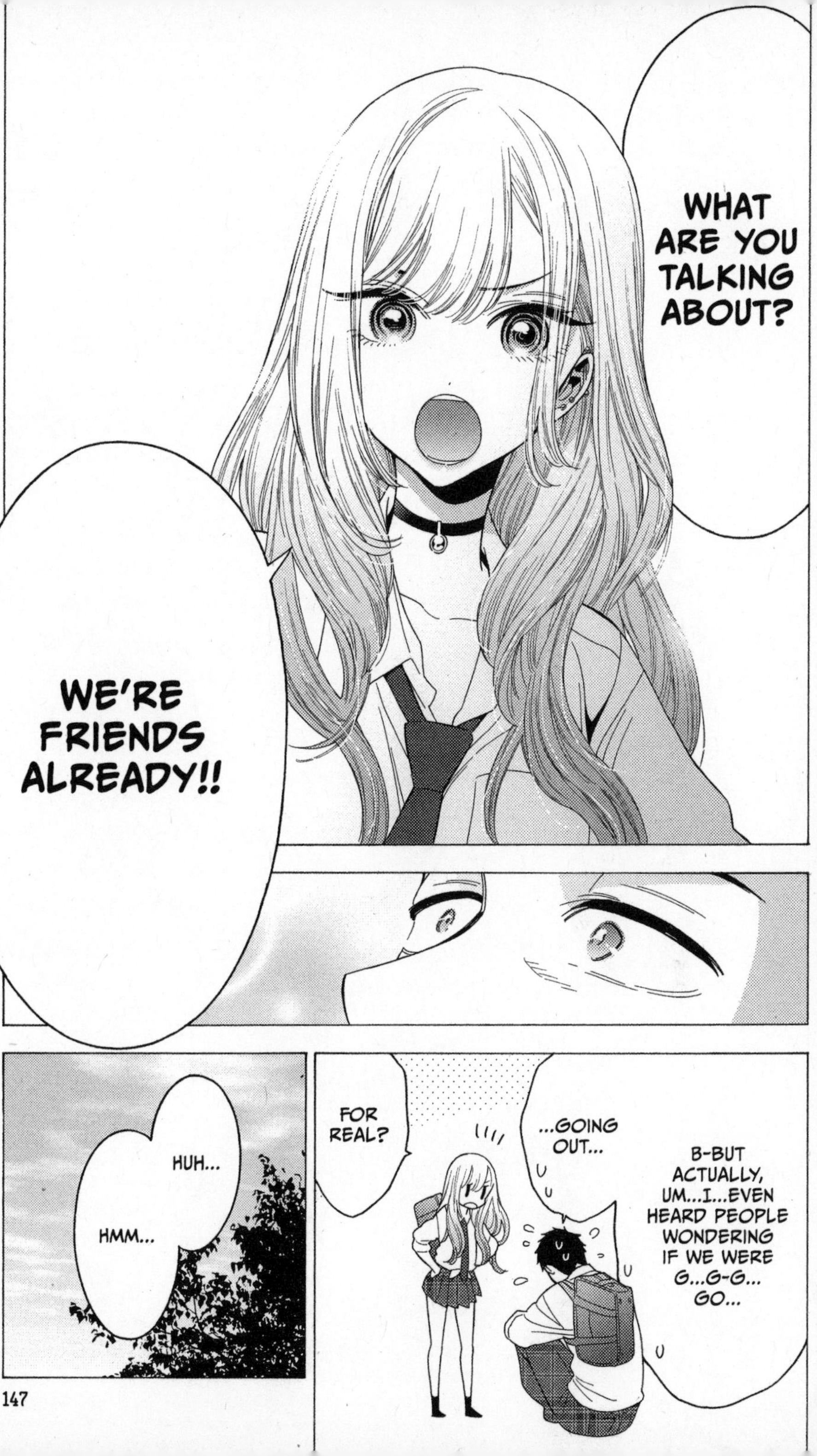
WHAT ARE YOU TALKING ABOUT?
WE'RE FRIENDS ALREADY!!
B-BUT ACTUALLY, UM...I...EVEN HEARD PEOPLE WONDERING IF WE WERE G...G-G... GO...
...GOING OUT...
FOR REAL?
HUH...
HMM...

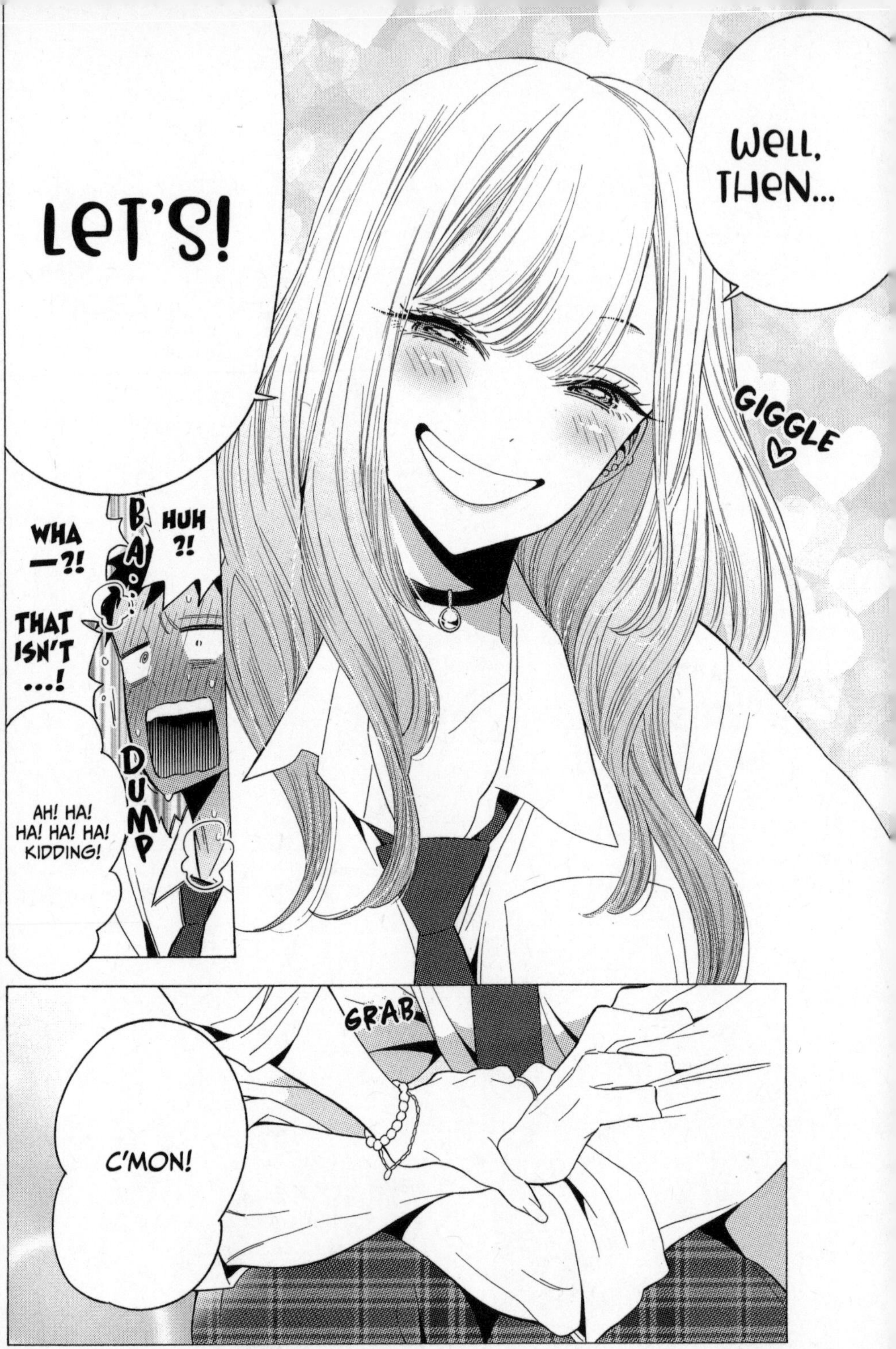

WELL, THEN...
LET'S!
GIGGLE ♡
HUH ?!
BA...
WHA —?!
THAT ISN'T ...!
DUMP
AH! HA! HA! HA! HA! KIDDING!
GRAB
C'MON!

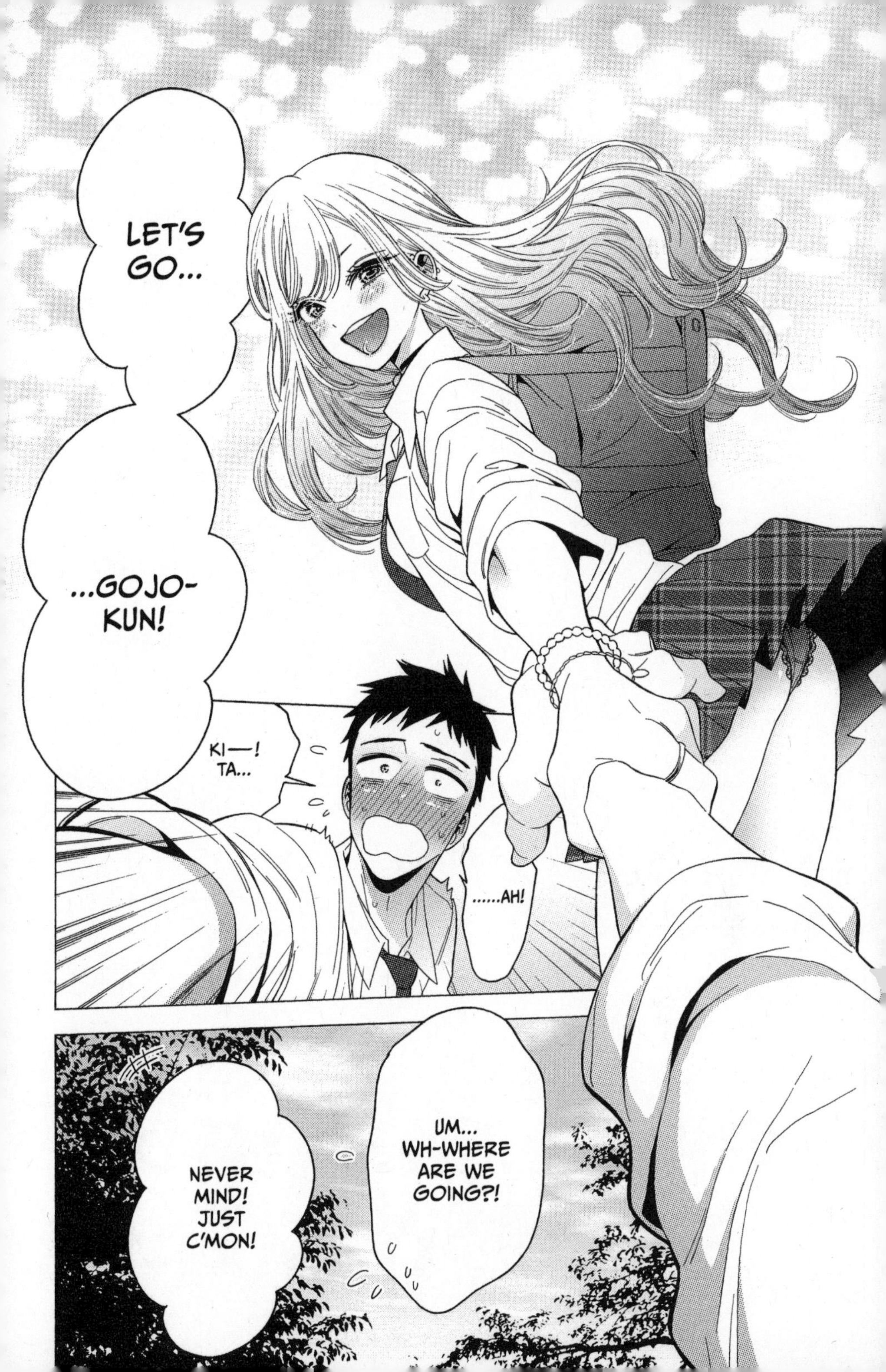
LET'S GO...
...GOJO-KUN!
KI—! TA...
......AH!
UM... WH-WHERE ARE WE GOING?!
NEVER MIND! JUST C'MON!

My DRESS-UP Darling

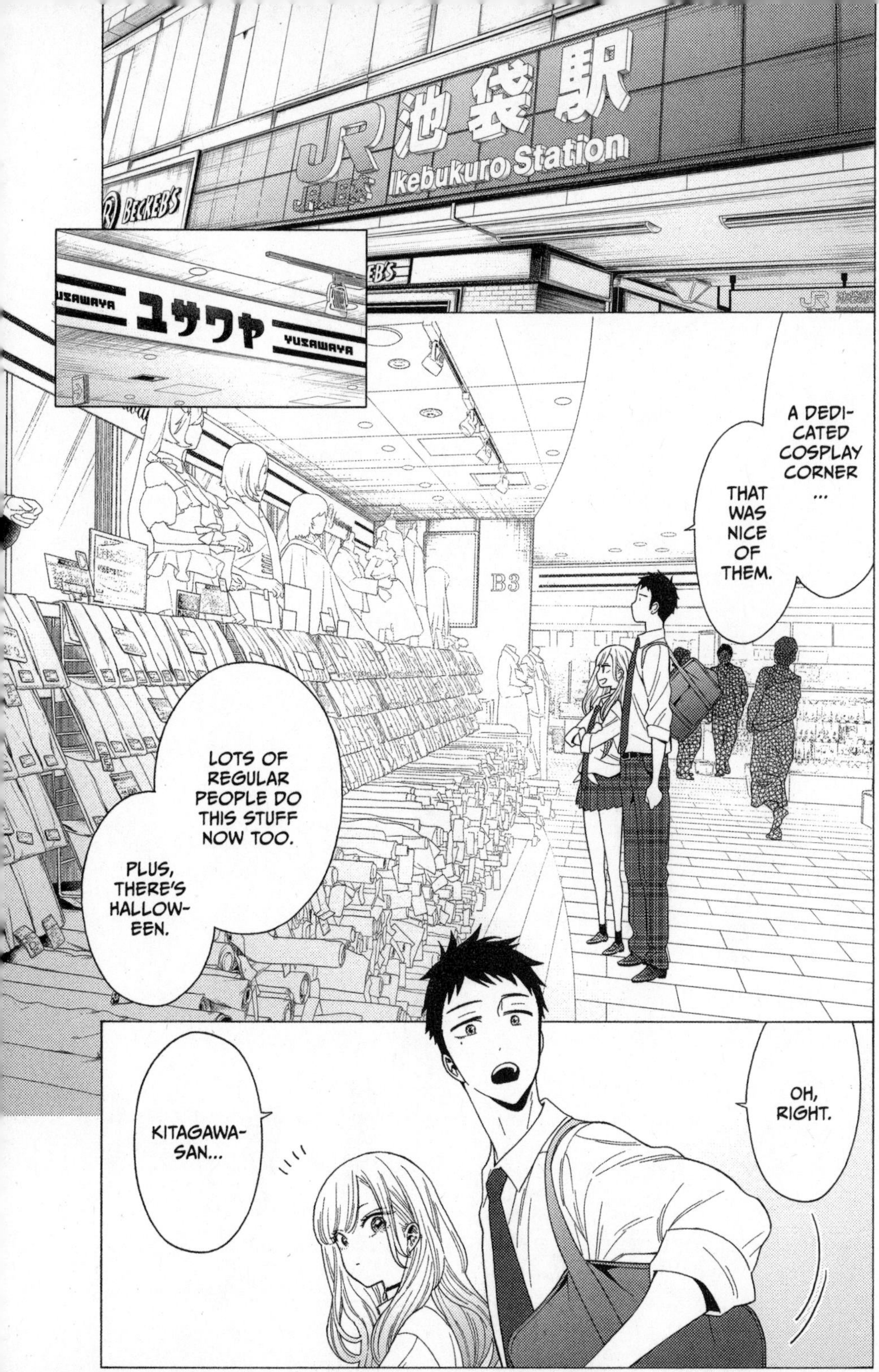
JR 池袋駅
Ikebukuro Station
BECKEB'S
ユサワヤ
YUSAWAYA
A DEDI-CATED COSPLAY CORNER ...
THAT WAS NICE OF THEM.
B3
LOTS OF REGULAR PEOPLE DO THIS STUFF NOW TOO.
PLUS, THERE'S HALLOW-EEN.
OH, RIGHT.
KITAGAWA-SAN...

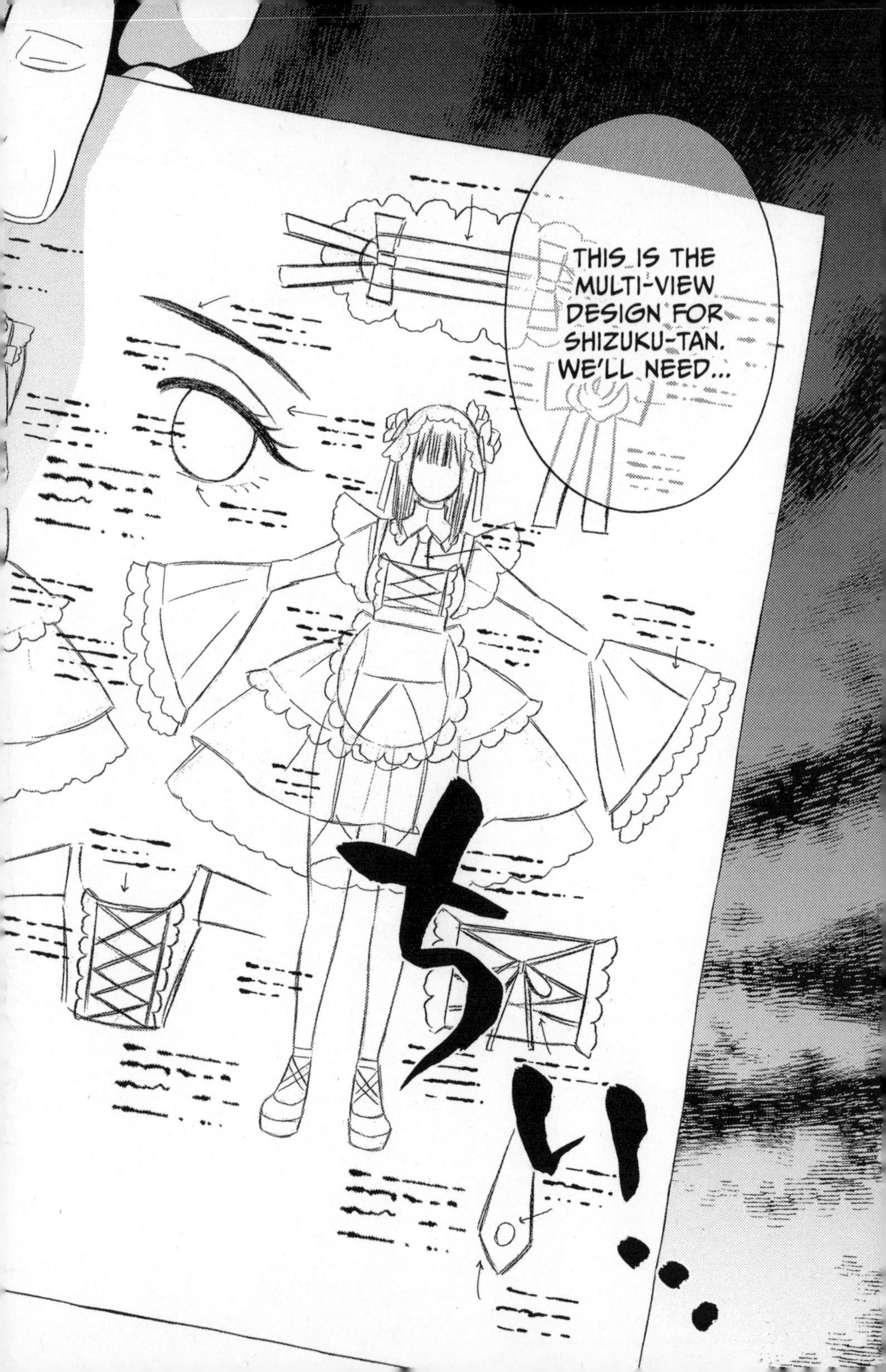
THIS IS THE MULTI-VIEW DESIGN FOR SHIZUKU-TAN. WE'LL NEED...
ちい...

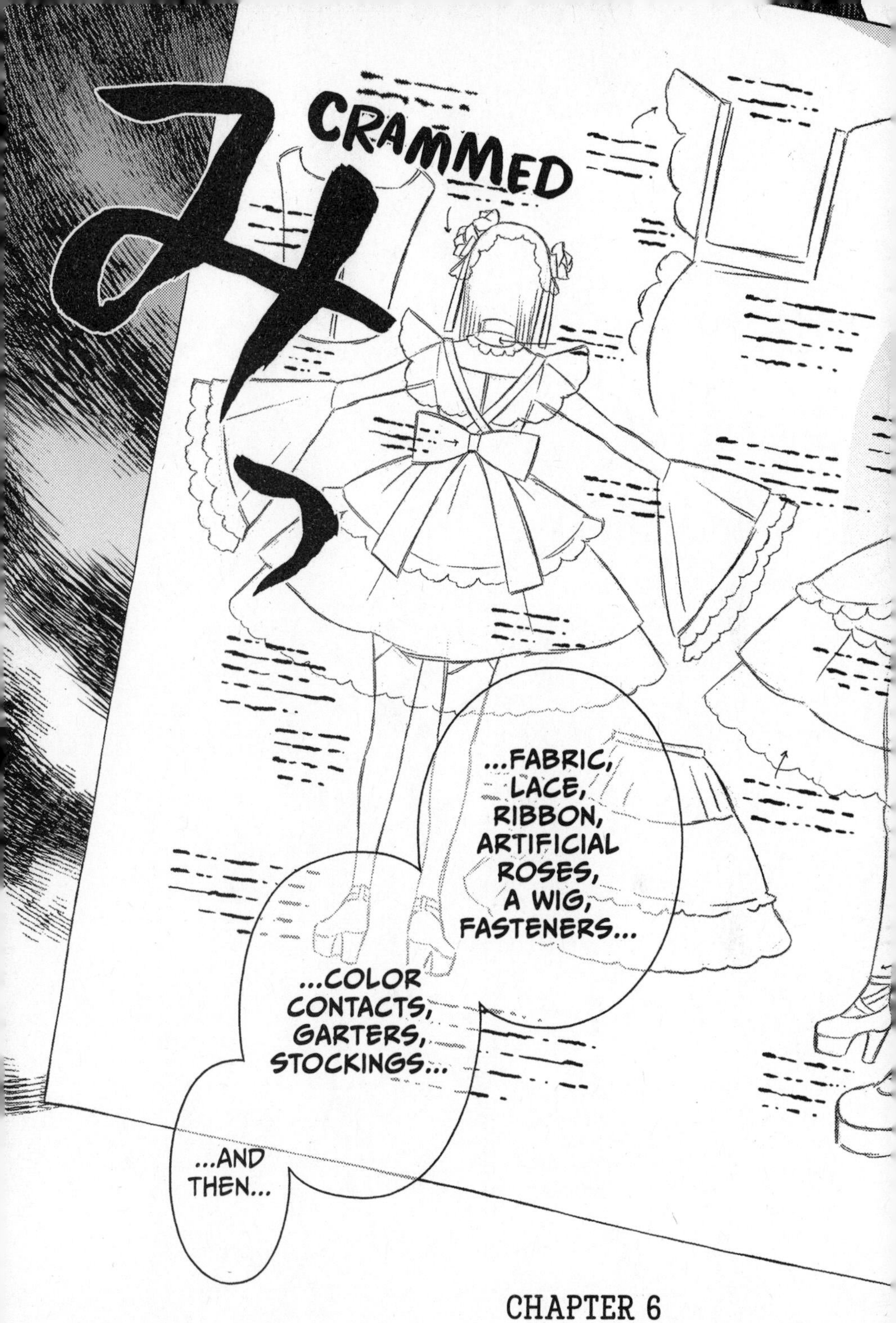
CRAMMED
...FABRIC, LACE, RIBBON, ARTIFICIAL ROSES, A WIG, FASTENERS...
...COLOR CONTACTS, GARTERS, STOCKINGS...
...AND THEN...

CHAPTER 6

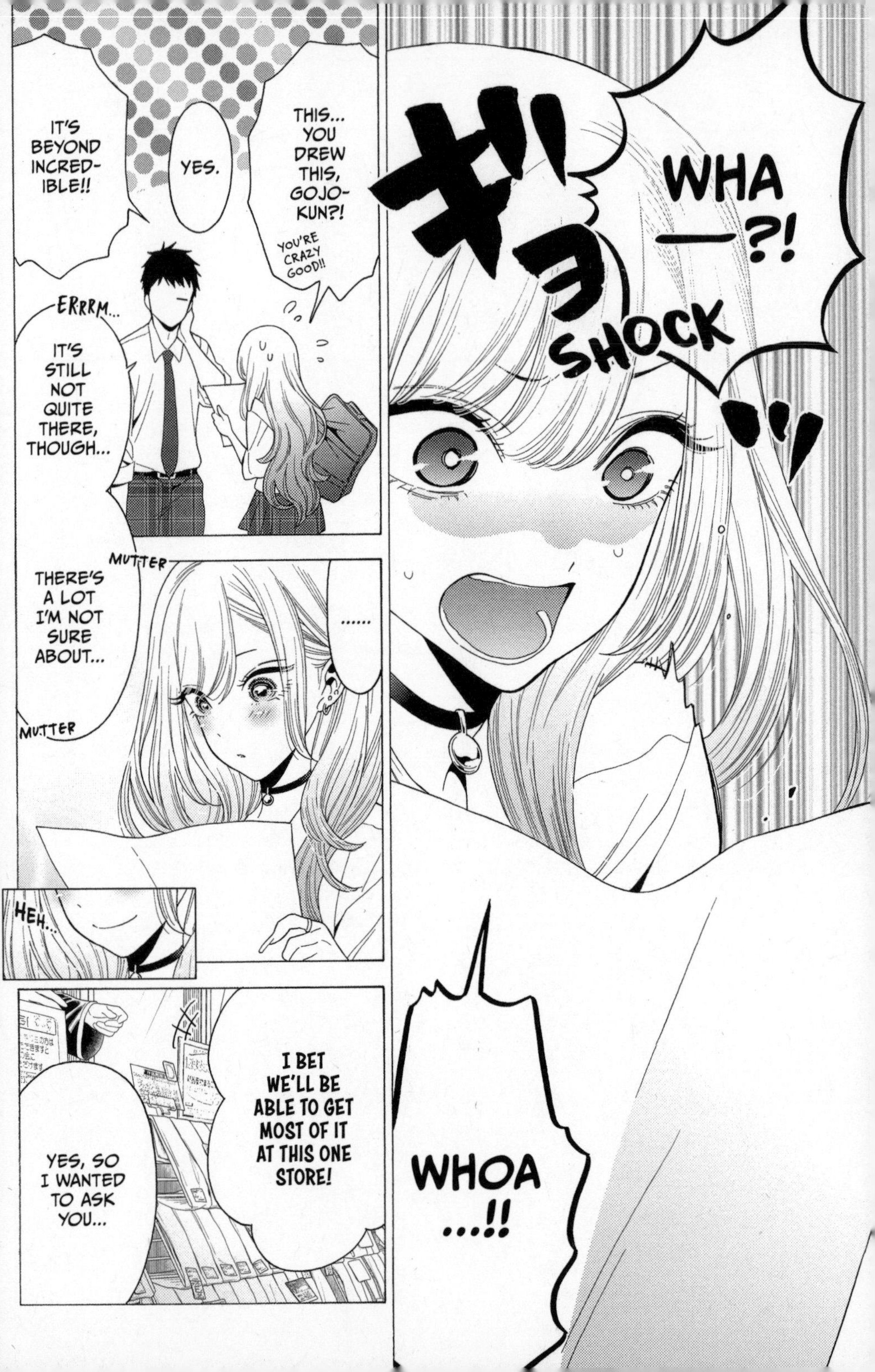
WHA—?!
ギョ
SHOCK
WHOA ...!!
THIS... YOU DREW THIS, GOJO-KUN?!
YES.
IT'S BEYOND INCREDIBLE!!
YOU'RE CRAZY GOOD!!
ERRRM...
IT'S STILL NOT QUITE THERE, THOUGH...
......
MUTTER
THERE'S A LOT I'M NOT SURE ABOUT...
MUTTER
HEH...
I BET WE'LL BE ABLE TO GET MOST OF IT AT THIS ONE STORE!
YES, SO I WANTED TO ASK YOU...

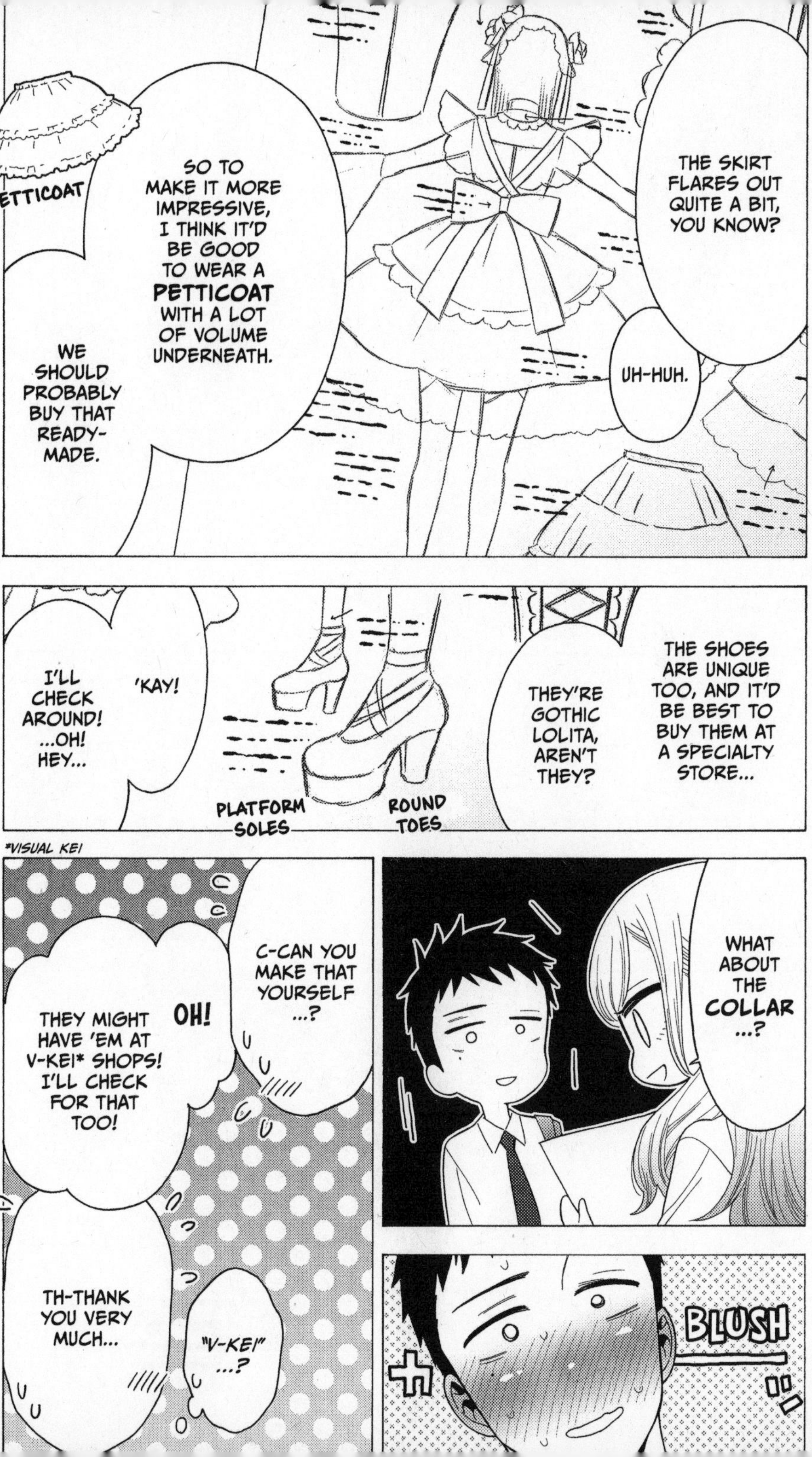
THE SKIRT FLARES OUT QUITE A BIT, YOU KNOW?
UH-HUH.
SO TO MAKE IT MORE IMPRESSIVE, I THINK IT'D BE GOOD TO WEAR A **PETTICOAT** WITH A LOT OF VOLUME UNDERNEATH.
PETTICOAT
WE SHOULD PROBABLY BUY THAT READY-MADE.
THE SHOES ARE UNIQUE TOO, AND IT'D BE BEST TO BUY THEM AT A SPECIALTY STORE...
THEY'RE GOTHIC LOLITA, AREN'T THEY?
ROUND TOES
PLATFORM SOLES
'KAY!
I'LL CHECK AROUND! ...OH! HEY...
WHAT ABOUT THE **COLLAR**...?
BLUSH
C-CAN YOU MAKE THAT YOURSELF...?
OH!
THEY MIGHT HAVE 'EM AT V-KEI* SHOPS! I'LL CHECK FOR THAT TOO!
"V-KEI"...?
TH-THANK YOU VERY MUCH...

*VISUAL KEI

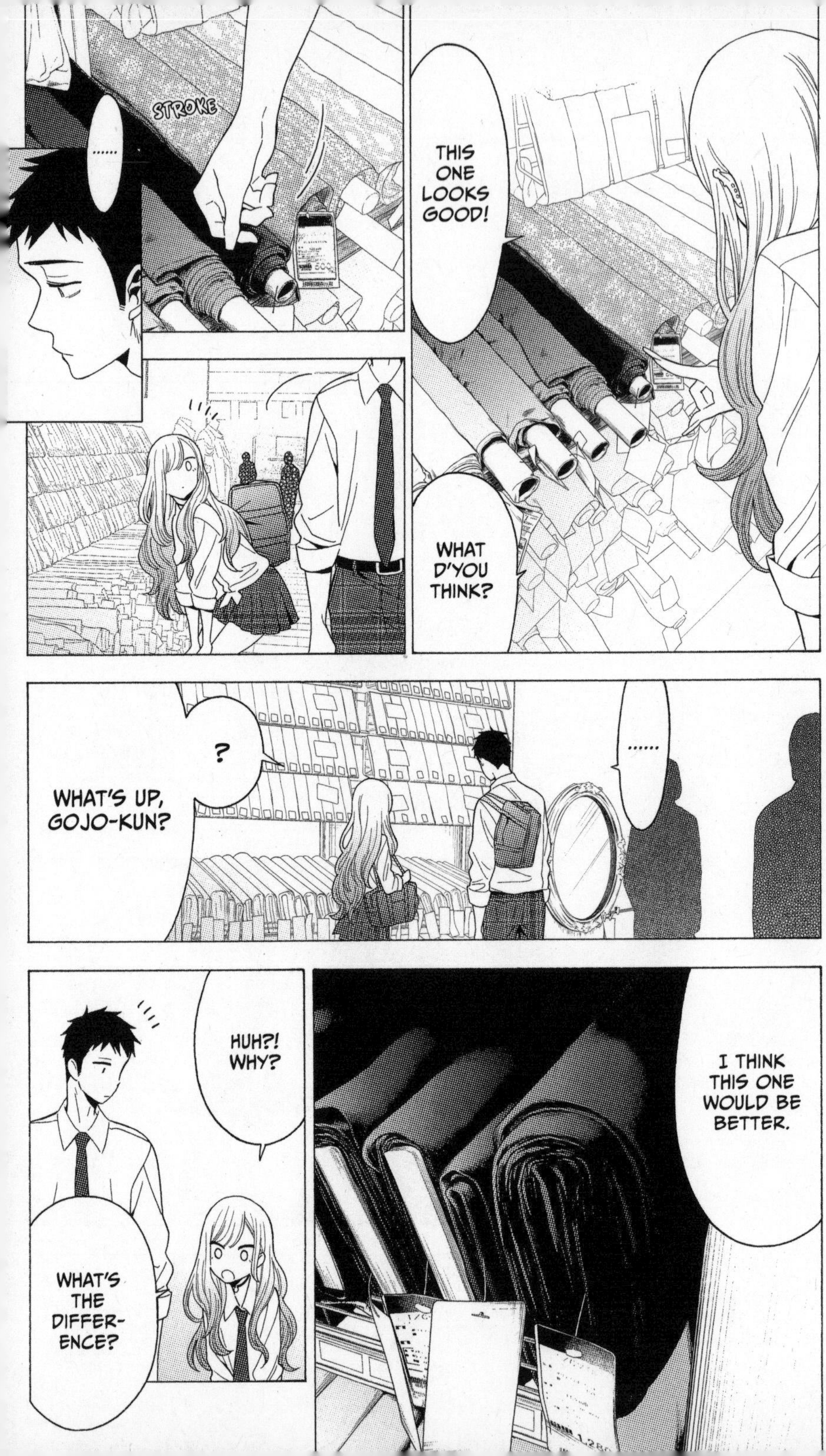
THIS ONE LOOKS GOOD!
WHAT D'YOU THINK?
STROKE
......
......
?
WHAT'S UP, GOJO-KUN?
I THINK THIS ONE WOULD BE BETTER.
HUH?! WHY?
WHAT'S THE DIFFER-ENCE?

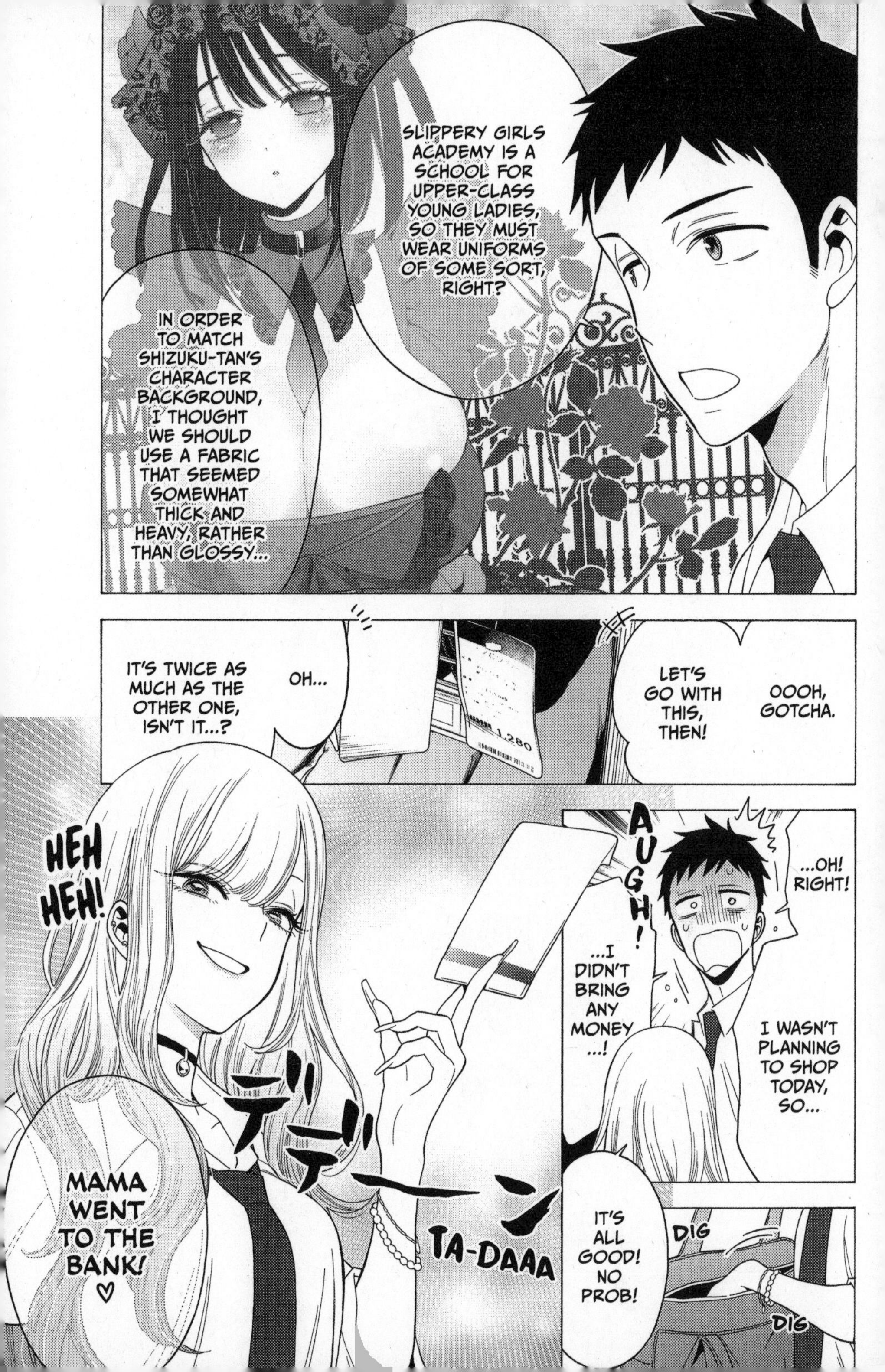
SLIPPERY GIRLS ACADEMY IS A SCHOOL FOR UPPER-CLASS YOUNG LADIES, SO THEY MUST WEAR UNIFORMS OF SOME SORT, RIGHT?
IN ORDER TO MATCH SHIZUKU-TAN'S CHARACTER BACKGROUND, I THOUGHT WE SHOULD USE A FABRIC THAT SEEMED SOMEWHAT THICK AND HEAVY, RATHER THAN GLOSSY...
OOOH, GOTCHA.
LET'S GO WITH THIS, THEN!
OH...
IT'S TWICE AS MUCH AS THE OTHER ONE, ISN'T IT...?
1,280
...OH! RIGHT!
AUGH!
...I DIDN'T BRING ANY MONEY ...!
I WASN'T PLANNING TO SHOP TODAY, SO...
DIG
DIG
IT'S ALL GOOD! NO PROB!
HEH HEH!
TA-DAAA
MAMA WENT TO THE BANK! ♡

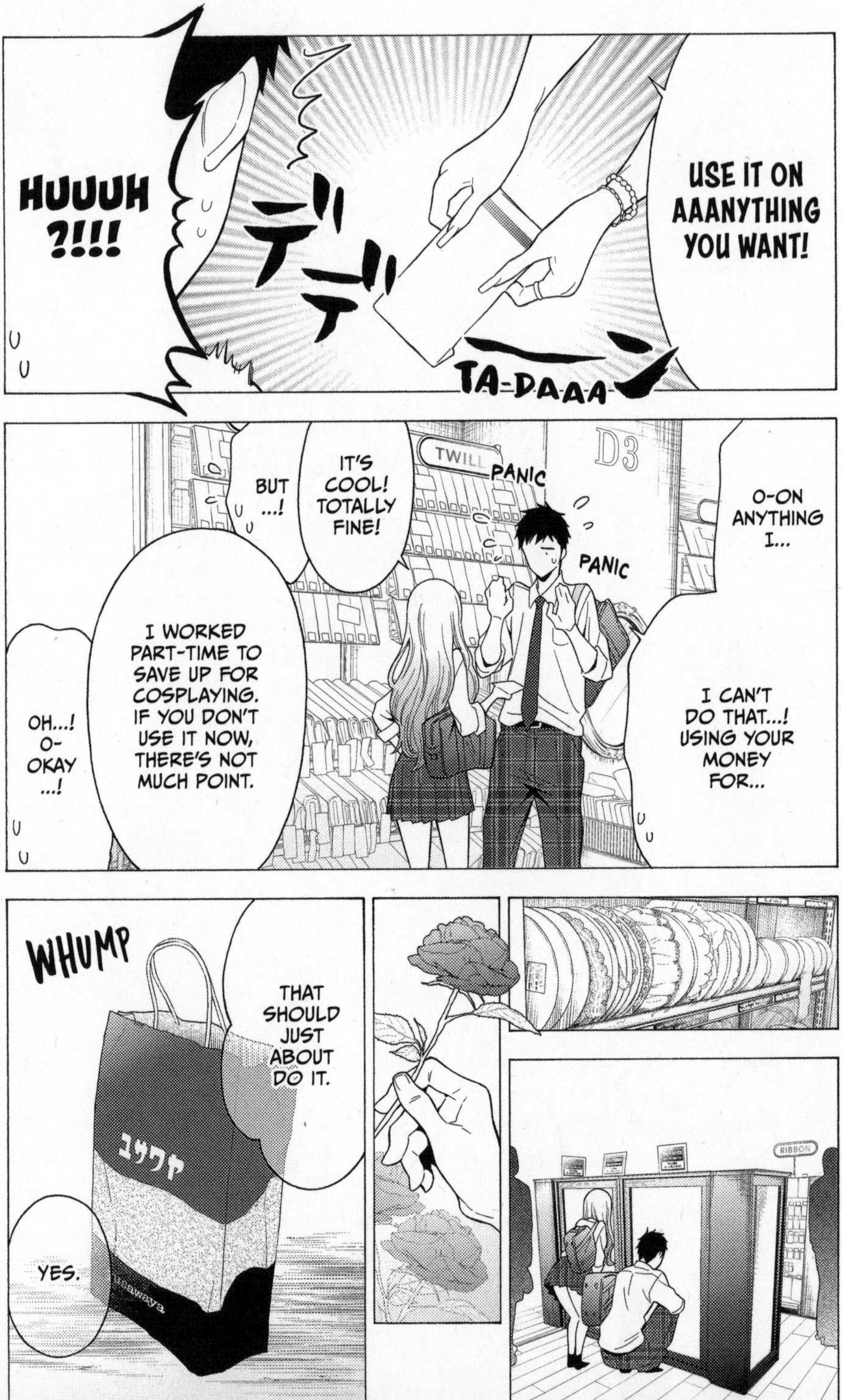
USE IT ON AAANYTHING YOU WANT!
TA-DAAA
HUUUH ?!!!
D3
TWILL
O-ON ANYTHING I...
I CAN'T DO THAT...! USING YOUR MONEY FOR...
PANIC
PANIC
IT'S COOL! TOTALLY FINE!
BUT ...!
I WORKED PART-TIME TO SAVE UP FOR COSPLAYING. IF YOU DON'T USE IT NOW, THERE'S NOT MUCH POINT.
OH...! O-OKAY ...!
RIBBON
THAT SHOULD JUST ABOUT DO IT.
WHUMP
ユザワヤ
YES.

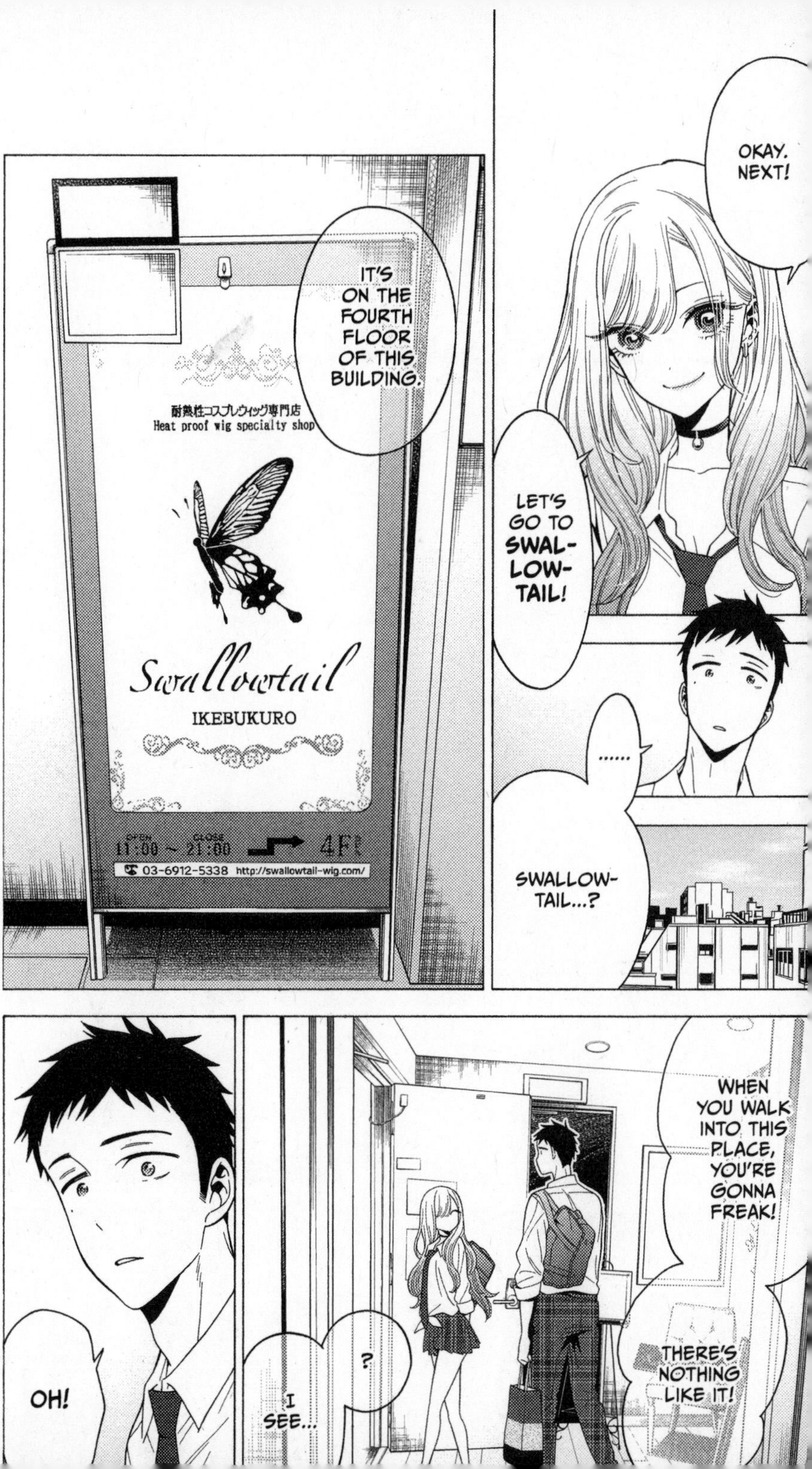
OKAY. NEXT!
LET'S GO TO SWAL-LOW-TAIL!
......
SWALLOW-TAIL...?
IT'S ON THE FOURTH FLOOR OF THIS BUILDING.
耐熱性コスプレウィッグ専門店
Heat proof wig specialty shop
Swallowtail
IKEBUKURO
OPEN 11:00 ~ CLOSE 21:00
4F
03-6912-5338 http://swallowtail-wig.com/
WHEN YOU WALK INTO THIS PLACE, YOU'RE GONNA FREAK!
THERE'S NOTHING LIKE IT!
?
I SEE...
OH!

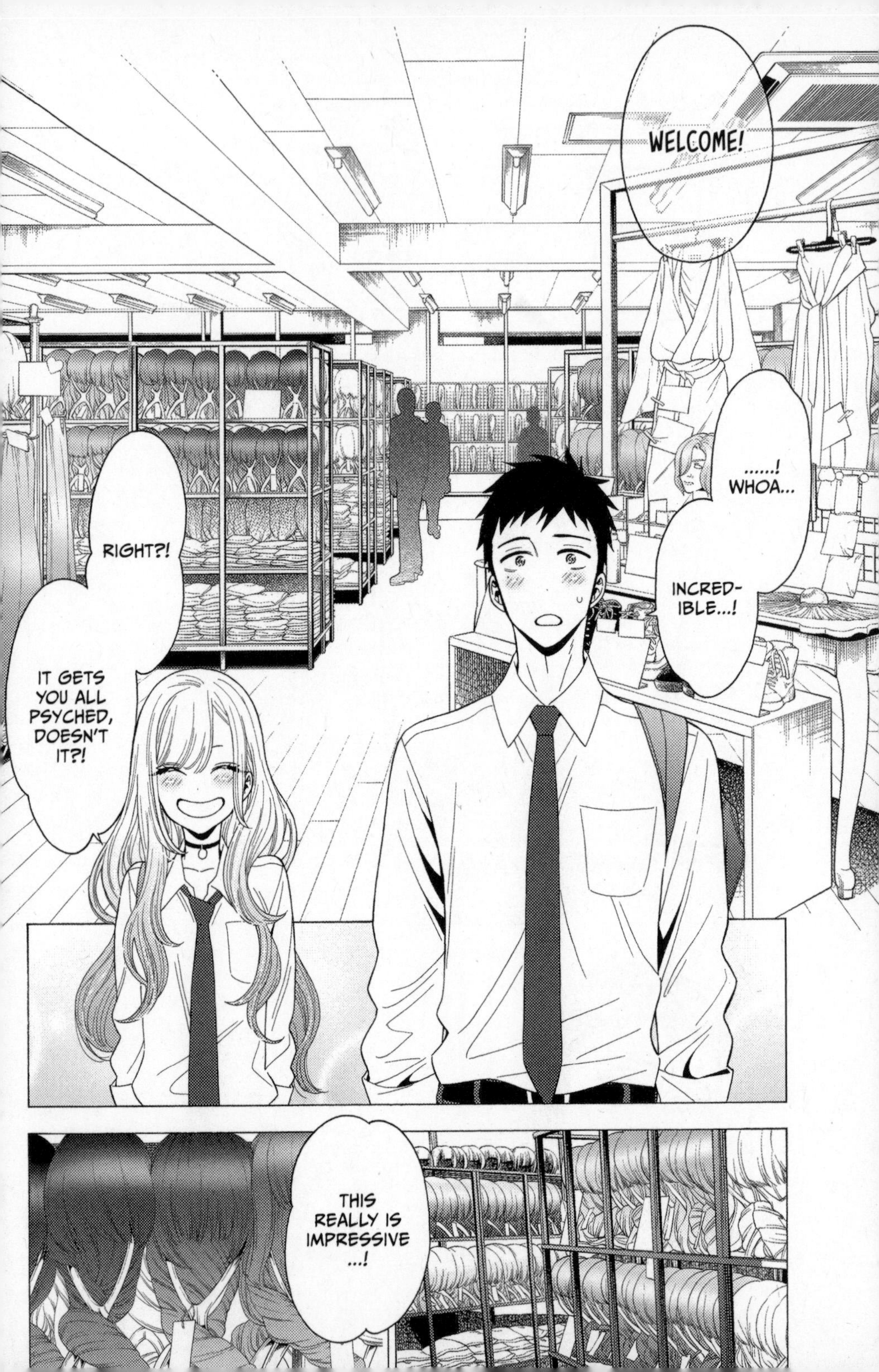
WELCOME!
......! WHOA...
INCRED-IBLE...!
RIGHT?!
IT GETS YOU ALL PSYCHED, DOESN'T IT?!
THIS REALLY IS IMPRESSIVE ...!

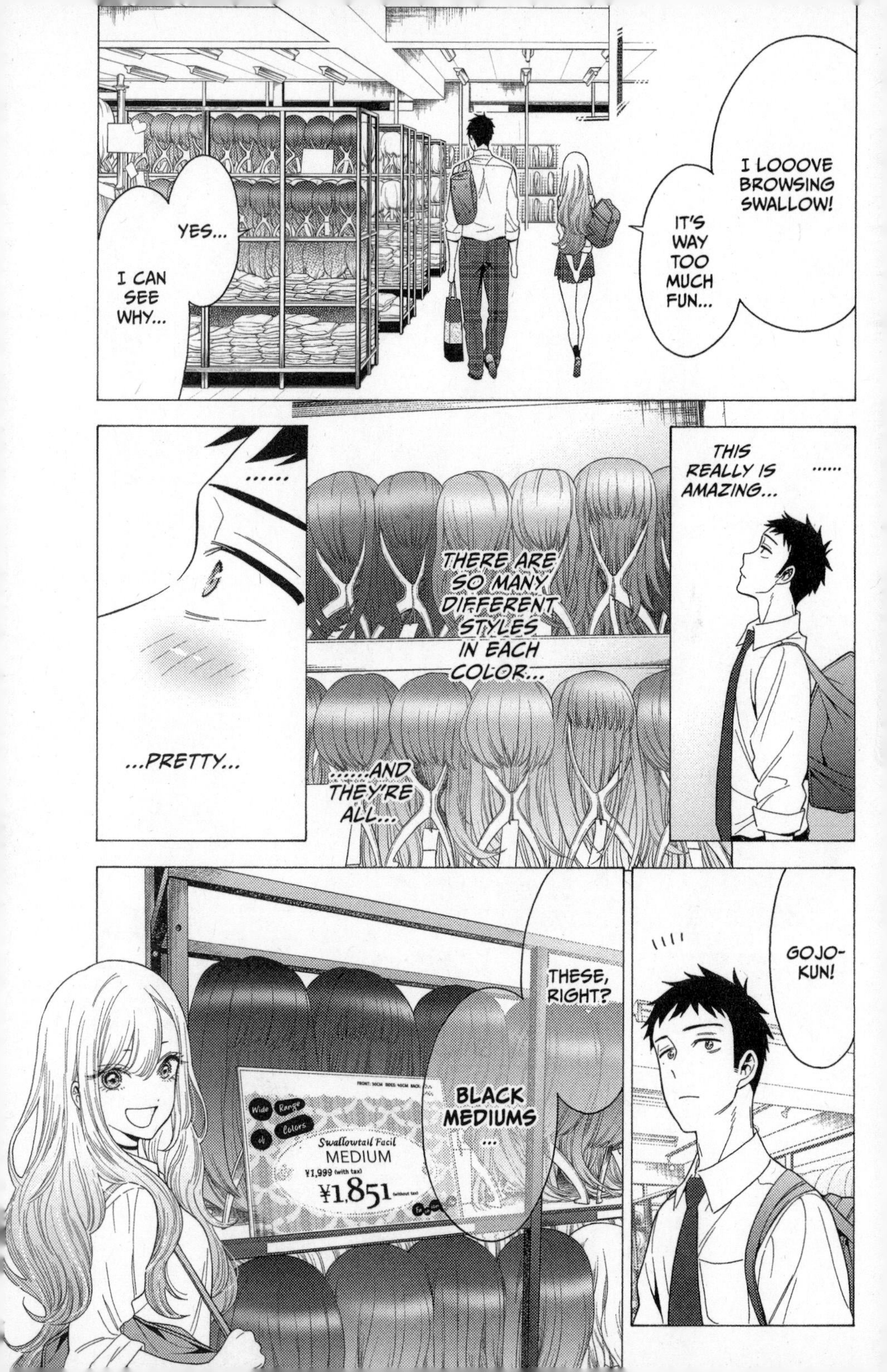
I LOOOVE BROWSING SWALLOW!
IT'S WAY TOO MUCH FUN...
YES...
I CAN SEE WHY...
THIS REALLY IS AMAZING...
......
THERE ARE SO MANY DIFFERENT STYLES IN EACH COLOR...
......AND THEY'RE ALL...
......
...PRETTY...
GOJO-KUN!
THESE, RIGHT?
BLACK MEDIUMS ...
Wide Range of Colors
Swallowtail Facil
MEDIUM
¥1,999 (with tax)
¥1,851 (without tax)

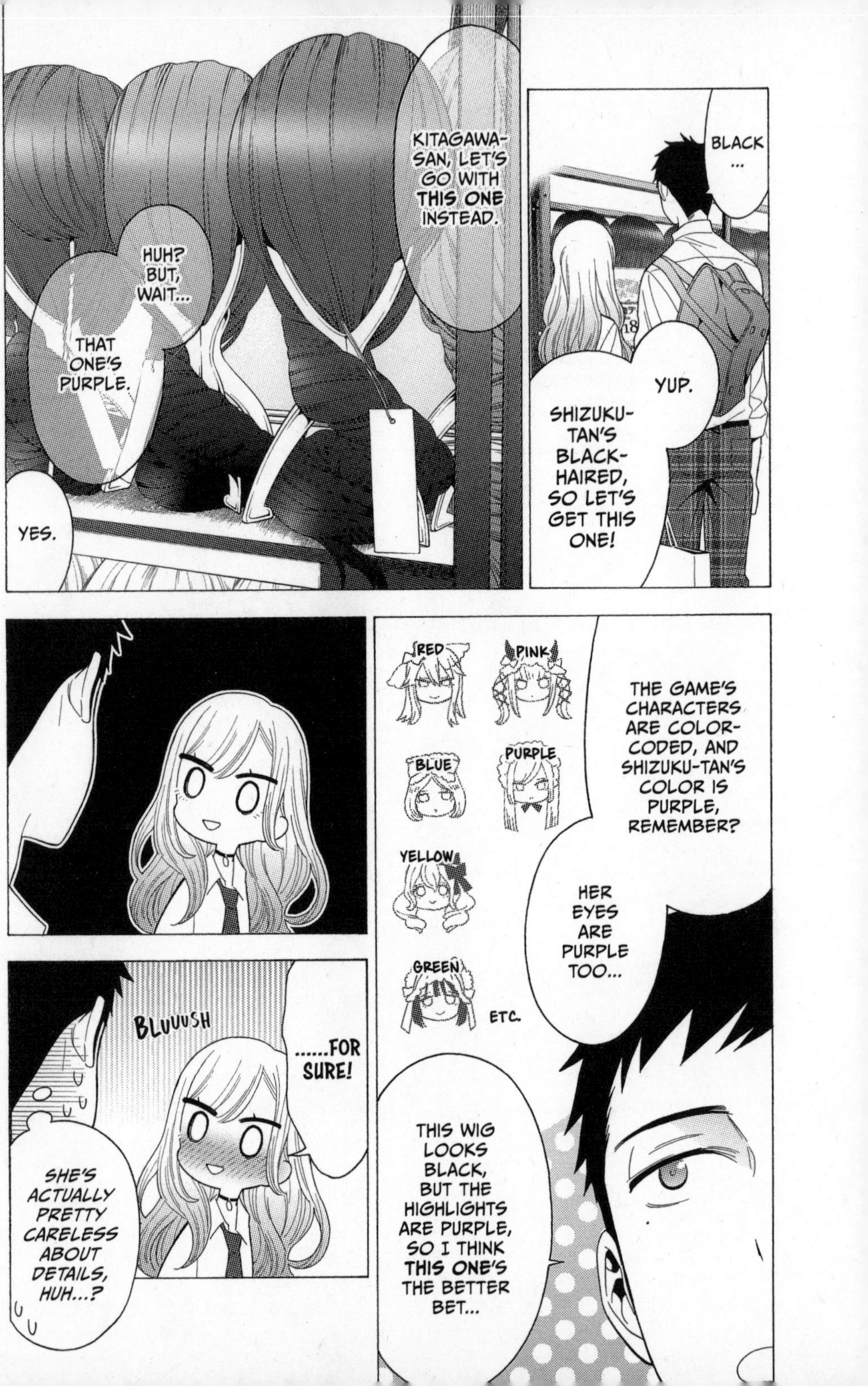
BLACK...
YUP.
SHIZUKU-TAN'S BLACK-HAIRED, SO LET'S GET THIS ONE!
KITAGAWA-SAN, LET'S GO WITH THIS ONE INSTEAD.
HUH? BUT, WAIT...
THAT ONE'S PURPLE.
YES.
THE GAME'S CHARACTERS ARE COLOR-CODED, AND SHIZUKU-TAN'S COLOR IS PURPLE, REMEMBER?
RED
PINK
BLUE
PURPLE
YELLOW
GREEN
ETC.
HER EYES ARE PURPLE TOO...
THIS WIG LOOKS BLACK, BUT THE HIGHLIGHTS ARE PURPLE, SO I THINK THIS ONE'S THE BETTER BET...
BLUUUSH
......FOR SURE!
SHE'S ACTUALLY PRETTY CARELESS ABOUT DETAILS, HUH...?

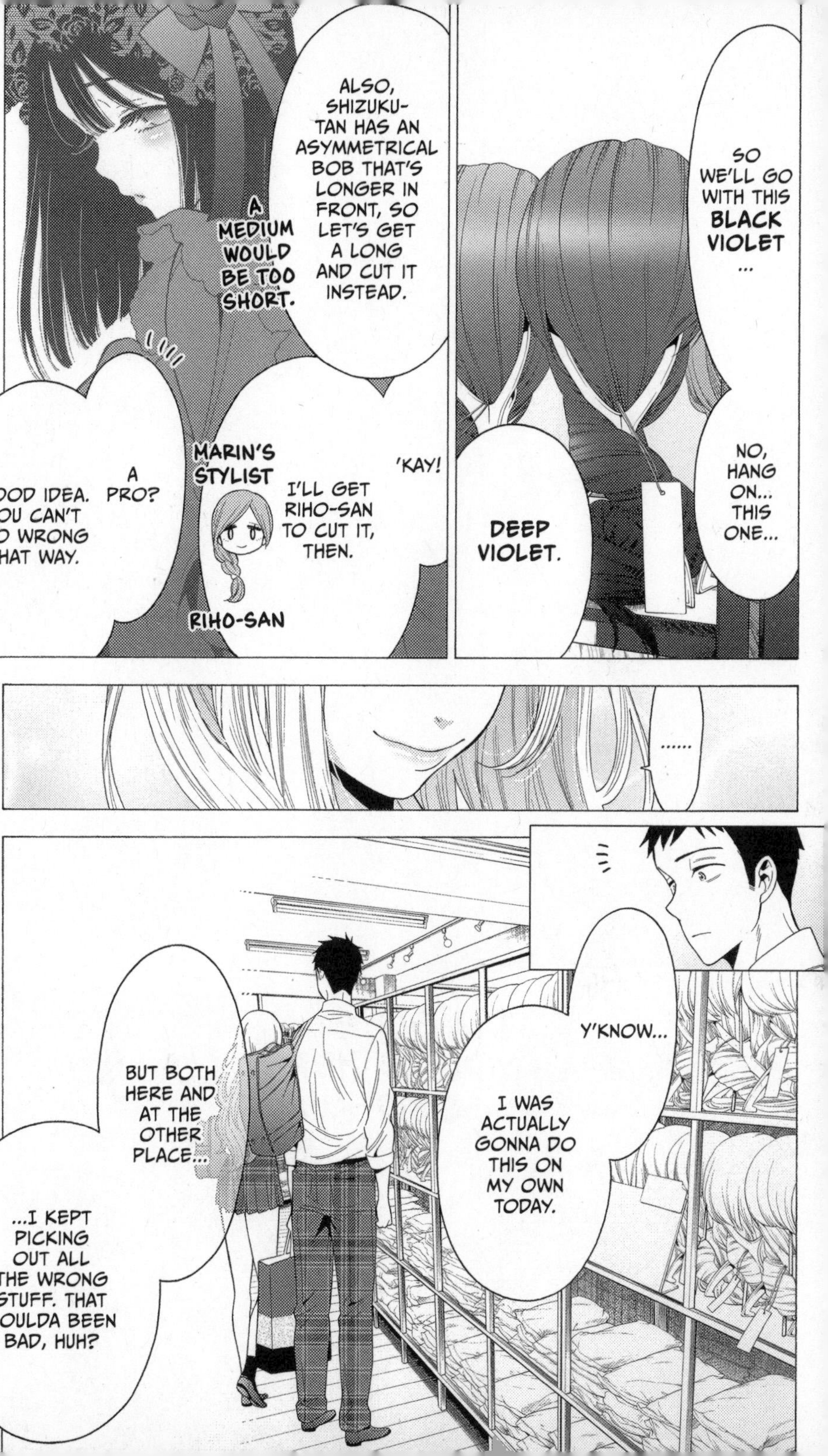
SO WE'LL GO WITH THIS BLACK VIOLET ...
NO, HANG ON... THIS ONE...
DEEP VIOLET.
ALSO, SHIZUKU-TAN HAS AN ASYMMETRICAL BOB THAT'S LONGER IN FRONT, SO LET'S GET A LONG AND CUT IT INSTEAD.
A MEDIUM WOULD BE TOO SHORT.
'KAY!
I'LL GET RIHO-SAN TO CUT IT, THEN.
MARIN'S STYLIST
RIHO-SAN
A PRO?
GOOD IDEA. YOU CAN'T GO WRONG THAT WAY.
......
Y'KNOW...
I WAS ACTUALLY GONNA DO THIS ON MY OWN TODAY.
BUT BOTH HERE AND AT THE OTHER PLACE...
...I KEPT PICKING OUT ALL THE WRONG STUFF. THAT COULDA BEEN BAD, HUH?

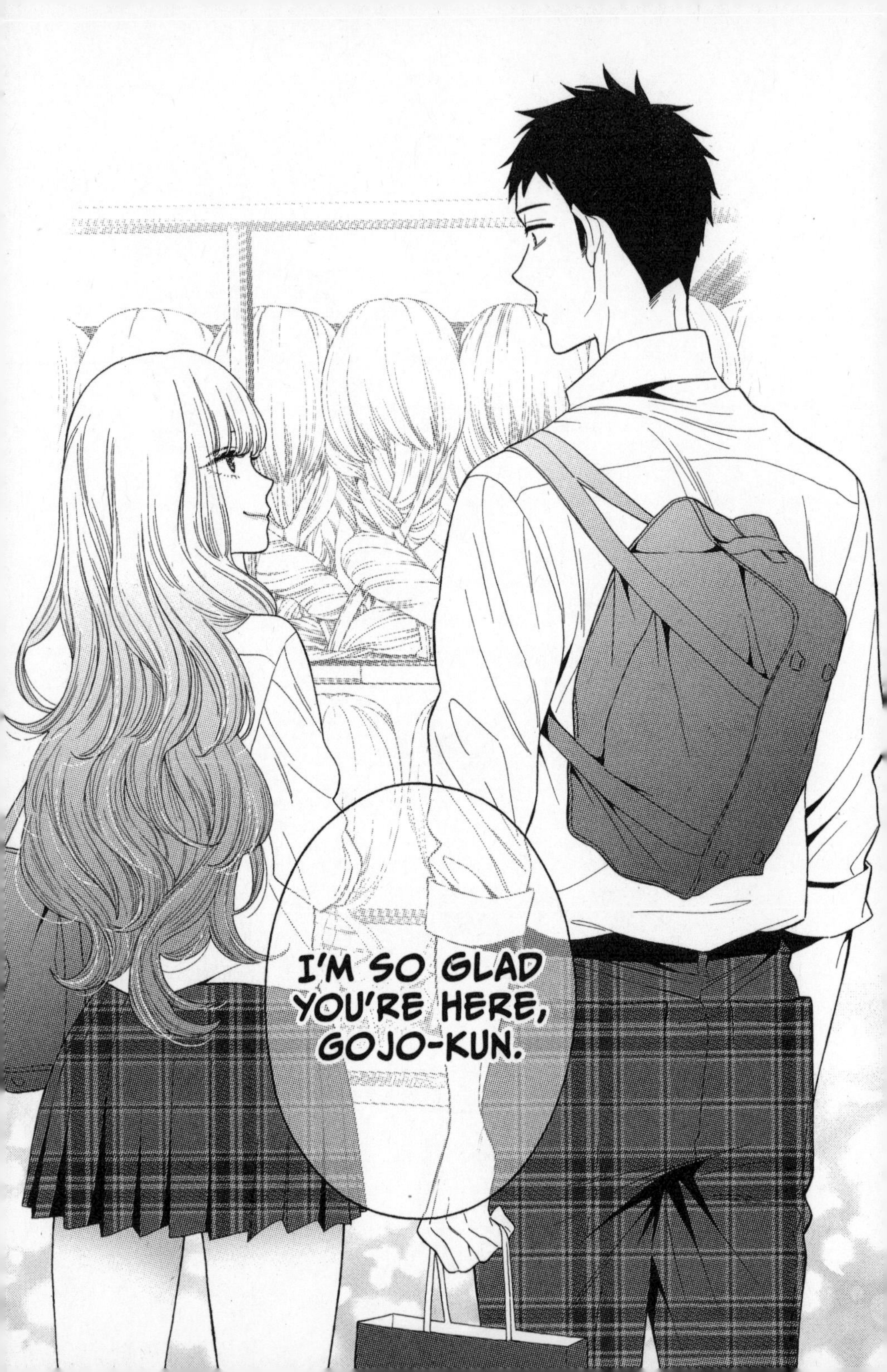
I'M SO GLAD YOU'RE HERE, GOJO-KUN.

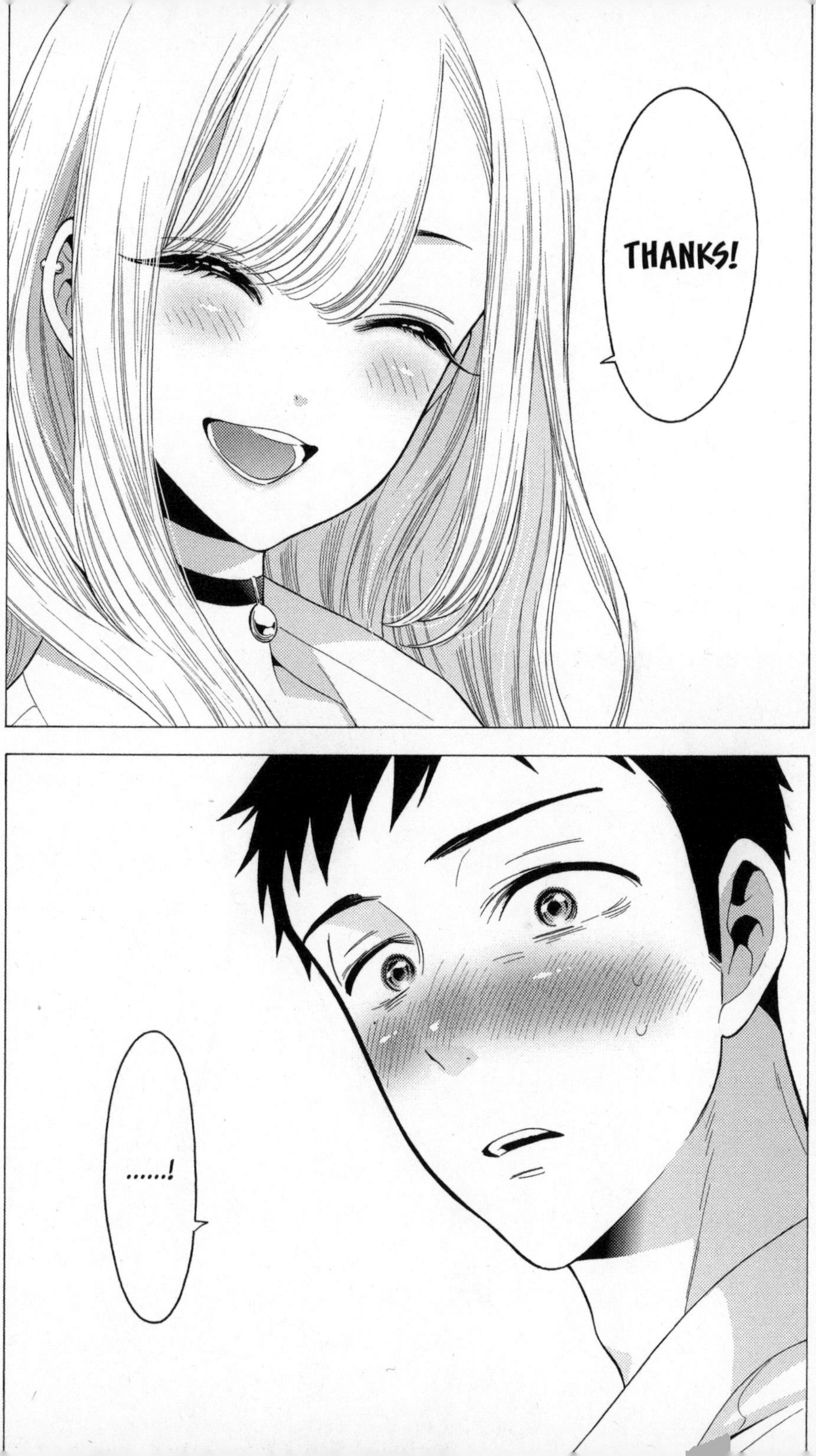
THANKS!
......!

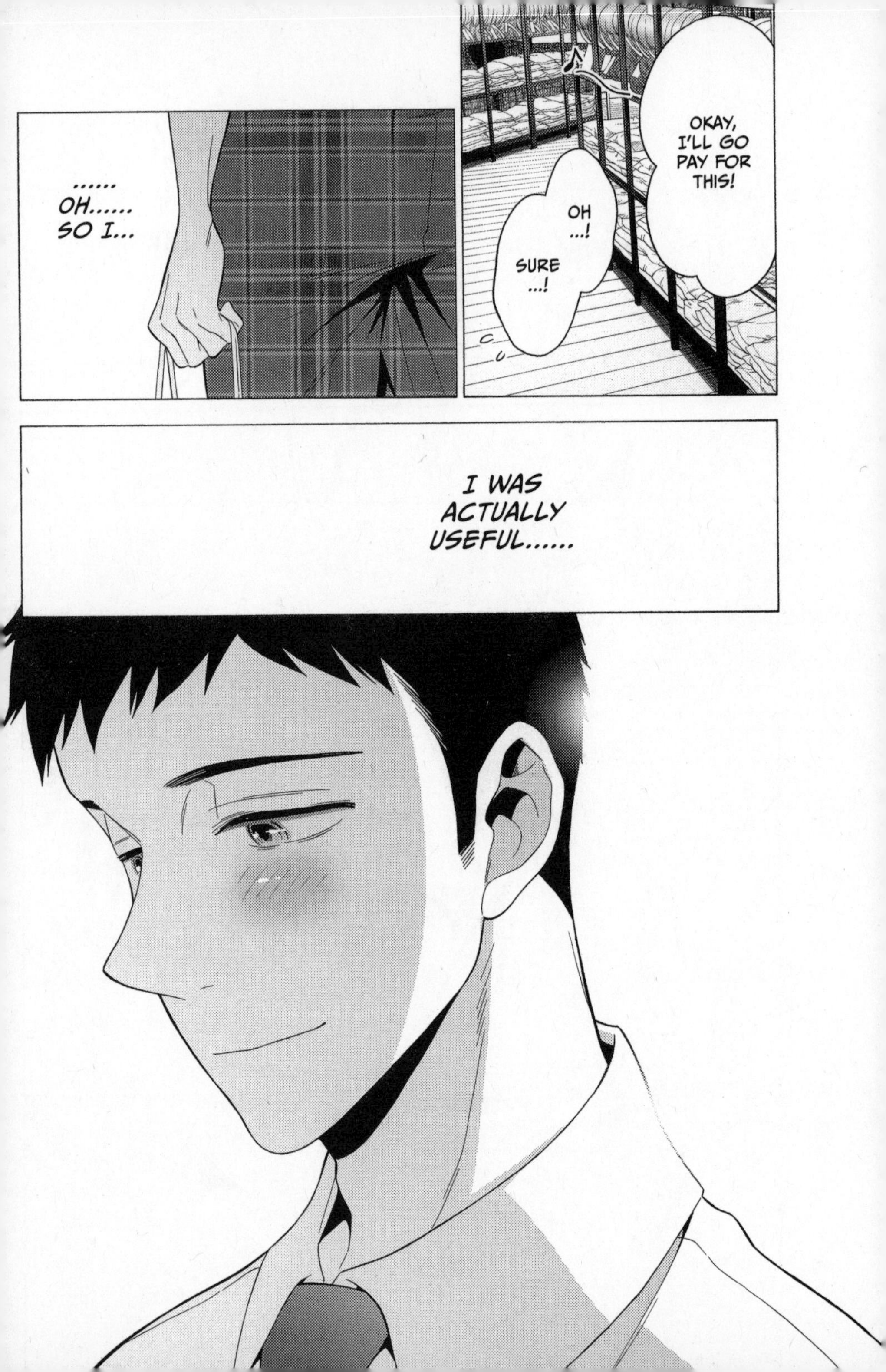
OKAY, I'LL GO PAY FOR THIS!
OH ...!
SURE ...!
...... OH...... SO I...
I WAS ACTUALLY USEFUL......

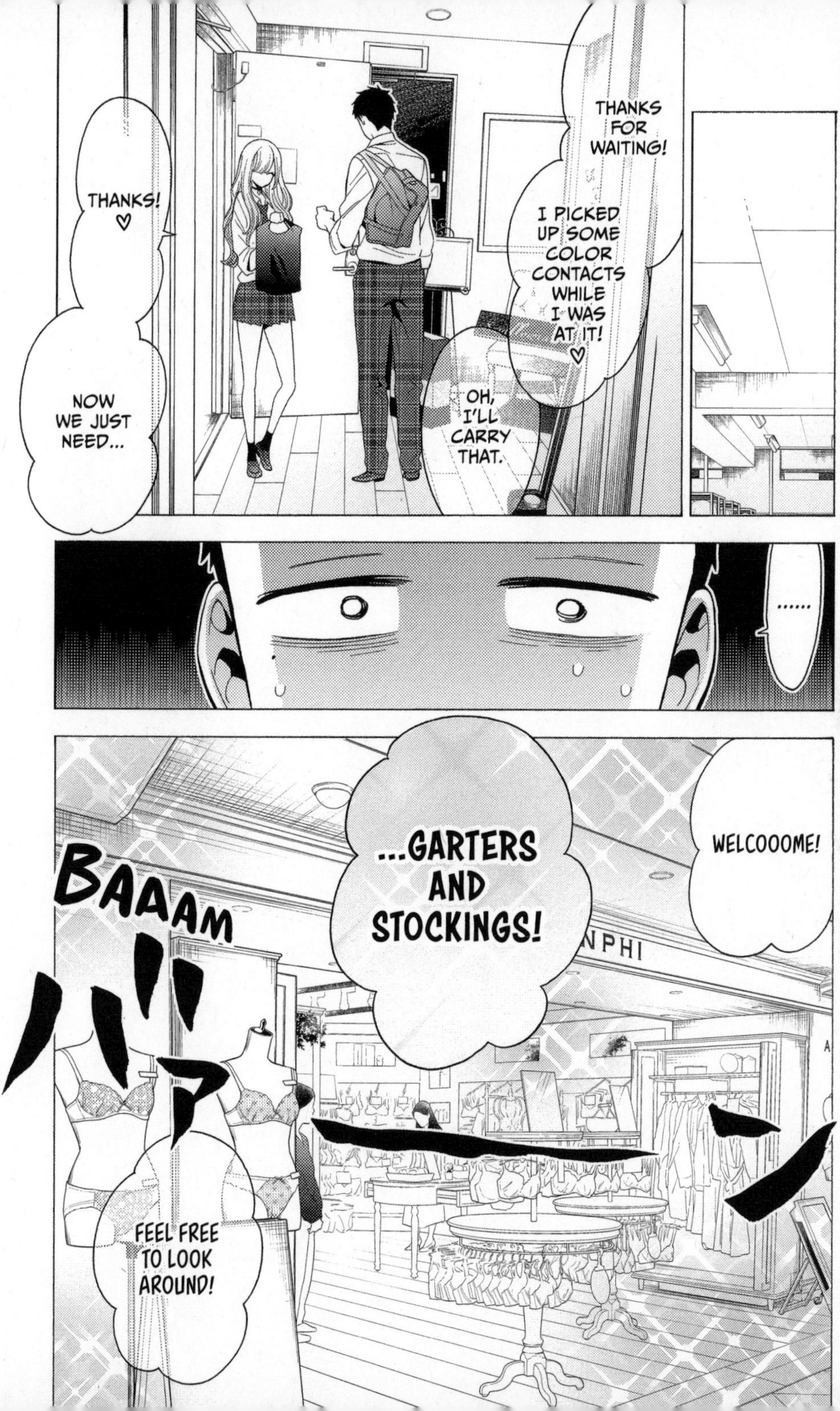
THANKS FOR WAITING!
I PICKED UP SOME COLOR CONTACTS WHILE I WAS AT IT! ♡
OH, I'LL CARRY THAT.
THANKS! ♡
NOW WE JUST NEED...
......
WELCOOOME!
...GARTERS AND STOCKINGS!
BAAAM
FEEL FREE TO LOOK AROUND!

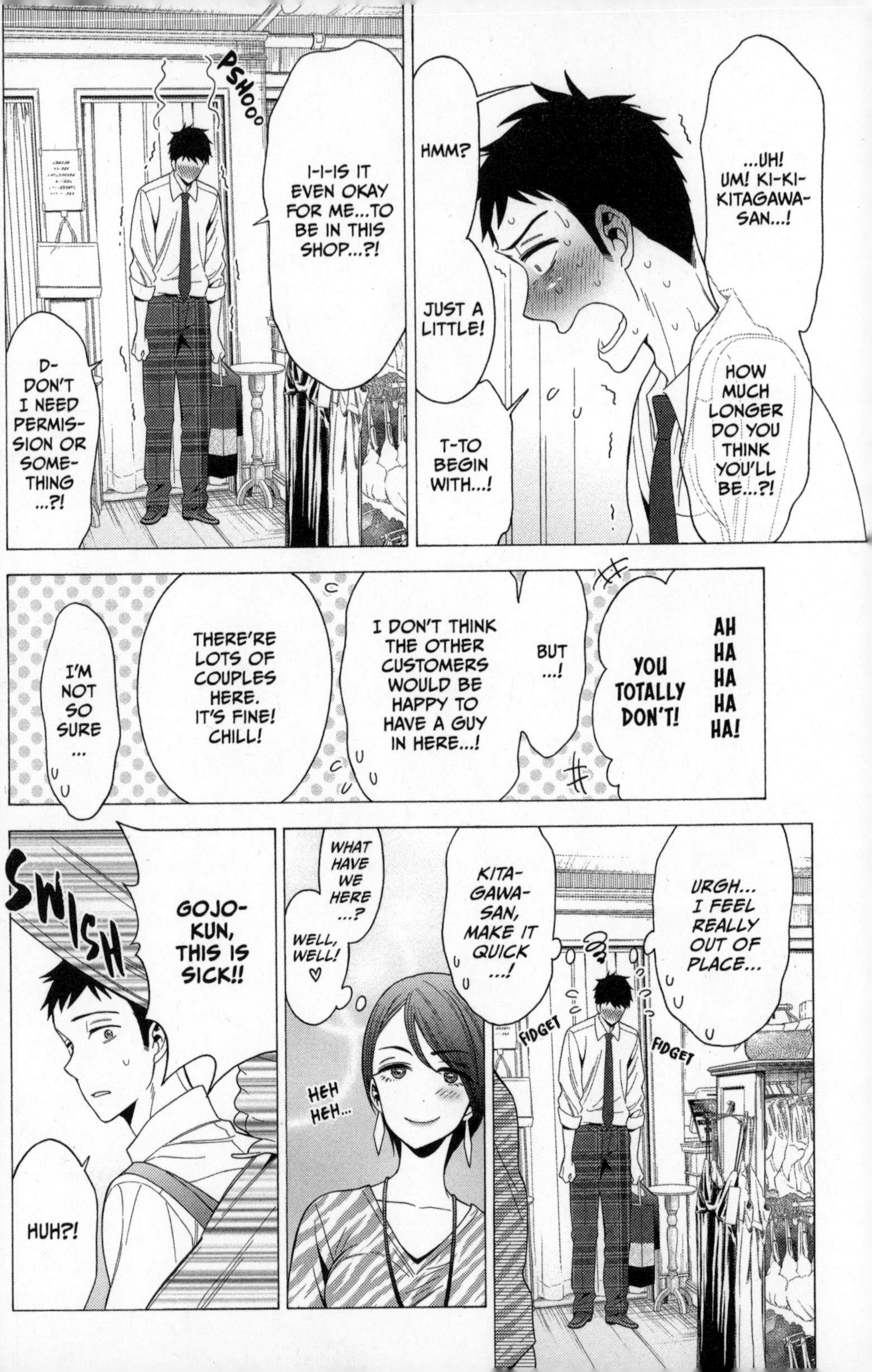
...UH! UM! KI-KI-KITAGAWA-SAN...!
HMM?
HOW MUCH LONGER DO YOU THINK YOU'LL BE...?!
JUST A LITTLE!
T-TO BEGIN WITH...!
PSHOOO
I-I-IS IT EVEN OKAY FOR ME...TO BE IN THIS SHOP...?!
D-DON'T I NEED PERMISSION OR SOMETHING...?!
AH HA HA HA HA HA!
YOU TOTALLY DON'T!
BUT...!
I DON'T THINK THE OTHER CUSTOMERS WOULD BE HAPPY TO HAVE A GUY IN HERE...!
THERE'RE LOTS OF COUPLES HERE. IT'S FINE! CHILL!
I'M NOT SO SURE...
URGH... I FEEL REALLY OUT OF PLACE...
KITA-GAWA-SAN, MAKE IT QUICK...!
FIDGET
FIDGET
WHAT HAVE WE HERE...?
WELL, WELL! ♡
HEH HEH...
SWISH
GOJO-KUN, THIS IS SICK!!
HUH?!

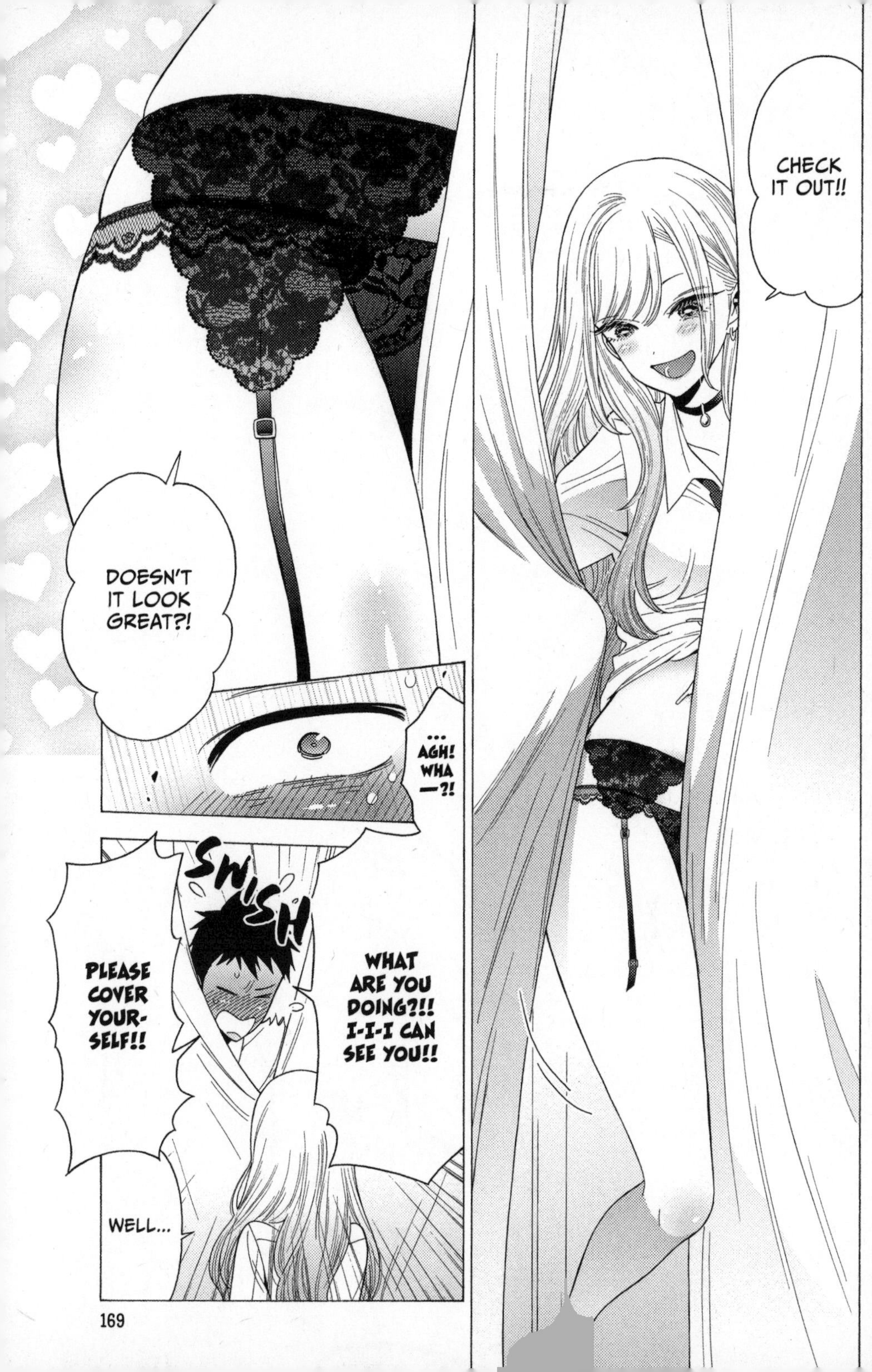
CHECK IT OUT!!
DOESN'T IT LOOK GREAT?!
...AGH! WHA—?!
SWISH
WHAT ARE YOU DOING?!! I-I-I CAN SEE YOU!!
PLEASE COVER YOUR-SELF!!
WELL...

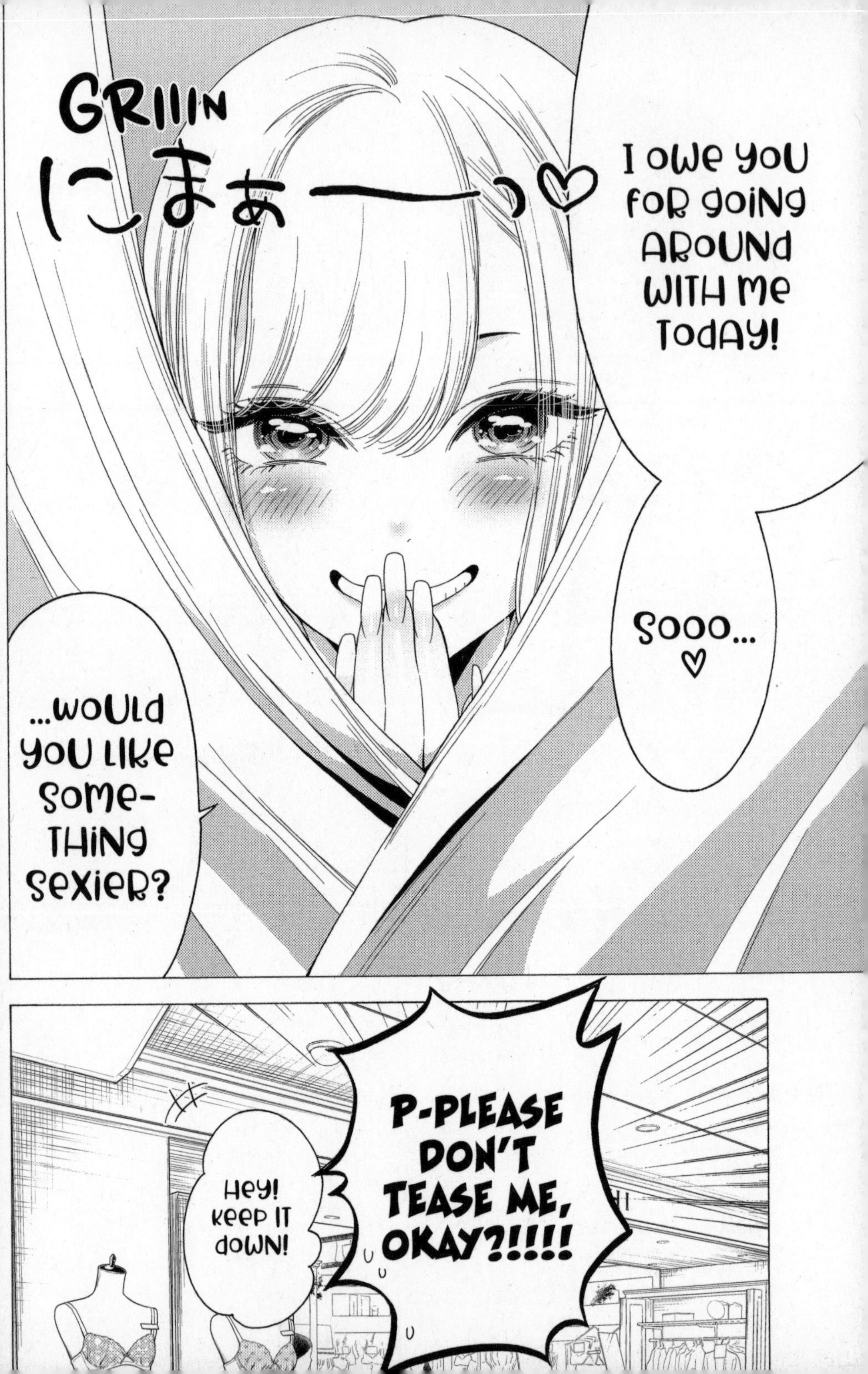
I OWE YOU FOR GOING AROUND WITH ME TODAY!
GRIIIN
にまぁーーっ♡
SOOO... ♡
...WOULD YOU LIKE SOME-THING SEXIER?
P-PLEASE DON'T TEASE ME, OKAY?!!!!!
HEY! KEEP IT DOWN!

My DRESS-UP Darling

CHAPTER 7

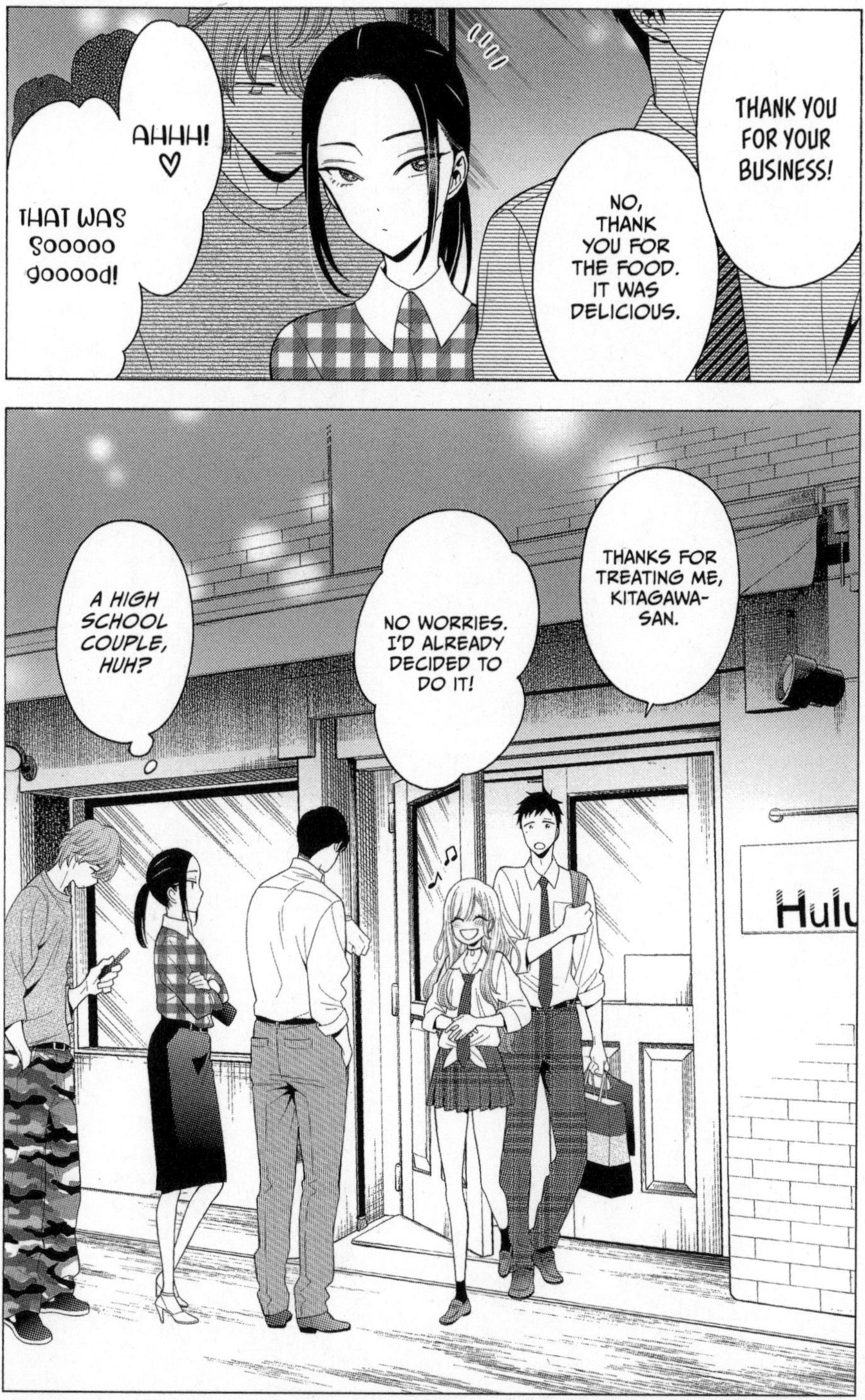
THANK YOU FOR YOUR BUSINESS!
NO, THANK YOU FOR THE FOOD. IT WAS DELICIOUS.
AHHH! ♡
THAT WAS Sooooo gooood!
THANKS FOR TREATING ME, KITAGAWA-SAN.
NO WORRIES. I'D ALREADY DECIDED TO DO IT!
A HIGH SCHOOL COUPLE, HUH?
Hulu

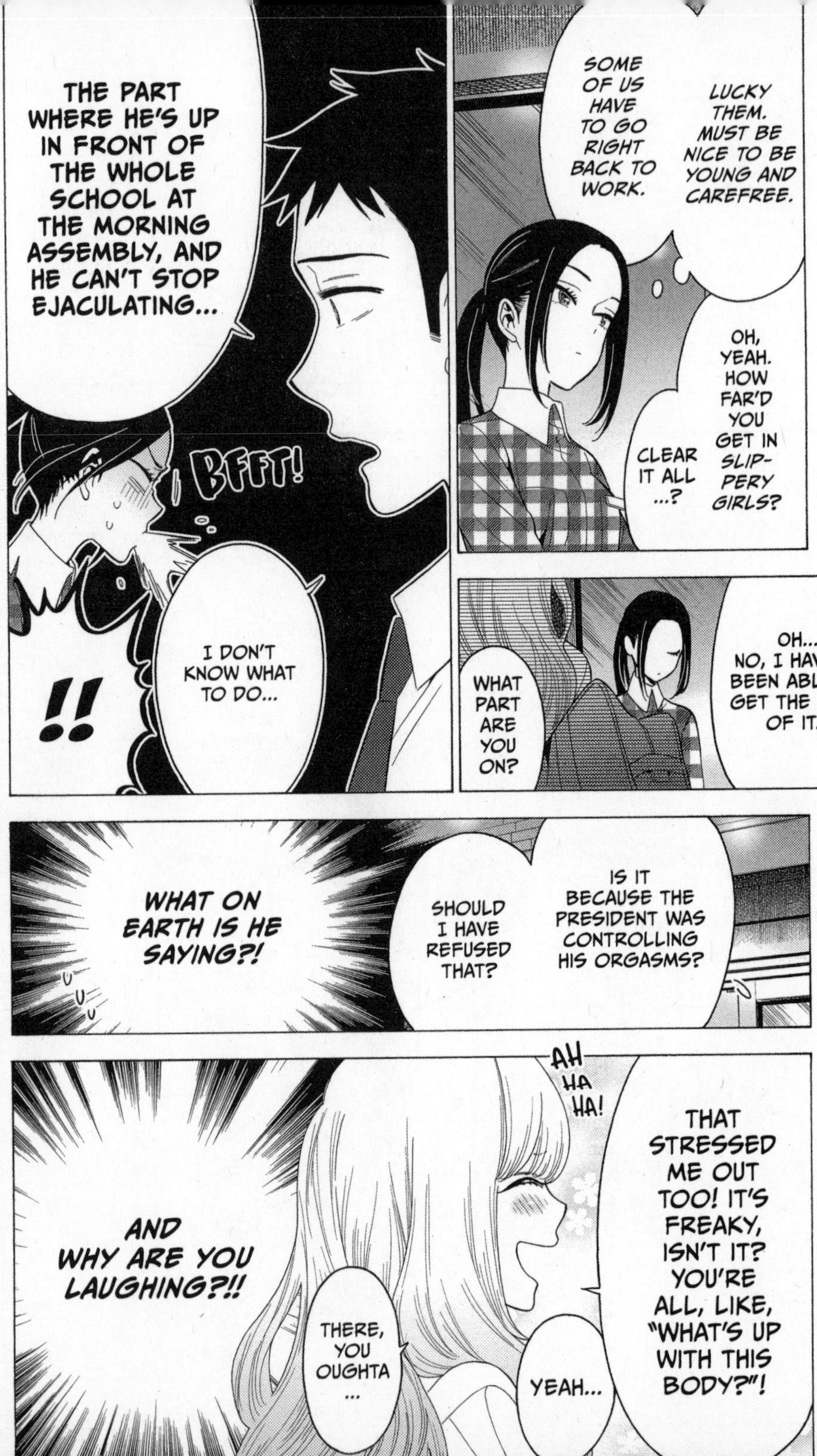
LUCKY THEM. MUST BE NICE TO BE YOUNG AND CAREFREE.
SOME OF US HAVE TO GO RIGHT BACK TO WORK.
OH, YEAH. HOW FAR'D YOU GET IN SLIP-PERY GIRLS?
CLEAR IT ALL ...?
OH... NO, I HAVEN'T BEEN ABLE TO GET THE HANG OF IT...
WHAT PART ARE YOU ON?
THE PART WHERE HE'S UP IN FRONT OF THE WHOLE SCHOOL AT THE MORNING ASSEMBLY, AND HE CAN'T STOP EJACULATING...
BFFT!
I DON'T KNOW WHAT TO DO...
!!
IS IT BECAUSE THE PRESIDENT WAS CONTROLLING HIS ORGASMS?
SHOULD I HAVE REFUSED THAT?
WHAT ON EARTH IS HE SAYING?!
AH HA HA!
THAT STRESSED ME OUT TOO! IT'S FREAKY, ISN'T IT? YOU'RE ALL, LIKE, "WHAT'S UP WITH THIS BODY?"!
YEAH...
THERE, YOU OUGHTA ...
AND WHY ARE YOU LAUGHING?!!

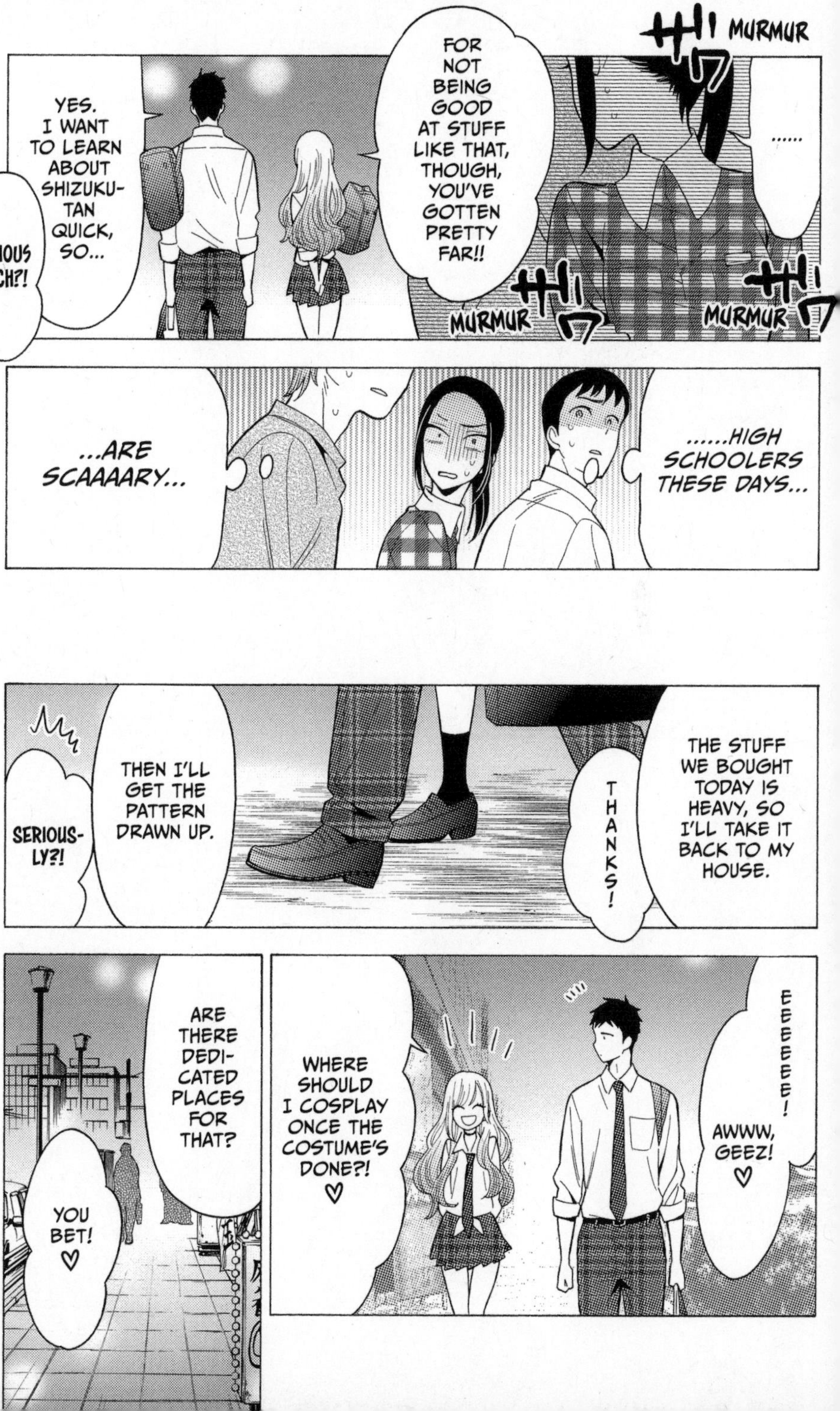
MURMUR
......
MURMUR
MURMUR
FOR NOT BEING GOOD AT STUFF LIKE THAT, THOUGH, YOU'VE GOTTEN PRETTY FAR!!
YES. I WANT TO LEARN ABOUT SHIZUKU-TAN QUICK, SO...
SERIOUS MUCH?!
......HIGH SCHOOLERS THESE DAYS...
...ARE SCAAAARY...
THE STUFF WE BOUGHT TODAY IS HEAVY, SO I'LL TAKE IT BACK TO MY HOUSE.
THANKS!
THEN I'LL GET THE PATTERN DRAWN UP.
SERIOUS-LY?!
EEEEEEE!
AWWW, GEEZ! ♡
WHERE SHOULD I COSPLAY ONCE THE COSTUME'S DONE?! ♡
ARE THERE DEDICATED PLACES FOR THAT?
YOU BET! ♡

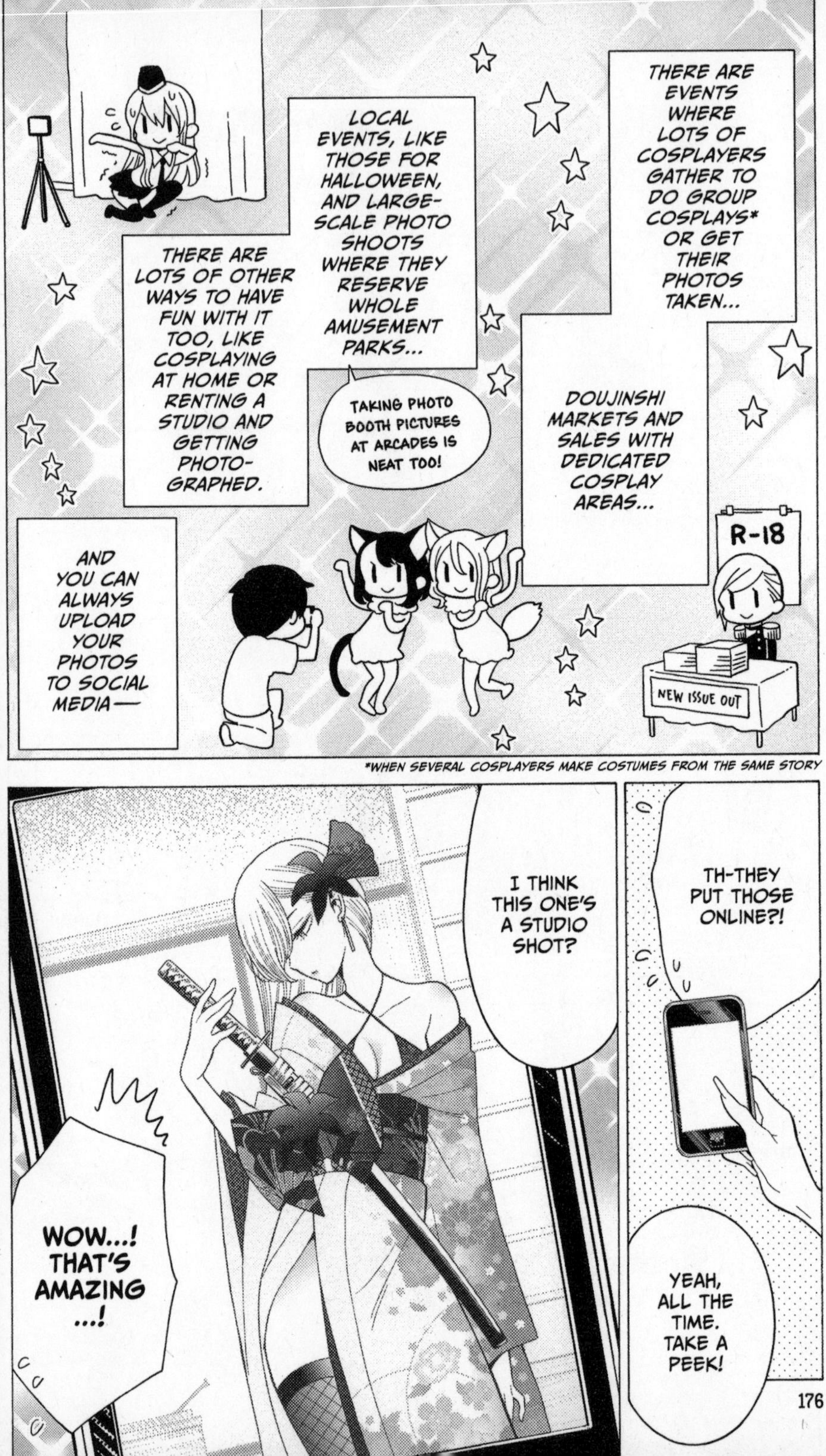
THERE ARE EVENTS WHERE LOTS OF COSPLAYERS GATHER TO DO GROUP COSPLAYS* OR GET THEIR PHOTOS TAKEN...
LOCAL EVENTS, LIKE THOSE FOR HALLOWEEN, AND LARGE-SCALE PHOTO SHOOTS WHERE THEY RESERVE WHOLE AMUSEMENT PARKS...
THERE ARE LOTS OF OTHER WAYS TO HAVE FUN WITH IT TOO, LIKE COSPLAYING AT HOME OR RENTING A STUDIO AND GETTING PHOTO-GRAPHED.
DOUJINSHI MARKETS AND SALES WITH DEDICATED COSPLAY AREAS...
TAKING PHOTO BOOTH PICTURES AT ARCADES IS NEAT TOO!
R-18
NEW ISSUE OUT
AND YOU CAN ALWAYS UPLOAD YOUR PHOTOS TO SOCIAL MEDIA—
TH-THEY PUT THOSE ONLINE?!
YEAH, ALL THE TIME. TAKE A PEEK!
I THINK THIS ONE'S A STUDIO SHOT?
WOW...! THAT'S AMAZING...!

*WHEN SEVERAL COSPLAYERS MAKE COSTUMES FROM THE SAME STORY

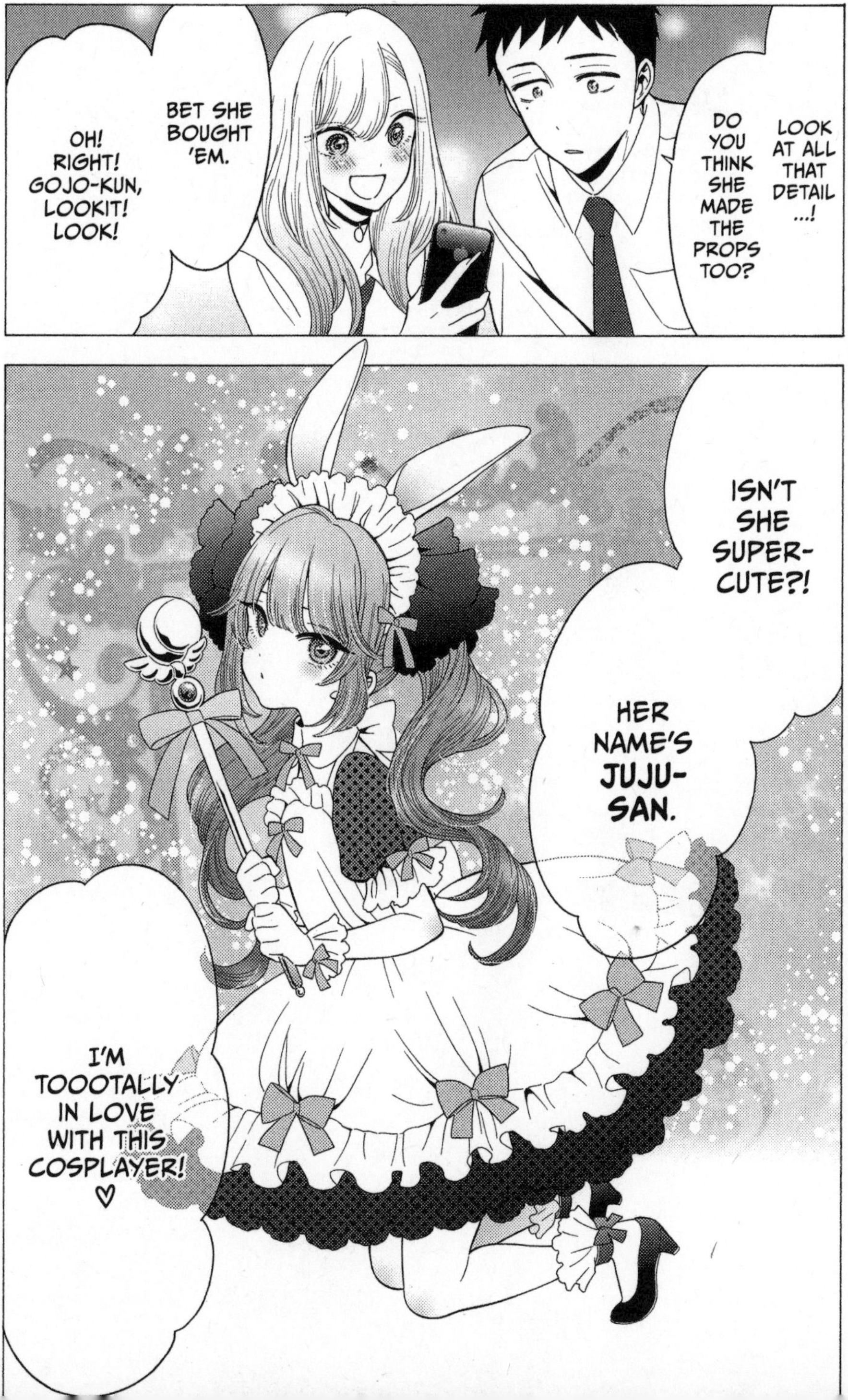
LOOK AT ALL THAT DETAIL ...!
DO YOU THINK SHE MADE THE PROPS TOO?
BET SHE BOUGHT 'EM.
OH! RIGHT! GOJO-KUN, LOOKIT! LOOK!
ISN'T SHE SUPER-CUTE?!
HER NAME'S JUJU-SAN.
I'M TOOOTALLY IN LOVE WITH THIS COSPLAYER! ♡

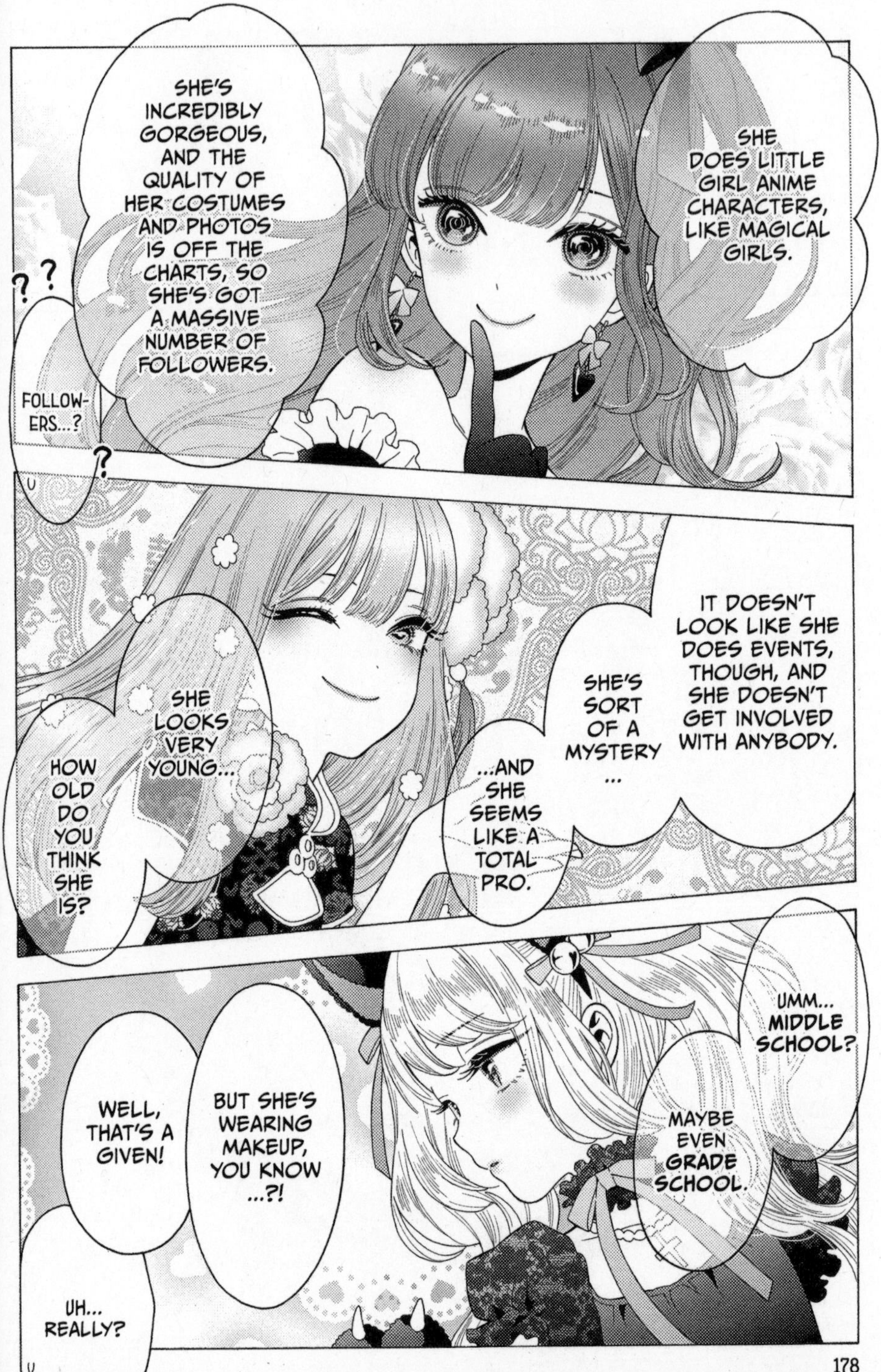
SHE DOES LITTLE GIRL ANIME CHARACTERS, LIKE MAGICAL GIRLS.
SHE'S INCREDIBLY GORGEOUS, AND THE QUALITY OF HER COSTUMES AND PHOTOS IS OFF THE CHARTS, SO SHE'S GOT A MASSIVE NUMBER OF FOLLOWERS.
? ?
FOLLOW-ERS...?
?
IT DOESN'T LOOK LIKE SHE DOES EVENTS, THOUGH, AND SHE DOESN'T GET INVOLVED WITH ANYBODY.
SHE'S SORT OF A MYSTERY ...
...AND SHE SEEMS LIKE A TOTAL PRO.
SHE LOOKS VERY YOUNG...
HOW OLD DO YOU THINK SHE IS?
UMM... MIDDLE SCHOOL?
MAYBE EVEN GRADE SCHOOL.
BUT SHE'S WEARING MAKEUP, YOU KNOW ...?!
WELL, THAT'S A GIVEN!
UH... REALLY?

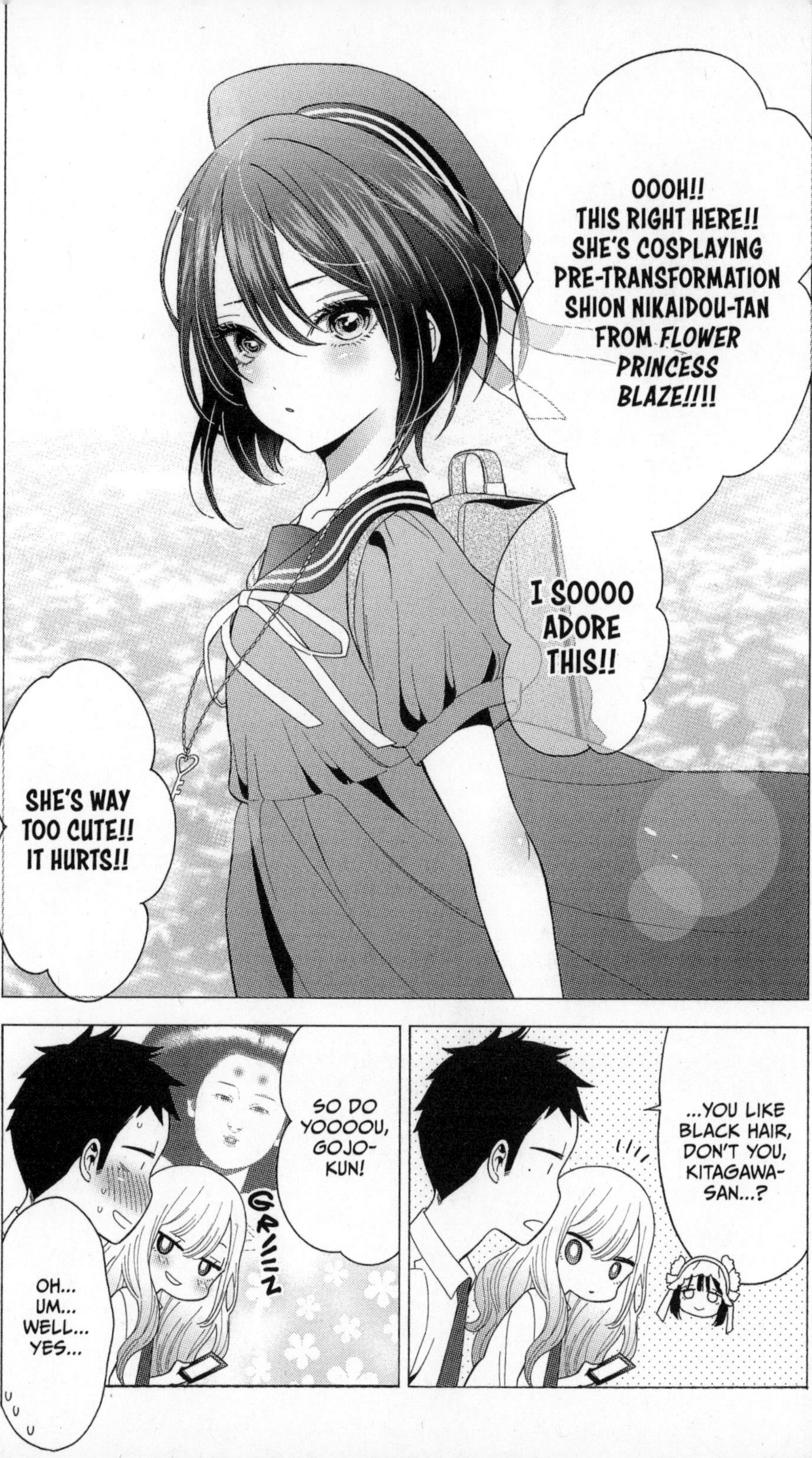
OOOH!! THIS RIGHT HERE!! SHE'S COSPLAYING PRE-TRANSFORMATION SHION NIKAIDOU-TAN FROM *FLOWER PRINCESS BLAZE*!!!!
I SOOOO ADORE THIS!!
SHE'S WAY TOO CUTE!! IT HURTS!!
...YOU LIKE BLACK HAIR, DON'T YOU, KITAGAWA-SAN...?
SO DO YOOOOU, GOJO-KUN!
GRIIIN
OH... UM... WELL... YES...

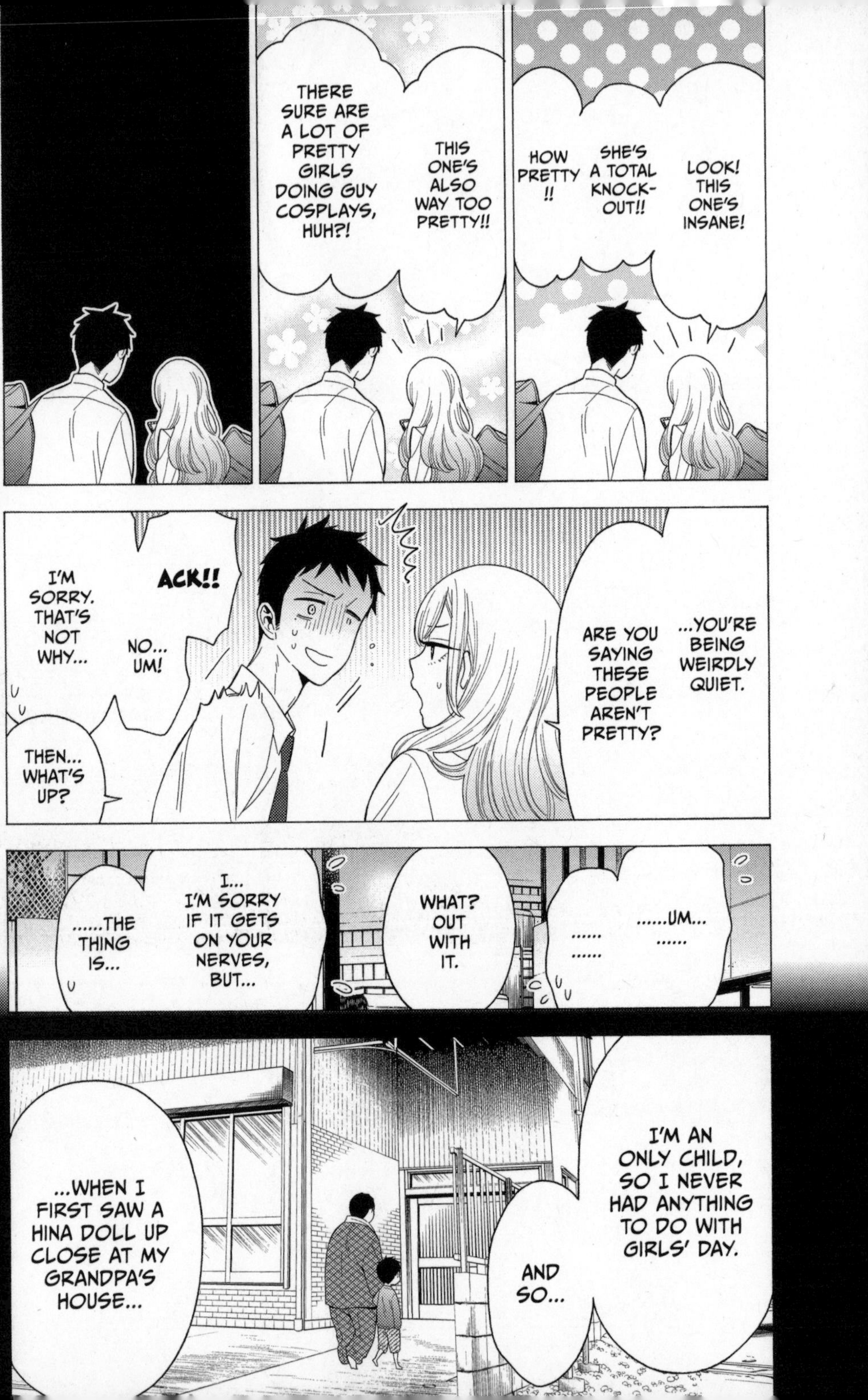
LOOK! THIS ONE'S INSANE!
SHE'S A TOTAL KNOCK-OUT!!
HOW PRETTY !!
THIS ONE'S ALSO WAY TOO PRETTY!!
THERE SURE ARE A LOT OF PRETTY GIRLS DOING GUY COSPLAYS, HUH?!
...YOU'RE BEING WEIRDLY QUIET.
ARE YOU SAYING THESE PEOPLE AREN'T PRETTY?
ACK!!
NO... UM!
I'M SORRY. THAT'S NOT WHY...
THEN... WHAT'S UP?
......UM... ......
....
WHAT? OUT WITH IT.
I... I'M SORRY IF IT GETS ON YOUR NERVES, BUT...
......THE THING IS...
I'M AN ONLY CHILD, SO I NEVER HAD ANYTHING TO DO WITH GIRLS' DAY.
AND SO...
...WHEN I FIRST SAW A HINA DOLL UP CLOSE AT MY GRANDPA'S HOUSE...

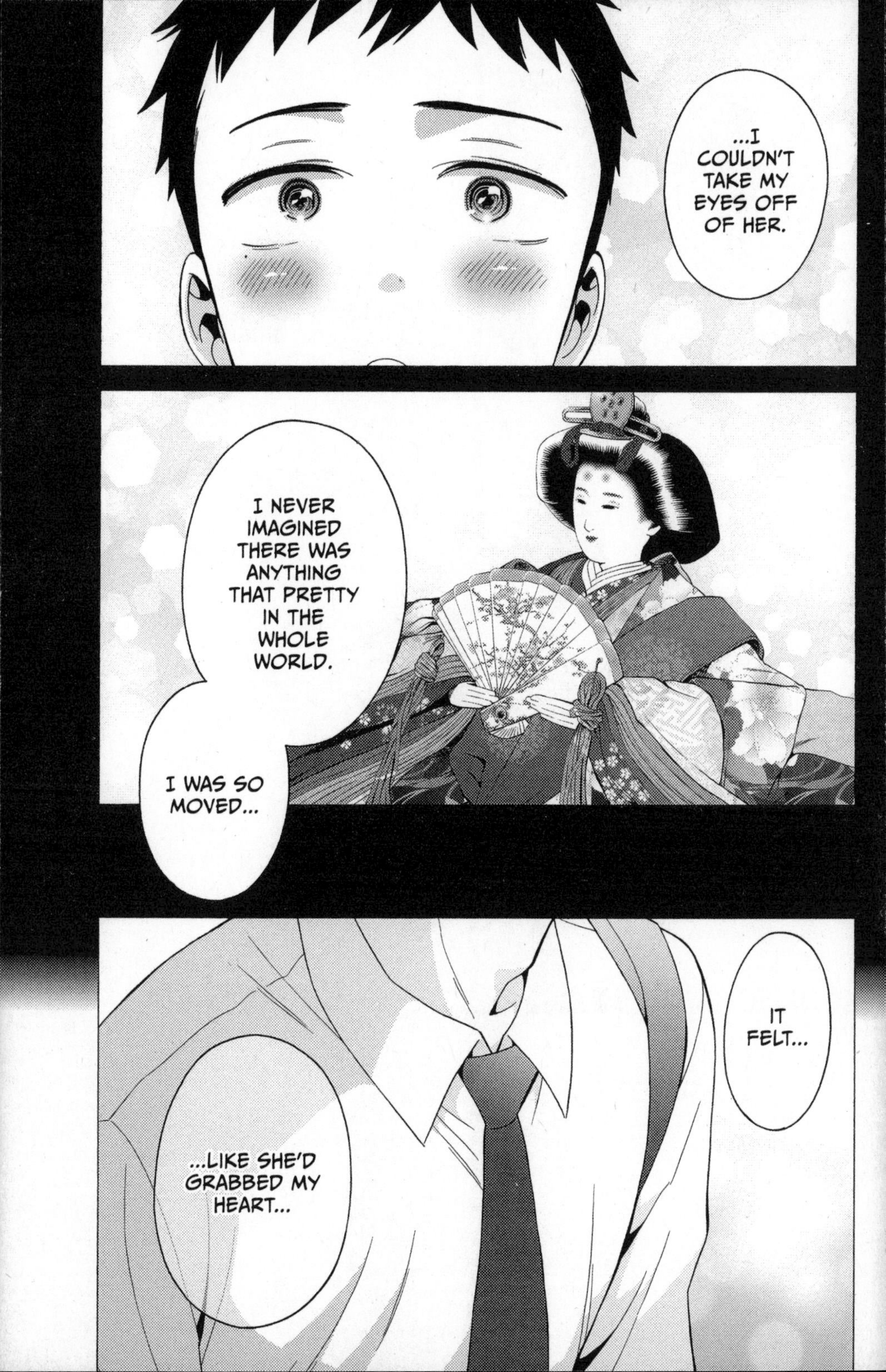
...I COULDN'T TAKE MY EYES OFF OF HER.
I NEVER IMAGINED THERE WAS ANYTHING THAT PRETTY IN THE WHOLE WORLD.
I WAS SO MOVED...
IT FELT...
...LIKE SHE'D GRABBED MY HEART...

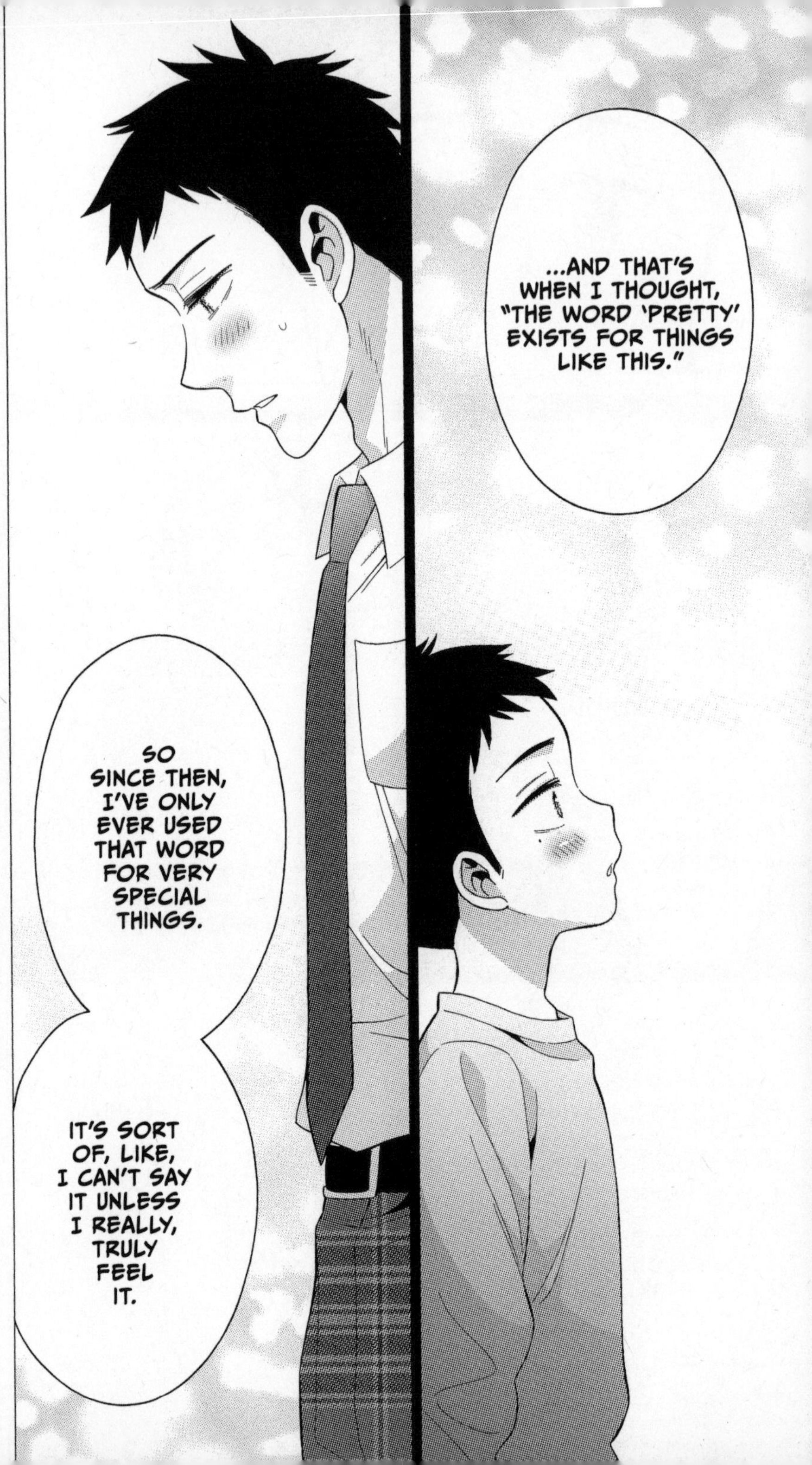
...AND THAT'S WHEN I THOUGHT, "THE WORD 'PRETTY' EXISTS FOR THINGS LIKE THIS."
SO SINCE THEN, I'VE ONLY EVER USED THAT WORD FOR VERY SPECIAL THINGS.
IT'S SORT OF, LIKE, I CAN'T SAY IT UNLESS I REALLY, TRULY FEEL IT.

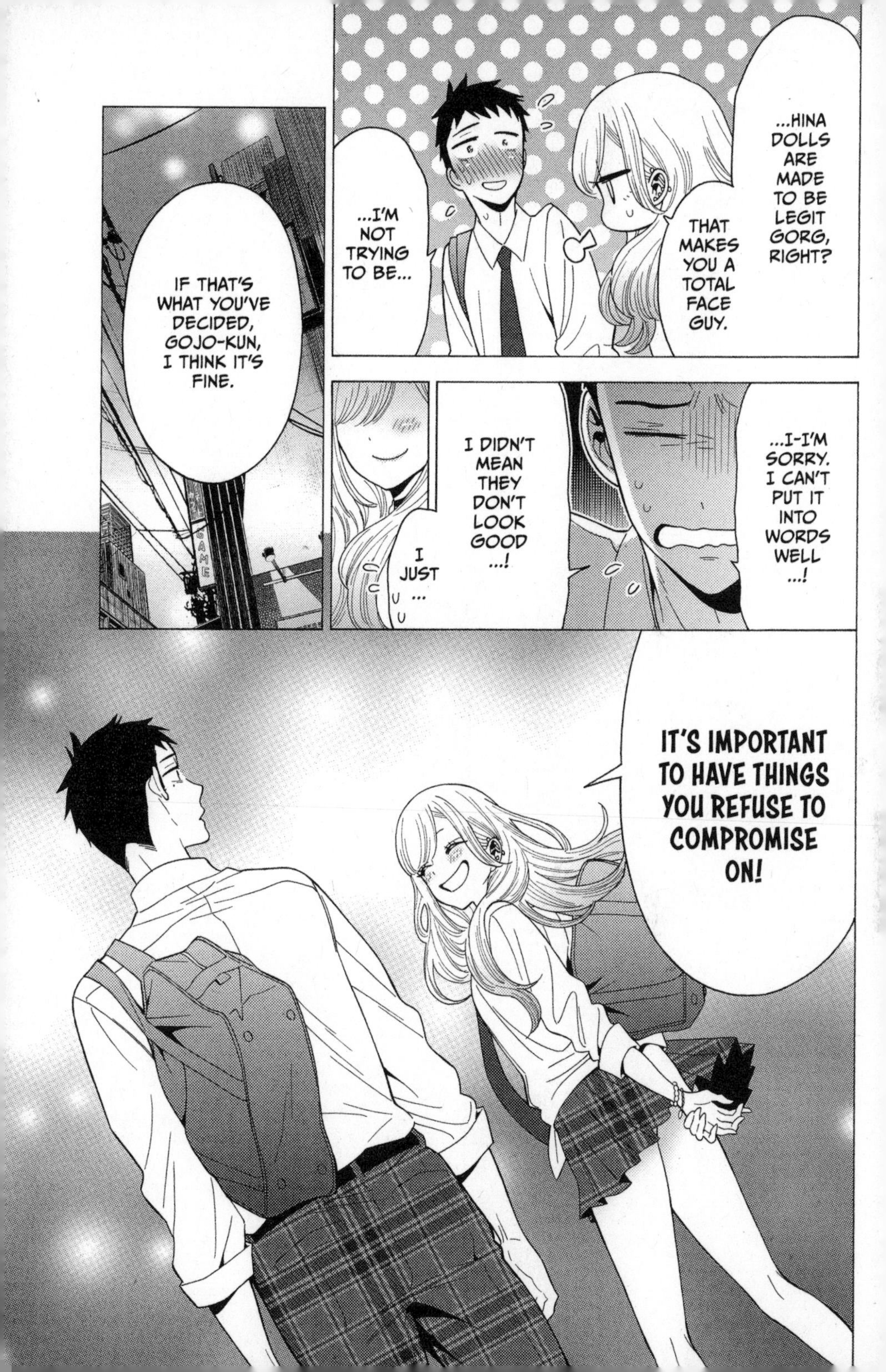
...HINA DOLLS ARE MADE TO BE LEGIT GORG, RIGHT?
THAT MAKES YOU A TOTAL FACE GUY.
...I'M NOT TRYING TO BE...
...I-I'M SORRY. I CAN'T PUT IT INTO WORDS WELL...!
I DIDN'T MEAN THEY DON'T LOOK GOOD...!
I JUST...
IF THAT'S WHAT YOU'VE DECIDED, GOJO-KUN, I THINK IT'S FINE.
GAME
IT'S IMPORTANT TO HAVE THINGS YOU REFUSE TO COMPROMISE ON!

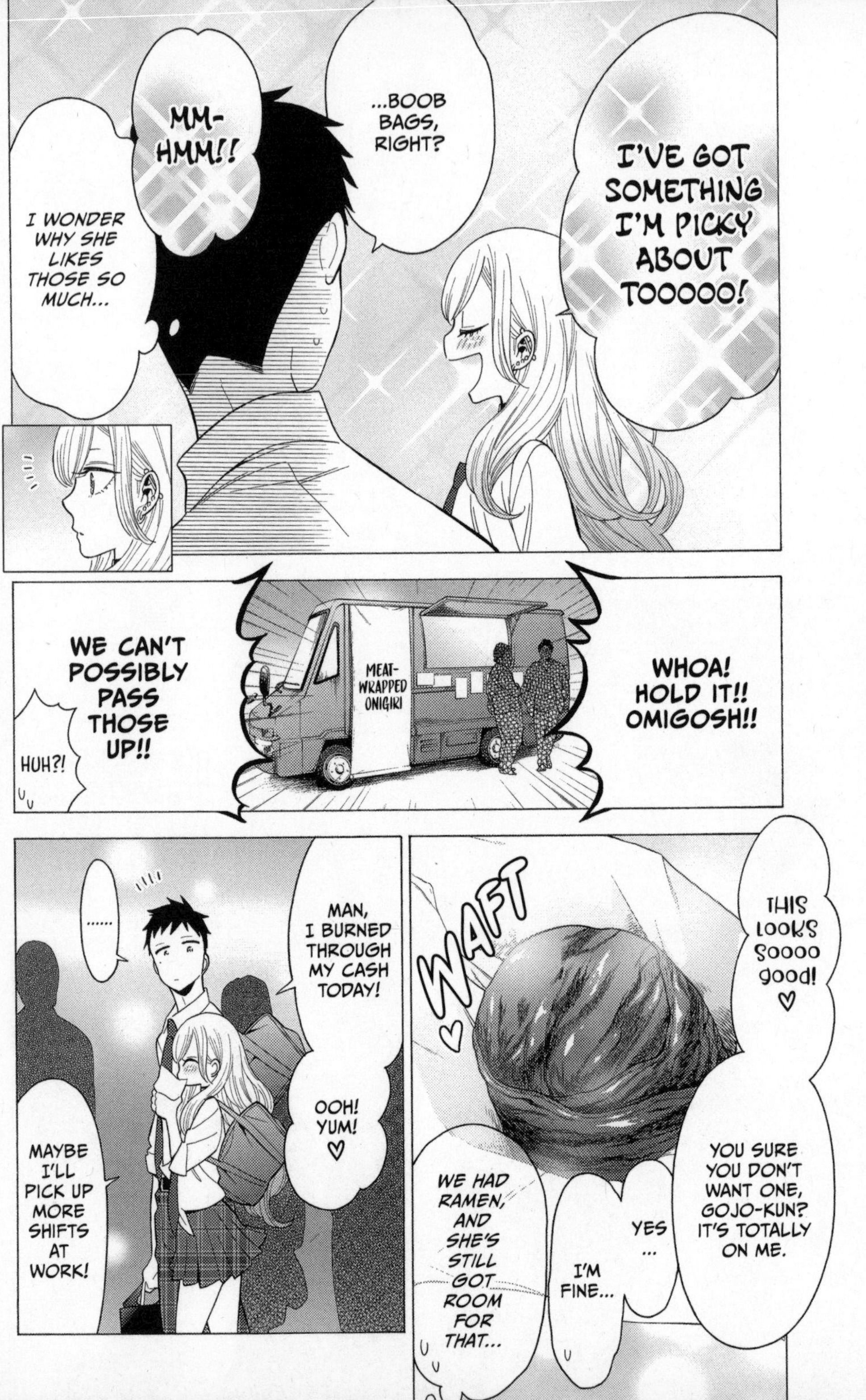
I'VE GOT SOMETHING I'M PICKY ABOUT TOOOOO!
...BOOB BAGS, RIGHT?
MM-HMM!!
I WONDER WHY SHE LIKES THOSE SO MUCH...
WHOA! HOLD IT!! OMIGOSH!!
MEAT-WRAPPED ONIGIRI
WE CAN'T POSSIBLY PASS THOSE UP!!
HUH?!
WAFT
THIS LOOKS SOOOO GOOD! ♡
YOU SURE YOU DON'T WANT ONE, GOJO-KUN? IT'S TOTALLY ON ME.
YES ...
I'M FINE...
WE HAD RAMEN, AND SHE'S STILL GOT ROOM FOR THAT...
MAN, I BURNED THROUGH MY CASH TODAY!
......
OOH! YUM! ♡
MAYBE I'LL PICK UP MORE SHIFTS AT WORK!

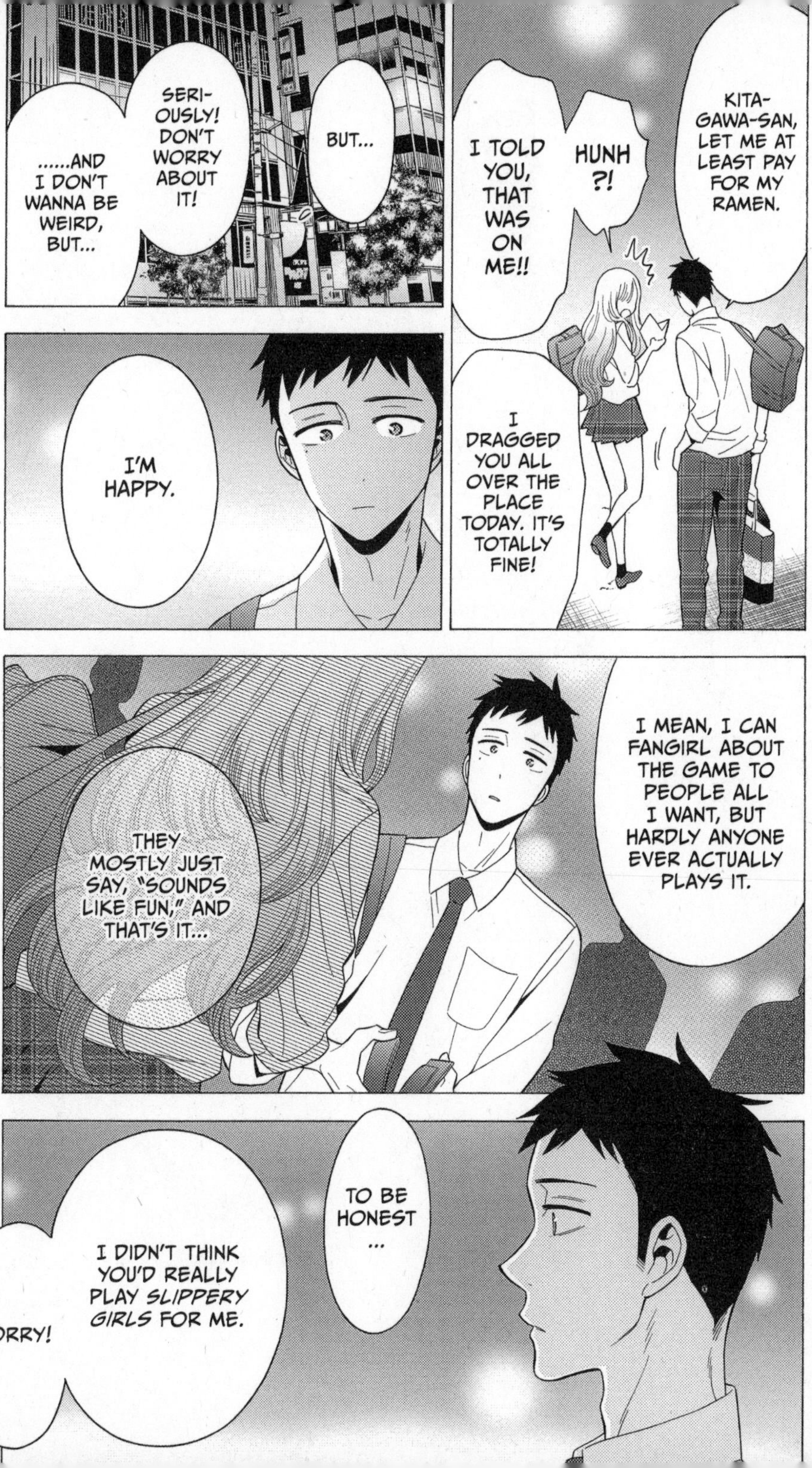
KITA-GAWA-SAN, LET ME AT LEAST PAY FOR MY RAMEN.
HUNH ?!
I TOLD YOU, THAT WAS ON ME!!
I DRAGGED YOU ALL OVER THE PLACE TODAY. IT'S TOTALLY FINE!
BUT...
SERI-OUSLY! DON'T WORRY ABOUT IT!
......AND I DON'T WANNA BE WEIRD, BUT...
I'M HAPPY.
I MEAN, I CAN FANGIRL ABOUT THE GAME TO PEOPLE ALL I WANT, BUT HARDLY ANYONE EVER ACTUALLY PLAYS IT.
THEY MOSTLY JUST SAY, "SOUNDS LIKE FUN," AND THAT'S IT...
TO BE HONEST ...
I DIDN'T THINK YOU'D REALLY PLAY *SLIPPERY GIRLS* FOR ME.
SORRY!

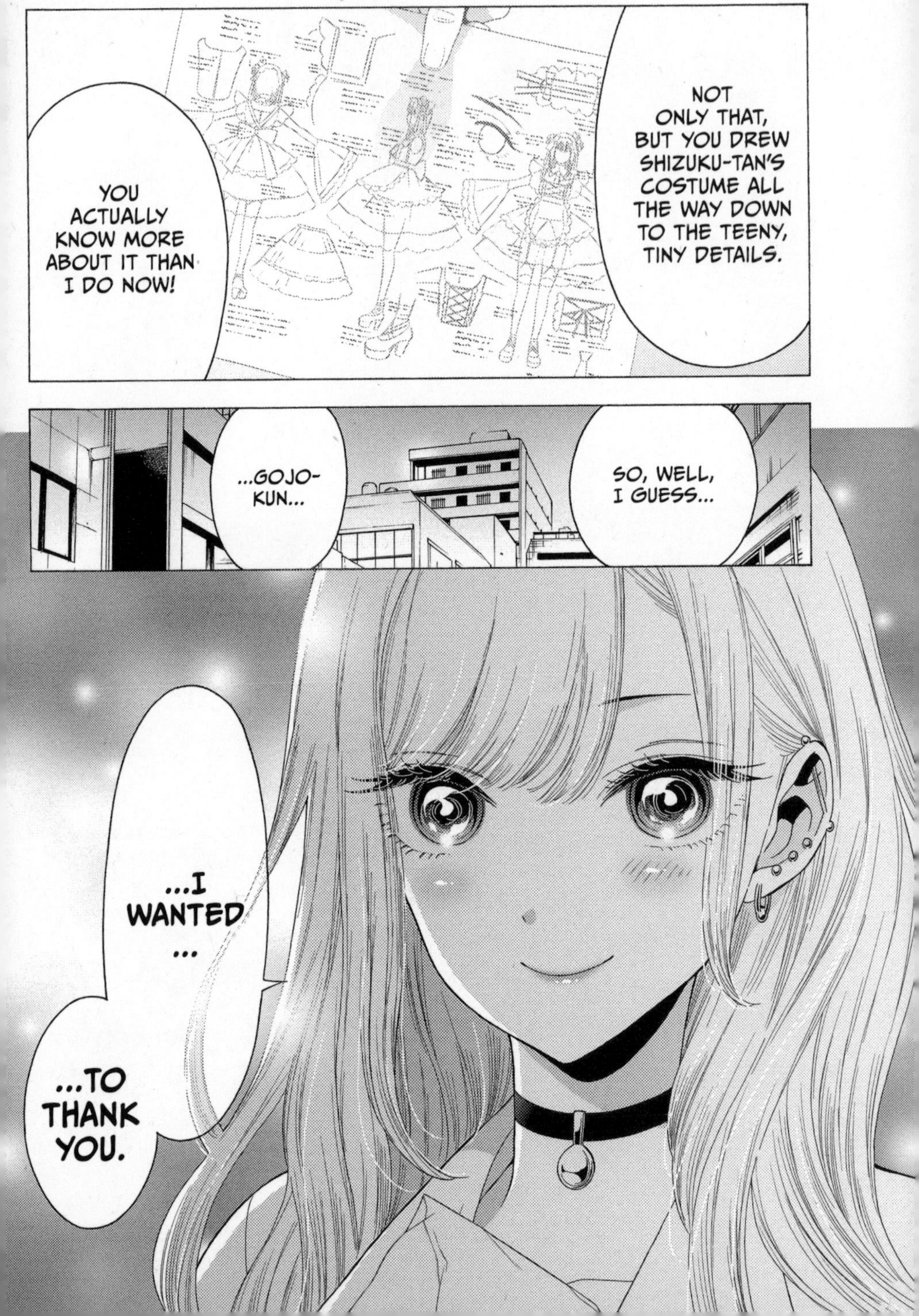
NOT ONLY THAT, BUT YOU DREW SHIZUKU-TAN'S COSTUME ALL THE WAY DOWN TO THE TEENY, TINY DETAILS.
YOU ACTUALLY KNOW MORE ABOUT IT THAN I DO NOW!
SO, WELL, I GUESS...
...GOJO-KUN...
...I WANTED ...
...TO THANK YOU.

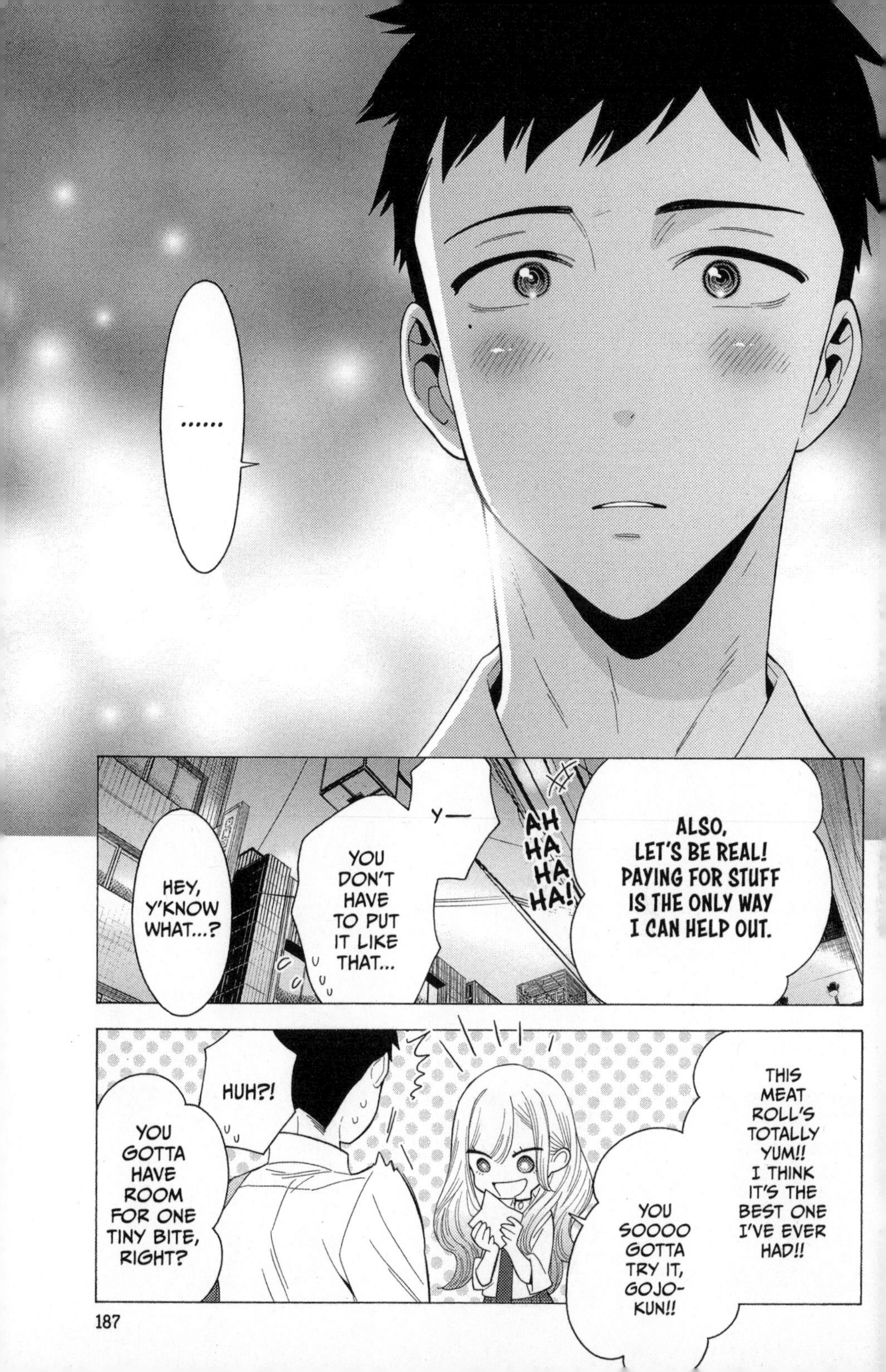
……
ALSO, LET'S BE REAL! PAYING FOR STUFF IS THE ONLY WAY I CAN HELP OUT.
AH HA HA HA!
Y—
YOU DON'T HAVE TO PUT IT LIKE THAT...
HEY, Y'KNOW WHAT...?
THIS MEAT ROLL'S TOTALLY YUM!! I THINK IT'S THE BEST ONE I'VE EVER HAD!!
YOU SOOOO GOTTA TRY IT, GOJO-KUN!!
HUH?!
YOU GOTTA HAVE ROOM FOR ONE TINY BITE, RIGHT?

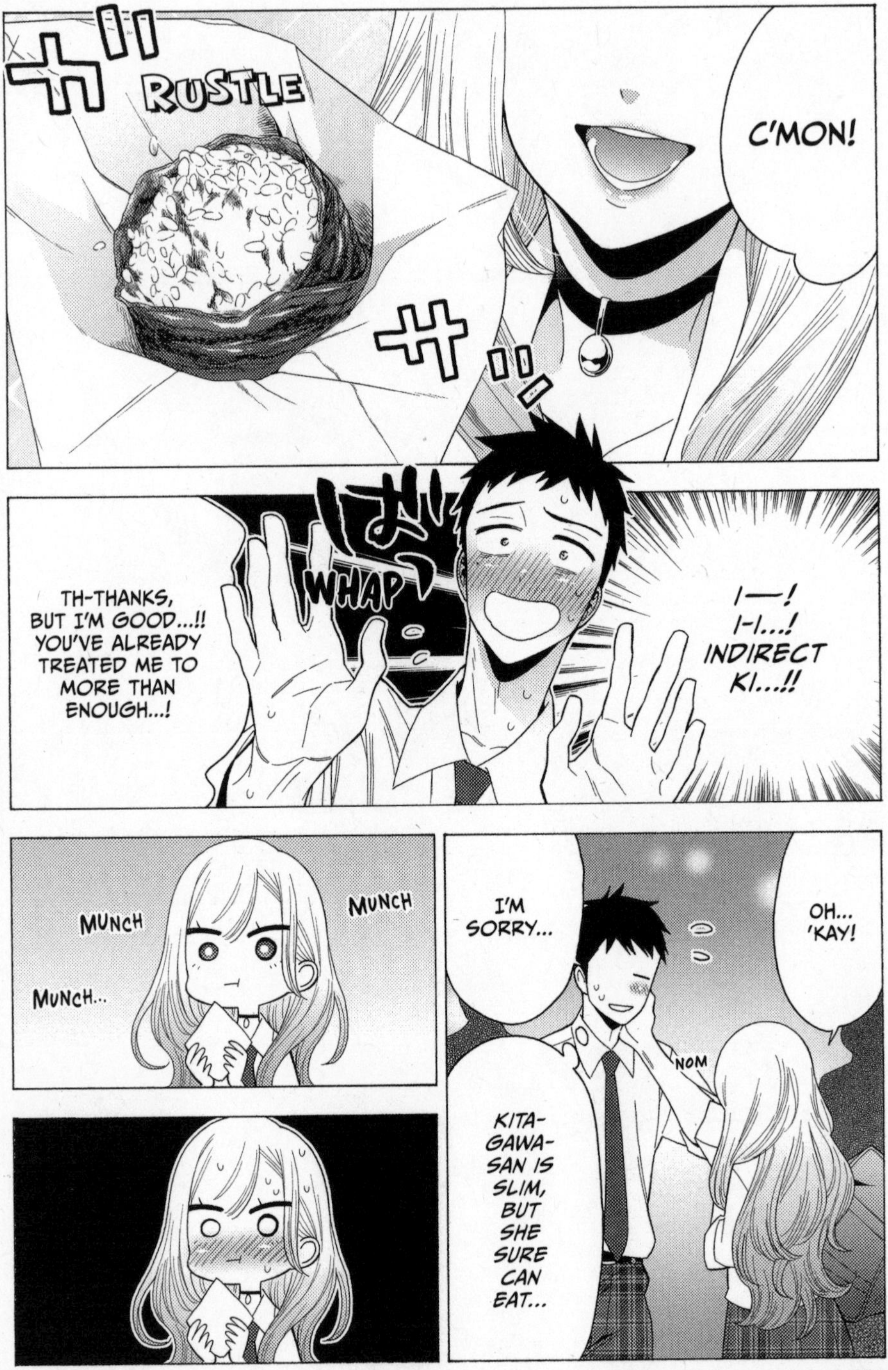
C'MON!
サッ
RUSTLE
サッ
I—!
I-I...!
INDIRECT
KI...!!
ばっ
WHAP
TH-THANKS,
BUT I'M GOOD...!!
YOU'VE ALREADY
TREATED ME TO
MORE THAN
ENOUGH...!
OH...
'KAY!
I'M
SORRY...
NOM
KITA-
GAWA-
SAN IS
SLIM,
BUT
SHE
SURE
CAN
EAT...
MUNCH
MUNCH
MUNCH...

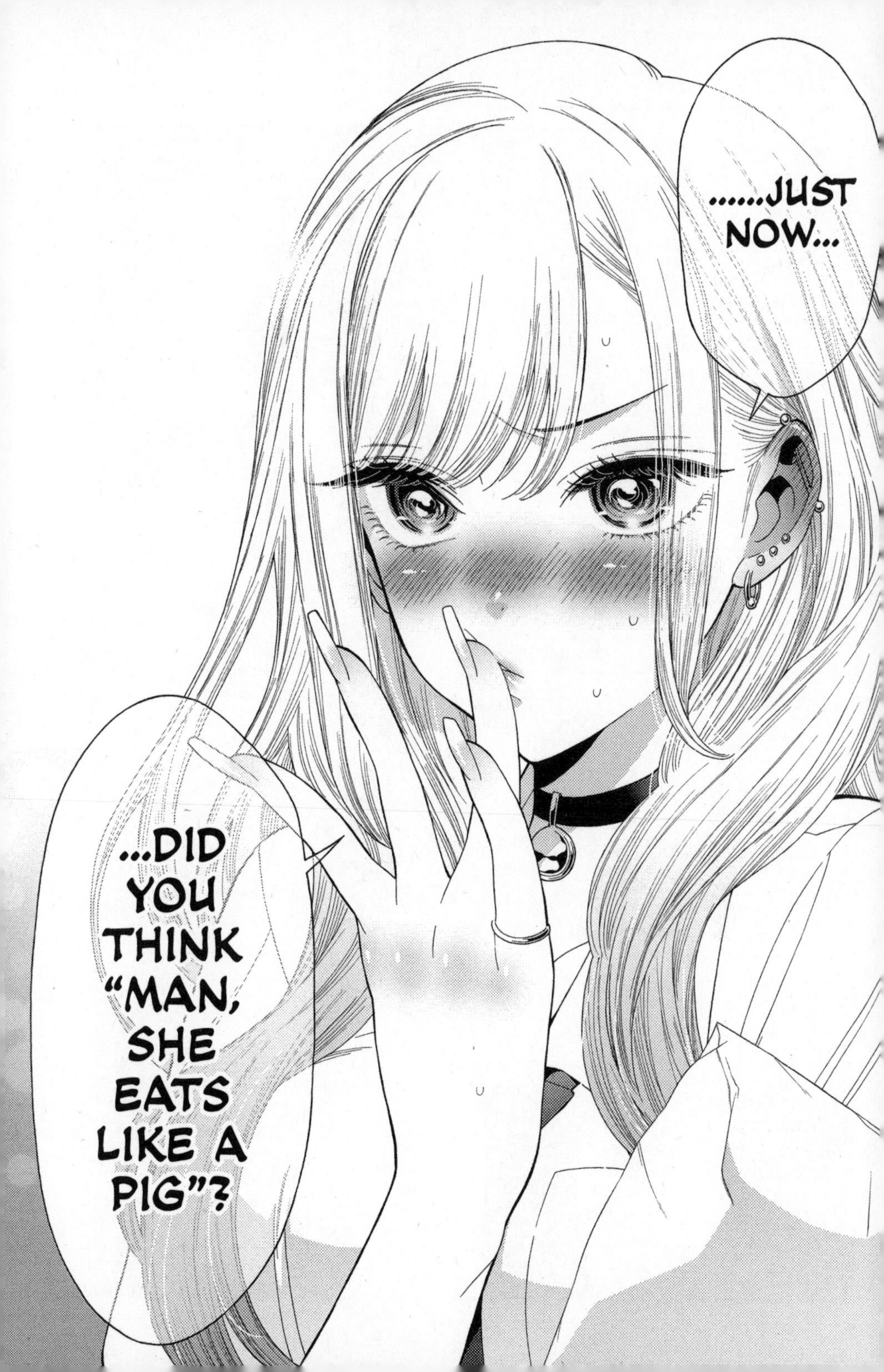
......JUST NOW...
...DID YOU THINK "MAN, SHE EATS LIKE A PIG"?

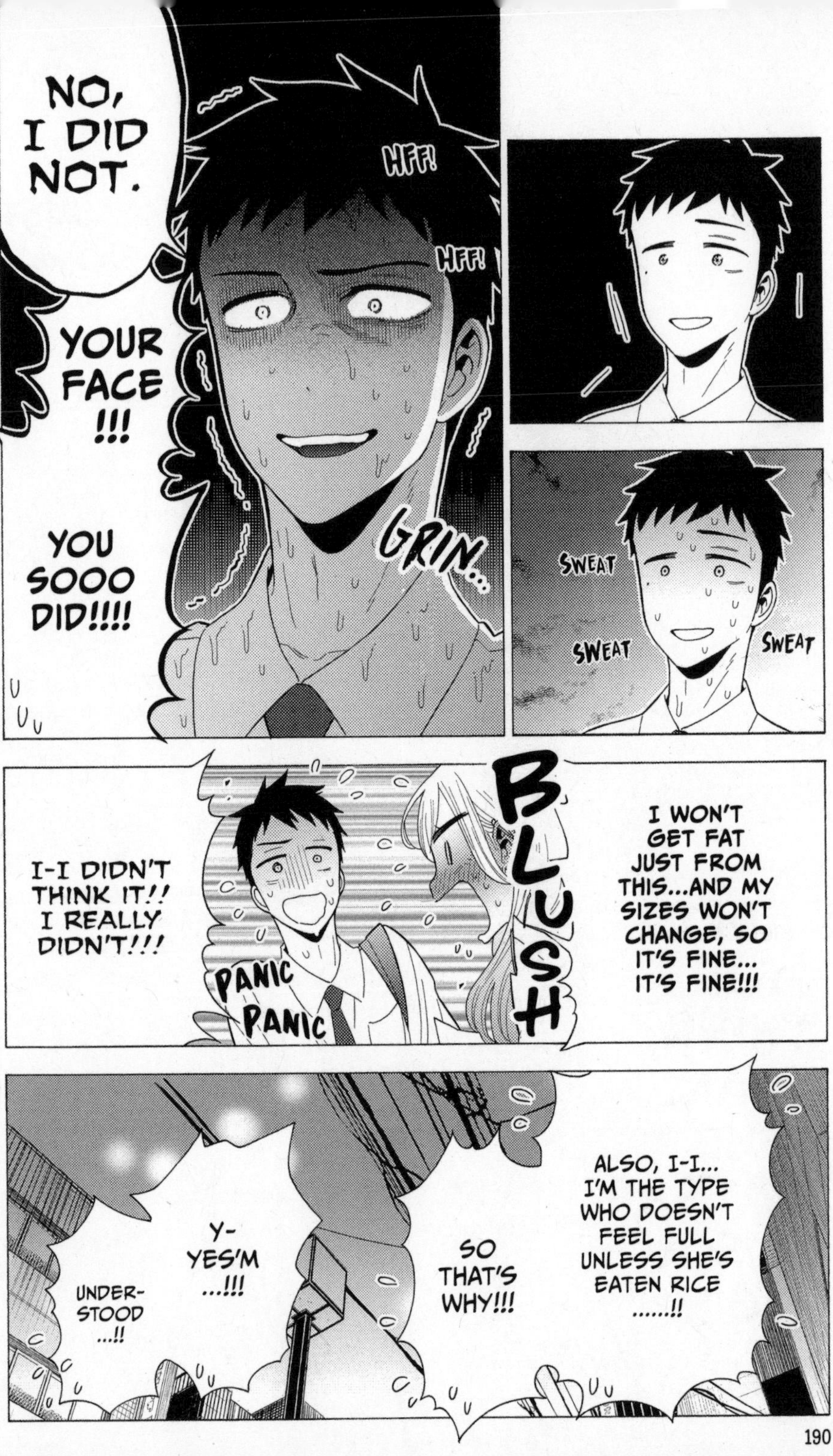
SWEAT
SWEAT
SWEAT
HFF!
HFF!
NO, I DID NOT.
YOUR FACE !!!
GRIN...
YOU SOOO DID!!!!
I WON'T GET FAT JUST FROM THIS...AND MY SIZES WON'T CHANGE, SO IT'S FINE... IT'S FINE!!!
BLUSH
PANIC PANIC
I-I DIDN'T THINK IT!! I REALLY DIDN'T!!!
ALSO, I-I... I'M THE TYPE WHO DOESN'T FEEL FULL UNLESS SHE'S EATEN RICE ......!!
SO THAT'S WHY!!!
Y-YES'M ...!!!
UNDER-STOOD ...!!

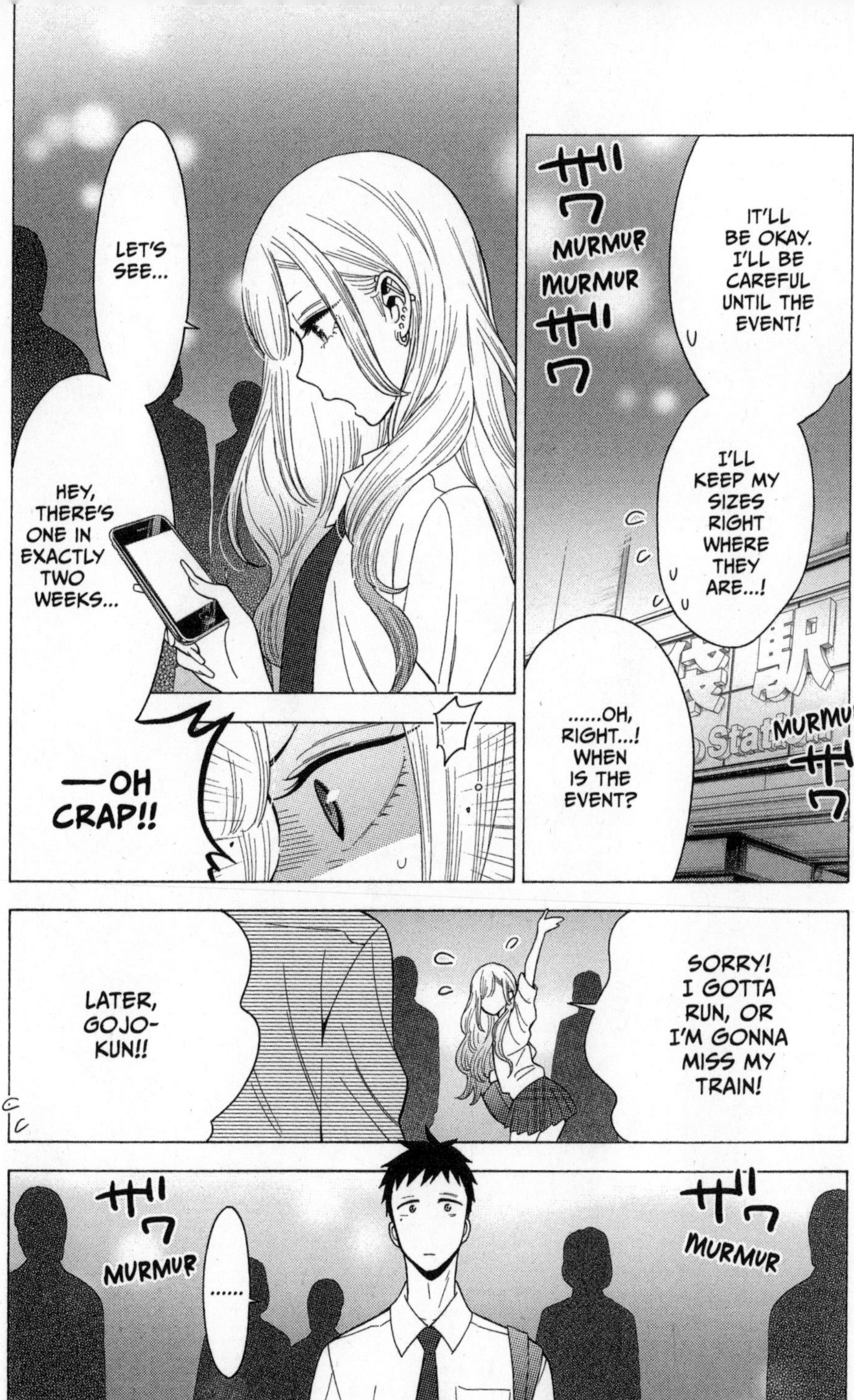
ザワ
MURMUR
MURMUR
ザワ
IT'LL BE OKAY. I'LL BE CAREFUL UNTIL THE EVENT!
I'LL KEEP MY SIZES RIGHT WHERE THEY ARE...!
......OH, RIGHT...! WHEN IS THE EVENT?
駅
Station
MURMUR
ザワ
LET'S SEE...
HEY, THERE'S ONE IN EXACTLY TWO WEEKS...
—OH CRAP!!
SORRY! I GOTTA RUN, OR I'M GONNA MISS MY TRAIN!
LATER, GOJO-KUN!!
ザワ
MURMUR
ザワ
MURMUR
......

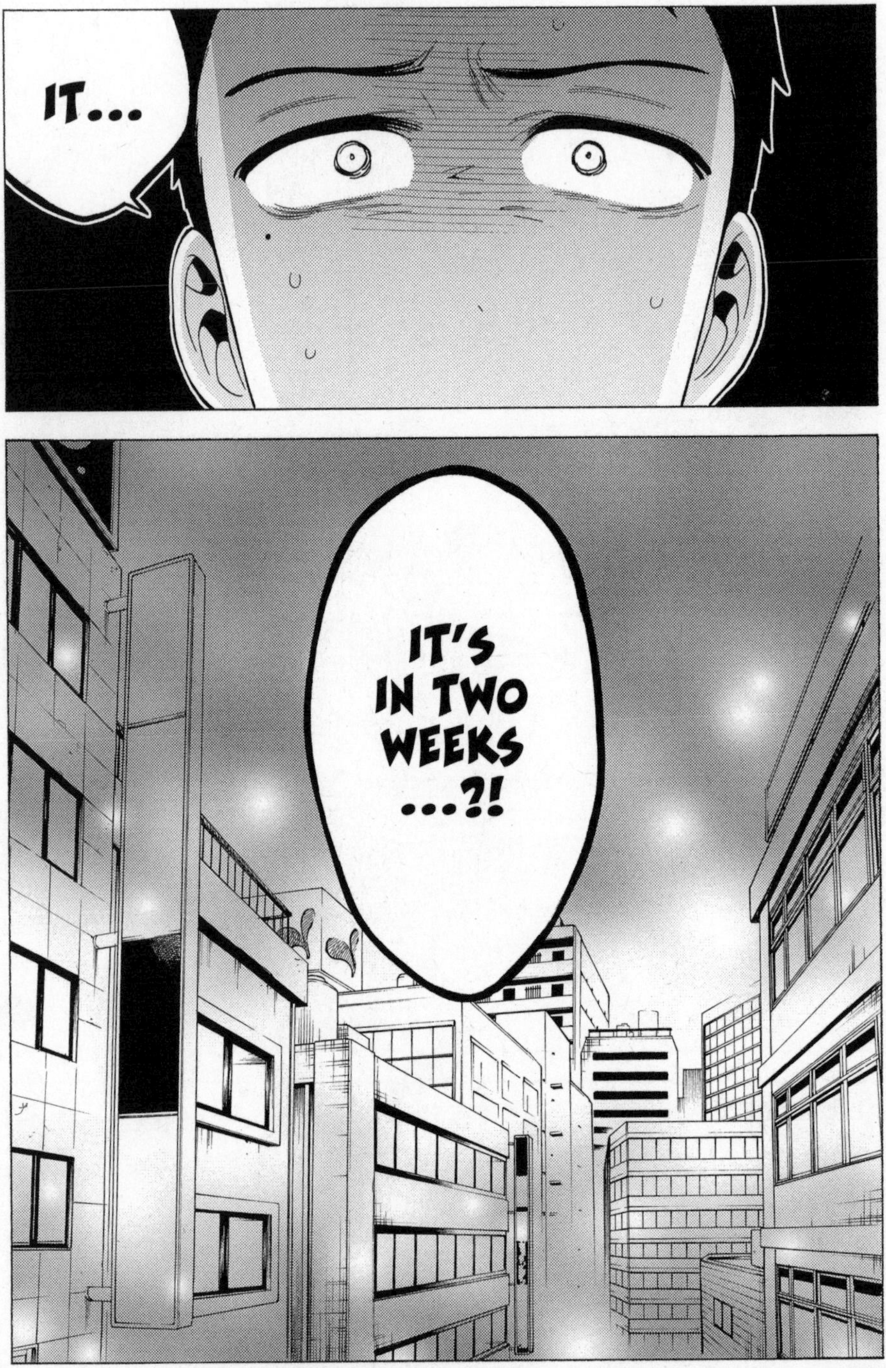
IT...
IT'S IN TWO WEEKS ...?!

My DRESS-UP Darling

AFTERWORD♥

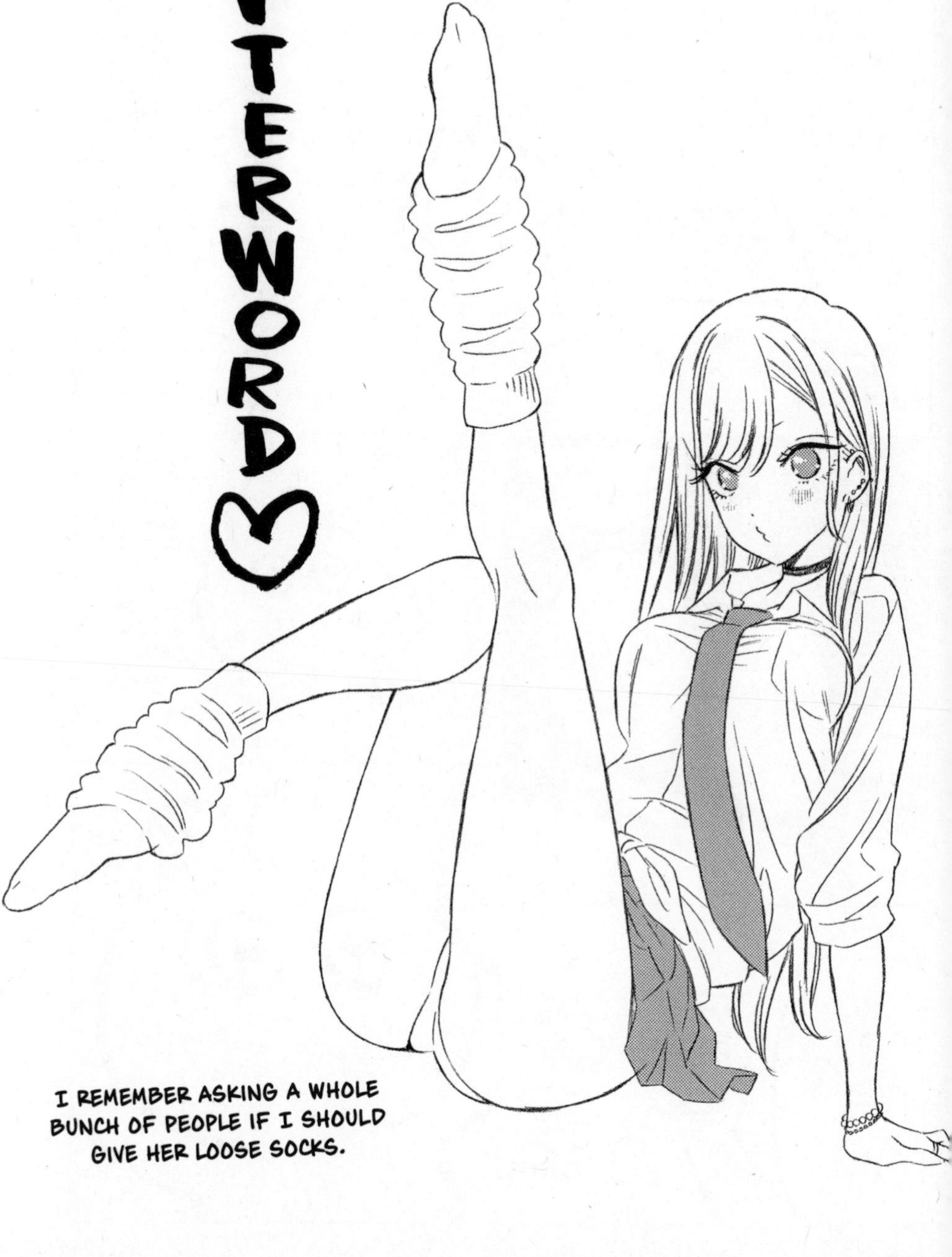

I REMEMBER ASKING A WHOLE BUNCH OF PEOPLE IF I SHOULD GIVE HER LOOSE SOCKS.

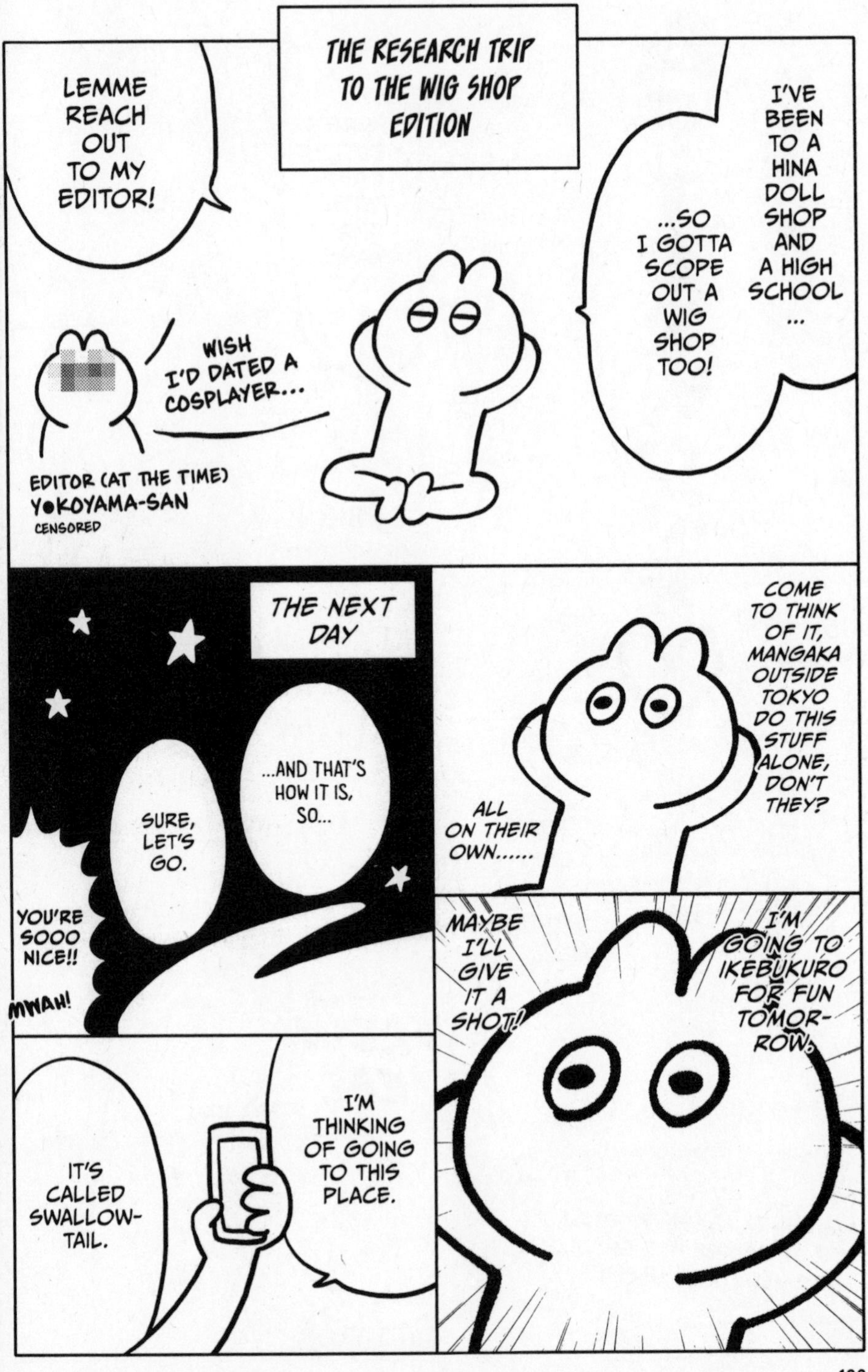
THE RESEARCH TRIP TO THE WIG SHOP EDITION
I'VE BEEN TO A HINA DOLL SHOP AND A HIGH SCHOOL...
...SO I GOTTA SCOPE OUT A WIG SHOP TOO!
LEMME REACH OUT TO MY EDITOR!
WISH I'D DATED A COSPLAYER...
EDITOR (AT THE TIME) Y●KOYAMA-SAN
CENSORED
COME TO THINK OF IT, MANGAKA OUTSIDE TOKYO DO THIS STUFF ALONE, DON'T THEY?
ALL ON THEIR OWN......
I'M GOING TO IKEBUKURO FOR FUN TOMORROW.
MAYBE I'LL GIVE IT A SHOT!
THE NEXT DAY
...AND THAT'S HOW IT IS, SO...
SURE, LET'S GO.
YOU'RE SOOO NICE!!
MWAH!
I'M THINKING OF GOING TO THIS PLACE.
IT'S CALLED SWALLOW-TAIL.

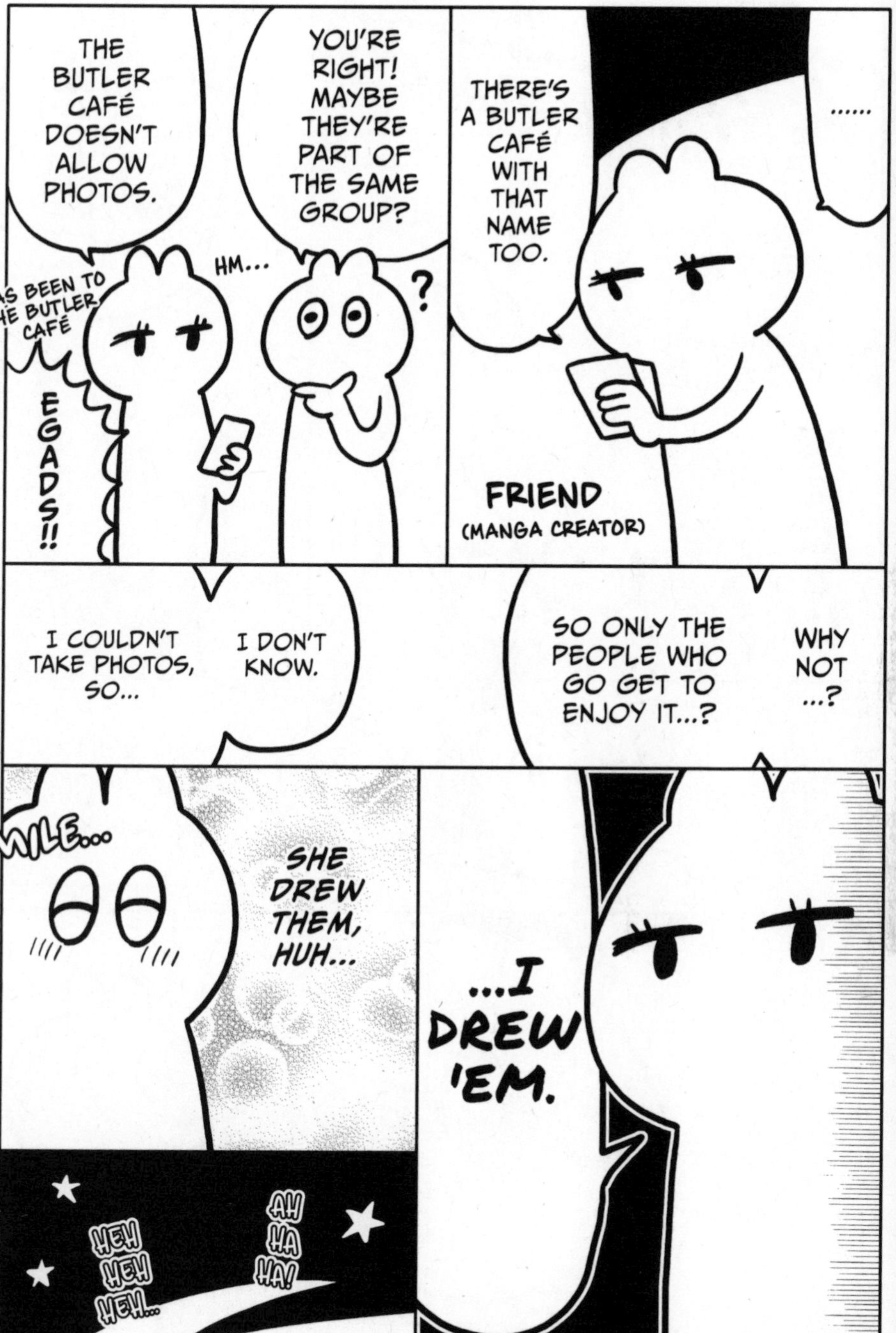
......
THERE'S A BUTLER CAFÉ WITH THAT NAME TOO.
FRIEND (MANGA CREATOR)
YOU'RE RIGHT! MAYBE THEY'RE PART OF THE SAME GROUP?
?
HM...
THE BUTLER CAFÉ DOESN'T ALLOW PHOTOS.
HAS BEEN TO THE BUTLER CAFÉ
EGADS!!
WHY NOT ...?
SO ONLY THE PEOPLE WHO GO GET TO ENJOY IT...?
I DON'T KNOW.
I COULDN'T TAKE PHOTOS, SO...
...I DREW 'EM.
SHE DREW THEM, HUH...
SMILE...
AH HA HA!
HEH HEH HEH...

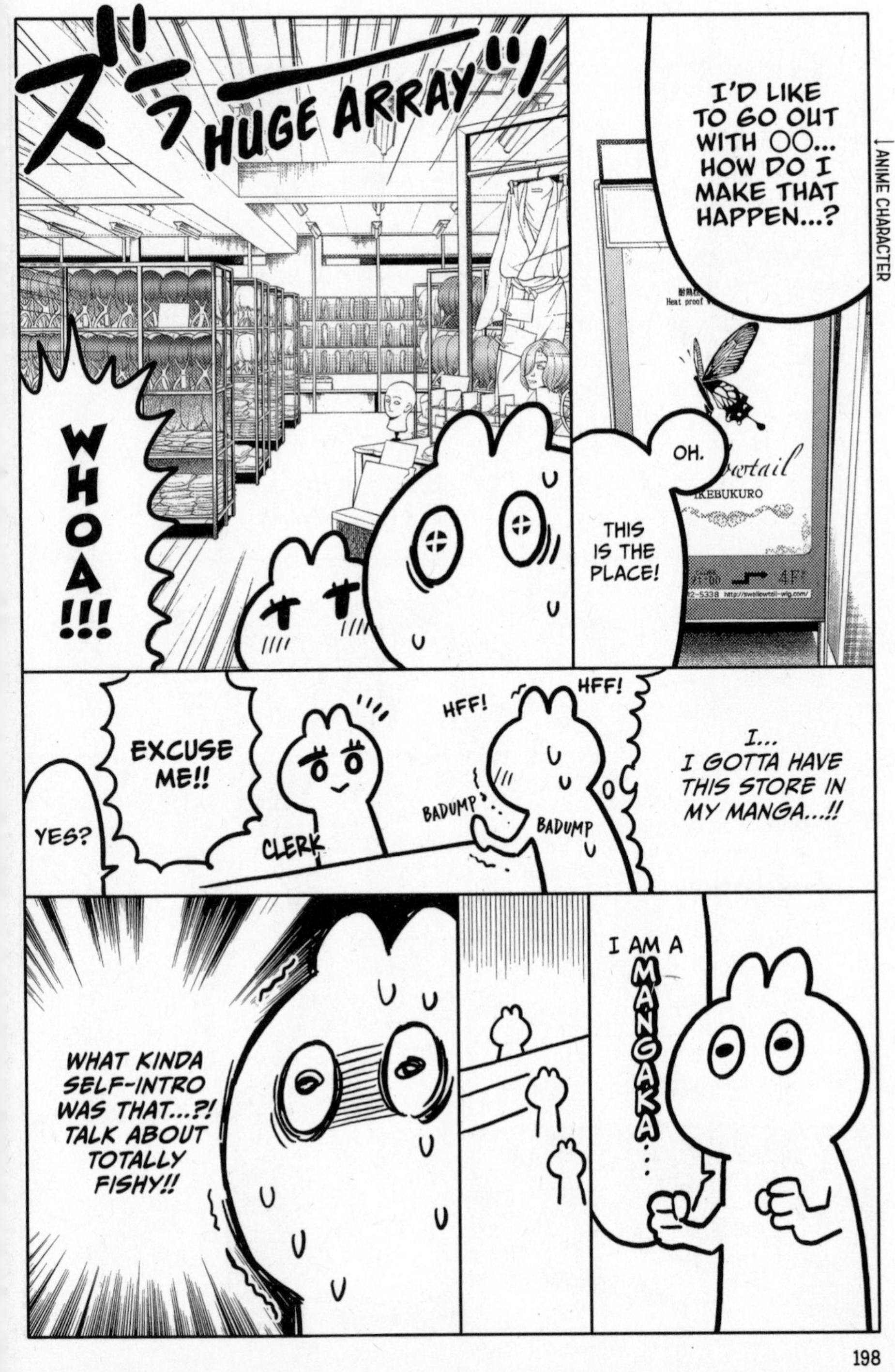
I'D LIKE TO GO OUT WITH ○○... HOW DO I MAKE THAT HAPPEN...?
OH.
THIS IS THE PLACE!
IKEBUKURO
ズラーーーッ HUGE ARRAY
WHOA!!!
I... I GOTTA HAVE THIS STORE IN MY MANGA...!!
HFF!
HFF!
BADUMP
BADUMP
EXCUSE ME!!
CLERK
YES?
I AM A MANGAKA...
WHAT KINDA SELF-INTRO WAS THAT...?! TALK ABOUT TOTALLY FISHY!!

↓ANIME CHARACTER

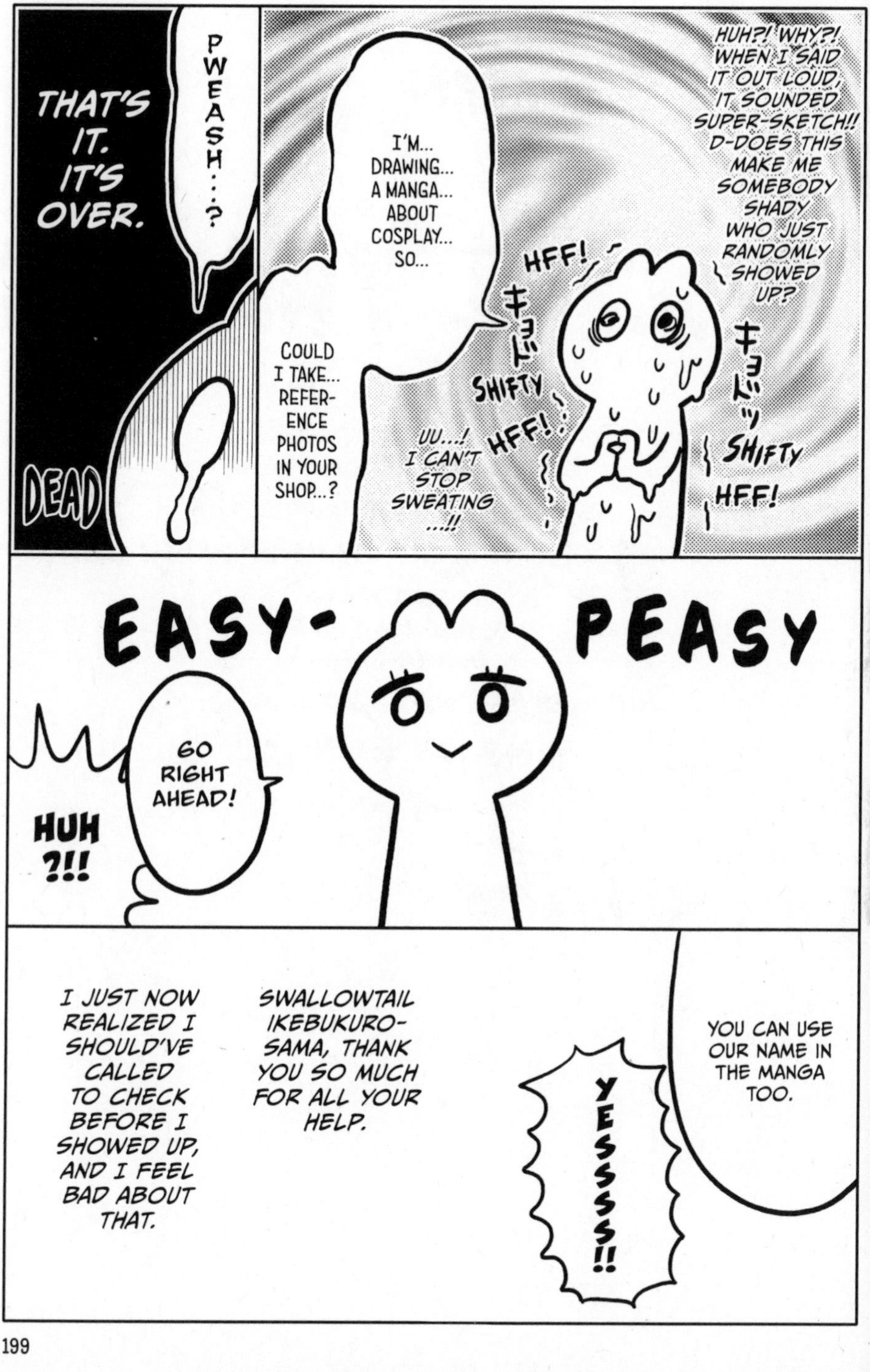
HUH?! WHY?! WHEN I SAID IT OUT LOUD, IT SOUNDED SUPER-SKETCH!! D-DOES THIS MAKE ME SOMEBODY SHADY WHO JUST RANDOMLY SHOWED UP?
キョドッ
SHIFTY
HFF!
I'M... DRAWING... A MANGA... ABOUT COSPLAY... SO...
HFF!
SHIFTY
HFF!
UU...! I CAN'T STOP SWEATING ...!!
COULD I TAKE... REFERENCE PHOTOS IN YOUR SHOP...?
PWEASH...?
THAT'S IT. IT'S OVER.
DEAD
EASY-PEASY
GO RIGHT AHEAD!
HUH ?!!
YOU CAN USE OUR NAME IN THE MANGA TOO.
YESSSSS!!
SWALLOWTAIL IKEBUKURO-SAMA, THANK YOU SO MUCH FOR ALL YOUR HELP.
I JUST NOW REALIZED I SHOULD'VE CALLED TO CHECK BEFORE I SHOWED UP, AND I FEEL BAD ABOUT THAT.

SPECIAL THANKS

SUZUKI DOLLS-SAMA

TOKYO METROPOLITAN
NOGYO HIGH SCHOOL-SAMA

SWALLOWTAIL IKEBUKURO-SAMA

ALL THE COSPLAYERS WHO LET ME INTERVIEW THEM

MY EDITORS—
YOKOYAMA-SAMA
OZAWA-SAMA

AND EVERYONE WHO READ THIS BOOK...

THANK YOU VERY MUCH!!

11/2018 FUKUDA

apart. If you only leave a little bit of room between the seam and the edge, it will stay together, but there will be no wiggle room for tailoring.

Page 40
The **tension dial** adjusts the tension of the stitch; longer stitches or thicker fabrics need less tension, shorter stitches and thinner fabrics need more. Changing the tension dial mid-seam will make the stitches look irregular or even pucker the fabric.

Page 58
Eroge is a slang term usually referring to visual novel games with erotic content.

Page 77
Leaving your futon out is the equivalent of not making your bed in the morning.

Page 114
Boob bag (*chichibukuro*) is cosplay lingo that refers to the area of the bodice right around the bust, especially when it's meant to particularly emphasize or exaggerate the shape of the breasts.

Page 151
Yusawaya is a nod to Yuzawaya, an actual crafts store in Ikebukuro that caters to cosplayers.

Page 155
In cosplay, **pannier** and **petticoat** tend to be used interchangeably; in Japanese, the biggest difference between the two is that panniers are meant to "bulk up" skirts and make them bell out more, while petticoats are made of smoother material and are intended to let the overskirt move with more freedom.

Page 155
Visual Kei (V-kei) refers to a Japanese music subculture that has been around since the 1980s and is characterized more by elaborate hairstyles and flamboyant costumes than the style of music played..

Page 159
Swallowtail Ikebukuro is another actual store in Tokyo. The URL on the sign will take you to its website!

Page 174
Ejaculation management is a form of dominance play wherein a guy isn't allowed to ejaculate without his partner's permission and must report it (and possibly receive some sort of punishment) if he does.

Page 176
The **R-18** on the sign behind the table means "adult content."

Page 180
Families only celebrate **Girls' Day** if they have a daughter, and the only reason to have a *hina* doll set is if you do celebrate.

Page 200
Though **Tokyo Metropolitan Nogyo High School** is the official school name, "Nogyo" can be translated to "Agricultural."

TRANSLATION NOTES

HONORIFICS

-san: The default honorific, roughly equivalent to Mr./Mrs./Ms./Miss in English. It can be used for coworkers, classmates, strangers, and acquaintances.

-sama: An honorific that conveys respect.

-kun: Less formal than -san, this is generally used for boys and younger men or by men when speaking to male peers. Occasionally used for girls and younger women as well.

-chan/-tan: An informal, affectionate honorific. It's mainly used for children, girls, and women and may be used for animals of either sex. It is only rarely used for men. The -tan variation is a cutesier version used almost exclusively by teenagers and members of various otaku subcultures.

No honorific: Usually indicates closeness.

GENERAL

Gyaru (from the English "gal") is a word used to describe a broad Japanese fashion subculture; the term originated around 1970, and its use peaked in the early 2000s. The term may also be used to refer to fashionable and trend-conscious high school girls, often with short skirts, bleached hair, and tans. In the Japanese edition, Marin is identified as a gal.

Page 3

Hina dolls are traditional ornamental dolls representing a fictional imperial couple and their court. They are displayed in their Heian period (794–1185) finery on tiered, red-carpeted altars for Girls' Day (also known as the Doll Festival), which takes place on March 3. A full set consists of fifteen dolls (the imperial couple, three court ladies, five male musicians, two ministers, and three guards) and a lot of very detailed accessories. As such, sets can be very expensive and are usually once-in-a-lifetime purchases. Although not every family has one, it's customary for grandparents to buy their granddaughter's *hina* dolls soon after she is born, rather than letting the burden fall on the new parents, but contemporary parents will sometimes buy their own set.

Page 13

The **duds** this kid is talking about are low rarity or unsatisfactory rewards from the kind of lottery found in mobile games.

Page 17

Salon models are people whose photographs are used in the catalogues, web pages, social media accounts, etc. of salons.

Page 40

Lining is a layer of fabric on the inside of a garment that gives it more substance and makes it less see-through.

Page 40

Backstitching is the act of reversing the sewing machine for a few stitches and sewing back over an existing row of stitches. This prevents the seam from unraveling and should be done at the start and end of most seams.

Page 40

A complete stitch requires thread from two places: a main spool of thread on top of the sewing machine, which comes down and through the needle, and a **bobbin** under the needle plate, which comes up through the plate and the machine's foot. A missing bobbin thread means an incomplete stitch.

Page 40

The distance from a line of stitches (or seam) to the raw edge of the fabric is known as the **seam allowance**. Sewing at the edge without leaving one means the stitches will unravel, and the seam will come

Read on for a sneak peek at Volume 2!

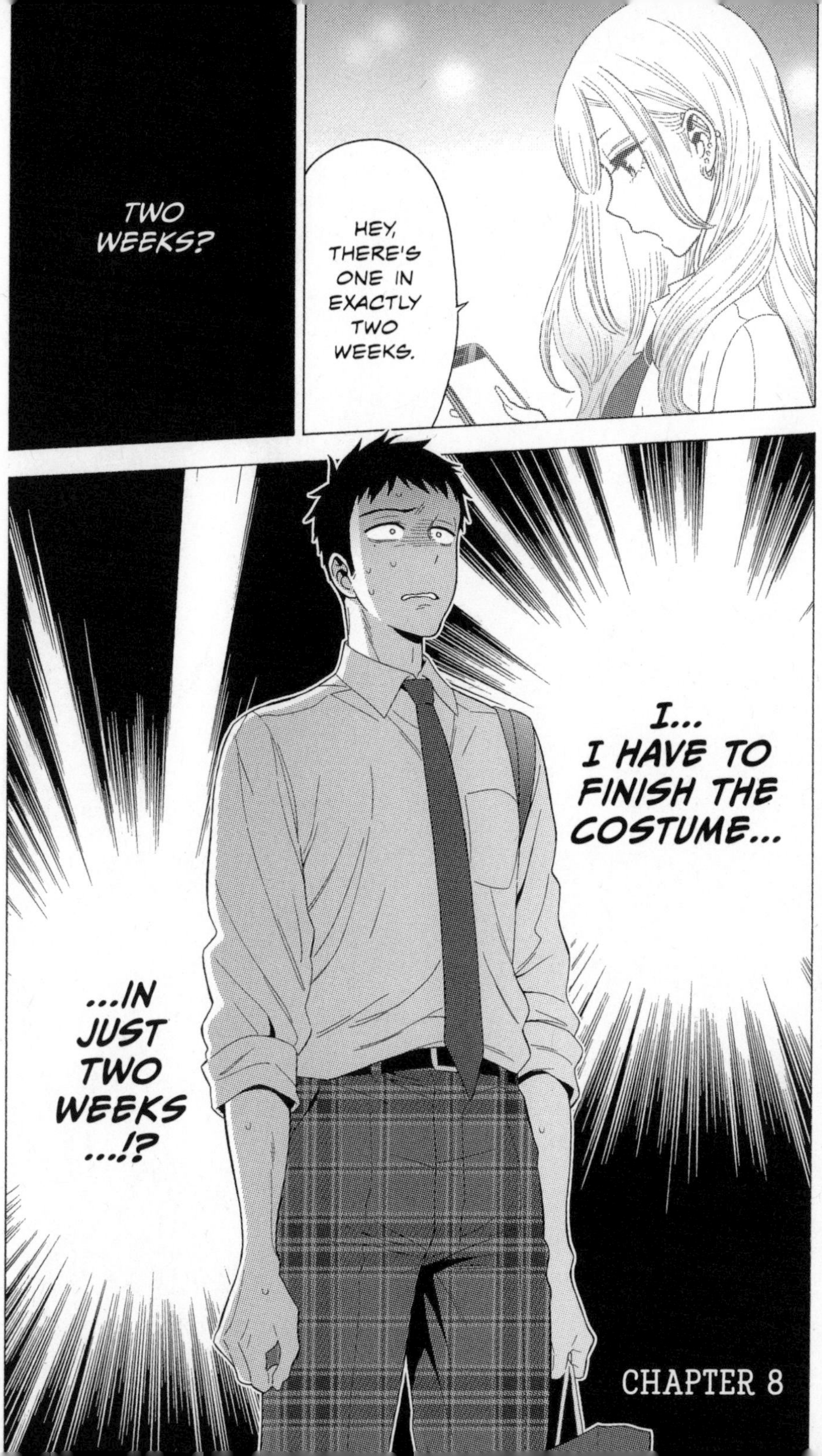
HEY, THERE'S ONE IN EXACTLY TWO WEEKS.
TWO WEEKS?
I... I HAVE TO FINISH THE COSTUME...
...IN JUST TWO WEEKS ...!?
CHAPTER 8

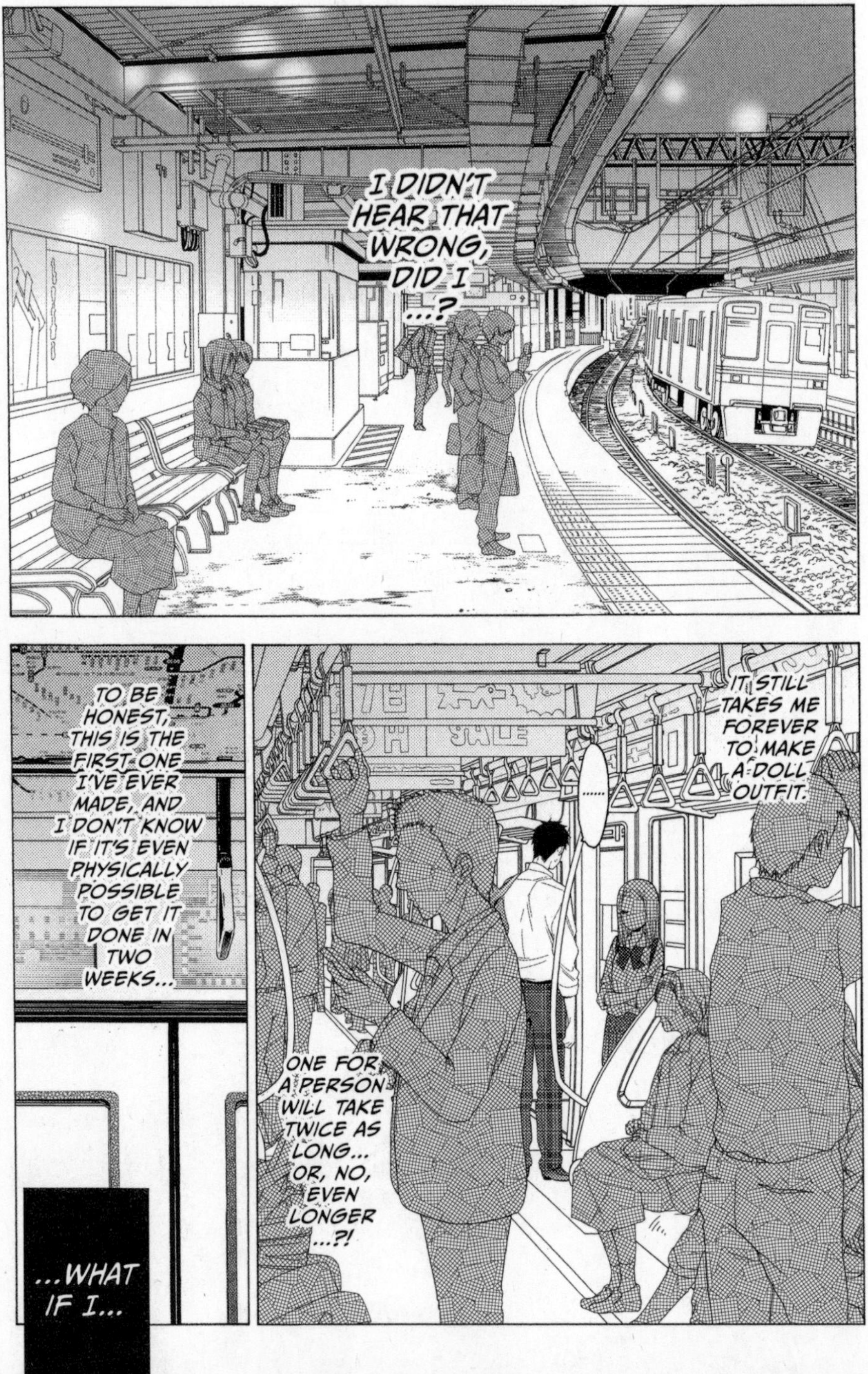
I DIDN'T HEAR THAT WRONG, DID I ...?
IT STILL TAKES ME FOREVER TO MAKE A DOLL OUTFIT.
......
ONE FOR A PERSON WILL TAKE TWICE AS LONG... OR, NO, EVEN LONGER ...?!
TO BE HONEST, THIS IS THE FIRST ONE I'VE EVER MADE, AND I DON'T KNOW IF IT'S EVEN PHYSICALLY POSSIBLE TO GET IT DONE IN TWO WEEKS...
...WHAT IF I...

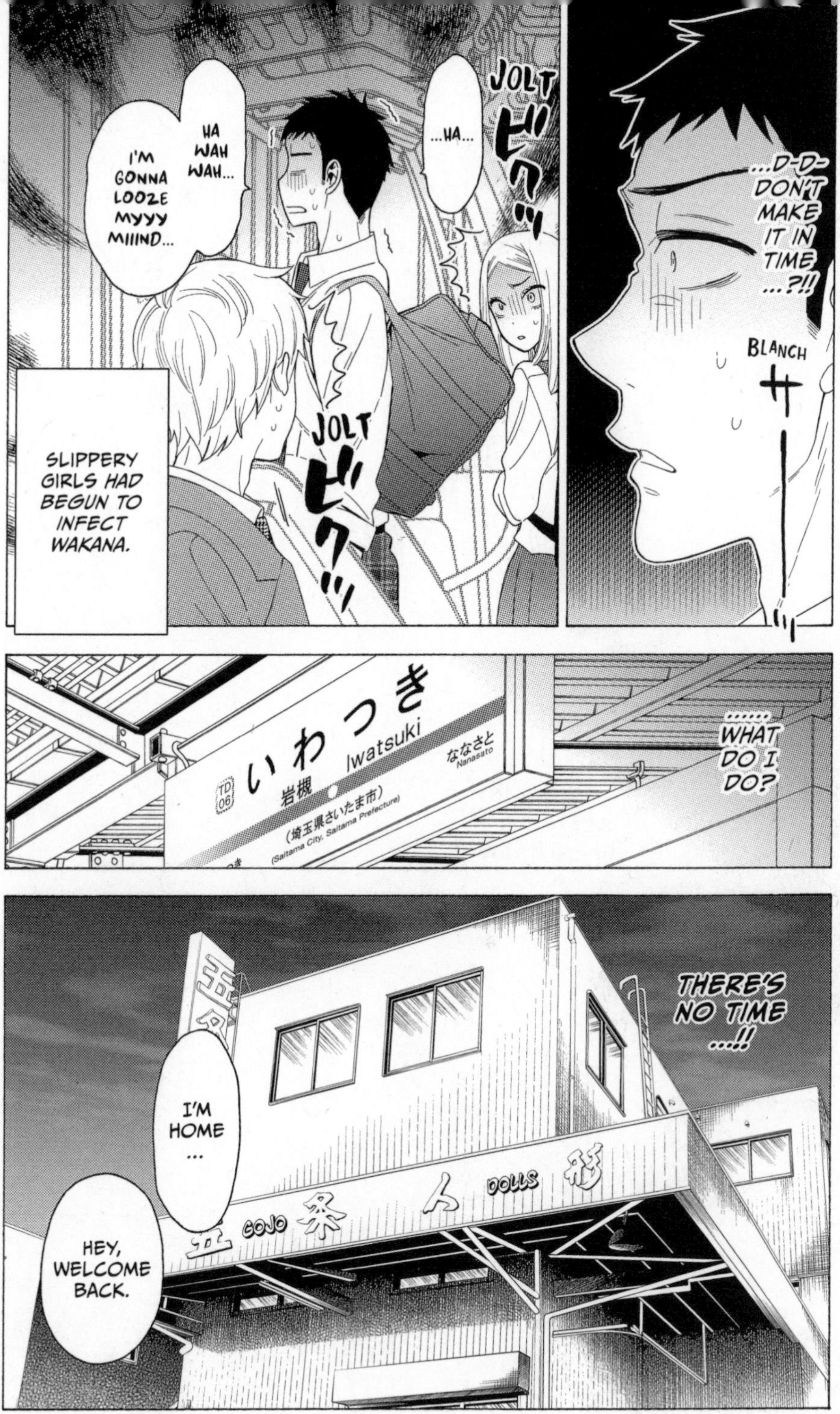
...D-D-DON'T MAKE IT IN TIME ...?!!
BLANCH
サー
JOLT
ビクッ
...HA...
HA WAH WAH...
I'M GONNA LOOZE MYYY MIIIND...
JOLT
ビクッ
SLIPPERY GIRLS HAD BEGUN TO INFECT WAKANA.
......WHAT DO I DO?
TD 06
いわつき
Iwatsuki
岩槻
ななさと
Nanasato
(埼玉県さいたま市)
(Saitama City, Saitama Prefecture)
THERE'S NO TIME ...!!
I'M HOME ...
HEY, WELCOME BACK.
五 GOJO 条 人 DOLLS 形

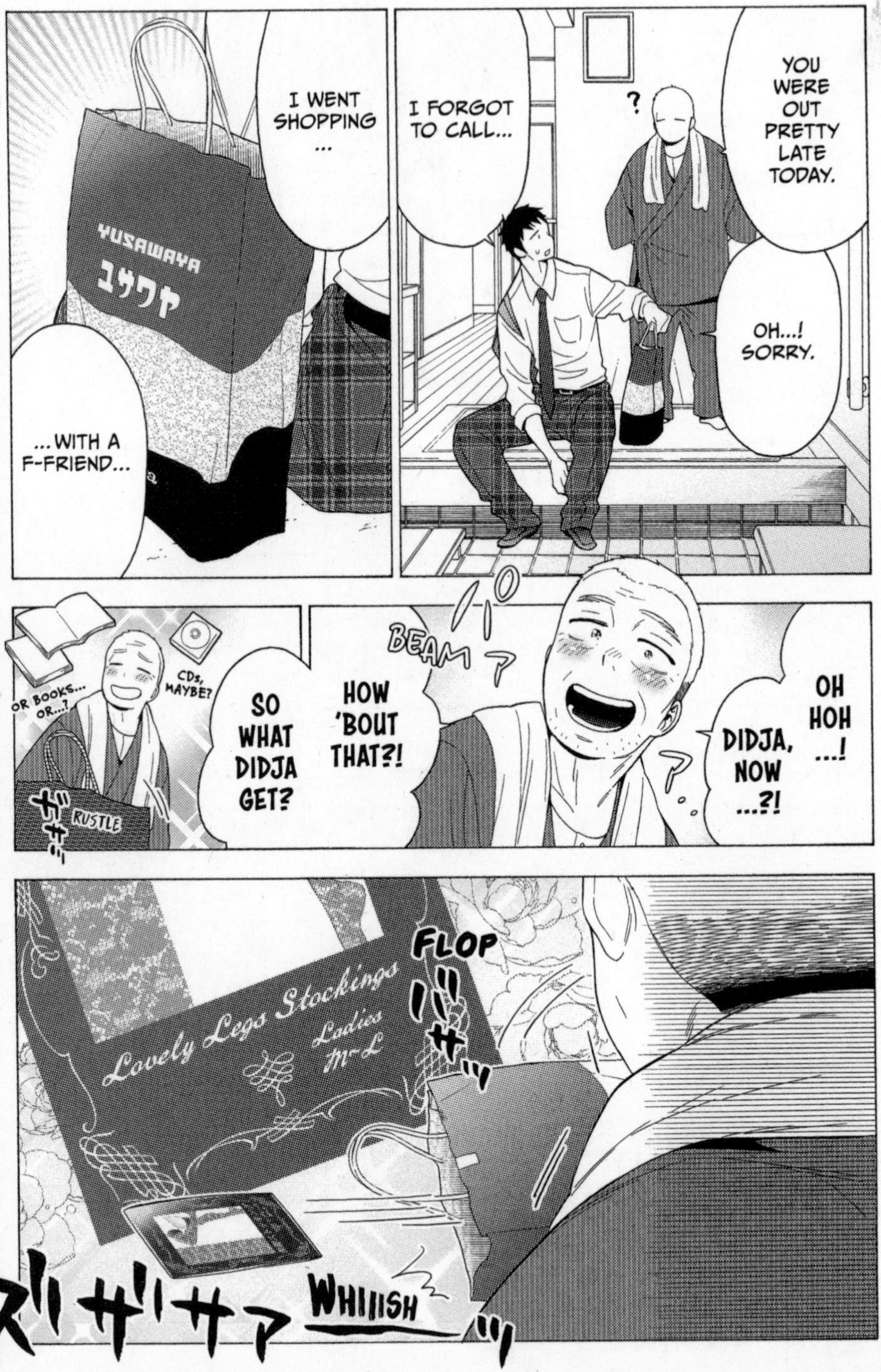
YOU WERE OUT PRETTY LATE TODAY.
?
OH...! SORRY.
I FORGOT TO CALL...
I WENT SHOPPING ...
YUSAWAYA
ユサワヤ
...WITH A F-FRIEND...
OH HOH ...!
DIDJA, NOW ...?!
BEAM
HOW 'BOUT THAT?!
SO WHAT DIDJA GET?
CDs, MAYBE?
OR BOOKS... OR...?
RUSTLE
FLOP
Lovely Legs Stockings
Ladies M-L
WHIIISH

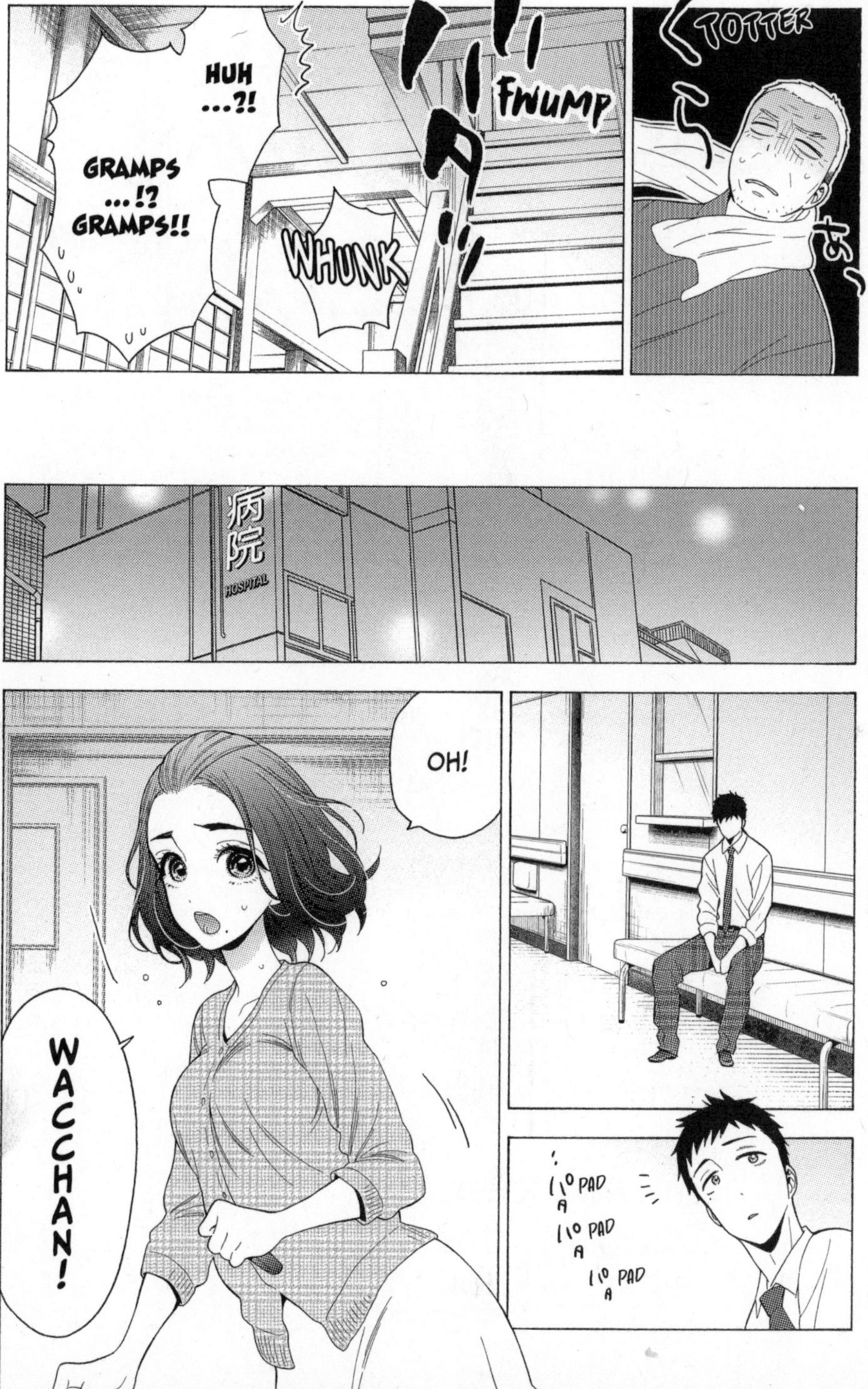
TOTTER
FWUMP
WHUNK
HUH ...?!
GRAMPS ...!? GRAMPS!!
病院
HOSPITAL
PAD
PAD
PAD
OH!
WACCHAN!

TO BE CONTINUED IN VOLUME 2 OF *MY DRESS-UP DARLING!*

My DRESS-UP Darling ①

Story and Art by Shinichi Fukuda

Translation: Taylor Engel
Lettering: Ken Kamura
Cover Design: Andrea Miller
Editor: Tania Biswas

MY DRESS-UP DARLING Volume 1
© 2018 Shinichi Fukuda/SQUARE ENIX CO., LTD.
First published in Japan in 2018 by SQUARE ENIX CO., LTD.
English translation rights arranged with
SQUARE ENIX CO., LTD. and SQUARE ENIX, INC.
English translation © 2020 by SQUARE ENIX CO., LTD.

ISBN: 978-1-64609-032-7

Library of Congress Cataloging-in-Publication
Data is on file with the publisher.

Printed in the U.S.A.

10 9 8 7

SQUARE ENIX
MANGA & BOOKS
www.square-enix-books.com